Golden Days

A PROJECT OF STUDENTS AND ALUMNAE
SOUTHERN WOMEN'S INSTITUTE
MISSISSIPPI UNIVERSITY FOR WOMEN

The Southern Women's Institute was funded by a $496,000 congressionally directed grant received through the assistance of U.S. Senator Thad Cochran. The grant was administered through the U.S. Department of Education.

PROJECT FOUNDERS AND ORAL HISTORY COMMITTEE, MUW ALUMNAE ASSOCIATION
Susan Rayner Puckett, Class of 1975
Barbara White, Class of 1975

SWI ORAL HISTORY PROJECT COORDINATOR
Sally Wells Black, Class of 2004

COORDINATOR OF INTERVIEW TRAINING AND ALUMNAE CONTACTS
Valleri Templeton Merrill, Class of 2006

SUPERVISING INTERN AND COORDINATOR OF PUBLICITY
Rachel Forester, Class of 2007

GRADUATE INTERN AND ASSISTANT FOR TRAINING
Sarah Sheffield, Class of 2006

INTERNS
Brandie Ashe, Class of 2007
Christie Collins, Class of 2007
Amber King, Class of 2007

VIDEOGRAPHER
Chris Jenkins, MUW Office of Public Affairs

INTERVIEWERS FOR THIS VOLUME
Cindle Fontan, Class of 2008
Rachel Forester
Amber King
Valleri Templeton Merrill
Jayde Peterson, Class of 2010
Leigh Pourciau, Class of 2008
Susan Puckett
Elizabeth Segal, Class of 2010
Sarah Sheffield
Barbara White

TRANSCRIBERS FOR THIS VOLUME
Brandie Ashe
Christie Collins
Amber King
Rachel Forester
Leigh Pourciau
Sarah Sheffield

CONSULTANTS
Martha Jo Ballard Mims, Class of 1963
Stephen Pieschel, MUW English Professor Emeritus
Mona Katharine Vance, Class of 2002

DIRECTOR OF THE SOUTHERN WOMEN'S INSTITUTE
Bridget Smith Pieschel, Class of 1979

Golden Days

Reminiscences of Alumnae, Mississippi State College for Women

SOUTHERN WOMEN'S INSTITUTE,
MISSISSIPPI UNIVERSITY FOR WOMEN

Introduction by Bridget Smith Pieschel

UNIVERSITY PRESS OF MISSISSIPPI
JACKSON

www.upress.state.ms.us

The University Press of Mississippi is a member of the Association of American University Presses.

All photographs courtesy of Mississippi University for Women.

Manufactured in the United States of America

First printing 2009
∞
Library of Congress Cataloging-in-Publication Data

Golden days : reminiscences of alumnae, Mississippi State College for Women / Southern Women's Institute, Mississippi University for Women ; introduction by Bridget Smith Pieschel.
p. cm. — (A project of students and alumnae)
Includes index.
ISBN 978-1-60473-097-5 (cloth : alk. paper) 1. Mississippi University for Women—History. 2. Mississippi State College for Women—Alumni and alumnae—Interviews. I. Pieschel, Bridget Smith, 1957– II. Mississippi University for Women. Alumnae Association.
LD7251.C688G65 2009
378.73—dc22 2008020143

British Library Cataloging-in-Publication Data available

Book and jacket design by David Alcorn, Alcorn Publication Design

In memory of Helen Perry Hopkins, Class of 1927

I looked in the glass
And saw myself as they would see me,
Old, lined, gray, and stooped.
I dreaded going back, though I
Loved my college and my friends of college days;
Some had continued with me through all my years.
And then I went, and in
The joy of reunion I almost forgot
How old I looked, how hurt with the years.
I said something of this to a dear friend.
She smiled gently and said to me,
"Go back, and look in the mirror again
And see yourself through our eyes.
You will see joy in living, a youthful spirit,
And your love of college and friends."
So I looked again,
And cherished my reunion.

HPH, 1982

Contents

*DECEASED

Introduction

"In navy blue we gave loud cheers
For Dr. Fant; I hear them plain
As autumn fades and winter nears.

~

But each with hope and vision clears
The path for others in the chain;
We come to toast the shining years
As autumn fades and winter nears."

RUTH MCCOY HARRIS, MISSISSIPPI STATE COLLEGE FOR WOMEN, CLASS OF 1927

"The memory is a living thing—it too is in transit. But during its moment, all that is remembered joins, and lives—the old and the young, the past and the present, the living and the dead."

EUDORA WELTY, MISSISSIPPI STATE COLLEGE FOR WOMEN, 1925–27

WHEN IT OPENED ITS DOORS TO ABOUT 350 STUDENTS IN 1885, the Mississippi Industrial Institute and College for White Girls (later Mississippi State College for Women and now Mississippi University for Women) was the first state-supported college for women in the United States. Those who find it difficult to believe that Mississippi would be the first in any type of educational achievement would also probably be surprised to learn that this public institution was the extension of a private college for women, the Columbus Female Institute, financially maintained continuously since 1847 by a group of stockholders who believed that Columbus girls and women needed more than a finishing school education. But localized private higher education for women was too narrow for Mississippi's needs. For very practical reasons, the all-male Mississippi legislature voted in 1884 to expend some of its limited appropriations on a state-supported college for women. As Representative Wiley Nash said in his persuasive speech supporting the bill, "This institute, if established, will be a Godsend, a blessing to the poor girls of the State. . . . The poor farmers of Mississippi can send their daughters; and here they can gain a good practical education. . . . Can we not do something for the poor girls of Mississippi so that they will be enabled by their honest effort and industry to begin with some prospect of success the great battle of life?"[1] As Nash and his colleagues knew, Mississippi faced dire economic straits. Although the state was already paying for public higher education for white men and African American men and women, thousands more women had no way of earning a living or supporting themselves other than through dependence on fathers, brothers, or husbands.

The II & C was created and survived because it was a unique educational hybrid of liberal arts college and vocational or professional school. In the middle of economic crisis, Mississippi had the foresight to recognize that women needed to learn not only to think for themselves but also to support themselves. The II & C's first president, Richard Watson Jones (1837–1914), who also taught physics and chemistry, headed an otherwise all-female faculty, women who influenced the political and educational life of Mississippians for many decades. Pauline Vandegraaff Orr (1861–1955), Mistress of English; Mary J. S. Callaway (1836–1907), Mistress of Mathematics; Ruth Roudebush (1862–1949), Mistress of Bookkeeping and Penmanship; and Sallie McLaurin (1848–1922), Mistress of Industrial and Decorative Arts, became powerful mentors for the young II & C graduates, who went on to teach, to attend graduate school, or to find places in the business world as bookkeepers or telegraphers. Many were active in the state and national women's suffrage movement, and Orr in particular urged her students to press for the vote for women. In fact, after retiring from teaching in 1913, Orr became a full-time suffragist, serving as president of the state association

1. Qtd. in Bridget Pieschel and Stephen Pieschel, *Loyal Daughters: One Hundred Years at Mississippi University for Women* (Jackson: University Press of Mississippi, 1984), 6.

and speaking the length of the eastern seaboard, using her connections with former students and faculty to further the cause.

Other early faculty members became household names in Mississippi because of their innovative teaching and their passion for their disciplines. Emma Ody Pohl, a legendary physical education teacher at the II & C/MSCW from 1907 until 1955, brought mandatory physical education courses to all students and created some of the most distinctive campus traditions, including the Junior-Freshman Wedding and the Zouave marching drill. Weenona Poindexter, music faculty member from 1894 until 1945, established the diploma in music and began decades of highly successful lyceum concerts by personally guaranteeing the funding for a 1905 performance on campus by renowned pianist Ignacy Jan Paderewski. Mabel Ward, hired in 1903 by President Andrew Kincannon, was one of the first home economics professors in Mississippi, and before she left the II & C in 1915, she created innovative programs, such as the Home Management Practice House, that set the standard for home economics departments all over the country.

Young women and girls, many of them barely fifteen years old, came to Columbus from all over the state. Most of them did not graduate because they lacked adequate preparation for the demanding curriculum; they returned to their hometowns after only a semester or two, at least a little better educated than before they packed their college trunks. But a few persevered. In 1889, the first ten graduates formed an alumnae association and went out to conquer their worlds.

For most of its history, the overcrowded, tightly restricted campus was a society unto itself. The earliest students, selected as the most likely educational prospects from their home counties, knew that their free education was a miraculous gift. Homesick and often overwhelmed by zealous teachers, struggling through chemistry or Latin or telegraphy, they told themselves and each other, "We are lucky to be here; we will make our parents proud; we will 'get a school' or 'get a place' and won't be a burden on anyone." To entertain themselves, they created societies and clubs, performed musicals and plays, invented ghost stories and secret rituals, composed school songs and yells, wrote poems and stories, idolized teachers and upperclasswomen, and imagined the future. Their time at this college bound them together in ways modern students often do not understand. For the rest of their lives, they saw themselves as connected to each other and to the school that changed the direction of their lives. Although the earliest alumnae are gone, their voices still resound in these oral histories, stories told by twenty women who graduated more than fifty years ago from the W. These shared memories of a place and time are crucial in understanding their significance. As Donald Ritchie explains, "Memory is the core of oral history, from which meaning can be extracted and preserved."[2] What are those meanings, and what do they reveal? The answers are as complex and as many-sided as history itself.

While MUW has always been steeped in tradition, this institution also has a history of innovation, beginning with the earliest emphasis on employment as well as higher education for its graduates. Its history is also surprisingly volatile, with years of repeated political threats to its existence, of public and private battles, as well as decades of growth, prosperity, and amicable political relationships. In fact, crises have almost been commonplace. From the first year of the II & C's operation through the 1890s, presidents, faculty, students, alumnae, community factions, and politicians clashed, usually as a consequence of tensions that arose between proponents of the collegiate curriculum and those who saw the school chiefly as a local institution or as a vocational school. The issue of a female president repeatedly surfaced, pushed by alumnae, women faculty, and students; an 1898 legislative investigative committee consequently banned the consideration of women for the highest position at the college.

As in all public education, financial problems always loomed, but they were even worse for a state women's college and were further inflamed by inequities in statewide appropriations and salary scales. When Mississippi's fortunes flagged, public officials, the press, and frustrated taxpayers invariably turned critical eyes on the women's

2. Donald A. Ritchie, *Doing Oral History: A Practical Guide*, 2nd ed. (New York: Oxford University Press, 2003), 19.

college, labeling the W as unnecessary and as too expensive for a poor state to maintain. In 1898, 1920, and 1952, the school barely survived overt closure or merger attempts, and the resulting unfavorable publicity, through the coordinated lobbying efforts of alumnae and the Columbus community. In 1930, loss of accreditation as a consequence of Governor Theodore Bilbo's purge of faculty and administrators at the state's universities, combined with the beginning of the Great Depression, the state's bankruptcy, and the resulting decline in enrollment, nearly devastated the institution. Enrollment surged through the 1950s and 1960s, but by the early 1970s, coeducation at public institutions was becoming more attractive to young women and more acceptable to their parents. Living a nearly cloistered life on campus was not always preferable or even possible. More women were delaying their educations or returning to school after beginning families or careers, raising college students' average age. The W's academic reputation remained strong, but like many women's colleges nationwide, it struggled to define its purpose: should it protect or liberate its students? And in the early 1980s, as Mississippi's public women's university neared its centennial, its single-sex status, the apparent reason for its existence, changed.

Throughout the W's history, significant change has sometimes been welcomed and sometimes resisted, but the school has adapted, survived, and even flourished through several substantial restructurings. In 1920, shortly before newly enfranchised II & C graduates elected their former college president, Henry Whitfield, governor of Mississippi, the Industrial Institute and College for White Girls became Mississippi State College for Women. The new name more clearly reflected the institution's merging of all professional training, including two-year certificate and diploma programs, with four-year bachelor's degrees. The elimination of the original name was happily prophetic, because in 1966 the college was finally racially integrated. The next noteworthy change was more subtle, but many MSCW graduates nonetheless found it jarring. By 1974, as all eight of Mississippi's public institutions of higher education began adding and strengthening graduate programs, MSCW became the Mississippi University for Women.

The most radical change in the institution's history occurred after a male applicant to the nursing program sued to be admitted on the basis of gender discrimination. Ironically, a school that had been established to equalize educational and employment opportunities for women lost a precedent-setting legal battle over gender equity. In 1982, the United States Supreme Court voted five to four to order MUW to admit male applicants to the School of Nursing. To avoid the expense of further legal challenges, the Board of Trustees, Mississippi Institutions of Higher Learning (IHL) ordered MUW to open all academic programs to men.

The change from single-sex to coeducation resulted in several years of uncertainty and turmoil about MUW's institutional identity, although men began to attend and to graduate almost immediately after the Supreme Court decision. At the same time MUW was adjusting to its new status, Mississippi was plunged into another severe budget crisis; higher education's response was not surprising. In 1986 the IHL voted in favor of closing the smallest state universities, MUW and Mississippi Valley State University, one of the state's historically black institutions. Joining forces with Valley alumni, MUW alumnae won another political battle, skillfully using the media and other means to exert fierce pressure on Mississippi legislators. The IHL reversed its decision to close Mississippi Valley State and MUW and in 1988 reaffirmed MUW's original mission of focusing on education, professional preparation, and leadership opportunities for women. The deliberate reaffirmation of the women's mission resulted largely from continued lobbying efforts by alumnae, who persuaded Mississippi's public officials, including the IHL, that the W's survival and growth were directly connected to its unique mission. In 1989, as a dynamic symbol of MUW's renewed focus on women's education, Clyda Stokes Rent became MUW's first female president.

Rent began an aggressive marketing plan that dramatically increased enrollment and resulted in significant fund-raising and national visibility. Her marketing efforts and the reaffirmation of the women's mission apparently did not occur at the expense of male students, many of whom were attracted to MUW by its academic reputation, its small campus environment, and its strong programs in areas where men were traditionally underrepresented, such as elementary education and nursing. However, in spite of MUW's documented success in balancing the women's mission with educating both female and male students, the merger/closure specter rose again later, in response to Mississippi's 1992 loss of the *Ayers v. Fordice* racial discrimination case.[3] W alumnae, this time in tandem with Rent's public relations genius, mobilized political and media pressure to ensure the university's survival.

Now coeducational for more than twenty-five years, the university retains its gender-specific name and women's-emphasis mission. It remains predominantly a women's institution, with male students making up between 15 and 18 percent of the total enrollment. Although a small percentage of the total campus population, male students appear to have found their niche: three men, David Ivey, Class of 1992, Trey Harper, Class of 1998, and Phillip Cockrell, Class of 2003, have served as president of the Student Government Association. Fraternities coexist with the women's social clubs, male and female students live and study together in the residence halls and in the residential Honors College, and men compete for and receive academic and leadership scholarships. Programs in nursing and in culinary arts are particularly attractive to male students seeking less traditional careers. Today, the Mississippi University for Women prides itself on its "tradition of excellence for women and men" and provides the reminder that it has been "admitting men since 1982" with every official mention of the university's name.

The twenty women interviewed for this collection now see their lives from multiple perspectives; they understand the present by recalling

3. In 1975, Jake Ayers filed suit against the state of Mississippi, saying that the state's three public historically black institutions of higher education were and had been consistently and deliberately funded at a lower level than the historically white universities. In 1992, the case reached the U.S. Supreme Court, which ordered the Fifth District Court of Appeals to take up the case again. The plaintiffs won, and Mississippi was ordered to remedy years of financial discrimination against the historically black institutions. In response, the IHL recommended that Mississippi Valley State University and Mississippi University for Women be merged with two other state institutions, a plan that would essentially have eliminated the two smallest universities.

and examining the events in their lives in the context of the W's past. They are the institution's collective history, and they have been significant determiners of that history, participants in its successes and its battles. Which of their recollections are more important, the facts of state or national events or the details about meals and collars? That determination depends on one's definition of history. Perhaps the most appropriate definition, at least for oral historians, is also one of the oldest: Cicero called history "the witness that testifies to the passing of time."[4] As witnesses, these women speak clearly about what is valuable to them as individuals and as women. Historian and professor of feminist studies Emily Honig reminds us that "oral history has become increasingly central to the writing of women's history."[5] The memories revealed in this volume clearly demonstrate that for these women, their college experiences marked their lives in similar ways and gave them a conspicuous consciousness of their difference from other women of their generation.

Many of the women interviewed for this collection have direct connections to the early faculty and administration. When Mary Ellen Weathersby Pope's older sisters were studying at the II & C, three original faculty members—Orr, Roudebush, and modern languages teacher Gessner Tutwiler Smith (1862–1934)—were still in the classroom. In 1889, Barbara McMillin Webb's paternal grandmother was one of the first women to earn an II & C industrial certificate. When Pope, Elizabeth Smith Gwin, and Juanita McCown Hight were at MSCW, Cora Walker, a member of the first graduating class and a student of Orr and Tutwiler, was still teaching chemistry. Gwin learned piano technique from Poindexter, whose mother had been a teacher at the Columbus Female Institute. Pope, Hight, and Emily Eugenia Summer were taught by alumna Mary Wilson, who was taught by Ward. Every woman in this volume vividly remembers the inimitable Pohl. While all of these recollections are based on memories rather than on statistics or researched

4. Cicero, *Pro Publio Sestio.*

5. Emily Honig, "Getting to the Source--Striking Lives: Oral History and the Politics of Memory," *Journal of Women's History* 9, no. 1 (1997): 139.

evidence, as oral *portraiteur* Studs Terkel reminds us, "in their rememberings are their truths."[6]

In 1954, barely two years after MSCW had survived yet another threat to its separate identity, a proposed merger with Mississippi State, the old chapel was named for Orr. Orr had been a controversial figure in her time, promoted by faculty and alumnae as a candidate for the presidency of MSCW, as were her colleague Mary Callaway and their former student Nellie Sutton Keirn, although more conservative factions apparently considered perilous Orr's forceful personality and her captivating influence. Of the three, she was the only one who did not serve as interim president or even as a dean. Self-exiled in New York City, Orr was too infirm to attend the dedication of the chapel but sent a letter of thanks, asserting that she knew her intellectual influence would survive in her students. At the ceremony, Myra Lindsey, Class of 1912, declared, "Some modern physicists say no sound made is ever lost. . . . Miss Orr's beautiful voice will never be lost to those who were fortunate enough to be her students."[7] It is not difficult to believe that we can still hear Orr, her colleagues, and their students speaking through this volume's interview subjects; after all, every one of them was taught by at least one woman who learned her craft from the original faculty members.

Although the graduation years for the interviewees range from 1926 to 1957, the common campus memories in this collection sound, echo, and reverberate: performing Pohl's rousing and militarily precise Zouave marches; singing the alma mater and "Hail to Thee" at every chapel meeting; eating family-style meals complete with white linen tablecloths and napkins in Shattuck Dining Hall; reveling in their exposure to a world of music, art, and drama unheard of in their hometowns; carrying the Magnolia Chain at graduation; expressing their gratitude for teachers who demanded more of them than they knew they had; describing friendships that have endured for fifty years or more.

6. Studs Terkel, *Hard Times: An Oral History of the Great Depression* (New York: Avon, 1970), 17.

7. Qtd. in Pieschel and Pieschel, *Loyal Daughters*, 176.

There are remarkable firsthand accounts of historical events, sometimes appearing in the middle of more ordinary recollections. As Philip Gardner points out, "People always have more to tell us than we expect."[8] Pope describes the drama of rising water and her escape from the Great Mississippi Flood of 1927. Hight recalls "standing in the lobby in Fant Hall when the first announcement came on the radio that President Franklin Roosevelt had closed the banks" at the beginning of the Great Depression. Hyacinth McCormick Hayman describes the Asian exhibits at the 1933 Chicago World's Fair. Summer remembers enduring an air raid warning while alone in a dark classroom building during World War II.

The opportunities to learn outside of the classroom were not lost on these women, and their recollections of campus programs and speakers are amazingly detailed. Hight heard Jascha Heifetz and John Philip Sousa's orchestra perform on campus and while in charge of the ticket office at Whitfield Auditorium spent an afternoon chatting with writer and explorer Richard Halliburton. Joan Meadows McLemore enjoyed Bob Hope, but author Frances Parkinson Keyes made more of an impression: "She heaved her bosom up on the lectern, and she started talking. That woman was one of the most fascinating speakers that I have ever heard. . . . I could've listened for hours." Lenore Loving Prather describes being a member of an enthusiastic student audience demanding four encores of "handsome, tall" opera star Jerome Hines. Prather was luckier than Nell Ann Pickett, who says her only regret about her time at MSCW is that she refused a weekend trip with friends to Tupelo to see an up-and-coming singer named Elvis Presley.

As students, these women knew that they were fortunate in their affordable education. Pope says bluntly that and she and her four sisters came to MSCW because it was a "cheap school." Her prudent working mother said to her children, "I'm going to educate these five girls, but the two boys will have to fend for themselves, [because the boys] can manage, but girls need an education." Katherine Lipscomb Worrell recounts her difficulty in paying even the very low tuition fees because of the pov-

8. Philip Gardner, "Oral History in Education: Teacher's Memory and Teacher's History," *History of Education* 32, no. 2 (2003): 184.

erty of her large farming family, in which she served as her "mother's nurse" for her numerous younger siblings. Until she moved into Main Dormitory at MSCW, she says, "I don't believe I'd ever had a bath in a bathtub. At home, we used a tin pan, a tin tub, every Saturday night." Summer recalls, "My family would talk about my twin brother going to college and how they were going to afford to send him to college, but my name was never mentioned." Her mother eventually intervened and said, "If that boy is going to college, this girl is going, too," persuading her husband that at the "inexpensive" MSCW, Summer could help earn her keep with a federal work scholarship. For McLemore, MSCW offered the same superior education as the prohibitively costly private women's colleges: "We didn't have to go to Ward-Belmont or some of those fancy schools a lot of girls from here went to, like Hollins College in Virginia . . . more expensive schools . . . Brenau, places like that." Transfer student Pickett had planned to move from her junior college to private Millsaps College, but she and her family quickly eliminated that option when they learned what the tuition would be there in comparison to state-supported MSCW.

These women believed that they had a responsibility to be self-supporting. In fact, as new graduates, they took it for granted that they had been prepared for an independent life, whether they married and had families or remained single. After graduation, they worked. Carmen Pearson Ronken matter-of-factly describes the strenuous feats she performed as a home demonstration agent in Leake County: "We had to show them how to slaughter the [cow]. I'd always take a sharp knife the county agent would go with me to help me cut up the meat. . . . However, sometimes I just did it myself, with a sharp saw—a meat saw." Hight remembers that "jobs were hard to get in 1934." However, she continues, she found a teaching position, because "back when I graduated, if you had five people who were applying for a job and only one of them was an MUW grad, the MUW girl got the job. That was the reputation it had." Hight remembers that she "made $75 a month my first year. The second year, I got $80. And about the beginning of the fourth year, it got to $85, and I got a chance to be home economist for the federal government for $160 a month. I thought I was going to be rich, but I had to buy a car, and my car payments were $25 a month." Mary Libby Payne graduated from law school and at first found that her gender limited her options:

> I couldn't get a job. . . . The law firms wanted to know how many words a minute I could type. They didn't want to think about me as an associate but as a typist, and that's the one subject that I made a C in. . . . I finally did get a job as a secretary for a lawyer. Why people don't tell you things like this beforehand, I don't know, but I was so desperately in need of a job—I later found out he had been disbarred and reinstated. Anyway, I had beaten him in a lawsuit. . . . It was sort of a trash suit, he thought, [thrown my way by another lawyer, and] the lawyer I defeated hired me to be his secretary, not a lawyer. He was to pay me fifty dollars a week. But if he was not there on Friday when he was supposed to give me my fifty dollars, we started a new week the next week. He thought he didn't owe me for the week before. That job got a little expensive for me.

Payne eventually opened her own law office after losing another job because she took a few weeks off from work to have a child.

As she neared graduation, Sylvia Duck Clark says she knew she would be "going to work somewhere," so she and an MSCW friend moved to Dallas, Texas: "That seemed like a big city to us. She had majored in library science, so she immediately got a job in the public library there. But they wouldn't let you teach there unless you had lived in Texas for a year. . . . I got a job in the library, too. I didn't intend to go anywhere with it, just be there long enough to be able to teach the next year. So we both took the teachers' test and passed it, and the next year, we got assigned to schools there." Beverly Koch Jones concludes, "We had such good role models on the campus. . . . [A]ll the deans were women. They were interested in developing us. The W made me mature and then realize that I was equipped [for life]."

These women became the leaders of their generation. Most stayed in Mississippi to work, to raise children, to volunteer, to crusade for causes, to blaze trails, to break gender barriers in organizations from church councils to chambers of commerce to courts of justice. Jones says that MSCW taught her "about service." She continues, "To give up yourself is sometimes hard for people, but here on the W campus, we were always giving to each other." Mary Elizabeth Barrett Francis says, "We were expected to do this, and we did it, and we've kept on doing it through life." Payne says that as a lawyer and judge, she "wanted to make a difference in people's lives. I wanted to give a voice to the voiceless. I wanted to see justice done to the poor." In 1966, Pope calmly drove a carload of African American MSCW students to a program at the University of Mississippi, persuading the owner of a segregated diner in Pontotoc to allow all of them inside to have coffee and use the restroom. As judges, Payne and Prather wrote groundbreaking law giving equitable property rights to women in divorce and protecting women from sexual harassment in the workplace.

These women still give back to their towns, their states, and their school, and they come back at Homecoming nearly every April as Golden Girls for whom the years fall away, at least for a day or so. They have given generously of themselves in these interviews. They are candid, serious, proud, modest, funny, moving, and perceptive. They believe, as Hayman said, that W women are "sisters under the skin." MSCW made a mark on them that has never faded, and they cherish their educational kinship as much as they value their blood kin. They know themselves and live in the present, not in a haze of nostalgia. But they also remember who they were and honor the institution that added value to their lives. We are all grateful for their "hearts' allegiance which never dies," as the W's fight song, "Hail to Thee," says, and for the treasure of their memories.

It is difficult to thank everyone who deserves it because this collection is the result of many people's efforts. It is a culmination of a partnership between the graduates and the students of Mississippi

University for Women and of a project begun by alumnae Susan Rayner Puckett and Barbara White. They launched the MUW Alumnae Association's oral history project in 2003 and committed themselves to preserving the memories of older alumnae, particularly the oldest living graduates. During the fall of 2004, they and MUW videographer Chris Jenkins filmed the first two interviews: Mary Ellen Weathersby Pope, Class of 1926 and Emily Eugenia Summer, Class of 1945.

MUW recognized the value of their efforts and supported the project with financial resources and personnel. Early in 2005, Susan, Barbara, and Chris began filming additional interviews for historical preservation and for presentation in edited versions at future Homecomings. Their interviews are the sources of six of the oral histories in this book and the partial source of two others.

Shortly after her arrival in 2002, President Claudia Limbert began to plan the creation of a campus women's center dedicated in part to recording and archiving valuable memories and historical documents. Her vision took the form of a grant request to the U.S. Department of Education, which provided nearly half a million dollars to establish the Southern Women's Institute in the summer of 2005. An important component of the new institute was the collection of oral histories, particularly those of alumnae who attended MUW at least fifty years earlier—the Golden Girls. The new oral history project was designed to offer educational opportunities for the present, since the interviewing, recording, and transcribing were to be conducted by MUW students. The grant provided not only funds for archive-quality recorders and other technology but also stipends for conducting the interviews and for the publication of this book.

The twenty oral histories in *Golden Days* illustrate the high quality and impressive breadth of all of the alumnae interviews that have been and are being collected for the MUW archives. The sharp details and reflective commentaries offered by the interviewees illustrate the significant historical value of the entire collection. A wealth of interview material is available for future research and publication. To a large extent, this first volume contains those completely transcribed interviews readily available for editing. Beyond the broader historical significance of this publication and of MUW's entire oral history collection, these stories are especially important in identifying and celebrating the specific and lasting effects of women's educational experiences at the Mississippi State College for Women. These preserved memories will strengthen the connection between the W's past and its future, a link symbolized by the Magnolia Chain that seniors carry every year at graduation.

We owe very special thanks to Sally Wells Black, who oversaw the beginning of the campus project. She researched similar programs, and she and student intern Valleri Templeton Merrill conducted the first training workshops for students. By the spring of 2006, interviews were in progress. The newly trained student interviewers coordinated their work with the MUW Alumnae Association Oral History Committee, scheduling joint interviews of alumnae who had graduated in the late 1920s and 1930s.

Student interviewers transcribed both video and sound recordings. Rachel Forester and Amber King began the transcriptions of existing videotape and of the digitized recordings. These two women proved amazingly adept, accurate, and patient, spending hours producing as many as forty pages of transcript per interview. They were later joined by Brandie Ashe, Leigh Pourciau, and Sarah Sheffield. These interns continued the demanding and labor-intensive process of contacting women and scheduling, conducting, and transcribing interviews, all the while keeping meticulous records.

After Sally Wells Black moved to Jackson, Val Templeton Merrill took over the project until her May 2006 graduation, when Rachel Forester assumed oversight. As a project for a graduate seminar, Ole Miss southern studies graduate student Sarah Sheffield trained new student volunteers in the fall of 2006 and coordinated interviews conducted during Homecoming of 2007. The following summer, Christie Collins documented and proofread the interviews and selected and scanned photographs. All of these women showed extraordinary dedication, professionalism, and resourcefulness. In addition, we are grateful to Mona Vance, Class of 2002, archivist for the Columbus-Lowndes

Public Library's Billups-Garth Archives, for her research skills and technical advice, and to Joshua Hollis, Class of 2007, MUW Office of Public Affairs, and David Brasher, Class of 2006, Columbus-Lowndes County Library's information technologist, for hands-on help in preparing fading yearbook photographs for book-quality publication.

Finally, we all owe particular thanks to Seetha Srinivasan at the University Press of Mississippi and to Ellen Goldlust-Gingrich. Without Seetha's advice, guidance, and support and Ellen's accurate, sensitive, and perceptive editing, the manuscript would not have become a book.

Bridget Smith Pieschel, Class of 1979
April 2008

Golden Days

Mary Ellen Weathersby Pope
Class of 1926

OCTOBER 14, 2004
INTERVIEWED BY BARBARA WHITE AND SUSAN PUCKETT
FILMED BY CHRIS JENKINS
TRANSCRIBED BY BRANDIE ASHE

MARY ELLEN WEATHERSBY WAS BORN TO Ellen Harrell Weathersby and Robert Lodwic Weathersby on April 14, 1905, in Liberty, Mississippi. Raised in Magnolia, she attended MSCW from 1922 to 1926, when she received a bachelor's of science degree in home economics. She had four sisters, all of whom earned degrees at MSCW—Nema Weathersby Colee, Class of 1915; Marguerite Weathersby Devall, Class of 1916; Robbie Weathersby Corder, Class of 1929; and Ann Weathersby Starnes, Class of 1931—as well as two brothers. During her time at the W, Mary Ellen Weathersby participated in the Home Economics Club and the Westminster Club for Presbyterian students. Under her senior picture in the *Meh Lady*, MSCW's yearbook, she is described as "a dependable combination of willingness to help, genial disposition, and ability to execute practical ideas." Between 1938 and 1973, Pope taught home economics at the W; she also spent two years as a student counselor. She earned a master's degree from the University of Minnesota in 1945. In 1949, she married widower Willis Pope (1895–1958), a bank executive. After her retirement, she was named assistant professor emerita, and in 2004 she received an honorary doctorate from MUW. She also received an MUW Medal of Excellence, an Alumnae Achievement Award, and a Celebration of Service Award from the Lowndes County chapter of the alumni association. Pope served as a director emerita of the MUW Foundation Board of Directors. She lived in Columbus until her death in March 2007.

MP: I lived in Liberty, Mississippi, for about three years. Then we moved from Liberty to Magnolia, which is about twenty-five miles from Liberty. My father had a mercantile business, he and his two brothers. They had this great big old brick store, and they had everything in it from potatoes to women's clothes. He had typhoid fever when I was three years old, and he was very ill. Back in those days, they didn't know how to treat it. He recovered, but he was an invalid after that. He realized he was not able to carry on with the store, so he and my mother—they had seven children—decided that they would sell his interest in the store, and they would move to Magnolia and buy this small hotel, and she would run the hotel and he would keep the books. My mother was a very bright, courageous woman who had never worked a day in her life. They moved us, and we went on the train from Liberty to McComb. Somebody met us there in a car and took us to Magnolia, which was seven miles south of McComb. The hotel was small and kind of a long, rectangular building. We lived on the right-hand side of the hotel. But on the left-hand side of the hotel, my mother had the office, and back of that was the dining room, and then back of that was the storage room, and then the kitchen was built at the back.

BW: What was the name of this hotel?
MP: It was already named Victoria, and Mother didn't change the name of it. She had a good cook—a man—and she had two boys that waited

on the tables, and we all lived in that hotel. It was strange. My mother would take time to see about us. She had a little baby at that time, so she had to have a nurse for the baby, but she carried on very well.

She was a person that believed in education. She had those five girls and two boys, and she would often say, "Now, I'm going to educate these five girls, but the two boys will have to fend for themselves." Because, she said, "they can manage, but girls need an education." So all five of us came to the W, and we all majored in a different field, and we were all teachers. That pleased her very much. I wanted to be a nurse, but she wouldn't let me. She said, "Nurses have to work too hard. They have to scrub floors and do dirty things like that, and I don't want you doing that."

BW: Why did she choose to send her daughters to the W?
MP: She sent all of us to the W because it was a cheap school and she could afford to send us there. My oldest sister finished in 1915, and then my next sister finished in 1916. She went only two years. She was the kind that wanted to get out and make money, so she took the two-year normal certificate, and she was a teacher. But we were all teachers.

There were two of us at the W for four years. I was there with my younger sister, and then she was there with the youngest girl. There were three little girls when we moved to the hotel, and we were the three I think that Mother worried about because the others were teenagers; in fact, Big Sister was in college. I never did call her anything but Big Sister because she was so much older than I was. I never called her by her name, which was Nema, which is unusual.

We enjoyed the life at the hotel. In those days, the salesmen were called drummers. Mother had such a good reputation for having clean sheets on the beds, the drummers would say. And she would make chocolate pies and fried chicken. She became famous for that. And those drummers made their schedules so that they could spend the night at Mrs. Weathersby's hotel.

I was a very naive fifteen-year-old who came to the W. I finished high school in three years. My mother planned all this because she knew we had just so much money, and she was planning ahead all of the time. So there always were two of us in college, and that was really a strain on her, I know. We didn't have a car.

BW: Did you go to a public school?
MP: Yes, I went to public school and finished high school, as I said, in three years. And at the W, they took me on probation, so I had to make certain grades in order to stay there because I didn't get a high school diploma. I just had finished enough courses that I could go in the W.

BW: What did you major in?
MP: I majored in home economics because my mother thought I was domestically inclined. In those days, you paid attention to what your mama said. She wanted me to major in home economics, and that's what I majored in. I never regretted it, except that I think some of my teachers regretted that I majored in home economics. I couldn't cook, I couldn't sew. In a big family like mine, you had to have a cook. I took nutrition. I took cooking classes. Miss Wilson[1] and Miss Scott[2] were in the home economics department. They took me under their wing, and they would give me projects in the summer so that I could learn more about cooking. I was really just timid, as I say, a naive girl, and I really struggled at the W because I was homesick so much of the time.

Let me tell you about the projects they would give us. Miss Wilson gave me one project—cooking for my family for a month. I had to buy the groceries, and I had to cook, and I had to clean up and just do everything that a mother has to do. I had a boyfriend over at Mississippi State who was doing some research with soybeans—soybeans were just coming in—and he would say, "Take this variety of soybeans and cook them, and tell me which variety your family likes the best." So I cooked those soybeans for that whole month, different varieties, and my brother,

1. Mary Wilson (1892–1988), Class of 1915, served as a faculty member and later as head of MSCW's home economics department from 1925 until 1961.
2. Julia Scott (1895–1977) joined MSCW in 1921 as instructor of clothing construction and remained a member of the home economics faculty until 1965.

who was just older than I, told my mother one day, "If Mary Ellen don't quit giving me that cow food, I'm gonna run away from home!" I had to have sewing, too. Miss Scott insisted that I do some sewing in the summer. But I loved the courses and enjoyed them.

In those years, the home ec majors had to take two years of chemistry. I had not had chemistry in high school, so I really struggled, and I had a teacher that I did not learn anything from the first year—Miss Cora Q. Walker.[3] She wore a wig, and we all were fascinated with that wig. We'd never seen a wig before. We'd think about doing tricks on her all the time, so we could get that wig off of her head. We'd try to turn the spigots so they'd shoot up and maybe hit her wig. I was a *W* in those days, so I sat on the last seat in the room. On Monday she'd question the girl in seat number 1—she'd go around the room. So I could figure out what question I was going to get on Friday. I'd learn that question, but that's all I'd learn. Oh, Miss Cora Q. Walker. We used to watch her walk to the theater. She loved Rudolph Valentino,[4] and she would sit for hours and see a show two or three times just so she could see Rudolph Valentino.

I took a lot of courses that related to agriculture. I took horticulture, and I took a course that taught us about raising chickens and things like that. And we had courses in child development and family relations and nutrition. Then I had to take a lot of science because I had a science minor. I took physics—just a half a year—but I had two years of chemistry. In the second year of chemistry, I did very well, but the first year I have to admit I didn't do very well.

BW: Do you remember any of the other teachers on campus?

MP: I remember Miss Pohl[5]—scared to death of her. She would yell at you. If we were supposed to be doing something with our right foot and we did it with our left, she'd say, "Weathersby, do you know your right

3. Cora Q. Walker (1865–1951), Class of 1889, was a member of II & C's first graduating class and taught chemistry at her alma mater from 1893 until 1933.
4. Rudolph Valentino (1895–1926) was a silent film star from 1914 until his death.
5. Emma Ody Pohl (1880–1966) joined II & C in 1907, when she was hired to develop the department of physical education. She taught that subject until her retirement in 1955.

foot from your left foot?" At that stage, when she would say that, I did not know my right foot from my left. I would just freeze! She was that kind of person. I was not one of her favorite pupils, because I wasn't very graceful, and I never was one of the dancers.

BW: Did you participate in Zouave?
MP: Oh, heavens, yes, four years. Really, Zouave was just exercise. We had some figures we would do, like waving arms. We were marching a lot, and then we would do exercises like toe touches. They really were just good exercise classes. But of course it was spectacular to see hundreds of people doing that. She would stand up on the fountain between Hastings-Simmons and Franklin Halls and direct us. She could see to the back row—we were in sections—and she could look way back, and if you were out of step, she could tell. She had a good mind, and we were going to do it right or we weren't going to do it at all. I think most people were scared of her, because she was pretty demanding. Later in life, I knew her after I married and my husband had died. I had gone back into teaching, and I would ride to school every morning. I had to pass right by the Alexandria Hotel, where she lived—in the 400 block of College Street, where the Alexandria Parking Lot is today. She'd be walking and I'd be riding, and she'd look at me and she'd shake a fist at me and she'd say, "Weathersby! Get out of that car and walk!" And I wasn't even Weathersby then, I was a Pope. But she never called me by my married name—I was always Weathersby. She was a character, but she was a wonderful person. She really was.

BW: Do any other teachers or students stand out in your mind?
MP: Helen Hopkins[6] was a real good friend of mine. And Helen was also a friend of Eudora Welty's.[7] Eudora was just in school two years. I didn't have much contact with her, because she was liberal arts, and I was more

6. Helen Perry Hopkins (1906–2000), Class of 1927, served briefly as a dormitory social adviser and held the position of MSCW alumnae secretary from 1929 until 1932.
7. Eudora Alice Welty (1909–2001), an internationally known writer, was a native of Jackson, Mississippi, who attended MSCW in 1926 and 1927 before transferring to the University of Wisconsin at Madison.

science. I don't want to misrepresent things about her, but she wasn't very happy at the W. I think she thought it was a poor girls' school, and she really was not interested in staying. She wanted to study journalism. We didn't have a journalism department, so she left and took journalism courses. She should have been at Randolph-Macon[8] or somewhere like that, generally, because we were a poor girls' school. We weren't poverty-stricken, but it was a cheap school. And I knew that was the reason that I was there—because it was a cheap school.

BW: Do you have any memories of the dining hall?
MP: Yes, we had family-style dining, and you had to be there by a certain time or the doors were closed on you—you couldn't get in. I didn't like to get up for breakfast, but I would just put on my raincoat over my pajamas and go. If anyone caught me doing that, I was in trouble.

BW: What did students usually wear?
MP: Oh, I had to wear a uniform. My two older sisters wore skirts and little basque waists, and the skirts had to have seven gores. They were wide, and they all had seven gores in them. Both my older sisters had to make their garments. They were all navy blue. But I didn't have to make mine. My mother was a good seamstress, and she made a lot of my clothes because she couldn't find what she wanted. Once a year, she would go down to New Orleans with my father and buy a lot of our clothes. She made me a dress that was satin-back crepe—slick on one side, shiny on one side, and just dull on the other side. My mama liked the slick side, so she made just a darling dress, I thought, on the shiny side. And I wore it, and I got a reprimand, because they said that Mama should have made it on the dull side. That made my mother mad. Oh, she was just ready to write Miss Keirn[9] and bless her out, because she had made that dress and she thought it was beautiful, and she didn't

8. Randolph-Macon Woman's College (now Randolph College), a highly regarded private school founded in 1891 in Lynchburg, Virginia.

9. Nellie Sutton Keirn (1885–1975), Class of 1906, was hired at II & C in 1906 as a teaching fellow. She taught until 1919, when she became dean, serving until 1955. She also held the post of acting president of MSCW in 1929–30.

think I should get a reprimand, but I did. So many reprimands would make a demerit, and so many demerits would make a confinement to campus, so you were in trouble if you got many.

BW: Did you have dances? Did boys come to visit?
MP: Yes. And of course, we danced with each other. The girls danced with the girls, because the boys would come for dates, but that was an ordeal, too. Dancing was really one of our big recreational activities, and we loved it. We did all kinds of dances because we didn't have anything else to do. After supper we would go into this big activity room and dance.

You could have a date once a month, I think it was. And if you were going to have a date, and you were going to a dance over at Mississippi State, your mother would have to write Miss Keirn and tell her that you could go. Then Miss Keirn had to write and approve, and then Miss Keirn would have to find out who you were going to stay with, just so you could spend the night. There would be six to eight of us in the room, three of us asleep in the bed and the rest of us asleep on the floor, and it would cost a dollar to stay there at these Starkville ladies' homes. But we looked forward to those times. If you got an invitation to a dance over at State, why, it was wonderful, because we didn't have boys. In 1938, I think it was, we started having formal dances with men. I was teaching by then. We started letting boys come for dances.

BW: What did most of the students expect to do when they finished school?
MP: Most of them were going to teach if they had to work. Now, some of them didn't like teaching. Some of them just said they would not teach. But there were not a lot of opportunities. I was lucky. I got a job over in the Delta. But my mother didn't want me to go. She said, "The mosquitoes are going to eat you up." I never had been to the Delta, but I wanted to go. I was going to Anguilla to teach, and they were going to give me a hundred dollars a month. That was more money than anybody else had offered me, so that was the way I convinced Mama I should go to Anguilla and teach. That was in 1926 and 1927.

I just had a wonderful time. The Delta people, they believe in a good time. And the boys—the men, I should say—looked forward to the teachers coming, and they were just wonderful to us. They'd take us to Vicksburg; then they'd take us to Greenville—we were between Vicksburg and Greenville. That would be on the weekend. Some of the boys would have cars, but usually we didn't go by ourselves, because if a boy had a car then he'd invite some other boys, and maybe we'd be six in a car to go to Vicksburg or to Greenville. I was teaching chemistry and home economics, and I had to work because I wasn't a very good chemistry student, and I was scared to death that those big old football boys were going to blow the place up. I'd go on Saturday and try out every experiment so that I would know how to do it to keep them from blowing up the place.

I guess it was in early February that they began to say, "If it doesn't quit raining, we're going to have a flood." I didn't pay any attention to them, because I didn't know what they were talking about, because I'd never seen a flood. And it just kept raining, so in March, we really got serious about the flood. People were just worried to death because the water was everywhere, and they were saying that they couldn't get the crops in, and it was really bad. I guess it was the end of March that they started saying, "If the levee breaks at Greenville, why, it'll come down here and we'll be flooded." I didn't pay much attention to that. I didn't know what they were talking about. Then, one night, the man and woman that I was living with said, "I believe that levee's going to break at Greenville." I still wasn't too concerned about it. In the night, though, I heard an unusual noise, and I didn't know what it was. I didn't get up to see. The next morning, I put my feet down on the floor, and I put my feet in water. The levee had broken, and the water had just gushed down to Anguilla. It was right in the path of the flood.[10] I got worried then.

So I went to breakfast, and the man I was living with was very nice, and he was trying to be calm and to keep us calm. He said, "I know that

10. On April 21, 1927, the levees broke, leading to the Great Mississippi Flood of 1927, the worst ever in U.S. history. Within ten days, one million acres of the Mississippi Delta were covered with water ten feet deep.

we got to get you teachers out of here, because there'd be no way for us to take care of you, since the water may even go as high as the ceiling." We were really worried, so about 10:00 he told us they had gotten boats to take us down to the railroad station so we could catch the train. They were getting us a special train to take us to Vicksburg. We got in these boats and we went to the station.

It's funny in a way. The woman that roomed with me had been in Anguilla a long time, and she was in love with this man, and he was just begging her and begging her to marry him. He said, "Marry me!" She said, "I just can't see our future in this flood, and I just don't think I better do that." But he was just begging her and begging her. She finally said, "No, I'm going to get in this boat and I'm going to go on to Vicksburg, and I'll come back." So we got in the boat. Then we went to the station, got off at the station, and we're waiting for the train, and there was Jack, still trying to persuade Bea to marry him. She still didn't want to get married. So then we got on the train. There was a man with a big pole on the cowcatcher of the train, and he stood on that and he would see if the crossties were still there because the tracks could have washed out. It took us five hours to go fifty miles, because it was just that tedious. We got to Rolling Fork, which is five miles from Anguilla, and there was Jack! And he said, "Bea, you've just got to get off of that train and come on and marry me." So she just grabbed her bag and got off the train, went back and married him. And they got along all right. They found a barn that they lived in for a while because that was the only place that they could stay. That was right romantic. I remember that very vividly because of her grabbing that bag and getting off that train and getting in that boat with him.

BW: How long did you stay in Vicksburg?

MP: I can't remember. It didn't take us too long to get a train to Jackson. But then there wasn't any way I could get home. My mother was just a wreck. She was just scared to death. There was a man in Magnolia who had a home on the coast as well as in Magnolia, and he had a big boat. He had told Mama that he would come get me. I don't know how he thought he could get there, but anyhow, he told her, so that kind of satisfied her until she found out that I was out of the flood and that I was coming home.

That was quite an event, I'll tell you. I remember that it made a very big impression on me because I'd never seen that much water in my life. And it is a scary thing just to look at. There was water everywhere, and you could see it rising. It was just rising up in that house. I don't know how high it got in that house, but it was coming pretty fast.

BW: When did you go to graduate school?

MP: I left Anguilla and went to Canton, Mississippi, and taught. I taught there five years. While I was in Canton, there were about five of us teachers that decided that we were going to see the world. We were going to start off by going to New York, so we saved our money and in the summer we all went to New York. One year we went by boat, because it was cheap. And then the rest of the time, though, we went by train. For two summers, I went to Columbia University, hoping that I would start a degree. They didn't know what home economics was at Columbia. They just didn't. I took some courses. I took one course because I had read a book that the teacher had written, so I thought, "I'll just get in this class, because I can go back and brag about having a class with Scribner," I think his name was. I never saw him. He went to Europe that summer, and a graduate student taught the class the whole time.

At Columbia we had classes that were on tiers because the class was large. I think there were about five hundred in that class. One of the assignments was that you were to tell about the educational program in your state, and how it was developing and so forth and so on. That frightened the life out of me, but I wrote to the Mississippi State Department of Education and told them what I had to do and to send me some literature. I really worked on my paper about the educational system in Mississippi, and I felt right proud of it. I thought, "But I'll never hear from him." Don't you know, the first day he called on Miss Weathersby from Mississippi for my report? Mississippians didn't go to New York in those days—that was back in the early 1930s. So I walked down those steps, and I was just trembling. I didn't know whether I was going to get through that or not. Anyhow, I said, since we had to tell who we were, "I'm Mary Ellen Weathersby from Magnolia, Mississippi." I had that southern voice—they just screamed. The whole class! So I gave my report, and I made an A, so it must have been all right. But I thought I was going to have a heart attack, I really did, because I was so scared. When we had an examination, I just knew I wasn't going to pass. There were a bunch of men in that class, and they were just cheating. I was just horrified. They just had brought all this material with them, and they just openly would look something up and write it down. I could hardly finish my paper for looking at them doing all this cheating. It really made me mad, because, hey, I was struggling, but that was the only way I finished—without cheating. I had my eyes opened to a lot of things in those classes. I went to Columbia two years, and I decided that if I really wanted an education, I'd better go somewhere else!

In New York, we'd go to school in the morning. There were five of us. We had an apartment, and we'd live in the apartment and fix our meals, some of them. And then in the afternoons, we would tour and go to the theater and do things like that. When I told my mother I was going to New York for two months, she said, "If you go to New York, you will take some courses at Columbia University." She said, "I just don't think it's really decent for you to go up there and just be loose on the town." So I had to take two courses at Columbia, and that's when I started in graduate school.

By the time I had gotten a job at the W, I realized I was going to have to have a master's degree, so I started going to the University of Minnesota. I had a friend up there, and she wrote me and said, "If you really want an education, come to the university." I started at the University of Minnesota. I really liked it, and I felt that I was getting a real good education. I went two summers, and then I had to go for a spring term and a winter term—they wouldn't let you get your degree just during the summer—which was the best thing that ever happened except that I almost froze to death. I enjoyed Minnesota, and I enjoyed my classes. I had wonderful teachers. I was in small classes.

That's where I had my first experience with integration. There was a black woman in one of my classes, and she was from Texas, a real nice woman and smart as she could be. Of course, I'd never had much contact with blacks in any way, except in the kitchen and with nurses and things like that. My mother used to help the black county home demonstration agent, and she would come to our house, but she would come in the back door, but I remember Mama giving her a cup of coffee. Mama was very—I would say she was liberal. So I was interested in this black woman because I think she was interested in me. I was the only southerner, except for her.

I ran around with four other women, and I called them "girls." That was back in the 1940s. They were just so interested in the fact that a southern girl had come north to get an education. They quizzed me and quizzed me and asked "How'd you get here?" and "Why did you come?" and so forth and so on. They decided they were going to test me as to how I felt really about this black woman. We all ate in the cafeteria, and one morning they decided they would go to the cafeteria, sit at a table, and then they were going to invite the black woman to eat with us so that when I came in, they could see what I would do. So I came bouncing in, and I looked over there and I thought, "I've never seen her at the table," this black woman. "I've never eaten with a black person, except for Jane, my maid, when I was a little girl." And I thought, "What am I going to do? Am I going to just snub her now?" But I kept thinking, "I've never eaten with a black person." That just kept looming up in my mind. So I went on down the line, but the closer I got to it, something said, "Now, listen. You just go and sit by her," because I figured they were tricking me and because we talked a lot about blacks and whites and their relationship, so I went and sat down by her. The conversation stopped. They didn't have a thing to say—didn't talk. We ate the meal in silence. Afterward, they said, "You know, you just ruined the whole thing." They said, "We just expected you to blow up and you didn't. You just sat down there and then ate." They said, "You just ruined the whole thing." And I said, "You think I'm going to have an explosion in the North with all of you northerners?"

The woman from Texas was such a nice person, and I had conversations with her after that. I think her name was Janie, and I said, "Janie, what are you going to do when you get finished?" She was working on a Ph.D. I said, "What are you going to do when you get your degree?" She said, "I've thought about it a lot," and she said, "I'm going back South." She said, "There I know my place, and up here I don't know whether I'm going to be accepted or not." She said, "Sometimes I am, and sometimes I'm not." And she said, "I just want the security of knowing whether or not people will accept me. I'm accepted as a black person in the South, and I might as well accept it." Which I thought was a very sensible way to look at things. So that was my first experience in integration.

BW: Do you remember any of the college presidents at MSCW?

MP: Yes, Dr. Parkinson.[11] And then I was under Hogarth,[12] too. Dr. Parkinson was very strict and very rigid in his administration. He would have been a wonderful administrator if he hadn't listened to Dera,[13] his wife. But she was a mess. Have you heard that before?

In the early 1940s, Dr. Parkinson decided that I should be a counselor and that I shouldn't be in home economics. I didn't know what a counselor was. And he said, "I'll raise your salary." He raised my salary a thousand dollars. In those days, that was a lot of money, because I had borrowed money to go to graduate school, and I was still working in the summers at the University of Minnesota. So I decided I would try it. I said, "Now, I don't know what I'm going to do." Then he said, "Every week you will come into the office on Monday, and we will write the job description for that week." That's what we did for a long time. I was the first student counselor, and I worked two years, but then I decided I had too many gray hairs on my head. Those girls—you

11. Burney Lynch Parkinson (1887–1972) served as president of MSCW from 1932 until 1952.
12. Charles Pinckney Hogarth (1911–1997) served as president of MSCW from 1952 until 1977.
13. Dera Dry Parkinson (1887–1979). In 1927, she became the first woman to earn a Ph.D. (in psychology) from the University of South Carolina.

talk about problems, the problems they have now? They had the same problems then. But Dr. Parkinson was real good to me. He'd say, "You just see what you think the problems are." Half of the time I was just letting freshmen cry on my shoulder and just listening, and things like that. For example, one girl that I had was really a psychiatric case, but I hadn't had enough psychology to know that she was a psychiatric case. She would write a letter to herself from this boy over at State—I don't know who he was—and then she'd go around town and mail it so it would come back to her that same day or the next morning. Then she would tell the girls, "Oh, listen to my letter." We would all meet in the post office with our mail, and she would read them this letter that she had written herself pretending that it was this boyfriend. She lived in a world of fantasy, and it was just terrible. It really was. I finally realized something was wrong. She wasn't passing her classes, and she spent so much time in this world of fantasy that she couldn't pass. I went to Dr. Parkinson, and I said, "Something's wrong, and I think we ought to tell her parents." And the girls were beginning to talk to me about her. Dr. Parkinson had her parents come, and he told them about our conversations and so forth, so they took her to a psychologist. I don't know what happened to her after that. But that is just to show you that there were girls who were having problems then, just like they're having right now.

Sometimes, though, Dr. Parkinson would take my job description to Dera, and she'd take a red pencil and write through the things that I could do and I couldn't do, and that would make me so mad! And I'd go in and tell Dr. Parkinson I was going to resign. I guess I resigned six or eight times. I was resigning all the time because I just couldn't take her! For example, she told me, "Now at the dances, you bring your ruler so that the boys and girls won't dance too close together." She was wanting me to measure the distance between the boys and the girls, those of them that danced. And the boys, one or two of them kind of caught on to it, and they'd dance right up to me and say, "Where's the ruler?" Of course, I had it, but I didn't have it my hand, and I tried to avoid Mrs. Parkinson. Of course, the Parkinsons were chaperoning, too! I'd avoid her as much as I could because she was such a nuisance.

Then Dr. Parkinson wanted me to write a curriculum on etiquette and teach the girls etiquette, so I did that. And then he wanted me to write one on sex education, and I told him I didn't know how to teach sex education. He said, "Get you some books and write the curriculum, and then we'll give this course." I said, "Dr. Parkinson, I don't want to do this. Why don't you get the hygiene teacher to do it?" "No, I want you to do it," he said. So then Dera of course would take what I wrote, and Dera would strike out—she didn't think they ought to know about reproduction or anything like that. I just had to do what she told me to do. Except that sometimes I'd kind of get off the subject and they'd ask questions that they'd want to know the answer for. So she didn't know what I taught. She wasn't in the class. She was really the bone of contention because there were certain ideas she had, and how to teach sex education was one of them. She didn't even approve of him telling me to write a course in it, because girls weren't supposed to know about things like that.

I would go home and my mother would say, "You have more long dresses than anybody I've ever seen!" But you see, we had many receptions and entertainments, and we had to wear a long dress, so I had more long dresses than I had short dresses. I had to have a long dress because I went to every function. That was one of my jobs. I had to learn every student's name, and that was a big job, too, since I wasn't used to learning people's names. And I'd have to sit at all of the tables in the dining hall so that I got all the way around, so I could see what kind of manners that the girls had. I was supposed to correct them. Sometimes I did and sometimes I didn't!

I left the W. I was teaching there and had taught there four years, but I just couldn't take that. I didn't know enough. I needed to go back to school. And I wanted to teach home economics, anyhow. I got an offer at Peabody,[14] so I just left and went to Peabody. I taught two years at Peabody, and then I went to Louisiana State University and taught

14. George Peabody College for Teachers in Nashville, Tennessee, now the Peabody College of Education and Human Development at Vanderbilt University.

two years, and then I came back to MSCW. Miss Wilson was head of the home economics department at the W, and she wanted me to come back because she was trying to develop a graduate program between Mississippi State and MSCW. That was during World War II. Miss Wilson had this vision that we should learn everything about conservation. She said that I could work with the agriculture department, and Mississippi State faculty could teach the agriculture—these were graduate courses—and I could teach the nutrition. I was supposed to develop a graduate curriculum between the two institutions. That's when I came back, but I was over at State and stayed two years, and then that's when I got married.

I don't know whether I should say this or not, but I think this new curriculum would have not been approved. The administration couldn't agree on if they took part of the courses at the W and part of the courses at State, then who got the credit for the student? And that's where it just bogged down, at the administrative level, and we never could get it off the ground. But it lasted two or three years, and then Mildred Witt[15] got her master's degree under the program, and several of the girls from the W got it. But it just shows you how selfish people are. I ought not to say that, but I'm going to say it.

BW: Tell me about teaching home economics. You pointed out earlier that it trains women for basically anything.

MP: I think that the teachers themselves had a lot to do with it. Their philosophy was that in all those courses, they were family-oriented. Life is so complex now, and with most or so many women working, it's hard really and truly to build on. I'm not being very coherent on this. But each of the teachers that I taught with had a philosophy, and they taught values. I don't know whether we're getting values now. We're mostly numbers. We've lost our identity, and that bothers me. I don't really know how we did it when we were teaching those classes, but I think about Miss Scott. Miss Scott had a philosophy that was just wonderful.

15. Mildred Rea Witt, Class of 1949, taught in MSCW's Department of Home Economics from 1952 until 1985.

And Miss Wilson had a wonderful philosophy of family education. And Thrath Curry[16] was a wonderful teacher, and she had a wonderful philosophy of education and family. There were some screwballs in there, too. We had some screwballs. And I shouldn't be too critical, because I'm not a part of it. But as I look at it as an older person, the changes—some of them I guess had to come. You just can't tell. Life is changing so much. We're just moving so fast.

BW: How many years did you teach home economics?
MP: I came back to MSCW in 1938 to teach home economics, and I was here until about 1943, and that's when I had to do what Dr. Parkinson wanted me to do for two years. Then that was when I left and went to Peabody. I was there two years, and I was at Louisiana State two years, and then I came back to Mississippi State and I was there three years, and that's when I married. I didn't teach while my husband was living. He didn't want me to, so that was all right with me. He lived eight years after we married, and after he died, Miss Wilson wanted me to come back to teach, so I went back into teaching again. I taught at the W that time another eight years. Then I retired. So I was in and out of the W about twenty-six years in all.

BW: What do you think are the greatest strengths of the W?
MP: There are some underlying things about the W that I can't put my finger on. In the first place, I think we attract a certain type of person. Then I think that they have people around them that help them develop. I think about values a lot, because I think it's so important that we learn values. And I think we're losing some of that now. We've just gotten so interested in making a living that we don't have enough time to really live. Some of those things that were taught in home economics were in an undercurrent. For example, I think about Miss Scott and Miss Wilson. They really made a woman out of me. I was just timid and

16. Thrath Curry served as dean of MSCW's School of Home Economics from 1979 until 1983.

scared to death and a crybaby. But Miss Wilson and Miss Scott, I think they recognized that I had potential. And they, for example, suggested that I have these extra projects, because I didn't know how to sew and I didn't know how to cook, and those were two essential things in home economics that you ought to know. So they gave me these little projects to do, and they were good for me. It's hard to say. I think there are a lot of things you can't describe that teachers had when I was at the W, and I think it's this closeness that I'm talking about. Now the poor teachers don't have time to really be sociable, and that's too bad.

BW: So you got a lot of personal attention from teachers at the W?
MP: Yes. And I think that's what the W does. I think that personal touch is very important. I don't know how much now they get it because the teachers have so much paperwork. I feel sorry for them. They're just buried with reports and paperwork and things like that.

BW: Tell me about integration and other changes in the student body while you were a faculty member.
MP: Let me give you an example of the first graduate class I taught just to show you how integration was difficult in coming. Segregation was just something that's inbred in us, and it's just hard to overcome. You know that they had the explosion up there at Ole Miss in 1962.[17] And in the summer of 1966, I was teaching a graduate class. I had three blacks and twelve whites. And I didn't know what was going to happen since I'd never taught an integrated class. The students came to class, and the three blacks sat on this side of the room; the twelve whites sat on this side of the room. A white student came up to me and she said, "Mrs. Pope, if you think I'm going to work with these blacks, you got another thought coming." She said, "I'll leave the class." And so I didn't answer her, and she said, "What are you going to say?" And I said, "Elizabeth, I'm here to teach, and they're paying me to teach. And if you choose a project and

17. Rioting occurred on the University of Mississippi campus following the federal government's order that James Meredith, an African American, be admitted to the school in the fall of 1962.

it's the same project as a black student chooses, and you all won't work together," I said, "then I'm not going to stop it." I said, "I'm gonna let the chips fall where they may." And she says, "I'll leave the class." And I said, "You'll have to leave the class then." So you see how we had those feelings, and it's hard to get rid of them.

We had a good class. It was interesting. In a graduate class, you have a lot of freedom. So one day, one of the girls came to the class and she said, "Mrs. Pope, there's a woman from Washington going to be at Ole Miss, and she's going to speak." She said, "I have heard her speak and she's a very good speaker."[18] She said, "Could our class go up there?" And I said yes, but I also said, "You all will have to provide your own transportation." So they said okay, they would. It was on a Monday morning that this was going to happen. I stressed the fact. I said, "Everybody gets her own transportation." I thought I had taken care of the situation. On Friday afternoon, before we were going on Monday, these three blacks came to my office and they said, "Mrs. Pope, may we ride with you to Ole Miss?" And I said, "Yes." Martha Jo Mims[19] was in my class, and so I called Martha Jo and I told her these girls—these women—wanted to ride with me and that I wanted her to go with me. I don't know why, but I wanted a white person with me, too. So we started out. They sat on the back seat and Martha Jo sat on the front seat with me. We got to Pontotoc and I stopped and I said, "This is where I usually go to the restroom and drink a cup of coffee. But I'm going in ahead of you." I said, "If they won't let us come in as a group, we won't go in the restaurant." So they agreed that that was okay. I went and I asked the man—I told him, "I have a group of people who are in a class, and I have blacks and whites." And he looked at me and scratched his head, and I said, "We want to come in and we want to get coffee and we want to go to the restroom. Will you let us come as a group?" And he looked at me and he said, "I guess so." We walked in, and that was

18. Martha Jo Ballard Mims remembers that the speaker was Bertha King, education program specialist, from the U.S. Office of Education.

19. Martha Jo Ballard Mims, Class of 1964, taught in the Department of Education and Home Economics at MSCW/MUW from 1967 until 2000.

when they used to have these seats at the counter. There were about six old farmers sitting across there. When we walked in, they just quit their coffee and looked at us. They did not take their eyes off of us the whole time we were there. That's the first time they'd ever seen that happen. And we were very conscious of what they were doing, and they were very conscious of what we were doing.

So we went on to Ole Miss. We went to the speaking. At 12:00, the three blacks came to me and they said, "Mrs. Pope, may we go to the cafeteria with you?" And I said, "Yes." We went to the cafeteria. I could hardly get my lunch. They were just all over me, just scared to death. But the interesting thing is that the people saw us come in, and they were just as interested in us since it was a first. It just hadn't happened; they weren't used to it either. So we ate our meal and we came on back, and after we got back, I was in my office and those three blacks came in. They said, "Mrs. Pope, we want to thank you for taking us." They said, "We would have no more taken our car on that campus," they said, "because we just didn't know what would happen." And I said, "I was glad to take you." But I'll tell you, I breathed a sigh of relief. I was scared, too. I didn't know what was going to happen. It was so new to all of us. But I got along okay.

Integration is something that's been hard. We're still accepting it. There's some in my family that don't accept it. And I can't convince them that blacks are people, too, and God made them just like he made us, and that we've got to accept them. I've taught some mighty smart ones. That was when I came back to teach the second time, in retirement. It was during the time when Head Start programs were starting, and the Housing Authority was building all of these apartments for the blacks. So I decided that I was going to teach adult education. Adult education was something new at that time. So we went out into the community and asked the Housing Authority if we could come in there and teach these people, as they moved in, how to use the appliances. They didn't know how to use gas; they didn't know how to use electricity. They'd always burned wood in this big old stove. We taught them all about any of the new equipment that they had. Then Head Start was starting a program and they needed teachers, and I helped teach those aides how to manage the Head Start program. I was teaching so that the student teachers could watch me teach, and then they would help me a little bit in it. We had one class in child development for the Head Start program, and we had a hundred in the class. But I didn't have a place to teach them. So I went and asked the administration at the W if I could bring an integrated class onto campus. They looked at me, and they said, "We don't know what Dr. Hogarth would think." I said, "Won't you find out?" And they said, "We're afraid he wouldn't let you do it." But this administrator that was really broad-minded said, "When are you going to have it?" And I said, "We'll teach these classes at night." In those days we didn't have classes at night on the campus. And he said, "It'll be at night." He said, "No one will know we're having blacks and whites together." But they had the best time. They would talk about, "We're going to college!" It was kind of pathetic to hear their conversation. But they were so proud to be a part of coming to the W for their classes. So those classes were integrated. And I had some funny experiences with them. They taught me as much as I taught them.

I never did teach high school integrated classes, because I moved up to teaching at the college level. The curriculum had changed a great deal from when I first taught at the W to when I came back after I married and my husband had died and Miss Wilson wanted me to teach again. That's when I really got busy about my graduate degree, because I knew I couldn't be at the W without a master's degree. So I finished it up. But everything at the W had so much changed. They didn't have the uniforms. They didn't have to have chaperones when they had dates. We used to have to have chaperones. And if you went out to eat, the boy would have to pay for the chaperone as well as you, and that was hard. It was terrible. And very expensive. You didn't have many dates! And then if you went just for a ride, why, you'd put her in the rumble seat. Cars used to have rumble seats.

BW: How did you find the chaperones?

MP: I had a favorite teacher that I used to get to chaperone. She was nice. She was very sympathetic, because we thought it was just really ridiculous for us to have to have a chaperone.

BW: What has filled your time since your retirement?

MP: I did a lot of community work. I started doing a lot in the church. I've been an elder in the Presbyterian Church three times, and I was the first woman to be an elder in my church. Then I've done a lot of work with the Meals on Wheels program. I used to help with that. And I used to work in the Alumnae Office, just part time. If they'd have an extra job, I'd come and do it. And I helped with campaigns like the cancer drives and the Easter Seals and things like that. Blue Cross/Blue Shield has a program called Ageless Heroes. Three years ago, somebody nominated me as "Vitality." They have four categories, and they nominated me as Miss Vitality. Of course, they'd have to take that away from me now because after I broke my hip, I'm not as vital as I used to be. But then I used to do a lot of exercise. I was in an exercise class, and I was in a swimming class.

BW: Tell me about the honorary doctorate you received from the W in 2004.

MP: That was the biggest surprise I ever got in my life. I just couldn't imagine it. I guess it was November 2003. It was during the Welty Symposium. Dr. Limbert[20] walked over to me and she said, "Don't leave until I tell you something." And so I didn't know what in the world she wanted. Then she said, "Let's go in this room where there's not so much talk." And she'd invited several of my friends to go with her. She sat me down. And she said, "I want to tell you something." I looked at her, and she said, "It's good!" She said, "The Board of Trustees has just approved your receiving an honorary doctorate." I began to cry! "That's a wonderful honor," I said, "but I don't deserve it." And she said, "That's all right." She said, "Other people think you deserve it." She said, "I'm telling you now. I'm not supposed to tell you, because I'm not

20. Claudia Limbert (b. 1940) became president of MUW in 2002.

supposed to tell until you receive it." But she said, "I couldn't keep it secret." She said, "I was just so excited." And she said, "We will give you your doctorate at commencement in May." And I just kept saying, "I'm not worthy, I'm not worthy." And she said, "Oh, that's all right. Don't worry about being worthy." And then it got out. I had so many friends congratulating me. And somebody said, "How does it feel to be ninety-eight years old?" And I said, "It feels great because I'm getting such an honor, and I had to be ninety-eight, actually ninety-nine, before I got it!" I said, "It's just wonderful!" Then they began to tell me the things that were going to happen.

We broke the ground for the new Marie Charlotte Stark recreation building, and we had a wonderful dinner. They got this tent, an electrified tent—just a beautiful tent—it was really very pretty. A friend of mine said, "I've seen a lot of tents, but I never saw one with chandeliers!" It really was beautiful. It really was nice. And the dinner was just lovely, and the whole program was lovely. Then the next day, why, I didn't know whether I was going to be able to make it. We have two commencements now, and I didn't know whether I could walk in both of them or not, but I did. I got along just fine. Of course, I had my cane. But I was walking, and that's something. And my hood is just beautiful. It's perfectly beautiful. It's light blue and dark blue; the stripes on it are light and dark blue. Now I don't know what I'm going do with it, except that I think I'm going to put it in a shadow box, because I can take care of it that way.

BW: I once heard that most people who become centenarians are optimists. What do you think is true about people who live such long lives?

MP: I think attitude has a lot to do with it. I think that keeping a positive attitude is very important. My mother always looked on the bright side of things. And I give my mother a lot of credit for the attitude that I have, because I usually can, if I talk to myself, get myself in the right mood if I get in a bad mood. So I try to think about how optimistic she was. Every difficulty she had, she would overcome some way and come through it. I think attitude is very important, and then I think keeping active. I think that you've got to keep interests. Like these people where I'm living, in this personal care home—they call it assisted living. Some of them go into the living room at 8:00 in the morning and turn on this big-screen television, and they stay there from 8:00 in the morning until 9:00 at night. The only thing they get up to do is go to the bathroom and go to meals. Now, that isn't living to me. I don't know how they do it. I think that you've got to keep active. I think you've got to keep a positive attitude, and I think you have got to have an interest of some kind.

BW: What do you want to do with the rest of your life, however long it may be?
MP: I want to serve the Lord as much as I can in my feeble way. I have had some experiences in my life that have caused me to get real close to the Lord. I've had some tragedies in my life, but I trusted in the Lord, and I've asked for his help, and he has helped me. When my husband died, that was a very traumatic experience for me, because I just thought we'd live a happy married life forever—you know how you just kind of live but you're not being very realistic? But I just kept on. I'd hit a wall. I just couldn't see my way around. But I just kept talking and praying, and God just brought me around.

BW: What advice would you give future generations of W graduates? What wisdom have you learned in your life?
MP: First thing I would say is to get close to the Lord and pray and put God first in your life. That's very important, and that's what I did.

I lost my husband; he died in 1959. Then in 1964, this man from Memphis wanted to marry me, and I told him I was going to be a career girl. And he said, "You've been a career girl long enough." But we dated a while. We didn't do much actual dating because he was in Memphis and I was here. He'd been a friend of the family's, and he just decided he was going to marry me, so he worried the life out of me. But then he died two weeks before we were to be married. I tell you this because I want you to know that you can get over tragedies. It isn't easy, but I know you can come through.

BW: So you'd tell young women today that you can get through tragedy?

MP: Yes, those two tragedies were pretty heart-rending, and I didn't think I was going to come through at all. But I did.

When I was teaching, I was living in another house. We had a real nice house when my husband was living, and when I went back to teaching, why, I used to have some of the girls up for meals, and I enjoyed doing that. I think those experiences were good for the girls and good for me, too.

Then my granddaughter[21] was going to the W, and she was majoring in speech. She came to me one day and she said, "Granny Ellen, I will change to home economics if you will be my adviser." And I said, "Betty, no. No, indeed!" I said, "I can't be your adviser." And she said, "Oh, Granny Ellen, yes, you can!" And she said, "I'm going over and ask Miss Spann[22] if she won't let me." So I said, "You ask her. I'm not going to ask her." So she asked Miss Spann if she could change her major and could she have me. Miss Spann said, "Yes, you can have her." Betty gave me a lot of trouble. For example, she'd change her curriculum and she'd change her courses. She hated chemistry. She took chemistry as the last course she took to graduate. And she was supposed to take it when she was a freshman. Every time I'd put it on the schedule, she'd go and change it. But anyhow, she was a good major, and I enjoyed her.

21. Betty Pope Waters, Class of 1975.

22. Mary Coleman Spann (1915–2003), Class of 1937, was first a faculty member in biology and later an administrator at MSCW/MUW from 1958 until 1981.

Elizabeth Spann Smith Gwin
Class of 1930

MARCH 18, 2006

INTERVIEWED BY SUSAN PUCKETT AND BARBARA WHITE

FILMED BY CHRIS JENKINS

TRANSCRIBED BY RACHEL FORESTER

BORN IN COLUMBUS ON MAY 24, 1909, to Charles Barnett Smith and May Rush Smith, Elizabeth Smith was already familiar with the W when she became a student. As a student she was a member of the Town Girls Club, the Black Crows, the Bach Society, the Spanish Club, her class volleyball team, and the Junior-Freshman Wedding (a ceremony to unite the two classes) and Wedding Chorus. She also served as president of the campus chapter of the Mississippi Historical Society. She presented a senior recital as part of her piano diploma and earned a bachelor of arts degree in Spanish. In her senior year, the editors of the MSCW yearbook, the *Meh Lady*, wrote, "She has good common sense, a clear mind and excellent judgment." After graduating, she taught music, married English professor Howell Holmes Gwin (1904–81) in 1931, and eventually moved to New York City with her husband and worked as a high fashion model. She subsequently returned to Mississippi and then served as the Mississippi executive director for Girl Scouts of America for twenty years. An Alumnae Achievement Award winner, she served as president of the MUW Alumnae Association in 1988–89. She lives in Starkville.

EG: My relationship with the W started when I was nine years old, because I took music lessons on the campus. The Department of Education was called the Normal Department in that time. I took music from the juniors and seniors who were majoring in music. And I did that until I was a junior in high school and it was suggested that I enroll as a college music student. So I had music with Miss Etta Atwell[1] to teach me, and I took subfreshman music when I was a junior in high school and freshman music when I was a senior in high school. So when I started at the W as a freshman, I entered as a sophomore music major. That made me able to get two degrees.

I was on the campus as a child all that time and had a wonderful time. We slid down the fire escapes when we finished our music lessons, and I got invited by cousins who were students to midnight feasts. The lights had to be out at 10:00, and we pulled all the shutters and hung sheets up and ate things that we call trash food now for midnight snacks. Because of this familiarity, the W held no great attraction for me to go as a college student. I took four years of Latin in high school, hoping I could go to Agnes Scott,[2] but I was sixteen and my father said I was too young to leave home. So I was enrolled as a W freshman early in the summer of 1926.

Our freshman class had four hundred in it; it was the largest class that had ever been. And there were not enough dormitory rooms for girls who lived in town, and many from over the state had to board in town. The town students wore uniforms, but we had to have colored collars, and having loved clothes all my life and wanting to be different,

1. Etta Atwell (1882–1978), Class of 1903, served as instructor of piano at II & C/MSCW from 1906 until 1932.

2. Agnes Scott College, a private women's liberal arts college in Decatur, Georgia, near Atlanta.

I designed myself a collar. It was hot pink organdy and it was pleated around. It was like a clown collar. And so I put that on my first time in uniform on the campus and thought I looked pretty stylish. But when I got home my neck looked as if I'd had a porcupine for a collar, it was so stuck with this organdy collar. That went aside and I got all these little pink and blue Peter Pan collars that most people had. We found we didn't look good. We really didn't. Because of the required uniforms, when we had money for a new dress, it was never a navy blue dress. For the uniforms, we'd take one of our old dresses and take it to the dye vat and have it dyed navy and wear it with these colored collars and colored coats.

We had one room on campus that was called the Town Girls Room. It was in old Industrial Hall,[3] which is where Carrier Chapel is now. This room had old broken-down wicker furniture in it, and it smelled like wet galoshes and stale cigarette smoke. Most of the town girls didn't go there. It seemed just so unfair to me. Between classes I went to the library and studied, and when I got home I took my uniform off and lived my own life with no social restrictions. Most town girls felt that way. We felt as if we weren't a part of the college since we weren't included in things. But when I was a junior, somebody told me that Miss Pohl[4] had put my name on the list of people she wanted to walk for the wedding.[5] So I went down and walked for the wedding and was chosen, and that's the first time I felt as if I really were an integral part of college. And of course the next year, the ones who had been in the wedding the year before were in the chorus for the next year's wedding. That was a big deal.

At Halloween, we had Hell Week. The week before Halloween, the seniors could do anything they wanted to with the juniors. I asked if I could be a part of that, and somebody invited me to stay on the campus

3. Industrial Hall was built in 1902 to house classrooms and laboratories for all of the vocational courses. It was demolished in the early 1950s.

4. Emma Ody Pohl (1880–1966) joined II & C in 1907, when she was hired to develop the department of physical education. She taught that subject until her retirement in 1955.

5. The symbolic and beautiful Junior-Freshman Wedding ceremony took place on campus between 1909 and 1948 and united the juniors and freshmen as sister classes. The older women were supposed to protect their "little sisters" from senior pranks, and when they became sophomores, the younger students made the magnolia chain for the seniors to carry at graduation.

that week. We had to carry their books; we had to copy their notes; it was like hazing in a sorority. At the end we had a great banquet, and that was part of the fun. But except for the wedding and Hell Week, most town students felt as if we were outsiders. We didn't have that great loyalty.

The president of the university was Dr. John Fant,[6] who was just a beautiful gentleman. Everybody loved Dr. Fant. He called my grandmother "Cousin" and she called him "Cousin John," but I never knew what the relationship was. Dr. Fant died the spring of my senior year, and Miss Nellie Keirn,[7] who was the dean, became the acting president. At commencement, our class, which still was a tremendously large class, sat in our places in our caps and gowns. Students—I guess they were monitors—had baskets of diplomas, and they stood at the end of the row and passed our diplomas down to us. We didn't even rise to receive our diplomas, much less be shaken hands with and be wished success in our graduation. This really kept commencement from being a great celebration of our four years of college.

When we had the Mag Chain,[8] the seniors didn't throw magnolia blossoms. They threw their white collars out, and the juniors were the ones who picked up the white collars. The seniors could wear white collars, juniors wore white collars with blue embroidery or stripes or lace or something. The Mag Chain ceremony was another time of great feeling of having accomplished something. I had two diplomas, since in addition to music I majored in Spanish, and I was one of three of the first Spanish majors who were at the W. Annie Payne Lott,[9] who was in my class and also president of the student body, was one, and Agnes

....

6. John Clayton Fant (1870–1929) served as president of MSCW from 1920 until his death.

7. Nellie Sutton Keirn (1885–1975), Class of 1906, was hired at II & C in 1906 as a teaching fellow. She taught until 1919, when she became dean, serving until 1955. She also held the post of acting president of MSCW in 1929–30.

8. In 1894, in imitation of some eastern schools, II & C graduating seniors carried a daisy chain from the steps of the old chapel to an outdoor ceremony. In 1913, seniors modified the tradition and carried a magnolia chain. The students still sing the traditional magnolia chain song and carry a magnolia chain at a special class day ceremony before commencement in May. At the end of the ceremony, the seniors rush to the piled chain to claim a bud or flower. Those who get either one will have good fortune, which has been variously defined over the years and for some generations involved being the first to marry.

9. Annie Payne Lott McAllister, Class of 1930, was elected president of the student body and Outstanding Student in her senior year.

Tesch[10] was the other major. Our junior year we had a native Spanish-speaking teacher. Her name was Senorita Josefina Villarreal,[11] and she was from Mexico. She so wanted to be from Spain that she taught the Castilian accent, which is not as pretty as just the regular Spanish accent. I used to visit my mother's twin sister in Corpus Christi every summer, and her help, of course, spoke Spanish. I always looked forward to talking to them, but they couldn't understand my Castilian accent, and I couldn't understand them, which was a blow because I thought I was pretty good at Spanish.

All the time I was at the W I realized I was getting a good education. The music education was just tremendous. Miss Poindexter[12] was head of the department, and our exams consisted of going into her studio and playing whatever the requirement was for that year. I remember as a junior in high school I played Bach's *Two Inventions*, and Miss Poindexter asked me questions about what key they were in and if I transposed them what key they would be in and so forth. So I knew that I was getting as good an education as probably I would have gotten at Agnes Scott. But I lacked the dormitory experience, and I lacked the close friendships that I would have made otherwise.

When we came back to Mississippi after twenty-five years in New York, we came to Mississippi State, so my interests of course were on State's campus. I didn't go over to Columbus very much except to see friends. But there was a local chapter of the alumnae association here, and I remember it was 1981 that I went to a meeting for the first time. Then it was suggested that I go over to a workshop that the alumnae were having at the W. So I did. I went that summer to a workshop, and Kay Cobb[13] was the president of the alumnae association, and there were people on the board who came from all over the state. I was so taken

....

10. Agnes Tesch Holesapple (1907–94), Class of 1929.
11. Josefina Villarreal Arnold (1895–?) served as an instructor of modern languages at MSCW from 1927 until 1932.
12. Weenona Poindexter (1866–1956) served as a faculty member and subsequently as head of the Music Department at II & C/MSCW from 1894 until 1945. Music Hall was named for her in 1947.
13. Kay Beevers Cobb (b. 1942), Class of 1963, served on the Mississippi Supreme Court from 1991 until 2007. From 2004 until the end of her tenure, she served as a presiding justice. She was the court's second female justice. She served as president of the MUW Alumnae Association 1983–84.

with their ability, the scope of their experiences, and their leadership that I thought, "This is pretty good!" So I became the president of the local chapter in Starkville the next year. In those days, the presidents of local chapters were invited to a luncheon that the alumnae had at Homecoming, and I gave my part each year. Then I was asked to be secretary of the alumnae association, and the next year I was treasurer, and the next year vice president, and the next year president-in-waiting or whatever they call that—president-to-be—and then president. And it was then that I had my first dormitory experience! We sat up all night and talked and ate potato chips and giggled.

The people I met and have met and loved and enjoyed and admired all these years, I met long after I was a student. Even though all my life I've lived on or close to a college campus, it took me that long to realize that the W has something that no other school has. I still feel that it is unique with the close relationship of faculty and students and with the small classes. The interest that the administrators take in people is just amazing to me. I appreciate the W and have loved it and will do everything I can to keep it at the glory that it's enjoying right now. I feel that right now it's just a really good place to be.

BW: Tell us a little bit about your parents and your early childhood.
EG: I was an only child, and my parents were very aware of how spoiled and ugly and unlikable only children were, so they went out of their way to make me—unselfish, maybe? Or thoughtful of others? My mother would push me out to be with people when it might have been more fun to stay with her. I went to Barrow School and then Lee High School and then to the W. I had been engaged for a couple of years to a young professor, and he was teaching at Northwestern, and I thought, "I have never been on my own. I have never managed money." If I needed something, I went uptown and charged it to my father. And I thought, "I am really not ready to have a household of my own." So I taught music for one year in Hollandale, in the Delta, and then married the next year, and we lived in Evanston, Illinois, for four years and then Howell left to go to Columbia. We stayed there for nine years, and we realized that

New York was not the place to bring up children. And so we came south, and went first to Macon, Georgia, which has Wesleyan College.[14] That place was so much like the W. We got there the fall that Madame Sun Yat-sen and her sister, Madame Chiang Kai-shek,[15] had visited there. They had both attended Wesleyan, and of course Macon was just enthralled with their having come back. That really was a delightful time in our lives. But Howell was head of the department, and he thought he needed to go to a bigger school. He had been invited over to Mississippi to teach summer school several summers at State, so we came over here. And it's been just a wonderful place to bring up children and a wonderful place to live.

BW: How did you meet your husband?

EG: After my freshman year at the W, my father said I could come to summer school at Mississippi State. And in those days, not many women came even to summer school except the people who were renewing their teacher's licenses. So a group of us came over to summer school and had a wonderful time. There were so many boys, we just had our pick of people. There was a young man on the campus who had just graduated and gotten his master's from the University of Virginia. His name was Howell Gwin. My class was under Mr. Brackin,[16] who taught English, and this other young English professor said to Mr. Brackin, "There's just one girl on the campus I'd like to meet, and she doesn't even notice me." And Mr. Brackin said, "There's a girl in my class I would love for you to meet because I think you'd really like her." And Howell said, "No, I don't want anybody else. I just want this young girl." And so at

14. Wesleyan College, chartered in 1836 as Georgia Female College, is a private women's school affiliated with the Methodist Church.

15. Soong Ch'ing-ling (1893–1981) graduated from Wesleyan College in 1913 and in 1915 married Sun Yat-sen (1866–1925), cofounder and leader of the Chinese Nationalist Party (Kuomintang). Her sister, Soong Mei-ling (ca. 1897–2003), attended Wesleyan College before transferring to Wellesley College, from which she graduated in 1917. She married future Chinese nationalist president Chiang Kai-shek (1887–1975) in 1927.

16. Thomas T. Brackin (1898–1972) taught English at Mississippi State from 1926 until World War II, when he left for USO work. He subsequently returned to the school and taught there until his retirement in 1960.

the end of summer school the two of them were at the post office when I passed by and they pointed to me and said, "That's the girl!" I didn't know all of that, of course, and then it was in February that Margaret Lloyd Vaughan[17]—she finished the year after I did—she was in love with somebody over here on the campus and she called me up and she said, "My fiancé can't get over this week because he doesn't have a way, but Professor Gwin said if you have a date with him, he'll bring him over for me to have my date." And I said, "Oh, no, he's a college teacher." He was always dressed just so. "Darling, I can't do that." And she started to cry because she was engaged to this cute boy who had promised Howell to get him a date with me. And I said, "Okay, I don't know how I'll manage, but I'll have a date with him." So on February 10, 1928, the three of them came to my house, and we just had a wonderful time. We talked and just had so much fun. I always told my parents good night, so I went back and I said, "I just met the most beautiful man I have ever seen, but he'll never come back. I know he'll never come back." On Valentine's Day, I got this little valentine with a horse on it and down below it said, "Don't say neigh." So he called me the next week, and that was the beginning. That was my sophomore year. I was eighteen years old. He was at State my junior year, but during my senior year he went back to do his first year on his doctorate at Columbia, and it was a good thing, because I had a senior piano recital to prepare for and I might not have if he had been nearer. My senior year he was at Columbia, and then I taught the next year. Then I married him, and we went to Northwestern.

BW: Is your childhood home in Columbus still in existence?

EG: Yes, yes. My mother lived in it for a long, long time, and when Howell retired over here, we had a choice of going back and living in her house or building a house here, because we had lived in a campus house, just a wonderful, old, great big twelve-foot-ceiling, two-story house. It was a wonderful place to bring up children. And so he made me decide. And I thought this: we need to stay over here where his professional

17. Margaret Lloyd Vaughan (1909–96), Class of 1931.

friends are. We already had this lot, so we decided to stay over here, and it was a wonderful decision.

BW: Tell us a little bit about Miss Pohl's Junior-Freshman Wedding ceremony.[18]

EG: I don't know how it began, but the freshmen were the girls, of course, and the juniors, the boys, and it was something that everybody wanted to do and we practiced. You would have thought it was going to be on the Broadway stage, we practiced so often. Even on Thanksgiving morning we had to practice for the wedding. My costume disintegrated, but I understand there is one in the museum still. They were white satin with rhinestones and knee britches, and I don't have a picture of that either—wish I did.

There's a story about Miss Pohl—everybody has stories about Miss Pohl, but there's one story I remember. Miss Pohl felt that at certain times of the month, girls should not exercise at all. So when we went to gym class, those girls laid down on the floor and took an exercise called "motion." It just happened that there was a history teacher called Dr. Mosher,[19] but it sounded a lot like "motion." He was middle-aged, the shyest man I have ever seen. He taught me freshman history. And every time we said the word "Dr. Mosher," everybody would giggle, and he certainly never knew what was so funny.

BW: Tell us about your life in New York City.

EG: I went to every museum. I went to everything I could go to. We lived right in the Columbia neighborhood on this one-block-long street. It was 118th Street. At one end of that one block was Columbia, and at the other end was Morningside Park, and the Columbia Library was just

18. The symbolic and beautiful Junior-Freshman Wedding ceremony took place on campus between 1909 and 1948 and united the juniors and freshmen as sister classes. The older women were supposed to protect their "little sisters" from senior pranks, and when they became sophomores, the younger students made the magnolia chain for the seniors to carry at graduation.

19. Orville W. Mosher Jr. (1885–1971) served as an associate professor of history at MSCW during the 1926–27 school year.

across the street. For a nickel I could get on the subway or a streetcar and go down to Times Square. Without a reservation for a ticket, I could go to a matinee for almost nothing in those days, so I got to see all the plays. We got to see the opening of *Porgy and Bess*.[20] And we saw *Gone with the Wind*,[21] but we had to pay four dollars to go to *Gone with the Wind*, when usually the movie ticket was twenty-five or fifty cents. We thought that was exorbitant, four dollars, with everything else so much cheaper than it is now. That time was called the Golden Age of New York. It's when Helen Hayes[22] was at her best. It was just a marvelous place to be. So I was out of the house most of the time. Then I started to work, and I worked a few years.

It was 1934 and 1935. It was really almost by accident that I got this job. John Robert Powers[23] was the guru of the modeling world at that time, and I didn't know enough to go to him. I just answered an ad from the *New York Times* and went to the studio. I knew he was a well-known designer, but that's all I knew about him, and so I walked in. I didn't see him, of course, but his secretary ushered me into a dressing room and said, "Put on this dress and let him see you." So I put on this gold and black dress that was too short on one side and too long on the other, and it was poorly made; it had no style at all. I took it off right quick, but apparently somehow he had seen me in that dress, because when I took it off and started for the elevator, he said, "Who told you you could leave?" And I said, "I just looked so awful in that dress." And he said, "If you could make that dress look as good as you did, then you've got a job with me."

I started the next Monday, working for him. There were four other girls who worked for him, and they weren't very cordial. So I did my job

20. *Porgy and Bess*, an opera with music by George Gershwin and lyrics by Ira Gershwin, concerns African American life in Charleston, South Carolina, and was first performed in 1935.

21. The film version of Margaret Mitchell's 1936 novel, *Gone with the Wind*, premiered in 1939.

22. Helen Hayes (1900–1993) was a well-known Broadway actress dubbed the First Lady of American Theater. Among her most notable roles was Mary Queen of Scots in *Mary of Scotland* in the mid-1930s.

23. John Robert Powers (1892–1977) was an American actor who in 1923 founded what became an enormously successful and powerful modeling agency.

and they did theirs, and I thought, "They've just been together so long, and I'm the new girl on the block," and I didn't think anything about it. After about a month, maybe not that long, they said, "We heard your accent, and we decided that you wouldn't carry your load because we had heard about southern girls not doing much work." And one of them said, "We thought you sat under a magnolia tree and sipped mint juleps all the time." But they said, "You carry your load, and we are glad to have you, and we are sorry we weren't very cordial to you." So I had a wonderful time. It was a fun job.

Howell was a little worried that I'd take off these magnificent clothes and be disappointed to put my nickel in the subway and come home and live. We lived in the third floor of a brownstone front, three flights up. We didn't have a refrigerator, but we put our milk out on the windowsill. We were young and saw that as a challenge, because we were working toward something. One day I came home from work, and there was a note that had been slipped under my door and it said, "Sorry to have missed you. Emma Ody Pohl." She had gotten my address from my father and had climbed those three flights of stairs to visit me. And I cried. I was so taken with her thoughtfulness and her wanting to come to see me and coming all the way up to Columbia to do that. So I missed her. But those were just great times. And I really hated to leave New York. I really did, because we had every advantage.

We had children soon after that. Our little boy went to nursery school—they called it nursery school in those days—at Riverside Church, which was Harry Emerson Fosdick's[24] church. My son, Howell, was two years old, and he got a scholarship. We were members of the church, and we were given a scholarship—otherwise, we couldn't have afforded it. The first day I took him up to one of his teachers—I think there were four or five teachers for about twenty little two-year-olds. The teacher said, "Now, don't expect us to mention God because children get the wrong impression of God and Jesus, and don't expect us to say

24. Harry Emerson Fosdick (1878–1969) was the liberal pastor of the interdenominational Riverside Church and was known for his progressive sermons and radio addresses.

a blessing before lunch or to say prayers." And one of us said, "Do you mind if we do, because we don't know how not to mention God and not say prayers?" And she said, "What you do is on your own, but we just don't believe in it." So we lived the way we always did with prayers at night, and we read stories, Bible stories. And one day Howell and I—he was about three, I guess—were sitting in front of the window and it was snowing so hard we couldn't see where the Deans lived on the next street, and their gardens were between us. The trees were covered in snow, and it was just beautiful. At one point the reddest cardinal I have ever seen lighted on one of the limbs, and my little boy, who was sitting by me, dropped his head and said, "Thank you, God." And I thought, "Those Riverside teachers are really missing out because they just don't understand the depth that three-year-olds can have."

We brought up our children there until they were one and six, and that's when we came to Wesleyan. One of the professors at Northwestern who had known my husband, Howell, when we were there had become president of Wesleyan, and so he came to New York and asked us to come down. Then Howell was head of the English department at Wesleyan College.

Macon, Georgia, was a lot like Columbus, and if you hadn't lived there for four generations, you really didn't belong. It was during World War II, and the largest installation in the world was near Wesleyan, Camp Wheeler. The Wesleyan and Macon people were really resentful of their wonderful old town having this surge of new people. Early in the fall, I was invited to a reception by one of the dowagers of Macon, and the only reason I was invited was that I was a member of Wesleyan and anybody connected with Wesleyan was in good stead. I went with the wife of one of the deans, and she introduced me as having just come from New York, and this lady who was all of five feet bristled a little bit and said, "And how do you like us down here?" And I said, "I was born in Columbus, Mississippi." So I was all right then. I was not a Yankee. I joined the American Association of University Women and the Music Club, and one of the faculty wives took me under her wing, and I had a really good time.

We had bought a house the summer before we went there. Howell bought it over the telephone, because there was nowhere in the world to live in Macon, Georgia. The president of Wesleyan called and said, "I have this brick house for sale, but you'll have to tell me within thirty minutes." So he described it. We were at the dinner table when he called, and then he called again before dinner was over and said, "I can't wait the rest of the thirty minutes. Do you want the house or not?" So we bought it over the telephone. And when Howell got there first—I stayed in Columbus until he had the place open—we found out that the place had been rented to ornamental bird raisers. So you can imagine what the house was like. Every weekend he had all the janitorial people from Wesleyan come and literally wash every inch of that house. But by the time we left seven years later, it was beautiful, a wonderful brick house with big rooms. We put in floor furnaces and it was comfortable, so life in Macon was just so delightful.

In fact, I told somebody the other day I've really lived a charmed life. I grew up in Columbus, where everything was so good, and I had such a wonderful growing up there, and a wonderful marriage and children, and now a retirement I'm enjoying. I miss people I love, but I love life, and I hope as long as I can be productive, I can live. I wonder sometimes why I'm still around. I'll be ninety-seven in two months. But if the Lord has some reason for me to be here, I hope he'll tell me so I can do it.

BW: When did you move back to Mississippi?
EG: I believe in 1950. We stayed in Columbus for two years because we couldn't find a place to live on the campus, so we stayed with my mother and moved over here in 1952.

BW: Tell us about your work with the Girl Scouts.
EG: That was sort of accidental, too. When my daughter was a Brownie, I did what Brownie mothers do. Then the executive director asked me to be on the board, and I didn't know a rank from a badge. I knew nothing about the program because I had not been a Girl Scout, but I learned

along with my daughter, and I was in my second term when one of the national people came to tell the executive director that she would no longer be needed. Girl Scouting was not doing very well. So she asked me if I would take the job part time, temporarily, and I thought I knew enough by then, since I had gone to enough meetings nationally and regionally, and I knew a little about the administration, so I accepted. She had me leave the room, and the board voted to have me do it. And I worked for twenty years as the executive director. We had seven counties and four hundred girls when I started, and when we ended we had nineteen counties and five thousand girls. But that was twenty years, and that was a lot of work. And in the meantime, we bought and built a camp, and I still do the handicapped camp in the summer. It's called the Elizabeth Gwin session, and for one week after regular camp, we have camp for the handicapped. I just live for that every summer. It's the most wonderful experience. But now that's the only activity I have with Girl Scouting.

BW: What was Mississippi State like in the 1950s?

EG: It was very different. There's been so much construction that people who come back, people who were here then, say it's almost unrecognizable because there's been so much building. The greatest difference I can see in State is it used to be an agricultural and mechanical school, A & M, and it changed its name before Mississippi State College for Women became Mississippi University for Women. It used to be that the Agriculture School was the most empowering school on campus; now I understand it's the smallest school that we have. We have this veterinary school now, which is tremendous. But one of the greatest things I see is the difference in the arts. So much more is being done; the art department is really outstanding, and we have an English department that has grown tremendously. Much more attention is given to those things, I am sure, because there are so many women here now. We have almost seventeen thousand now enrolled, and it's so big that it's lost some of the feeling that it used to have, which the W always had, and to a much greater extent than State ever had. But the classes are big here, and so much of it is lecture. There's no relationship between students and faculty, and it's just a big university now, which means it's lost a lot of its charm.

BW: How did you feel when the W was threatened with closure in the late 1980s?
EG: When I think about those years with Dr. Strobel[25] when we almost lost the W, I know I will never forget them. Dr. Strobel was a tremendous person; he was so smart. And at the end of his administration, he realized that what he had to give was not exactly what the W needed at that point. But working with him was so good. We would go to Jackson and lobby for the W and talk to the legislators, and write letters and visit in homes with members of the Board of Institutions of Higher Learning in Mississippi (IHL). I was talking to Bryce Griffis[26] the other day, who was on the board for twelve years, and he said, "Remember when you used to sit in my living room and tell me how good the W was?" But I think we made our point. We made them realize that if they lost the W, they would be losing something very special to Mississippi and to the girls of Mississippi. So it was wonderful when we knew it was safe. And then, a couple of years after that, our mission was questioned, and we said our mission is for women, even if we admit men. And that was a real fight. And we met and we finally persuaded the IHL board. I feel maybe that was one of the hardest battles we had, but we won. And that was a challenge. Maybe all schools have something going on that has to be fought for and proved to be right, but I think it's time the W didn't have any more. It's had enough.

BW: What are you doing now?
EG: I'm really busy. I think I've had every job in the church. I did a video for the church the other day, and they told me to name the jobs I've had, and I've done everything from cook meals for two-year-olds to being

....

25. Dr. James W. Strobel (b. 1932) served as president of MUW from 1977 until 1988.
26. Bryce Griffis, of Starkville, Mississippi, served on the IHL board from 1980 to 1992, holding the position of board president in 1986–87.

a lay reader for two years, which was a real challenge. I still belong to the University Woman's Club and they have little satellite groups. One is a gourmet group, and I'm hostess next Wednesday for the gourmet group. We meet once a month—we have eighteen members, and two people are hosts. We make out the menu and send the recipes out to the others, and they bring what we ask them to bring, and that's real fun. We see people that you don't see any other time but maybe that once a month. And then I belong to a little knit-and-stitch group. We talk more than we knit, but that's a fun group. And there's a book review group that's active, and once a month we have a great big luncheon where everybody's invited and we have good, good programs for that. And then for friends, I love to cook and I have a lot of company. Since there aren't really very many people who really like to cook, they invite me out to eat, and it's wonderful to me because I don't get out except when I'm invited. I just cook at home. So I'm busy all the time, and that's what keeps people going. There was somebody in my Sunday school class several Sundays ago and she said, "I just dread afternoons. I just wait for them to be over so I can go to bed." And I thought, "Why don't you go in the kitchen and make some cookies and take them to a shut-in or something?" There are so many things to do. That's one of the things I do. I try to have people in nursing homes who are able to come over to visit, because I can't take too much responsibility if they aren't on their own. I have them come and spend the day with me. They love to get out of that atmosphere and talk about what they used to do. Most of us old people like to talk about what we did in our youth, so that does me more good than it does them, really. But time does not hang heavy. And I hope as long as I live I can be independent.

BW: What do you think is your secret to your longevity? I saw something once that said that almost all people who live to be one hundred years old are optimists.

EG: I am. I've always been. And I've always been conscious of my blessings, and I think that whatever happens to me now, I should never complain because I've had it so easy, so good, so pleasant. And I just hope as long as I live, I can be productive. But nobody in my family ever lived to be ninety-seven, which is what I will be on the twenty-fourth of May.

BW: What have you learned in life that you would like to share with future generations of W graduates? What are the lessons of life?

EG: I'll have to think about that a minute. I think maybe thoughtfulness or love of people would be the greatest thing. Forget about yourself and think what you could do that would make life easier for somebody else. I think that was taught to me as I was growing up. Until I married, I had two grandmothers living. And I knew both my grandfathers. They were so with it and didn't seem old. In those days, they didn't like for people to know how old they were. My grandmother used to say, "It's really nobody's business how old I am." And when her daughter, my aunt, gave her a birthday party and there were seventy-five burning candles on that cake, she wasn't all that happy because she didn't want people to know she was seventy-five. I didn't always tell people my age—not that I cared. If anybody had asked I would have told. But on my seventieth Homecoming, I was ninety. And most people in my class were ninety-one or ninety-two, so I thought, "I'm not going to let them think I'm ninety-two years old, I'm just ninety!"

Juanita McCown Hight
Class of 1934

APRIL 1, 2006

INTERVIEWED BY CINDLE FONTAN, LEIGH POURCIAU, SUSAN PUCKETT, AND BARBARA WHITE

FILMED BY CHRIS JENKINS

TRANSCRIBED BY RACHEL FORESTER AND AMBER KING

JUANITA MCCOWN WAS BORN IN PLATTSBURG, MISSISSIPPI, on August 26, 1913, the daughter of James Monroe McCown, a school administrator, and Ada Green McCown. Juanita McCown graduated from the W in 1934 with a bachelor's of science degree in home economics. She was involved in many groups on campus, including the Home Economics Club, the Chemistry Club, the Vesper Choir, the baseball team, the field hockey team, student government, and the President's Council. She was also active in the Theatre Guild, serving as master workman, as stage manager, and, in her senior year, as president. In 1940, she married William H. Hight (1902–82) of Louisville, Mississippi, the son of the long-time owner and editor of the *Winston County Journal.* When his father died in 1943, Billy Hight took over as the paper's editor. A very active civic and church leader, Juanita Hight worked with her husband on the *Journal* for many years. She served as president of the Mississippi Presswomen's Association in 1953–54 and on the

> board of the National Federation of Presswomen. She organized and ran the church library at First Baptist Church in Louisville and served as a founder and president of the State Church Library Association. The quotation under her senior photograph in the yearbook, the *Meh Lady*, reads, "She does an astonishing number of things well and is one of the truest and staunchest of allies." She has a home in Louisville but currently lives in Noxapater.

JH: When I was born, my daddy worked this side of Philadelphia, and Mama went over and stayed with him during the school year. After I was born, she stayed at home. When he would come home on weekends, he would try to take me and I'd cry and wouldn't let him hold me, so he said he was not going to ever do anything to keep his family from knowing him. Then it just happened to be that one of Mama's uncles who had a store at Plattsburg had died, so Papa bought that, and that's what he did for a living until I was seven years old. Then, since I would have had to ride a school wagon for five miles to go to school, he sold his store and moved to Philadelphia and went to work for a department store so that I wouldn't have to ride the school wagon.

SP: Tell us about your early schooling.
JH: It was at Philadelphia, and I don't remember much about it. There were lots of children I played with, and I know we had a little gang, about six of us, and we went home with each other on Sunday for dinner. In 1928, when I was fifteen, we moved to Noxapater, and that just nearly killed me. That's one of the worst things I remember. I spent most of the next year going back to Grandma's. I was only there at Noxapater two years and finished high school at the Winston County Agricultural High School.

SP: Why did you decide to go to the W?
JH: Papa all but made me. I didn't want to go. Back then, there was a Dodd College[1] in Shreveport that had done a lot of publicity, and I was

1. Dodd College was a private liberal arts junior college for women that existed between 1927 and 1942 in Shreveport, Louisiana.

just dead set on going to Dodd College. But Papa told me if I would go to the W one year, I could go anywhere I wanted to after that. I reckon he was using his psychology, because after I got there, I didn't want to be anywhere else. When it came time at the end of the year to sign up for a room for your sophomore year, I was the first one in line. I really did like the W. I had sort of a good introduction, too, because Mrs. Horton[2] lived at Noxapater, and her sister was Miss Mary Wilson,[3] who was head of the home economics department. I was going to major in home ec, so Mrs. Horton told Miss Wilson to be good to me, and that helped a little. And then Helen Perry[4] was already graduated and was a social adviser, and my family had been partners with her parents in business, so they told her to look after me. I had Miss Wilson and Helen Perry on my side to start with.

BW: How did you select a home economics major, and what other options did you have?

JH: I never did really consider anything except home ec because I liked my home ec in high school, and the two teachers that I had in high school were really influential in getting me to go into home ec in college. Back then, when you majored in home ec, you had to minor in science. Later I said, "It's a good thing I didn't have bacteriology until my senior year, or I probably would have majored in that, I liked it so well." We had to take little glass dishes of agar out—that was one of our projects—take it out and expose it somewhere and bring it back to the lab and let it develop and then see what germs we'd picked up. I was good friends with people over in the administration building. Mr. Trotter[5] was a business manager, and Dr. Williams[6] was the registrar. So he got

2. Anna J. Wilson Horton (1894–1979).
3. Mary Wilson (1892–1988), Class of 1915, served as a faculty member and later as head of the home economics department at MSCW from 1925 until 1961.
4. Helen Perry Hopkins (1906–2000), Class of 1927, served briefly as a dormitory social adviser and held the position of MSCW alumnae secretary from 1929 until 1932.
5. William Chamberlain Trotter (1890–1968) served as MSCW's financial secretary from 1932 until 1936.
6. Dr. Robert L. Williams (1904–?) served as MSCW's registrar from 1932 until 1936 and taught a course in psychology every year as an assistant professor of education.

me to bring one glass dish over there and asked Dr. Williams to take it and leave it in his kitchen overnight. Then when he brought it back to me, Mr. Trotter carried it and put it in bathrooms and all sorts of places where it would pick up dirty things. And then when I developed it, it was just full of germs. And we showed it to Dr. Williams and told him that's what was growing in his kitchen.

CF: What was your favorite subject at the W?
JH: Oh, I think spoken English, and I took one class in journalism—they didn't have but one. We had two male teachers then, Mr. Benny Alleman[7] and Mr. Robert Dawes.[8] And everybody wanted to be in their classes because they were young men. I took journalism because Benny Alleman taught it, and then I took second-year spoken English because Robert Dawes taught it.

CF: What was your least favorite subject while you were there?
JH: Chemistry—I didn't like it.

BW: Who were some of your favorite teachers?
JH: Dorothy Oldham[9] was my world history teacher my freshman year. We digressed every day because she would tell us some more about William Faulkner because her sister, Estelle, had just married William Faulkner. We had those tall radiators, and she would stand up there and stroke those radiators every day in class and tell us the latest things on Faulkner. When I visited the Faulkner home last year, I told the young man about Dorothy, and he said that she was the curator of Faulkner's home until she died. But she was an interesting teacher.

Louise Thomas[10] taught what we called spoken English back then. And she was also the head of Theatre Guild. I just happened to get her my freshman year in spoken English, and we hit it off. I liked her so

7. Benson Suesserott Alleman (1904–61) taught journalism at MSCW between 1931 and 1934.
8. Robert G. Dawes (1907–78) taught "Spoken English" at MSCW in 1931 and 1932.
9. Dorothy Oldham (1906–68) taught history at MSCW in 1930–31.
10. Louise Thomas Miller (1904–85) taught "spoken English" at MSCW from 1924 until 1934.

much that I got interested in Theatre Guild. I didn't like the acting part, but I was in costume and stage design. And one time, I don't know whether it was the end of my freshman year or my sophomore year, I was the stage manager for *Little Women*,[11] and they let me have the college truck, and I went all over town and didn't have any more sense than to ask people to lend me their antiques to fix the stage with. And they didn't have any more gumption than to let me have them—even one of these old-timey organs! After it was all over, I thought about how crazy I was. But anyway, it worked out all right. I enjoyed doing costumes and stage settings, and my senior year, I was president of the Theatre Guild.

BW: I understand you brought a drama fraternity to campus.
JH: Alpha Psi Omega. We chartered that my senior year, and we had to learn the Greek alphabet before we could join. I couldn't say two words now.

BW: What else did you do while you were a student?
JH: We got to take trips. We'd ride the C & G Railroad over to Greenwood or Greenville. And of course, Miss Pohl's[12] niece, Marie Charlotte Stark,[13] and I were real good friends, and I knew her real well. We used to laugh at Miss Pohl. She'd wash her hair herself and go to the beauty shop and sit under a dryer and get it dried and then come out and it'd just go in all directions. And then she said she'd been to the beauty shop!

BW: What was dormitory life like?
JH: It was real nice. My first year was in what they called Main then, now Callaway Hall. Miss Callaway[14] was our housemother. And I had known

11. Probably Marian De Forest's stage version, first produced in 1912, of Louisa May Alcott's 1868 novel, *Little Women*.
12. Emma Ody Pohl (1880–1966) joined II & C in 1907, when she was hired to develop the department of physical education. She taught that subject until her retirement in 1955.
13. Marie Charlotte Stark (1914–2004), Class of 1933.
14. Celeste Lusk Callaway (1864–1948) served as matron and superintendent of dormitories at II & C/MSCW from 1901 until 1932.

her before I went up there, so that helped a little bit, too. I can't remember her name, but there was a woman who went around and checked on everybody all during the night.[15] When she'd land on our floor and get on the other end of the hall, we'd take the elevator up to another floor, and she'd have to walk up the steps to get it.

Our crowd lived on fourth floor Shattuck after sophomore year, and I'm sure you can't believe it, but we were not allowed to have a radio in our room. About ten of us went together and bought us a radio and we fixed up one of the rooms for a sitting room. We got the maid on the hall to watch for Miss Perry when she came up so we could throw a raincoat or a blanket or something over the radio so Miss Perry wouldn't see it. But she missed her one time, and Miss Perry caught our radio up there. I teased her a lot about it in later years, but she made us sell it to the class and move it down to the lobby.

CF: Did you decorate your dorm room?

JH: Yes. We didn't have any closets in the room, and—cretonne was a flowered cloth back then—we all had cretonne curtains. We'd do off a corner of the room and fix us a closet out of it. Of course, my roommate and I were high school friends, so we got together on our bedspreads and so forth, and they let us do anything we wanted to, I think, but there wasn't much to do. But I remember those cretonne curtains were the main decorations.

BW: Were boys allowed on campus? What was your social life like?

JH: They had to sign in to get to come in, but I didn't really have dates much then, so I was not involved in that. And we didn't get to come home but three times a year, I believe. The first time we could come home was Thanksgiving.

BW: What do you remember about the administrators?

15. Probably Bess Hearon (aka Herron) (1893–1965), who was hired in 1919 as an elevator operator and whom students in the dormitory considered a night watchman. By 1929, her official title was assistant superintendent of dormitories.

JH: Mr. Sutherland[16] was there at first, and he was there just two years, and then Dr. Parkinson[17] came. And I don't really know how I got into going over to the Administration Office as much as I did, but I knew the Parkinsons real well. I was on the President's Council, and they had formal dinners for us at their house once a month. And Mr. Trotter was the business administrator. One time, I believe it was my junior year, they paid me a hundred dollars and I handled all the tickets for the lyceums. I especially remember Heifetz,[18] the violinist, and his wife was Florence Vidor,[19] and we just thought her movies were so glamorous. And King Vidor,[20] who was a big mogul in Hollywood, was her brother. We were more interested in Florence Vidor than we were in Heifetz.

BW: He came to campus?

JH: Yes, he did a concert there, and I remember handing him a stack of bills. We took the money we took in for the tickets and paid him. I paid him eight hundred dollars. And I did all that myself. We had to go to the president's home for a reception after the concert, and Florence Vidor talked real precise, and she said, "You have not seen Mississippi until you have seen the Poindexter Music Hall." She bragged on that.

BW: What other cultural activities went on during your time at the W?

JH: Richard Halliburton[21] was there, and I got to talk to him. He stayed with me in the ticket office about two hours one day, and I just enjoyed talking to him. And it wasn't many years after that until he disappeared and nobody ever found him. We also had Paderewski[22] there. We had

....

16. Robert E. Lee Sutherland (1878–1961) served as president of MSCW from 1930 until 1932.
17. Burney Lynch Parkinson (1887–1972) served as president of MSCW from 1932 until 1952.
18. Jascha Heifetz (1901–1987) gave a violin concert on campus on December 10, 1932.
19. Florence Vidor (1895–1977) was chiefly known as a very successful silent film actress.
20. King Vidor (1894–1982), a film director whose career lasted more than seventy years, was actually Florence Vidor's first husband.
21. Richard Halliburton (1900–1939) was a popular writer who often wrote about his adventurous travels and died at sea when his ship was lost in a typhoon.
22. Ignacy Jan Paderewski (1860–1941) was a renowned Polish pianist who performed on campus in February 1905, a concert that remained much talked about for decades thereafter.

real fine lyceums back then. And John Philip Sousa,[23] only a couple of years before he died, was there with his band. Played all those marches!

BW: Tell us about Zouave.

JH: Oh, we got to do Zouave a lot. We did it every year when I was up there. It was a chore to practice, and Miss Pohl would stand up on that fountain, and she could see all the way across campus if somebody was out of step. And she stopped them for me a time or two. But life was great at the W.

I was on the baseball team. I had long hair then, and I didn't have much time between my swimming class and my next class to get out and do anything with my hair, so I just got the doctor at home to give me permission to not take swimming because it was supposedly bad for me. But I really did like baseball, and I played on the baseball team. And the field hockey team. We just played different classes: we didn't go anywhere outside of our college.

Back then, they used to have Hell Week and I remember that was just terrible, the way they paddled those girls and carried on. The seniors whipped the juniors.

CF: How was your first experience with a roommate?

JH: She was the girl I had been with at Noxapater for two years, that I'd lived with in Noxapater—Hazel McCay[24] was her name. Reneau Hall was new that year, and Virginia Franks[25] was her cousin, and she had a room down at Reneau. Of course we had to have our lights out about thirty minutes before the upper classmen. Each student at Reneau had two beds, one on the sleeping porch and one in the room, and Hazel and I would go down and spend about two or three nights a week with Virginia just to get away from the freshman dormitory. I remember sleeping on the sleeping porch, and it was wide open, screens but no

23. John Philip Sousa (1854–1932) was an American composer known for his marches. He performed at MSCW on October 21, 1930.
24. Hazel McCay Watkins (1909–94), Class of 1934.
25. Virginia Franks Oakley (1910–92), Class of 1932.

windows, and we were up there one time, and it snowed, and it was cold, but we did enjoy it.

BW: What was the purpose of the sleeping porches? Was it because of the heat?
JH: I don't know. They had sleeping porches on two of the dormitories. And the girls had a bed in the room and one on the sleeping porch, too. But they soon did away with them. I don't know why.

SP: What did you usually wear to class?
JH: Oh, skirts and smocks. They all had to be navy blue. We all had a bunch of smocks and a bunch of skirts, and the one that got up first got the one they wanted—with your roommates. But it was not heard of to wear pants. Of course, a whole lot of time, I wore my raincoat to breakfast. You could have a raincoat any color, and I'd roll up my pajama legs and wear my raincoat to breakfast.

SP: Do you recall any world events from those years?
JH: I remember I was standing in the lobby in Fant Hall when the first announcement came on the radio that President Franklin Roosevelt had closed the banks.[26] We were just all in panic. I had five dollars to my name, and I think the banks stayed closed about two weeks. Everybody was panicky because we didn't have any money. I remember when World War II came along, and we used to listen on the radio to all that was going on. A few years ago, when they had the Gulf War, we watched it on television—a lot of difference.

BW: Tell us some more about the role of the social adviser.
JH: They just looked after us and made us behave. We had to sign in and out in their office before we could go to town. We had to sign in to come

....

26. On March 5, 1933, one day after his inauguration as U.S. president, Franklin Roosevelt ordered all banks closed to prevent further panicked withdrawals of funds. He then called Congress into session to pass emergency banking legislation, and within a few weeks, most banks reopened.

back when we came back. They were just sort of our guardians, I reckon, to be sure we didn't get into something wrong.

SP: Did you get to campus by car or train?
JH: Most of the time they just carried me in the car, and it was gravel roads all the way. You had to go to Ackerman and from Ackerman to Sturgis to Starkville and on. One time I rode the C & G Railroad to Mathiston and then changed to the GM & O Railroad down to Noxapater, and it was an ordeal. But I had a little brother two years younger than I was, and back then you could drive earlier. I learned to drive when I was thirteen, and he was driving at twelve, and they would let him come get me.

One time Mr. Painter[27]—I said I was glad I never did have him because he didn't know I wasn't so smart—but Mr. and Mrs. Painter were friends. I just got to know him and Mrs. Painter, and we were good friends. One time the Theatre Guild got up a bus to go to Birmingham to see *Green Pastures*,[28] and then after we got it all planned and everything, Louise Thomas had to be in Birmingham for a speech meeting, and they put me in charge of the bus to go over there. We had one ticket left, and I gave it to Mr. Painter. As we pulled out for the bus to leave, Dr. Parkinson said, "Miss McCown, you better watch out. You'll lose Mr. Painter before you get to Birmingham." And sure enough, we stopped at University of Alabama Student Union to get refreshments and just to stay around a little while, and Mr. Painter spied the head of the English department at Alabama. He got up and went over and sat at the table with him, and when we got ready to leave, he said, "I believe I'll just stay and ride on over with so-and-so." And so we lost him, but he had to come to us when we got there because we had his ticket, and he was sitting with us.

....

27. Lawrence Gilpin Painter (1878–1956) taught English at II & C/MSCW from 1913 until 1952, serving as chair of the department for most of his tenure. His wife was Edna Mitchell Painter (1893–1975), Class of 1915.
28. *The Green Pastures*, Mark Connelly's play that won a Pulitzer prize for drama in 1930, was based on a book of folk tales, *Ol' Man Adam an' His Chillun* (1928).

But anyway, after that he was real helpful, kept on trying to do something for me, and jobs were hard to get in 1934. A lot of people couldn't get jobs. It was still the depression. I was going up the sidewalk and met Mr. Painter and a school superintendent from somewhere over in the Delta. He was looking for somebody to teach Latin and music, and Mr. Painter told him to hire me, I was the very one. And of course I set him straight right away, but I got another job teaching at Bogue Chitto down between Brookhaven and McComb my first year. Then the next year, I got to Taylorsville. I was just trying to get as close back home as I could. And then the next year, I got to Louisville, and that is where I've been ever since.

SP: What was teaching like in those small towns?
JH: We just had classes, and we had to teach sewing and cooking. I didn't really want to teach but had to do something. That's about all you could do for a living back then in 1937. It just happened that Ruth Wallace[29] was from Bogue Chitto, and I knew her real well, and she got to be head of the home economics department for the whole state. The next year, she got me and two other teachers in the state to go over to Mississippi State and stay for six weeks and rewrite the course of study for home economics for Mississippi. We had the head of the home economics department from the University of Texas there to advise us and then the head of the English department from the University of Virginia to correct all of our English. We thought that was something else.

When I was teaching in Louisville, I made $75 a month my first year. The second year, I got $80. And about the beginning of the fourth year, it got to $85, and I got a chance to be home economist for the federal government for $160 a month. I thought I was going to be rich, but I had to buy a car, and my car payments were $25 a month. I did that for sixteen months, and then I married.

29. Ruth M. Wallace (1907–93), Class of 1929.

SP: Could you tell us about your work as a home economist for the Farmer's Home Administration?

JH: I was working in Stone County at Wiggins, and we dealt with the people who borrowed money from the federal government to farm, and my part was to work with the women and children. I remember one time the children were having tonsillitis all the time and missing school. I worked with a doctor, a surgeon in Gulfport, and got him to agree to do tonsillectomies for all of them for about either ten or twenty dollars apiece—I've forgotten. He was going to do them all the same day. Then I wrote a request for the money to pay for that. In the meantime, I had an appendectomy and was out, and instead of sending the money to the office, they sent the checks to the people individually, and they had spent the money when I got back. But I talked the doctor into going ahead and doing the tonsillectomies. Then we had canning demonstrations and all that stuff.

BW: How did the depression affect Mississippi? Did it affect your life a lot?

JH: It sure did. We were poor and didn't know it, because everybody else was, too. When I married in 1940, bacon was fifteen cents and coffee fifteen cents a pound. Billy gave me five dollars a week to buy groceries with, and I bought all our groceries and had fifty cents left over. I spent that fifty cents to go to the beauty shop. Now it's twenty dollars to go to the beauty shop, but it was fifty cents back then.

SP: Tell us about your husband.

JH: His daddy was the editor of the *Winston County Journal*, and he had started it in 1892. Billy was the only one of his sons that would go in with him and help him. Billy went to Mississippi State and then quit school before he graduated to come help his daddy at the paper. When his daddy died in 1943, Billy became the editor, and that's when I went down to answer the telephone and wound up for about sixteen years doing everything except setting the type and writing the editorials. But I enjoyed my newspaper work.

BW: What did you do for the paper?

JH: I wrote news, and I made the mistake one day when I was out collecting news of writing an ad, and from then on, Billy had me writing ads—selling ads and writing them for the paper. And I just wrote news items. In the county papers back then, they had what we called locals—that was who went visiting where and so forth. Then he made me write a front-page column, and it was funny things or things like that which had happened to somebody here in the county. I remember one time Mary Louise Fair[30] asked her husband, Johnny[31]—he and Bill Bennett[32] were going to Meridian—and Mary Louise asked him to pick her up a casserole at Learner's Jewelry in Meridian. She had one, and she wanted another one like it, and she said, "All you'll have to do is go in and tell them you want my casserole. I'll call them, and they'll have it ready." They saw Lerner's Dress Shop and went in there. He asked for a casserole, and the girl didn't know what he was talking about, and he didn't either, and finally he turned to Bill Bennett and said, "What in the H—— is a casserole, anyway?" And Bill said, "I don't know, but it's got something to do with asparagus." So I wrote a paragraph on that in my column—things like that.

SP: Did your column have a name?

JH: "Afterthoughts." I was real active in the Mississippi Presswomen, and we of course had annual meetings. In 1957, I believe, we entertained the National Federation of Presswomen, and I was cochairman of that and then was chairman of the postconvention tour. We had four buses of women from all over the United States going on that bus tour. I see now where postconvention tours cost so much; it cost them ten dollars apiece to go, and we were gone about three days, I think. We went to Vicksburg and from there to Natchez and spent the night in Natchez, and the Natchez Pilgrimage Women entertained them. Then we went on to Pass Christian and Gulfport and stopped at the yacht clubs. Then we stayed

30. Mary Louise Richardson Fair (1911–90), Class of 1931.
31. John Fair (1909–71).
32. William Edgar Bennett (1900–1995).

at the Buena Vista Hotel, and Jimmie Love[33] gave us a seafood jamboree, and we toured Ingalls Shipyards. But before we went, I wanted everything to make a good impression. I happened to know the man who was executive secretary or director of the Mississippi Highway Department, and I called him up and asked him to have the highway workers to clean the highways all the way—I gave him our route—from here to Pascagoula and back to Hattiesburg and back to Jackson. And they did it. They clipped them and picked up all the trash, and it was just the cleanest we'd ever seen. Governor J. P. Coleman[34] gave a hundred dollars for a prize for somebody to write the best article on Mississippi, and I've got a box of those papers in the attic now. They all went home and wrote something. I don't remember who won, but we got a lot of good publicity.

BW: What was it like to be a working woman, and what opportunities for advancement did you have?

JH: I reckon because my husband was the editor, it was a husband-and-wife team in the newspaper business. The wife had to work to make ends meet, really. I remember going to Chicago to a meeting: I was on the National Board for the National Federation of Presswomen. I was going to Memphis to fly out, and Billy told me whatever I did, not to fly at night, to go in the daytime. But I got up there and found out it would cost me half as much to get a ticket to go at midnight than it would cost in the daylight, so I went at midnight and got there. I had reservations at the Sherman Hotel. It was about 2:00 in the morning when we got to Chicago, and this Chinaman with a long moustache was driving the limo that carried about eight or ten people from the airport into town. He let everybody out, and I was still left in there by myself. I was scared to death. I could just see him taking me off somewhere and dumping me. He was nice as he could be and carried me right on, but he sure looked like a villain. I never did tell Billy that I flew at night.

33. James S. Love Jr. (1910–72) was a Gulf Coast businessman who operated the well-known White House Hotel and Buena Vista Hotel. He also founded Biloxi's first television station, WLOX.

34. James Plemon Coleman (1914–91) served as Mississippi's governor from 1956 until 1960.

Besides work, Junior Auxiliary was a big thing, and I was the first president in Louisville in about 1948 or 1949. And then I worked with the heart association. For about twenty years, I was the memorial gifts chairman and also did a lot of work with cerebral palsy. And my church work was real important to me.

BW: I understand you were quite influential in church media ministry. Tell us about that.

JH: I was the chairman of the planning committee when we built the new education building at First Baptist Church and then chairman of the furnishings committee. They had had a library, but it had been packed up while we were building the new building, and we unpacked it and got it going. Several years after that, it was just on the local level more or less. Janet Jordan in Jackson and Miss Jones who was the head of the Baptist bookstore in Jackson wanted to have a state organization and asked me to help them, and I did. We had our first meeting in Jackson and the second meeting in Louisville. Janet was the first president, and I was the second president of the state church library organization. I'm going this coming Friday night down to Garraway[35] to a state meeting just for fun.

While I was still at the *Winston County Journal*, I was the correspondent for the *Memphis Commercial Appeal* and the *Birmingham News* and the *Jackson Daily*. I remember an interesting thing: somebody had robbed a jewelry store in Kansas City, and an all-points bulletin was out for him for two or three days, and nobody could find him. One night about midnight, the sheriff called Billy and told him he had that jewel thief up there; did he want to come interview him? So I jumped up and went with him, and he just had tables of diamonds, and he let me try them all on. Anyway, it dawned on me after an hour or two that the *Commercial Appeal* would like to know it, too, so I just went out in the hall and called them, and they got the scoop on everybody about catching the jewel thief. That was one experience. We got to go to luncheons

35. Camp Garraway in Clinton, Mississippi, is operated by the Baptist Church.

for the correspondents then—we always went when they had the tri-state fair in Memphis and had a luncheon at the Peabody Hotel.[36] I didn't do as much for the *Birmingham News* as I did for the *Jackson Daily* and the *Commercial Appeal.*

CF: When you came to the W your freshman year, what were your first thoughts of Columbus?

JH: I didn't have any, I don't reckon. I thought it was a big town, and we had to wear gloves and hats to go to town. I did get to know the McGaheys,[37] because Miss Thomas was living over there, and she used to let me come spend the night with her a lot, and they were real nice. When Billy and I stopped by to see them one time right after we married, Mr. McGahey ran out, and he said, "I've got to go get you what I give all my girls," and he gave me a marble biscuit girl.

Did I tell you about going to the Indian Fair?[38] The *Commercial* sent me down there to get a write-up on the Indian princess, and of course I went the afternoon before. They had the contest that night. And I took pictures of all the girls who were contestants and sent them to the *Commercial Appeal.* Then they had the pictures before the contest ended, and all they had to do was find out who won. They did a whole big page spread on it.

When I was a little girl, there was an Indian family living on Grandpa's place out at Plattsburg, and Zionie was the little girl's name.[39] She used to pull me in my little red wagon. When I was going to the Indian Fair, I asked Mama, "Reckon Zionie would be there?" And when I asked the man who was in charge of the fair if he knew Zionie Bell, he said, "Yes, and yonder's her sister right over there. She can tell you

36. The Peabody Hotel, a historic luxury hotel in Memphis, Tennessee, opened in 1925.

37. Thomas A. McGahey (1885–1958), the proprietor of a marble works, and his wife, Hortense Wood McGahey (1883–1974).

38. The Mississippi Band of Choctaws has a federal reservation near Philadelphia, Mississippi (Neshoba County).

39. Onie Bell (b. 1916) is recorded in the 1920 U.S. Census as living with her parents, James and Winnie Bell, not far from Juanita McCown's paternal grandparents' farm. The Bell family is designated "Indian."

where she is." When I went out to the bleachers looking around, I just sat down, and I looked and right behind me was this beautiful Indian girl with all these ruffles and beads. I told her, "I'm looking for Zionie Bell." She said, "Me Zionie! Me Zionie!" I said, "This is Juanita, Zionie." And she knew immediately because she grabbed me around the neck and said, "Tell me about Miss Stella and Mr. John Henry," my grandparents, who lived where she had lived. And then she had to go get Rob, her brother, and they just hugged me and carried on. I had a good time.

SP: What is your life like today?
JH: I go to church and the grocery store. That's about it.

BW: Are you still active in your organizations?
JH: To some extent. I became librarian emerita about three years ago, I think. I was church librarian for thirty-five years. I still go up there, and they ask me a few things once in a while, but I'm not as active as I used to be. I'm more active in the Jackson Stitchery Guild than anything, and I go to meetings once a month in Jackson. For about twenty-three years, we've been having a retreat at Lake Tiak-O'Khata in Louisville. I started it, and I'm still chairman of it. This year, we had fifty women. They used to come on Monday morning and go home on Wednesday afternoon. This year, we had four that came on Saturday, and twenty-five came on Sunday, and then the rest of them came Monday, but we had fifty altogether. We'd eat and sew and eat and sew. They have a good time out there.

SP: How did the W change your life? What you think is special about the W?
JH: I just think it's great. I don't know how to say it otherwise. They had a great faculty, and the teachers were so good to the students. The classes were small, and your teachers knew you. And the curriculum is good, and if anybody will apply themselves, they can really get themselves fortified for life at the W. Back when I graduated, if you had five people who were applying for a job and only one of them was an MUW grad,

the MUW girl got the job. That was the reputation it had. And I've enjoyed recruiting. There are several little girls up there now, especially in the nursing school, that I recruited.

BW: What wisdom would you share with future generations of W students?
JH: You're getting mighty deep for me now. I just think the W gives you a good foundation. And I know when Sylvia[40] was wanting to go to Blue Mountain[41] and her argument to me was, "I want to go to a Christian college." I said, "They have Christians at MSCW, too." We had a good YMCA program then, and then the Baptist Student Union, and then the Methodists and whatever the other religious organizations. The W will prepare you for life.

CF: How do you feel about the W admitting men?
JH: It's all right with me now, but I sure did hate it when it started. But I don't want to ever change the name. Just like Dr. Rent[42] always said: "Mississippi University for Women and a few good men."

CF: What would be your best advice to a current W girl?
JH: Study hard, make good grades, and take part in extracurricular activities. It's so different compared to what it was then. But I think it's a great school, and I would advise anybody to go there and study and be involved in the activities of the school.

40. Sylvia Camille Duck Clark (b. 1934), Class of 1956. See the interview with her in this volume.
41. Blue Mountain College, originally a women's school, is a private Baptist college located near Ripley, Mississippi.
42. Clyda Stokes Rent (b. 1943), MUW's first noninterim female president, held the post from 1989 until 2001.

Hyacinth McCormick Hayman
Class of 1935

JUNE 21, 2006

INTERVIEWED BY AMBER KING, WITH ASSISTANCE FROM ELIZABETH HAYMAN CARITE AND SANDRA HAYMAN.

TRANSCRIBED BY RACHEL FORESTER

HYACINTH MCCORMICK WAS BORN ON JUNE 7, 1913, in Gulfport, to George Francis McCormick and Hyacinth Yerger McCormick. While she was a child, her household included her maternal grandparents, Rucks and Hyacinth Yerger, and her great-grandmother, Hyacinth McGuire. At MSCW, she majored in English and Latin and participated in numerous events and organizations, including the Latin Club; the Archery Club; the Coast Club; the Theatre Guild; the Vesper Choir; the Tea Room Committee; the International Relations Club; and the Lantern, Torch, and Star and Sceptre honor societies. She also served as vice president of the freshman class, as a junior participant in the Junior-Freshman Wedding, a ceremony to unite the two classes; on the President's Council; and as editor of the yearbook, the *Meh Lady*, during her senior year. She was selected as a senior chaperone and performed "singlesticks" in the Zouave drill. Her classmates elected her Most Charming in 1935. Of her, the 1935 *Meh Lady* says, "Her loveliness is not only of face, but of disposition; her sweetness is not only of voice, but of character; her fineness is not of the surface, but of depth." In 1937, she married educational administrator C. Edwin Hayman (1913–74) of McComb. Hyacinth Hayman served as president of the MUW Alumnae Association from 1958 through 1960 and on the MUW Foundation Board and was a longtime member of the Jackson Metro Area Chapter of the MUW Alumnae Association. She was a recipient of both the MUW Alumnae Achievement Award and the MUW Medal of Excellence. She lived in Clinton, Mississippi, until her death in July 2006.

HH: I had a wonderful senior English teacher in Gulfport, and she had been to the W. She was a great influence on me and on several of my friends, and we all went to the W and had a good time. She was right; it was the school for us.

AK: What was your first day like?
HH: The first day was wretched in a way, not because I was going to the W, but since I lived in Gulfport, we had to change trains four times to get to Columbus. So we spent the day chasing trains, getting on new trains, and we got there late in the afternoon and they had dinner, or supper, outdoors. And everybody sat on the ground and had a picnic supper. Of course all of us who were freshmen—and that was the majority of people on the campus at that time—were all homesick by that time, late in the afternoon and a hard day behind us. I can remember looking around, and everybody was crying. But then we had a senior, I guess she was—an upperclassman, anyway—who had a perfectly gorgeous voice. And she got up and began singing, and she got everybody to sing with her, and all of a sudden that homesickness just disappeared. We were all just having a good time, and so as far as I was concerned, it never did come back. I loved it from the very beginning, after I got through that first sandwich.

AK: What kind of songs did you sing?

HH: I remember one of them was "When You Come to the End of a Perfect Day,"[1] and we thought that had not been a perfect day with the changes we'd had to make. But really it was a wonderful school. It is a wonderful school. And I am so proud of the fact that I have a degree from it.

AK: Do you remember your first day of classes?

HH: No, not particularly. I can't distinguish an actual first day, but I do know that we met at Whitfield Hall—I guess they still do that—and they gave a rundown on everything, where we were supposed to be and what we were supposed to do, that sort of thing. And then from there we were taken to classes, just to meet the professor and so on.

AK: What did you think of all the rules?

HH: I thought they were good. I had rules at home. Truly, it never did bother me at all, because I had grown up in a family that was particular, and I don't remember that it bothered too many of us. There were a few, of course, always, but most of the girls were perfectly happy and enjoyed being there. And we were so lucky to have a good place to go, since that was depression time.

AK: What sorts of things did you do on weekends?

HH: I stayed on campus and went to church on Sunday. I went to St. Paul's Episcopal Church, at the corner of College Street and Fourth Street South in Columbus. And I didn't go home very much because I lived at such a distance. Believe me, from Gulfport to Columbus in

....

1. Carrie Jacobs-Bond, "A Perfect Day" (1909). The first verse is as follows:
When you come to the end of a perfect day
And you sit alone with your thought
While the chimes ring out with a carol gay
For the joy that the day has brought.
Do you think what the end of a perfect day
Can mean to a tired heart
When the sun goes down with a flaming ray
And the dear hearts have to part?

those days was a whole day. It took a day to go and a day to come, and so you didn't have any time at home. The coast girls pretty much stayed on campus.

SH: How did you travel between your home and Columbus?
HH: I had a friend who had a brother who was at State, and he had a car of some sort. It was a little dilapidated, but it was fine. He took us from the coast to Columbus and back, and of course we paid him for transportation. We got to be very familiar with the little car. It was fun.

AK: Did you do a lot of dating?
HH: Not too much the first couple of years; I did some after that. Dating was a serious prospect then. You've heard, I know, the tales about having to date in the parlors with the chaperones there and all that. And we had senior chaperones too. I was a senior chaperone, and I know I counted every telephone pole in Columbus, because when a couple would go riding, we'd have to be in the car with them, and we'd had to double-date, so that gave us five people in the car. So I was always on the edge of the seat, of course, one edge. And I would look out the window the whole time we were gone, passing the time and giving them a little privacy, too. But it was fun; we enjoyed it. And that was really an improvement over what it had been, because until we got to be a senior chaperone, we couldn't go out. We had to chaperone, but we had to stay in the dorm, in the parlor. After we got to be senior chaperones, then we could go riding. And that was good.

AK: What kind of uniform did you have to wear?
HH: Navy blue. We wore a solid navy blue when we were freshmen, and the next year we could add some white trimming and the next year we could have a white collar with navy blue on it and our senior year we could have a solid white collar, so everybody knew what class we were.

SH: Were they skirts or pants?
HH: Oh goodness, they were skirts!

SH: And they came all the way to your ankles, didn't they?
HH: Not completely. Some of them did, depending on how dressy it was. The girl who was the most stylish was Katherine Austin,[2] and oh, she did have the prettiest clothes. Her sister was one of the professors there, Miss Luna Austin,[3] and then her sister, Dorothy Austin,[4] was the one who had taught me in high school that really influenced me to go, and then Katherine was in the same class as me, so we were good friends.

AK: And you worked with Miss Pohl?[5]
HH: That was wonderful; one of the best experiences of my life. I think people were more afraid of her than was warranted. But she was absolutely wonderful, and I not only worked for her at the W, but two summers, after my junior year and after my senior year, I went to the University of Virginia, where she taught, and she got me a scholarship for those two summers up there. That was wonderful, because my grandfather had been there, and so he was excited I would get to go too. She was a wonderful, wonderful woman, Miss Pohl was. She was a bundle of energy, for sure. And she was extremely talented in dancing and other phases of P.E., too. She had a wonderful department with various activities taught, and she ran a really good ship. I think everybody was inclined to be a little—not scared of her, I don't mean that, but in awe of her. Let me put it that way, because she was so wonderful. I just thoroughly enjoyed working in the department and having those two summers, too.

AK: What did you do in your free time?
HH: We did the usual things, visiting back and forth in the dorms, and we went to the Goose,[6] and when we got to be seniors, we could sit at the cute girls' table in the Goose. You couldn't do that until you were

2. Katherine Karol Austin Williams (1913–2005), Class of 1935.
3. Luna Austin (1895–1985), Class of 1916, taught hygiene at MSCW from 1923 to 1961.
4. Dorothy Austin Wilson (1906–2000), Class of 1927.
5. Emma Ody Pohl (1880–1966) joined II & C in 1907, when she was hired to develop the department of physical education. She taught that subject until her retirement in 1955.
6. The Golden Goose Tearoom, located on the first floor of the Student Activities Building (formerly the Henry Whitfield Gymnasium), demolished in the late 1960s.

a senior. They had a big round table. It was a great big round table, and we couldn't sit there unless we'd been invited to sit there. That was kind of tacky, wasn't it? But anyway, it worked just fine. Everybody got to sit there that wanted to. So oftentimes between classes we'd meet a group and take the time for a Coca-Cola or something like that. The Goose was a big gathering spot when I was there.

AK: What was your favorite place on campus?
HH: I'm inclined to say the gym, because I worked there so much, but I also thought the parlors in the dorms were very, very pretty. And we just kind of congregated in a girl's room if she had a box come from home. That was the big thing. If we saw somebody at the post office with a box, we were pretty much aware of the fact that we were going to have a party.

AK: What came in those boxes?
HH: Whatever would ship—cookies and cake and stuff that wouldn't tear up too much. Candy. It was nearly always sweet stuff that made us all happy.

AK: Tell me about some of your friends.
HH: I had a very close friend that I had grown up with in Gulfport, and we roomed together at the W. Her name was Marie Louise Mohler.[7] She graduated a year before I did. After we finished, both of us married and went different directions, and then in the latter part of our lives, we both wound up here—she was in Jackson, and I was in Clinton. But she died several years ago. That was really a lifelong friendship that was very, very meaningful. And I still have a lot of good friends that went to the W. Of course I think the alumnae association has done so much to keep us all in touch, and I think that it's just been wonderful to take care of us. In some ways, it really is just like going home when I go back, even after all these years. I haven't been back since the cyclone

7. Marie L. Mohler Hathorn (1913–2002), Class of 1934.

hit,[8] but I would like to see the campus. It's like going to the coast after Hurricane Katrina. I want to go and I don't want to go. And that's the way I feel about the W. I would like to see what damage was done, but then I don't want to see it.

AK: Did you get a new roommate after Marie Louise Mohler graduated?
HH: Yes, Sarah Frances Mitchell[9] from Tupelo. And we had a good senior year together. And then as fate would have it, I lived in Amory for a while and I was close enough to have some more contact with Sarah Frances, so that was good, too.

AK: Who were some of your other friends?
HH: Carmen Ronken[10] and Mary Libby Payne.[11] There was a girl from Gulfport there who was named Mary Drane Wood,[12] and she was a good friend when I was in school, and Betty Fenwick[13] from Kosciusko. There were so many that were just real close friends. It was not so big then, and not so busy. Your personal life wasn't as busy as it is today. So you had time to develop friendships. And we did that.

AK: Did you like any teachers in particular?
HH: Of course Miss Pohl. And I was a Latin major: Dr. Gladys Martin[14] was head of the ancient languages department there, and then in the English department, Miss Elise Moore[15] and Lucy Banks,[16] who happened

8. On November 10, 2002, a category 3 tornado moved diagonally from the southwest corner of campus to the northeast corner and then on through Columbus. The Pohl Health and Kinesiology building, including the gym, was demolished, and the newly renovated Fine Arts Building, Reneau Hall, and Peyton Residence Hall were seriously damaged. Most of the buildings on campus suffered some damage.
9. Sarah Frances Mitchell, Class of 1935.
10. Carmen Pearson Ronken (1914–2006), Class of 1937. See the interview with her in this volume.
11. Mary Elizabeth Bickerstaff Payne, (b. 1932) Class of 1954. See the interview with her in this volume.
12. Mary Drane Wood McDonald (1915–81), Class of 1935.
13. Betty Tims Fenwick Thompson (1913–2004), Class of 1935.
14. Gladys Martin (1891–1979) taught ancient languages at MSCW from 1926 until 1952.
15. Elise Hill Moore (1897–1996) taught English at MSCW from 1921 until 1967.
16. Lucy Young Banks (1895–1993), Class of 1916, taught English at MSCW from 1932 until 1965.

to be a cousin, too. We really were pretty close to all of the professors. The classes were relatively small. And life was so much simpler and quieter than it is today, so we really had time to develop friendships among the students and among the faculty too. The Parkinsons[17] were very also good friends of mine.

AK: Tell me about a typical day.

HH: A typical day was first get up and hie yourself to the breakfast table—if you wanted to eat. And it was early—I think breakfast was 7:00, maybe 7:30, but it was early in the morning. If you didn't want to eat, of course you didn't go. Then we had classes all morning and then lunch and then oftentimes afternoon classes. That was particularly true if you had something like tennis or swimming—things of that nature. And then you had your supper and went back to the dorm and you had closed dorm for a couple of hours or so, long enough to get your homework done. Then it was time to go to bed, because you had to get up early. The days were very simple, I suppose, in comparison to now. But we enjoyed it, and I truly loved it. I wouldn't take anything for having gone to the W.

SH: You were a delegate to the National Collegiate Press Association meeting at Chicago during your senior year?

HH: That was because I was editor of the annual. They sent the editor and business manager of the newspaper and the annual to the convention up there. And that was quite a trip, quite an experience. We were there most of a week, and it was when the World's Fair[18] was also there. We got to go to that, too. That was wonderful. They had exhibits from the various countries there. We couldn't see all of them because we didn't have that much free time. But I can remember going to the Oriental ones—I don't remember whether it was China or Japan—and being cap-

....

17. Burney Lynch Parkinson (1887–1972) served as president of MSCW from 1932 until 1952. His wife was Dera Dry Parkinson (1887–1979), who in 1927 became the first woman to earn a Ph.D. (in psychology) from the University of South Carolina.

18. The Century of Progress International Exposition opened in Chicago in May 1933 and closed in October 1934.

tivated by all the pretty china that they had, china ornaments and so on. But it was fun. We had a good time. That was before you did a whole lot of traveling, so that was really a trip for us.

AK: Do you have any favorite memories?
HH: I don't know that I'd say I had any favorite ones. They're all pretty special. I remember the association with the Parkinsons and with faculty and the fact that Dr. Parkinson made it feasible and possible for the girls to get to know the faculty and faculty to know the girls, too. They were very much interested in that particular aspect. They had receptions, it seems to me, once a month, but it might not have been that often, over in the activity room in the Student Activities Building. Everybody wore their very best clothes, wore their hats and gloves, and went down the receiving line—the whole bit. They were teaching us what to do in later life, supposedly.

SH: What do you think about the W accepting men?
HH: That's a hard question. I wish they hadn't, but I can understand why. It just got to the point where they needed coeducation, I guess. I don't know. I've never quite gone the whole bit with it, but anyway I think they're doing all right now. When I was there, after dinner somebody played the piano and you could dance in the dining hall, but you had to dance with another girl because there were not any men.

AK: What advice would you give to the students who are there now?
HH: I'd say just take advantage of the opportunity that you have and do your best to live up to the reputation of the W.

AK: How would you describe the W's reputation?
HH: I think, taking advantage of all of the knowledge that is being given to you and then combining that with the good manners that you have learned and then coming out able to hold your own with anybody. That may not sound very good, but that's what I mean. It means that you were on that upper level, because they had seen to it that you had got there.

AK: Did you feel that you had been really prepared for life?
HH: Yes, yes. I certainly did.

AK: What have you done since you graduated?
HH: I taught school. I married a man who became a superintendent, and we were school people. And just regular life, I guess. It's nice to have good granddaughters. And I will say we had a wonderful life. My husband went to Ole Miss, so we were always involved with the state schools, and he was a really fine educator, so that was really the focus of our life—education—and then taking care of the children. I just had one son, but he had three.

After we graduated, I think all we really had to do when we got in a group and wanted to break the ice was to ask, "Did you go to the W?" And we'd say, "Yes." Immediately you have a bond there that you can talk about, and you're not strangers anymore, you're sisters under the skin. I do think that the influence has followed me forever, all my life, since the W. In a way, in the back of my mind, when something comes up, I think, "I wonder what we would have done at the W or what we should do." Then you get to thinking of how it worked there, and you've got the background for figuring it out, and things are going to be fine.

I moved around the state with my husband, and I never was a stranger in any town because as soon as I got there, the W got there. I can remember moving several times and getting into the house late in the afternoon, a strange house, coming home and then looking in the kitchen, and the whole kitchen was filled with good food people had brought. The table was set, and everything was ready. And as far as somebody was able to do, they had got the house straight. But it was always the W girls who did that. They are sisters under the skin. I am grateful that I had the experience of going.

Katherine Lipscomb Worrell
Class of 1936

JULY 19, 2006
INTERVIEWED BY AMBER KING, WITH ASSISTANCE FROM BROOKE WORRELL
TRANSCRIBED BY RACHEL FORESTER

KATHERINE LIPSCOMB, BORN JULY 17, 1913, in Mashulaville, Mississippi, was the fourth of eleven children born to Jasper Holmes Lipscomb and Mary Elizabeth Jernigan Lipscomb. Katherine Lipscomb came to MSCW from rural Noxubee County, Mississippi, in the fall of 1930, but family financial strain and a serious injury delayed her graduation until 1936. After graduation, she began teaching at Lynville High School in Preston, Mississippi, and a few years later she moved to Lebanon School in Hinds County as principal and teacher. In 1942, she married George Brooke Worrell (1909–84), a local farmer who left to serve in the U.S. Navy one week after the couple's marriage. She subsequently raised a family while continuing to teach. In the 1970s, she began a second career as a journalist, writing a regular column for the *Hinds County Gazette* on news from Learned-Lebanon. She lives in Utica and remains active in the Learned Presbyterian Church, her garden club, and a number of

> other organizations, including the Sixty-Plus group in Utica and the Hinds County MUW Alumnae Chapter. The 1936 yearbook, the *Meh Lady*, says of her, "Delightfully abrupt, outspoken and frank—she has a keen sense of the ridiculous and a kindly sense of humor that is entirely her own."

KW: We lived five miles from Fern Springs and five miles from Mashulaville, halfway between Columbus and Philadelphia, seventeen miles from the railroad—real rural. I finished high school at Noxubee County Agricultural High School in Mashulaville in 1930. Then I went to MSCW. I had eighty dollars pinned with a safety pin inside my girdle when we got on the train in Macon. We had to change trains in Artesia and then go to Columbus. The Columbus folks didn't want the trains to change there because they said the Mississippi State College boys would steal all their fruit, so they made the trains change in Artesia.

When I got to MSCW, we were met at the train. I had two hatboxes I had gotten for high school graduation. I didn't have many navy blue clothes, and we had to wear a uniform, navy blue. But I took all my clothes and the laundry dyed them navy blue. A lot of the clothes had figures on them and they didn't dye well, but we wore them anyhow. I roomed in number 51 Main Dormitory (now Callaway Hall). One of the girls at orientation week, Hudean Windham,[1] sat out on the sidewalk and cried because she couldn't find her way back to the room. But she was real smart. She made a good teacher.

AK: What was the dorm like?

KW: I thought the room would have pennants and everything in it. There wasn't a thing in that old room but naked mattresses—two beds with naked mattresses on them—and two chairs, and one end was for a closet. The bathroom was way down the hall. I don't believe I'd ever had a bath in a bathtub. At home, we used a tin pan, a tin tub, every Saturday night.

1. Hudean Windham Burkhalter, Class of 1934.

The first week of school we had chapel, and one head of a department said, "Jesus grew in wisdom and stature and in favor with God and man."[2] Every one of the department heads took a different verse. We had that program, I remember, in Whitfield Auditorium. We ate in Shattuck Hall. Everybody didn't go to breakfast, but I never missed a meal.

AK: What classes did you take during your first year?
KW: I took English and French and history and physical education. I made an A on Miss Pohl's[3] dancing. Folks was terrified of Miss Pohl. She was a little bitty woman with long hair, but she was a strict teacher. If a girl was chewing gum, man, she would eat them up alive! I never thought of chewing gum or doing anything wrong.

We'd have dances in the Student Activities Building. You had to go in your sock feet. The floor was highly polished, just as pretty as could be. We had dances at Mississippi A & M, too. I love to dance, and we'd dance the night away.

We had to have a formal dress. Often we had to go to the lyceum and then go to the reception at the Student Activities Building. One of the teachers stood in the receiving line and said, "I killed my husband in bed last night." We never paid any attention to what they said. She did that for fun. But we had to know how to act at a reception. And that's good training, too.

In the Music Hall I heard such terrible screaming, "Ooo-ooh, ooo-ooohh." They were practicing voice, but I didn't have any idea what they were hollering about.

AK: Did you ever get to go home?
KW: We'd get homesick but didn't come home until Thanksgiving. I remember going back after Christmas, I cried all the way to the train because I was facing examinations and they were hard, hard, hard, I thought. But I made it through the first year.

2. Luke 2:52.
3. Emma Ody Pohl (1880–1966) joined II & C in 1907, when she was hired to develop the department of physical education. She taught that subject until her retirement in 1955.

AK: What happened after that first year?

KW: In the second year, the depression was on, so Uncle Jim[4] invited me to come and live at their house and go to Mississippi State—A & M then—and I did. During the third year, I didn't go anywhere. The fourth year, I went to Nashville. At the time I finished high school, in our church, we had a lady who went to Scarritt College,[5] and she had arranged for two folks to go to Scarritt College. But one of the folks that was supposed to go was secretly married, and her husband objected to her going off, so the lady asked Mama, "Couldn't Katherine go?" And Mama said, "Why, yes." I had plenty of clothes, so I went to Nashville, and we went to Scarritt College.

Then I got a call saying, "Katherine Lipscomb call 881." It scared me. I didn't know much about talking on the phone. I called, and an old lady in Columbus said she had met my mother and she wanted me to come to see her. So we went to see her, and she was mighty nice to us. She came and got me and took me to her house, and I finished MSCW living at her house. When I graduated, she said I did not look like a graduate, and I certainly didn't talk like a graduate. She'd beat my ears down; she was hard on me, but she was good for me too. I graduated and I've been doing fine ever since. She and I even went to the University of North Carolina (the Tar Heels) at Chapel Hill one summer.

A girl I had taught with in Kemper County told the school where she worked that I could teach school, and they offered me a job. So I came to Hinds County to Lebanon school. I was the principal of the school and taught the fourth, fifth, and sixth grades in one room. Since I was the principal, I got five dollars more pay than the other teacher. It was just a two-teacher school. The teacher that got me the job was mean as a dog. She'd just boss us: she'd come stomping down the hall and open the door and say to a student, "Come here, you!" I said, "Wait a minute, I'm his teacher. You can't order him out." But I was scared of her, and everybody else was, too.

4. James K. Lipscomb, brother of Jasper Lipscomb.

5. Scarritt College for Christian Workers in Nashville, Tennessee, funded in part by the Women's Missionary Society of the Methodist Church, trained young people for missionary work.

We had to work to help issue sugar ration books during the World War II. One Saturday evening, I needed help, so they told me who to call to help. I called and notified George. He was a farmer. He didn't come on Sunday, but he was there early Monday morning and he had to sit at my table to learn what to do. Someone had brought some dominoes, and we played dominoes when we weren't writing sugar ration books. George played for blood, and I wasn't about to let him beat me, so we fell in love that week.

And the next year, in 1942, we got married. I've been living here ever since. He went to the war and he was wounded. He had the dengue fever in New Guinea. When he came back, I didn't hear from him for weeks and weeks and weeks. I didn't know whether he was living or not. Then I got a letter from the Red Cross saying that they had visited him that day. He was in Fort Worth, Texas. So I went to Fort Worth, but I had to wait several days before I could see him. Then when they brought him in, he was held up between two men nurses and he was barefooted and had his pants held up by a string. The first thing he said to me was. "How do I know you're my wife?" And I said, "I've got your initials in my wedding ring." And he started crying. He said they took his ring away from him.

But the next day he came out eating a cookie. He had been to the PX, and he was getting better. And in six weeks we came back to Lebanon, Mississippi. We had four children. Our oldest little boy, George Lipscomb—Bud, we called him—died when he was five years old. The doctor said, "Have Christmas early because he won't live." And he died the day after Christmas. My husband, George, had to go back to the state hospital in Whitfield a lot of times because he was sick. He died in 1984.

AK: What did the freshmen have to wear at the W?

KW: The freshmen had to wear solid navy blue. You could get on the train anywhere and tell the girls from their uniform. I was proud of it. And the sophomores could have a little white on their collar—navy blue collar, but it had a little white on it. And the juniors had a lot of white on theirs, but seniors had solid white collars, and on College Day, the seniors gave their white collars to the juniors and we had a Magnolia Chain.[6] They came from the Music Hall carrying the chain and the collars and sang. Oh, and we had a Zouave drill. I was taller than most girls, and we lined up, had fifty in a row, and I was on the end of my row. And we had to make a circle, walk around, and we had to take long steps. And Miss Pohl stood on the fountain and she'd holler, "Left, Lipscomb! Left, Lipscomb!" Lipscomb was going as far as she could step. And then we had to lie down, had to go down, put our hand down and keep our knees straight and every time I had to fall, it was in an anthill—the ants just covered me. Somebody said, "Why didn't you tell her about it?" I said, "Ooh, I wouldn't have told Miss Pohl for anything. She'd eat me up alive." But I lived through it.

For fun, we could go to Mississippi State to the football game. The train would come into the campus and we'd get on the train and go to the game and come back for a dollar. That was good.

AK: Tell me about swimming.
KW: I didn't know how to swim. We'd been in the creek, but the creek was never deep enough. It was just sand bottom, and we'd cover ourselves with sand and then wash it off in the creek but couldn't swim. At the W, we had to go swimming and learn all the strokes. They were hard—the Australian crawl and all that. But I made an A on swimming. I failed tennis.[7]

For physical education you had to have your picture made in the rough—naked. You stood in front of a wall.[8] And I had my identification ticket in my hand. It looked like I was deformed or something, with

6. In 1894, in imitation of some eastern schools, II & C graduating seniors carried a daisy chain from the steps of the old chapel to an outdoor ceremony. In 1913, seniors modified the tradition and carried a magnolia chain. The students still sing the traditional magnolia chain song and carry a magnolia chain at a special class day ceremony before commencement in May. At the end of the ceremony, the seniors rush to the piled chain to claim a bud or flower. Those who get either one will have good fortune, which has been variously defined over the years and for some generations involved being the first to marry.
7. Katherine Worrell's daughter, Nancy Jane Worrell Belknap, Class of 1968, played on the tennis team at the W.
8. Students were x-rayed to determine their posture. Girls with the best posture were named to the "vertically elite" group and were photographed for the newspaper.

that ticket in my hand. But one shoulder was higher than the other one, and they tried to correct it. I had been Mama's nurse, and I used to carry a baby on my hip, so I was one-sided. They'd make you stretch up on the wall. Physical education meant a whole lot to MSCW. And that's still true. The way you carry yourself is important.

Oh, and we had to stand on our head in gym. We had rings—jump up and catch a ring and swing this way and turn this one loose and grab the other one and swing that way. And we had to stand on our head, and I didn't do mine right. I know one woman, she just died last year, she could still stand on her head—Avis Clark.[9] But I nearly broke my neck.

Then I got sick and I couldn't sleep. I had nine different diseases. I went to nine different doctors and they'd give me nine different diseases. And finally Uncle Jess[10] said to come to Memphis and he'd take me to a specialist. So we went to a specialist and they kept looking in my eyes; they thought I had a tumor of the brain. And they operated on my brain. They bored four holes in my head and sawed in between it and laid it back over my eye. But I didn't have a tumor.

They put my head off the table and it wasn't comfortable, so I turned the thing around. I looked down and blood was dripping there. The doctor scolded the nurse and said, "You shaped it wrong." I said, "The nurse didn't do that, I did that. It's more comfortable this way." So they operated on my head, but I didn't have a tumor. A man came from home, saw in the paper where I was in the hospital, and he came to see us. And he came back there and looked and me, and he said, "I declare, Mr. Jasper. Don't she look bad?" My face was swollen and just red. Daddy said they sewed my head up like he sewed a baseball, stitched it just like they did a baseball. I stayed in Memphis over a year at my uncle's and got well enough to come home.

BW: What got you well?

KW: Oh, a red-headed Irish woman named Kathleen said to take me to an osteopath.

9. Avis Morrison Clark (1917–2005), Class of 1939.
10. Jesse Lipscomb, brother of Jasper Lipscomb.

BW: Chiropractor, they say these days.
KW: She said it would help me rest. So I went to her, and she said, "What did they do about your neck?" I said, "There's nothing wrong with my neck." She said, "That's where your trouble is." I had tried to stand on my head and got my neck out of line. So she rubbed me every day for, I reckon, six months. And one day, it was April the twelfth, my head quit hurting. And that was a real relief. I haven't had that headache since.

AK: So that's what it was the whole time?
KW: Yes. It was my senior year in college; I had nearly broke my neck.

AK: Were you finished with school?
KW: No, no. I wasn't through. I had to go back. And I had paid for my diploma. It cost ten dollars, and I had paid for it, and when I went back I told them I'd already paid for my diploma, and they caused a big stir, but I didn't have to pay for another one. I've been doing all right since. My mama believed in chiropractors.

AK: Tell me about your French class.
KW: Oh, my French class. French was horrible. I made a low B on French. When I'd get through reading, I'd ask the teacher[11] if she could think in French. She said, "Of course!" She could do French like she could English. When I'd get through reading, she'd throw her hand on her head and fall back against the board and say, "What a struggle." It was a struggle, too.

AK: What was your favorite class?
KW: History, I reckon. I loved the Greeks and the Romans. One of my schoolboys, he didn't give a hoot about history. He never brought a tablet, no pencil to class the whole time he was going to me, but he took a backpack trip, walking trip through Europe, and he wrote me a letter.

11. Probably Ellen Crawford (1874–1967), who taught French at II & C/MSCW from 1913 until 1934. In 1929, she also became a resident social adviser, and she continued in that position through 1936.

I was so proud to hear from that boy. He said, "I couldn't come to Greece without thinking about you." And he went to the Taj Mahal and everywhere. And he wrote to me, and I was so proud. And another boy that didn't care for history went to Alaska and he went fishing and hunting and he wrote to me. That was the highlight of that year.

Bena Virden[12] was my English teacher. She was a pretty lady. I got called to the dean's office.[13] The dean said, "You're nearly failing English." I said, "I can't spell." I'd do all right on the one I had to prepare for the week. But when we'd come to class, she'd write a subject on the board and then we had to write on it. Like *culture*—she'd write *culture* up there, and then we had to write. She'd read my paper to the class because the content was good, but it'd have an F on the outside of it because of the spelling, and that was embarrassing. But I got through. I was terrified when I had to go to the dean's office. That was the only time I ever got called. When we got to MSCW, a lot of girls had to go to subfreshman English. I didn't have to. I just got by by the skin of my teeth.

AK: Do you have any other stories about Miss Pohl?

KW: My daddy said he would have thought more of MSCW if he hadn't seen Miss Pohl in the lineup. She'd go to the beauty parlor, but she would comb her hair out and it just stood behind her like I don't know what. She was tall and thin with that hair standing behind her. She had a robe on with all her honors on it. But with that hair standing behind her, she looked just like—

We had to sit in chapel according to our name, and I was under the balcony the first year, my freshman year. But my senior year I was pretty close to the front. The girl that sat next to me was Evelyn Little,[14] and she was from Carpenter. And once when we went to a ballgame at Hinds, I saw her, I knew those eyes, and she spoke to me. I remembered Evelyn

12. Bena Virden Broyles (1908–56), Class of 1927, taught English from 1927 until 1932.

13. Nellie Sutton Keirn (1885–1975), Class of 1906, was hired at II & C in 1906 as a teaching fellow. She taught until 1919, when she became dean, serving until 1955. She also held the post of acting president of MSCW in 1929–30.

14. Evelyn Little Williams (aka Beatrice Little) (1914–82), Class of 1934.

Little, and I introduced her to George. She said, "I've known George Worrell much longer than you have."

AK: Have you stayed in contact with a lot of people?
KW: Yes. I belonged to a lot of senior citizens' groups—Sixty-Plus in Utica—and I did belong to the country club in Raymond, but I don't have a way to go anymore. Then we go to prayer meeting, go to the Methodist church, and teach a Sunday school class in the Presbyterian church. And that's about all.

AK: What kinds of songs did people sing when you were in college?
KW: Oh, we sang "Danny Boy."[15] I loved "Danny Boy." And we sang

> Mississippi State so fair,
> Thy loyal daughters sing to thee,
> our college beyond compare.
> Oh, hail to thee, Oh, hail to thee,
> Thy name an emblem of light.
> We rally to thee, to the yellow and white.
> The Spirit of our M.S.C. is one of loyalty and true fidelity.
> We raise our voice to you with all our hearts.
> Sing sis-a-boom!
> Sis-a-boom!
> Rah! Rah! Rah![16]

And then you put your arms around the girls and sway.

We also took junior cooking. MSCW said every woman must know how to cook. When I took junior cooking, I had to go from the cooking school clear across the college to the ivy-covered hall way over

....

15. "Danny Boy" is a popular song written by Fred Weatherly in 1910 and set to a traditional tune, "Londonderry Air."
16. "Hail to Thee," MSCW's fight song, was written in 1920 by Eola Williams (Class of 1920) and Jane Williams (Class of 1921).

yonder[17] to take biology. It was a terrible rush. We were supposed to crack our eggs into a cup before we put them in our batter, but one day I didn't have time, and I broke a rotten egg in my bread. I didn't make a good grade on cooking either. I roomed with a girl who was going to be a home ec teacher and she failed chemistry, though. Chemistry was hard.

AK: Did you take chemistry?
KW: No, I didn't take chemistry. I didn't take any sciences except biology. I remember I put down shark for whale—we had specimens to identify.

BW: Tell her about the time you all went to the movies, Mama.
KW: Governor Bilbo had fired all the teachers and then Mississippi's colleges were taken off of the accreditation list.[18] A man was at MSCW to see about it, and the seniors had a week off. That was Little Hell Week[19] for the juniors, so all the juniors broke out and went to the picture show one night. The man was there to see if we were fit to get back on the accreditation list. And the show wouldn't open. So we stood outside and sang, "We won't go home till morning; we came to see the show." The president[20] came and just begged us to go back to our dorms, and we wouldn't do it. We sang, "Won't go home till morning, we came to see the show." That wasn't good for us, but we got back on the accredited list.

BW: What song did the seniors sing to the juniors during Little Hell Week?

....

17. Science Hall, a four-story brick classroom building that stood in the 1400 block of campus facing College Street, just east of Franklin Hall.
18. Governor Theodore Bilbo (1877–1947) gained control of the college board of trustees with his handpicked appointees. In 1930, more than 150 faculty and staff were fired from Mississippi institutions of higher education, including ten faculty members and four staff members at MSCW. In reaction to Bilbo's political interference in education, the Southern Association of Colleges revoked the accreditation of four Mississippi colleges, including MSCW.
19. During Little Hell Week, seniors hazed juniors; it was scheduled for the last week in October to include Halloween.
20. Burney Lynch Parkinson (1887–1972) served as president of MSCW from 1932 until 1952.

KW:

Did you ever think when the hearse goes by
That it won't be long before you and I
Will be riding by in a big black hack
And won't be thinking of coming back?
And they'll put you down in a deep dark hole
And leave you there to decay and mold.
And your teeth fall out and your eyes fall in
And the worms crawl over your mouth and chin.
And they'll bring their friends and their friend's friends, too
And they'll make a horrible goo of you.

Wasn't that a cheerful song?

AK: Did anyone from the W really affect you, really change your life?
KW: Dr. Blanche Lockard[21] was an MSCW girl, and she was my doctor. She was an obstetrician. They said I'd have to go to the hospital because I was so old—they said I couldn't have my babies at home. So she said, "Do you have anybody in town that you could stay with?" They were afraid for me to come so far. So I stayed at my brother's house, and on Monday morning I thought I was sick [in labor] and went to get in the car, and it wouldn't start. I had to go to the man next door, and he took me, and he knew a shortcut to the hospital because I was in such a hurry. We went the shortcut, and there the train was backing up. We had to wait a long time for the train. They got me to the hospital, and that was on Monday morning. And Brooke wasn't born until Thursday. All that time. They didn't give me anything to eat from Monday until Thursday. I asked Dr. Lockard, "Why don't they feed me?" They thought any minute I'd have the baby, but I didn't have the baby. So after Brooke was born, they gave me brussels sprouts. Ooh, that was horrible. I was too weak to feed myself.

21. Blanche Lockard (1912–2003), Class of 1934.

AK: What did you think when the W started admitting men?
KW: I did not like it. I still don't like it. And I saw in the paper where a man was head of the student government [22]—I surely resented that.

AK: You liked it being an all-girl school?
KW: Yes, sir, yes, sir. It's still Mississippi's Sweetest Collection of Women, I think. MSCW is a great school, even if they do have men. A lot of the students I went to school with have gone on and made good. I belong to the Hinds County Alumnae Chapter of MSCW, but I don't get to go anymore, so I haven't been in a long time. But we enjoyed seeing everyone, and the president of the college would always attend that meeting.

....

22. Three men—David Ivey, Class of 1992, Trey Harper, Class of 1998, and Phillip Cockrell, Class of 2003—have served as the W's student government president.

Carmen Pearson Ronken
Class of 1937

MARCH 8, 2005
INTERVIEWED BY SUSAN PUCKETT AND BARBARA WHITE
FILMED BY CHRIS JENKINS
TRANSCRIBED BY BRANDIE ASHE

CARMEN PEARSON WAS BORN ON NOVEMBER 23, 1914, in Conehatta, Mississippi, one of seven children of Edward Pearson and Addie Wilkins Pearson. Carmen Pearson spent two years at Decatur Junior College (now East Central Community College) before transferring to MSCW, where she majored in home economics. She was active in the Home Economics Club, the Junior Forum, and the senior Y Group. According to the 1937 yearbook, the *Meh Lady*, "Mature thought comes from her rare silence and pensiveness." After graduation, she spent several years working in Mississippi as home demonstration agent and for the State Board of Health and the Department of Education. She later completed a master's degree in public health at Boston's Simmons School of Social Work and Harvard Medical School. In 1954, she married Noel M. Ronken (1902–78), who did applied research in plant science. She held leadership positions in a variety of organizations, including the American Home Economics

Association, American Women in Radio and Television, and the State Nutrition Council. She was very active in civic leadership, and in 2001 the Mississippi legislature passed a resolution "commending Ms. Carmen Ronken for her many years of outstanding community service" and "her tireless devotion to improving the quality of life of those around her." She lived in Jackson until her death in November 2006.

CR: Conehatta, Mississippi, is over in Newton County, and it's out in the Choctaw area. The name *Conehatta* means "polecat" in the Indian language. We really had more Indians than we had white people in our community.

BW: Did you socialize with them at all?
CR: Oh, yes. We'd go to their church, because they had the first organ in the area, and they had someone that had learned to play that organ and played it beautifully. This was on Sunday. Also, on Saturday night, they would meet and have a social hour at that church, play the organ and beat the drums. Then after they'd started the drum beating, you'd hear them singing, and they were dancing the Indian dance. And it was beautiful—just beautiful. We liked to go watch it, but lots of times my mother and I would sit on the big front porch at our house just so we could hear them. We'd enjoy it so very much.

BW: Were the Indians very poor?
CR: Oh, yes, they were poor. But the government came in and started a school for them. And when they started that school, many of them learned and were very smart—very smart. And some of them, now their children and grandchildren are leaders in the tribe over around Philadelphia in that area.

BW: Where did you go to school as a child?
CR: I went to the little consolidated school in Conehatta. It was one of the first consolidated schools in the area. And I could walk. I'd go across

the pasture because there was a path. We had no buses at that time.

BW: How many students were in the school?

CR: We had about three hundred, maybe four hundred. It was a big school because children came in from far and near.

BW: Tell me about your parents and your brothers and sisters. What kind of work did your parents do?

CR: My father passed away when I was eleven years old, but he worked with the county government. He was what we called a county supervisor. When I was a child, my oldest brothers and sisters were married and away from home. The youngest—I and my three brothers and one sister—lived at home at that time. One of my brothers was in the First World War in 1918, and of course we were all looking forward to the time that he came home. He came home, and he married and had children. And my other siblings lived around different places but not too far away. We lived near enough that we'd get together at Christmastimes and have a reunion—all of the family, with the big Christmas tree in the Christmas parlor, the living room. We didn't call it a living room, it was the front room to the house, so we called it the big hall. My father would go to the little town of Lake, Mississippi, and get on the train and go to New Orleans right after Thanksgiving every year and buy the Christmas presents for everybody. And we just couldn't wait. And sometimes, we'd think he and Mama were asleep, and we'd slip in there early and try to feel the presents we had for Christmas morning.

BW: Tell me about your mother's life.

CR: Mama was busy cooking and having food on the table, because she never knew how many she was going to have for dinner. When my father would leave from the little store—he had a little office up there—he'd ask everybody up there to come home and have lunch or dinner with him. And she never knew how many she was going to have for that meal—never, ever. But she always made plenty, and she always had tea cakes in the big old bowl; it was always filled. She never let that tea cake bowl get empty. We always knew when we got home from school we could go in there and get us a tea cake and a sweet potato and go out on the back steps and eat them. We'd go back out on the back steps and eat so we wouldn't mess up the kitchen, or Mama would have to clean it up. The potatoes would still be warm because they were inside a wood oven. We used wood back in those days to do our cooking, and it was called the stove. Today it's called a range. We'd go get a sweet potato and get us some butter and get us a tea cake, and that was a good midafternoon lunch.

BW: After your father's death, did your mother work or stay home?
CR: She had to stay home. However, she was what you call a midwife. A midwife was someone that the country doctor called when someone was going to have a baby; she'd go help him. He always would call my mama. Of course, she got no pay for it. But she went and helped him deliver babies, because there was no hospital to go to. The only place you could go, it was what they called Whitfield, or the asylum, back in those days, but they couldn't take everybody. So she would help him, no matter what time, day or night.

BW: When did you graduate from high school?
CR: I graduated from high school in 1933. Then I went to Decatur Junior College for two years, even though I had signed up to go to the W. I didn't get to go on account of my mother, who needed some help at home. She got sick and was partly paralyzed for a while, and I just couldn't go away and leave her.

BW: What did you study at Decatur?
CR: Home economics. It was really home economics. We studied all the things that families need. They need it now, really, worse than ever, because we need to manage our money; we need to know how to sew—at least know how to mend clothes. Back then we learned to make things, and we even had to make our cover. My mama was a wonderful quilt maker. She would even make her own designs for the quilts. Some of those quilts we had for many, many years, That was our cover, and it really kept us warm.

BW: How did the depression affect your life?

CR: I had to borrow money to go to school on, and I still didn't have any money to pay my board at the W. So I started working in the dining room—asked for a job working for Miss—what was her name?[1] She was the dietician there for years, and then she came to the State Board of Health and worked as a dietician for a good long while. She always had the white tablecloths and the fresh flowers in the dining room.

BW: When you finished at Decatur and came to the W, what were your first impressions?

CR: I just thought it was the prettiest place I'd ever seen. I remember the bell tower, and I thought that was the prettiest thing. It was just beautiful. The campus was just gorgeous. I thought I'd got into heaven, almost.

BW: What courses did you take?

CR: I took home economics—all the home economics courses. And Miss Scott[2] was one of my clothing teachers for years and years. And I had to take basic chemistry; then I had to take organic chemistry. But they were wonderful courses, and when we got out of them, we knew something about them, too.

BW: Tell me about your social life.

CR: We all looked forward to when our boyfriends would come. We had to sign up for the dating parlor, and we'd do that weeks ahead of time so we'd be sure to get a parlor, because it was hard to get one. The boys would come over from State, and I had a friend that came from my hometown one time, and he got to the W and he asked them if they knew me, if they knew a person by the name of Pearson, and they asked what was the first name, and he told them. They said, "We never heard of that name before." I told them later that he knew me by my country name.

1. Probably Ethel M. Summerour (1903–92), Class of 1926, who managed the Golden Goose tearoom in 1930 and later returned to MSCW to become dietician.
2. Julia Scott (1895–1977) joined MSCW in 1921 as instructor of clothing construction and remained a member of the home economics faculty until 1965.

When I got to a city like Columbus, I had a different name. I quit using my old name except when I was back in my home area, but some people still call me by that name. And I'll say, "Now, quit calling me by the country name!" You wouldn't believe what it was. It was Crucye. But at the W, I was called Carmen. My brother had a horse that was his favorite thing when he went away to war, and he named that horse Crucye! For years and years that horse was around, even after my father and my brothers were gone.

BW: What rules did you have to follow at the W?
CR: We had to be friendly. You were asked to speak to people. If you went out on the campus and you didn't speak, Miss Pohl[3] would tell us, "Will you stop and speak to me?" She called me by name since she knew all our names. And she said, "Don't go around on this campus without speaking to people. You must be friendly. And when you go off the campus, you must be friendly." And we'd go to town, in Columbus, and we spoke to everybody—just everybody. Didn't matter who it was. Most people in the stores knew our names, too. They made it a habit of learning the names of the people on the campus. It was fun to go. Of course, we had our gloves and hats on. If Miss Pohl saw someone chewing gum, she'd call her name and tell her to throw it away. And from that day to now, I can't understand people chewing gum in public. And teachers! I see teachers that chew gum! They think nothing of it. But we didn't chew gum.

BW: Did you participate in Zouave?
CR: Oh, that was a fun day. We had a good time at graduation. We looked forward to Zoauve. And we also helped make the Magnolia Chain.[4] For days we'd work on that chain. We'd have just an hour off—we had to

3. Emma Ody Pohl (1880–1966) joined II & C in 1907, when she was hired to develop the department of physical education. She taught that subject until her retirement in 1955.
4. In 1894, in imitation of some eastern schools, II & C graduating seniors carried a daisy chain from the steps of the old chapel to an outdoor ceremony. In 1913, seniors modified the tradition and carried a magnolia chain. The students still sing the traditional magnolia chain song and carry a magnolia chain at a special class day ceremony before commencement in May. At the end of the ceremony, the seniors rush to the piled chain to claim a bud or flower. Those who get either one will have good fortune, which has been variously defined over the years and for some generations involved being the first to marry.

sign up to go help build the chain. It would be spread out all the way from Peyton Dormitory around to Shattuck—all around..

BW: Where did you get the magnolias?
CR: A lot of them came from the campus. And also off the lawn of the dormitory that they built when they needed extra space—they had many magnolias there, and there were magnolias from all over town. They would even bring them down from as far as Amory.

BW: What was dormitory life like?
CR: We had a good time. Of course, we had study hours, and we had to be in our room during study hour. If you were going to study with someone, you had to get permission to go to her room, and they'd come back and check on you and see if you got back to your room when you were supposed to.

BW: What did you do for fun?
CW: We went to the gym, and we learned to swim. You had to learn to swim. I almost didn't get my diploma because I couldn't swim! I swam like I was swimming in the pond back home, the way I had learned to swim—dog-paddling. And then I got up there, and we had to do it just right—those strokes, just so. To the last day, I didn't know whether I was going to get my diploma or not because I thought I might fail the swimming test. But I finally passed it.

BW: What teacher was in charge of swimming?
CR: Miss Pohl.

BW: Who was president when you were there?
CR: Dr. Parkinson.[5] He was very, very formal, and Mrs. Parkinson,[6] too. We would invite them to what we called the Practice House, where we

....

5. Burney Lynch Parkinson (1887–1972) served as president of MSCW from 1932 until 1952.
6. Dera Dry Parkinson (1887–1979). In 1927, she became the first woman to earn a Ph.D. (in psychology) from the University of South Carolina.

had to go live six weeks when we were senior home economics students to learn how to run a home. So we would invite them to come to dinner, and when we'd invite them, we knew it had to be just perfect. Many times we would think, "Oh, how are we going to get through this and do it right, according to what is supposed to be done?" Because we knew we were getting a grade on it. The Parkinsons were very, very formal. However, we enjoyed them, and we learned a lot from them in how to be friendly as well as about being conservative and proper.

BW: What did you do after you graduated from the W?
CR: When I was growing up, I had been a member of the 4-H Club, and the person who taught us at that particular time was called a home demonstration agent. I would look at my home demonstration agent and say, "Oh, if I could be like you someday, I'd be so happy! I just wish I could be like you." Except I remembered I didn't want to have the dust behind my ears like she'd have, going over the dusty gravel roads. I was the second home demonstration agent in Leake County, Mississippi.

BW: What was your job like?
CR: For example, we had to show people how to make mattresses using surplus cotton. That's one big thing we did. And we had to can beef—the meat—because you couldn't buy it canned in the stores at that time. We had to teach people how to do their own canning. We had to show them how to slaughter the animal. I'd always take a sharp knife—the county agent would go with me to help me cut up the meat. But if he didn't, I'd get some strong-armed man. However, sometimes I just did it myself, with a sharp saw—a meat saw.

BW: What kind of animal?
CR: Most of the time it was beef, but sometimes chicken. We'd hang the chicken—take it outside. They always had a clothesline out in the yard, because we had wells for water. We'd hang up the animal and we'd pour hot water over that slaughtered chicken or the pig or cow, and clean them like that, and then we'd cut them up. And we'd can it, using real cans.

Then we got to using jars—glass jars—that could be used in pressure cookers. Many country people had pressure cookers, because it was necessary if they had food to preserve for year-round.

BW: Did most people lack refrigeration at that time?
CR: Yes. What they had was just an ice refrigerator. We all used ice after they got to making ice at the icehouses. One place in the little town would make the ice—they'd have a deep well and get the water that way and then make ice. And you'd go up to the little store and get the ice with their tongs, and you'd have to have a little red wagon or wheelbarrow to put that ice in to take it down the road to your house. Then you'd put it in the little container in the icebox. You'd have to drive a hole in the floor of the house, and as the ice melted, it drained through there.

BW: Did you demonstrate other things?
CR: We taught home management. We taught them how to manage their money. We'd ask them to make a budget for a family. At the home management house at MSCW, we had planned meals and other household expenses on a budget, so we had learned budgeting there.

BW: What were living conditions like out in the county? Were people very poor?
CR: They had outdoor toilets, and they had a clothesline hanging where they did washing and a big old washtub outside that they'd heat the water in. They had good meals, but they didn't have the variety that we have now. It's so much different now. People still call me and ask me questions about food, and I say, "Oh, I'll tell you what I know, but I'm so far behind now, because I haven't been back to school lately!" You have to keep up. And food has changed so much in the way people serve it.

BW: What did you do next?
CR: I went to graduate school at Harvard in the 1950s. I told my mama and my older sister, who kind of took over and helped my mother after my father died, that I wasn't going to unpack my trunk until after the

first semester, because I might have to come home! But I didn't. I got to stay and had a wonderful time. Of course there weren't many women on that campus. We would go to what was called the Radcliffe Club. I lived with a family on Beacon Hill because a friend of mine who had gone there had also lived with this family. This family was from Scotland originally, but they had come and made Boston their home. She taught music on the campus and had a beautiful voice. She'd invite me to go to the recitals. I had to take music appreciation, of course, when I was at the W, so I had learned to love good music, and until this day, I love all kinds of music.

BR: What did you study at Harvard?
CR: Nutrition. But I was in the School of Public Health, because nutrition was a major in the School of Public Health. That was a time when it was hard to get any schools to see the importance of teaching doctors anything about nutrition. Medical doctors, back in those days, knew nothing about nutrition, because they had not been required to take it. Public health nurses learned about nutrition. I was at Harvard two years.

BW: How did World War II affect life in Mississippi?
CR: We all had a rationing card, and we'd get just so much sugar, so many pairs of shoes. You had to have that rationing card to buy things. It was money to us at that time.

BW: When you left Leake County, where did you go to work next?
CR: I went to Greenville, Mississippi.

BW: Was Delta life any different from what you had been used to?
CR: Yes. I remember when I went down the hill at Yazoo City—I had to go across the bridge to go on into that flat country. I got over there, and it was just a straight road, and I was used to all the crooks and turns, so I got on that road and I thought, "Good gracious alive, where am I going?" When I got up there and was beginning to meet people, sometimes they'd look at me and say, in a real quiet voice, "I'm from the hills, too. I came from the hills, too." But then they would say, "You're going to like

it over here; they're lovely people." And they were. They were just lovely. Nice and friendly. There were lots of farmers in the Delta at that time—many, many farmers. It was big business.

BW: What was social life like there?
CR: People had a good time. They loved their neighbors, and they had good times together. They would get together for parties. When I worked up in the Tunica County area, everybody would go to Memphis just to get a cup of coffee, almost. I was in the Delta from 1940 to about 1954, when I came to Jackson.

BW: Did you meet your husband in the Delta?
CR: Yes. He worked with grain, growing it—experimental work.

BW: And when you married him, you left the Delta?
CR: Yes, and then we came to Jackson. In Jackson I worked with the State Board of Health and the Department of Education.

BW: What did you do for them?
CR: I helped the county health officers and the county school superintendents in learning how to treat pellagra, which is a disease we had among the poor people in Mississippi, and not only there, but even among the wealthy.

BW: What caused pellagra?
CR: It was a deficiency in their diets. The main things missing were vitamin B and vitamin A. The disease was widespread and it was serious.

BW: So you gave lectures on how to incorporate these foods into your diet to prevent this disease?
CR: Yes.

BW: How many years did you work in and around Jackson?
CR: When I was with the consumer marketing program, I had the

metropolitan area primarily. But then when I went to the district to work, I worked all over the district, in Southwest Mississippi.

BW: Tell me about the consumer marketing program.
CR: The consumer marketing program was one that was started because the home extension office had a marketing program. I had known the head of it, because he had been the county agent where I was a 4-H girl at one time. So when I started the home demonstration work and had taught several years, he pleaded with me to come to Jackson to do consumer work with products that were being grown by farmers, products that they couldn't sell.

BW: Like what?
CR: Cantaloupe. They had grown them—the research department had found an area where they would grow, but after the farmers started growing the cantaloupes and had a good many of them, they couldn't sell them because people didn't know what to do with them! So I had to get busy and get all the recipes together I could on how to use cantaloupe. So I did. And then the next thing I knew, he was calling me telling me to get off that telephone and stop telling people to use cantaloupe because they had sold them all, and they didn't have any more, and he didn't want to have to go outside the state to buy them because they wanted them to be a Mississippi project. But people kept begging for them, so Mississippi started taking cantaloupes from other states where they were being grown at that particular time, and that was when the farmer's market started here in Jackson, the old farmer's market, where a few farmers still bring food to sell.

BW: What other jobs did you have?
CR: I was a district agent. I had twenty counties in Southwest Mississippi, and I visited them, on an average, once a month at least. And then it began to get so horrible, since I had to keep so many records. Back then, of course, we had separate colored agents and white agents, but then it was changed, and after integration, we had both county agents and

home demonstration agents who were colored. They had programs that did marvelous jobs, and we still have them now in different counties. Some of the black agents are leaders of the programs in counties and doing a great job with them. After integration, we started work with Alcorn[7]—a cooperative program with them—and we also worked with Jackson State.[8]

BW: What are the most striking changes you see between women today and women sixty or seventy years ago?
CR: Most people now believe that women can do things in a business. Of course, women do work differently in many ways. But still, they can be good mothers and good businesspersons too if they can use good management and their budgets will allow. Now sometimes it's necessary for both husbands and wives to work because of economic conditions.

BW: What racial and societal changes have you seen during your life?
CR: I've seen many, many changes. For instance, last week there was a program where the different groups in downtown Jackson were meeting together to work out ways that they could do things better. And so I just see good things happening now, where blacks and whites are cooperating and we're all getting things done together. It's slow, but we're getting it done.

BW: What changes have you seen at the W since you were a student?
CR: There's just been so many, and a lot of them have been for the good—I think most of them have been. But sometimes it's hard, because at my age, it's hard to change, and it's hard to forget what things were like and not to judge a school by what it was. But now we have to change, because times change, and we have to have schools that are for everyone. Now, for example, most schools have a good preschool program, and they have young children on the campus. I love children of all ages.

7. Alcorn University, founded in 1871, was the first state-supported higher educational institution for African Americans, and it remains predominantly black.
8. Jackson State University is a historically black university founded in 1877.

I don't want people to say, "She just lives in the past," because I do want to live day to day and look to the future as being a good time and to help children. Now I have many small children who come to my back door and knock on it and call me the butterfly lady. I have a butterfly out on my wall that stays there year-round, and they'll come up and knock on my door, and they know I'll always have something to give them. I always keep something for the children. Right now, I do not have very many young ones around me, because I've lived here a long time, but their grandchildren and great-grandchildren, they come. And many of them live out of town, but they come back to see me. And I do try to help lots of shut-ins that can't get out, and every morning when I get up, I say to the Lord, "Help me do some good for somebody today." I try to say that also every night when I go to bed. And thank him for the good night I've had, because he's been so good to me in allowing me to have as good health as I have had.

BW: Have you been back to the W many times since you graduated?
CR: Oh, yes. For years, I didn't miss a reunion until after my mother was real sick or my husband was ill for a good long while.

BW: What were the W Homecomings like?
CR: Oh, they were wonderful. It was something we would look forward to year-round. Going on the campus at the W, and going to the tea-room.[9] That was a big attraction. The Goose! Mary Ida Flowers[10] was at the Goose, and she was in charge of that, and she did a marvelous job. And then, of course, the music department. I looked forward to going to the musical programs on the campus.

BW: Did you have a lot of good friendships with W alumni?
CR: Oh, yes. But the sad thing is, in Jackson, I'm one of the oldest, I guess, or among the oldest. I'm not the oldest, but I'm one of the few

9. The Golden Goose Tearoom, located on the first floor of the Student Activities Building (formerly the Henry Whitfield Gymnasium), demolished in the late 1960s.
10. Mary Ida Flowers (1916–97), Class of 1938.

that's left now from the 1930s. So Hyacinth Hayman[11] and I stay in touch all the time—very seldom a week passes but what we are not in contact with each another. And then Eloise Scott,[12] who was a legislator from the Pontotoc area, lived with me for most of the years that she was serving in the legislature. When she served in the legislature, I looked forward to having her because she kept me up with legislation and how it operates and so forth. Right now, I read the paper with interest, because I want to read what the legislature is doing and how they're doing it. Sometimes I agree, and sometimes I don't. But I like to know what's going on, I like to keep up. I even like the sports. I like baseball. I love baseball. And I love those St. Louis Cardinals. I really do. And I watch them. And if there's a game on, I always hope that the pastor finishes church in time so that I can get home and see most of that game. We go to early church and get home and to see the game. I like that.

BW: What lessons has life taught you that would share with future W graduates?

CR: I think it's still a marvelous school. It's a small school compared to some of the others, but still, it's the kind of school that's needed, because we have many students today that go there and they are not just a number—they are known by their professors and they call them by name, and that means so much, so much today. That's what I like about the W. And I think it's nice that we have men going there that want to go, but I still think a lot of emphasis should be put on women's education, because there are so many women that need the kind of education that the W gives. But the men are welcome.

....

11. Hyacinth McCormick Hayman (1913–2006), Class of 1935. See the interview with her in this volume.
12. Eloise Hale Scott (b. 1933), Class of 1953, served in the Mississippi House of Representatives from 1988 until 2003.

Emily Eugenia Summer
Class of 1945

OCTOBER 15, 2004

INTERVIEWED BY SUSAN PUCKETT AND BARBARA WHITE

FILMED BY CHRIS JENKINS

TRANSCRIBED BY CHRISTIE COLLINS AND SARAH SHEFFIELD

EMILY EUGENIA SUMMER WAS BORN ON JUNE 13, 1923, to Charles E. Summer and Emily O'Rorke Summer of Newton, Mississippi. Eugenia Summer came to MSCW from Yazoo City and served in numerous campus leadership roles, including holding the post of class treasurer during her freshman year and of president of the student body during her senior year. Also as a senior, she was elected Miss MSCW. After graduating with a major in history and a minor in art, she received a master's degree from Columbia University with an emphasis in painting. She also studied at the Art Institute of Chicago, the California College of Arts and Crafts, Seattle University, and the Penland School of Arts. She began teaching at MSCW in 1949 and in 1982 became head of the Division of Fine and Performing Arts. When she retired in 1987, she was awarded emerita status. In 2002, MUW named the art gallery in the new Fine Arts Building in her honor. She has received the MUW Medal of Excellence and the Lowndes

County Alumni Chapter's Celebration of Service award. In 2005, MUW conferred on her one of its rare honorary doctoral degrees. Her art has been shown in more than eighty juried national exhibitions throughout the United States. She lives in Columbus.

BW: Why did you attend the W?

ES: I didn't think I would ever get to college. My family would talk about my twin brother going to college and how they were going to afford to send him to college, but my name was never mentioned. In high school, I took secretarial work, and I thought I would go directly into a job. And then one day, about a year before I came to the W, I remember at lunch—we called it dinner back then since the big meal was in the middle of the day. We had this wonderful big table in our kitchen in our big house in Yazoo City. My daddy would walk home to dinner, and we would all sit down together. My brother and I were in the eleventh grade in school, and they started talking about how my brother was going to apply to Millsaps College.[1] Then all of a sudden, my mother hit the table—bang!—with her hand, and we knew when she did that she had something to say. Everybody was supposed to put down our forks and listen to what Mama had to say. So she hit the table, and we came to attention. She said, "Now, I just want to say one thing here. If that boy is going to college, this girl is going, too." I nearly fell under the table. I had never heard my name mentioned with college to that point. She said, "I've been doing a little research, and we can send her to MSCW." She said, "It will be very inexpensive because they don't charge a lot of tuition there, and she can get a National Youth Administration scholarship." That was a work scholarship that was instigated by the Roosevelt program. So I really say that I'm a Roosevelt scholar because I got that work scholarship, and I've always been grateful for it.

When I entered MSCW in the fall of 1941, that was the trailing end of the depression, and nobody had much money. I worked for a professor

1. Millsaps College, founded in 1890, is a Methodist-run liberal arts college in Jackson, Mississippi.

in English the first semester and a professor in the speech department the second semester. And I tell you, I decided that working for professors was not what I wanted to continue to do. They are tough birds to work for, and I wanted out. But I had to have a job, so I applied to work in the dining hall, and that paid the highest—it paid everything. It was a learning experience in itself because I found out who didn't like the soybeans and the other dishes we were served at lunch. You find out a lot of things about people when you serve food to them. I found out who were really great people and who were picky ones or the not so great ones. But I made a lot of friends among the people working in the dining hall. It was tough work since we had to be over there at 6:00 in the morning to eat breakfast, and then we had to set up our tables. We served two tables, about twelve people each, and we had to set up our tables and get ready at precisely 7:00 A.M. to bring the food out. Then we had to stay afterward and clean the dirty dishes. We did this three times a day, of course, but as I said, I learned an awful lot from doing that and made a lot of very close friends. I still keep in touch with two of those people who were working in the dining hall with me. We became really close friends; I wouldn't give anything for them.

BW: What do you remember about your first year on campus? Do you have any stories about dorm life?
ES: I do—but they were about things that I'm not too proud of right now. Should I tell them? My mother said she had a lot more fun going to school at Saint Mary of the Pines Convent in Chatawa, Mississippi.[2] She had some northern nuns there that really knew how to have fun. They had dances Saturday night, and the boys from New Orleans would come up. Were we having dances every Saturday night? No, we weren't, not by a long shot! So, anyway, whatever we could think up to relieve the monotony of trying to abide by the rules that we really didn't like, we thought was pretty much fair game.

2. Saint Mary of the Pines was a Catholic boarding school in Chatawa, a small town in Pike County, near the Mississippi-Louisiana border.

We had a social adviser, for example, that really did just bother the heck out of us. The rules were bad enough. For example, on Sunday afternoon, we had what was called Meditation. Isn't that quaint? It was from 2:00 to 4:00. We had to be in our rooms "meditating," supposedly, but of course we were in our rooms just agitating to leave. I had two roommates, and they were both from Yazoo City, Dicey Carr[3] and Mary Stigler,[4] and they would pretty much go along with these things that I would think up. They thought I was kind of funny, so I would purposely think up funny things to do. I decided one time that I would dramatize the studying we were doing during Meditation and that I would also sort of complain about the lack of lightbulbs in the ceiling. We needed a new lightbulb, and we couldn't get it. We couldn't get them to put it in, and the ceiling was too high in Callaway for us to do it. So, this social adviser had a habit of coming around—now people would sue the you-know-what out of her—but she would fling our doors open. She would knock, fling the door open, and see what we were up to. We decided we would be up to something, just to put her on. So we stacked a table on top of our study table and then a chair on top of that, and I climbed up on all that. I was sitting trying to look like I was trying to read a book, and the lightbulb was right above my head. We knew she would come fling the door open, because she always did. I had to sit there for a while because she never came at the same time, since she wanted to find what you were up to. So she flung the door open, and she looked at me up there and looked at the situation, and she said, "What are you doing up there?" I said, "I'm meditating and reading"—I think I had my Bible—"I'm meditating and reading my Bible, but the light is so dim that I had to get up here to be able to read it. We really do need a new lightbulb." So, anyway, she closed the door like nothing was happening. We got a bang out of doing this.

So we began to think up other things, and one of them we thought of I won't tell you because it has some bad language in it. Not that we

3. Dicey Dodds Carr Barbour, a freshman from Yazoo City in 1941–42.
4. Mary Stribling Stigler Thompson, a freshman from Yazoo City in 1941–42.

were saying it, but we were doing this slogan in calligraphy when she flung open the door. We were all three sitting there writing these things in red fingernail polish, and it was bad language. So anyway, she took a look at this and said, "Oh, dear," and closed the door. She didn't really know what to make of us, since we weren't really doing things that she could nail us on for the violation of some rule. Anyway, we enjoyed giving her a hard time. We had to be in the dormitory by 10:00 at night, and we had to be in the bed, with lights out, by 10:30. And she would come around and fling the door open to see if we were in bed or getting in bed or whatever. Then she made up a rule that we could not go the bathroom at 11:00, because she heard too much flushing between 10:30 and 11:00, so she said, "Just get it done before 10:30." So I decided that I would go around and tell everybody in Callaway that at precisely 11:00 we were going to flush every toilet in that dormitory. We synchronized our watches, and we snuck out the door and tippy-toed into these bathrooms and manned our post— or womaned our post, as you would say. So at precisely 11:00, we flushed those toilets. It sounded like Niagara Falls, because everything echoed in that dormitory. So it sounded like we wanted it to, and then we tippy-toed back to bed. Of course, she came roaring up there slinging open doors, saying, "I heard that!" Nobody said a word. Our response was total silence. So anyway, things of that sort went on. That really wasn't anything she could reprimand us for formally. If we got two reprimands, we got a week's restriction to campus. So we made sure that we didn't do anything that was against a specific rule, but she wrote reports every week, as required, to send to the president, who was Dr. Parkinson.[5] A number of years later, someone got hold of those reports, and we read them. We could tell she sort of knew that I might be a ringleader in all this. And she said, "To think these are supposed to be some of the best freshmen in this class." By that time, I had been elected secretary of the freshman class, and as it turned out in the end, strangely, I was elected president of the student body my senior year. Then I thought it was time for me to stop doing all this foolishness,

5. Burney Lynch Parkinson (1887–1972) served as president of MSCW from 1932 until 1952.

but people said "Don't stop," since it was just about the only fun we had!

SP: What was World War II like on campus?
ES: Pearl Harbor happened my freshman year, and D-Day happened very soon after my senior year, so I was there the four years of World War II. The strange thing was that we didn't have radios in our room, much less television. There weren't really many ways we could find out what was going on. We could go to the library and read the *New York Times*, which I did. But you know the news that would be printed in the newspapers then would already be old—it was what had happened maybe a week or two before. There was no reporting like we get every day, day by day, in a war like Iraq. It's astounding how we know what happens within an hour of its happening. Then I look back on the days of World War II and how little we knew of it here. My twin brother was in the South Pacific for four and a half years, and recently I told that to somebody, and she said, "He got to come home often, didn't he?" And I said, "Absolutely not." I said, "You don't understand. He went over there on a ship from Los Angeles, and it took a number of days to go by ship, a big battleship, and that's how they got to the war zone."

He was assigned to a small island in the South Pacific. He was a pilot, and we were constantly worried about his welfare. There would be times when two or three weeks would pass before we would get a letter from him, and one time, it was almost six months. And so we were getting more and more afraid every day that we were going to have somebody in a uniform knock on my mother's door at home, but finally we got a small packet of letters from him, and what happened to hold up that mail, we'll never know. We didn't know then; we don't know now. My brother was selected to fly some missions to China. He sent me a beautiful kimono, and of course the government shipped it for him. And he sent a brass flower container, and he sent me some embroidered slippers from China. I thought, "What is he doing in China?" I got those things before I had heard from him, but he never said what he did in China. And he didn't talk much about the war after he had got home.

And I would ask him about things, because I was really curious; I wanted to know about his war experience. I asked, "Now, those missions that you flew to China, what was that about?" And he said, "I can't tell you." And I said, "Not even now?" "No," he said, "I swore to secrecy forever." And he said, "I will never talk about those. I cannot talk about that at all." But he had flown several missions to China, and his letter would say, "I hope you got the things from China," but it would never say why he was in China.

So World War II was very strange, and I remember that my mother would telephone me once a month, and her message most of the time to me was, "Eugenia, I know that recruiters are coming to that campus to recruit women to work in factories or to join the military." She said, "I know the recruiters are coming there. My advice to you is, don't listen to them. Your twin brother is in the South Pacific, and I may never see him again, and I just can't bear it if the two of you were there. So please don't go." She would say, "He is sending back part of his military pay to help pay for you to go to college." And he would write me and say, "Don't interrupt your education, because this may be the only chance you will get to go to college."

SP: Did the campus sponsor activities for the war effort?

ES: We rolled bandages. We had to wash our hands and make them sterile and put on surgical gloves and sit there for hours folding these bandages. We did a lot of that. Miss Pohl[6] was the one that taught us how to do that. She went during the war and took a course in a lot of different things so she could come back to organize the campus to respond to the war effort. And then people who could knit would knit socks, sweaters, and caps. Then we raised a lot of money by selling war stamps. We would buy stamps for twenty-five cents each, and we had a little book we could paste them in after we had bought them. We could buy them at the post office, and of course people could buy war bonds, but we didn't

6. Emma Ody Pohl (1880–1966) joined II & C in 1907, when she was hired to develop the department of physical education. She taught that subject until her retirement in 1955.

have money to buy war bonds. But many a Saturday night we would have an entertainment of some sort over in the gym—I'm talking about the old gym—and we would sell war stamps for admission. So everyone that would come would buy at least one twenty-five-cent war stamp or more. When we filled our book, we had to keep it for, I think, five years or ten before we could get the money back. And so it was a savings plan for us and in small ways would help pay for the war in Europe. Right now, I really think that if people were asked to sacrifice something and do something to help the war in Iraq, people would feel different about it. We felt involved in World War II. I can remember that these affairs in the gym provided entertainment for us. I remember the faculty having what they called the Faculty Follies, and they would put on a program at least two times a month. We advertised one time that Miss Lucy Banks[7] would come as a flapper, and she was very much a lady. She was wonderful, and she did come as a flapper. It was so amazing; she came in, and someone was playing some jazz on the piano. She came in swinging a bunch of beads, and she had drawn her lips on with lipstick. We just thought it was remarkable.

We were very close-knit during that time because we couldn't leave the campus very often. Tires were rationed; people didn't have tires to do a lot of running around. Gasoline was rationed. Food was rationed. Sugar was rationed. All kinds of meats were rationed. Rationing meant that the person who managed the financial affairs of the household, for which my mother assumed the responsibility, had to apply to get a ration book to go to the grocery store. I think we could have bacon maybe once a month, a pound of bacon. Other forms of meat were severely rationed. At MSCW we didn't have much meat in the dining hall, so the dietician had to invent main dishes. Sometimes we just had vegetarian meals. Most of us were willing to go without meats, but some folks didn't. I thought that was very inappropriate not to support the war, to complain about what we had to eat, because at least we had something to eat. But we had to give up a lot of things.

7. Lucy Young Banks (1895–1993), Class of 1916, taught English at MSCW from 1932 until 1965.

SP: Did you ever worry about an invasion of the United States?
ES: I can remember how frightened we would be when the siren on the top of Fant Library, which is now the administration building (Welty Hall), would go off. We would have to turn off every light on this campus. Every light had to go off. And then we had to go to preassigned places on the campus to sit on the floor in a hallway, just leaning against the wall, people lined up close together and not saying a word. We could not talk. We could not do anything but sit there until the siren went off and signaled the end of the air raid. We could hear airplanes overhead, and we never knew until it was over if these were airplanes that were going to drop bombs. We took it very seriously. We would sit there and kind of look up at the dark and the sky, and the airplanes would fly by. Most time they were from the air base. Columbus Air Force Base was founded my freshman year. So they would fly over Columbus looking for lights, and if they had seen a light on this campus, it would have been bad news for the W. They would publish a list in the paper the next day about violations, lights being on. If they saw a house with a light on—they were flying very low—they could pinpoint it. They would have found out what house it was. They would have found out what dormitory it was. These air raids would last about an hour and a half, because we were taught what to do if a real invasion was under way, which was a possibility.

BW: Was there real danger?
ES: We were constantly told that Columbus, because of the air base, was a prime target, so we were well aware of the danger. I can remember one time in the summer I was up here. We didn't have summer school back then, but I was up here working. There was a special summer session for the home economics department because they were working on recipes to cope with having to give up so many kinds of foods. They were also taking part in a study on plastic dishes, because during World War II was the first time we had plastic dishes. And they were pretty sorry. Sometimes they would melt or warp in really hot water, so the home economics faculty was trying out different kinds of plastics in dishes. I was up here

working for Miss Wilson,[8] who headed the home economics department, and among other duties, I had to close up the home economics building, Martin Hall. I had to close that building after 10:00 at night, and all those people had to leave that building. Then I had to lock up the library and food laboratories and turn out all the lights and get out of there. One time, we had an air raid warning just as I had turned out all the lights in that building. There I was in that big building by myself, and I sat down in a hall against the wall. I looked at the sky and heard these airplanes flying over and I thought, "Oh, I'm going to die right here by myself. I don't even have anybody to touch." I was scared to death.

SP: Tell us about academic life.

ES: The classes were really tough then. We had really tough teachers. Of course, the teachers at the W are still tough, and they ought to be. They ought to demand a lot from their students. We always used to say it was possible to get into MSCW, but it was much harder to get out with a degree. We were in class even on Saturday mornings from 8:00 to 12:00. We had classes until 5:00 every day, and of course, the daylight savings time started during that war, too. That would mean darker nights earlier. But I really did enjoy Dr. Minnie Clare Boyd.[9] She was a teacher that influenced my life profoundly. She lived just around the corner from where I live now. But of course, I didn't live in this house then, I lived in a dormitory. I think there were six of us history majors in my class. She and Miss Lottie Howard[10] were both very tough teachers. I can remember studying so hard for their tests and exams. My goodness! Dr. Boyd gave the same kind of test every time, and the exam was just a bigger deal of the same format. She would have a test with four discussion questions. She would not have true-false or fill-in-the-blanks or anything like that.

8. Mary Wilson (1892–1988), Class of 1915, served as a faculty member and later as head of the home economics department at MSCW from 1925 until 1961.
9. Minnie Clare Boyd (1898–1983) taught history at MSCW from 1934 until 1963, serving as head of the department until 1948.
10. Lottie Howard (1888–1969), Class of 1911, taught history at MSCW from 1915 until 1950.

She would just put down four large topics, and we were supposed to write a short essay on each in an hour's time. So you really had to know what you were doing to finish that in an hour. I studied by anticipating what she was going to ask, and I would write out a question like I was making out the test. And I finally caught on to the things she liked to ask about. It helped to list out six or eight questions and try in advance to decide what the answer was going to be, because when we got in there, we had to start writing immediately, and we just really had to write ferociously. We had to get right on target.

BW: Do you have any memories of Dr. Parkinson?
ES: Oh, do I! I was president of the student body my senior year. He was so strict, and he had a wife[11] that didn't trust anybody, it seemed. She meddled in faculty members' private lives. Maybe I shouldn't say that, but it's true. It was kind of miserable on this campus for faculty members and for students because the two of them were so strict. She was much stricter than he was. And he would agree to things the students wanted, and then he would say that he had to think it over. We knew what that meant! It meant he had to go home and talk to his wife, and he would come back the next day and say, "I don't think that's a good idea at all." So forget that! When I was a senior, students would come to me and say, "We want this and we want that," and I would say, "We'll just have to think of a way to try to convince Dr. Parkinson." So Amanda Bridgforth[12] from Yazoo City and I decided that we were going to try to get a jukebox in the Goose.[13] Now that seems like a small thing, but when you don't have much entertainment at all on campus, it's important. The Goose was in a building that's been torn down now, unfortunately. It was a wonderful place, and it was sort of a gathering place for students and a hanging-out place to make friends. Students wanted a nickelodeon,

11. Dera Dry Parkinson (1887–1979). In 1927, she became the first woman to earn a Ph.D. (in psychology) from the University of South Carolina.
12. Amanda Bridgforth Williams (1923–ca. 1975), Class of 1945, served as editor of the *Meh Lady* during her senior year.
13. The Golden Goose Tearoom, located on the first floor of the Student Activities Building (formerly the Henry Whitfield Gymnasium), demolished in the late 1960s.

a.k.a. jukebox, in the Goose. I said, "Amanda, let's do this research to find out what it'll cost and how we can get a jukebox in the Goose." We found out there was a place down the street on College, a good bit down the way, sort of out of bounds for us. But I said, "Let's go down to the Fairway Amusement Company and talk to those people about what it will cost to have a jukebox in the Goose, because Dr. Parkinson would say that we can't afford it." We didn't know anything about it except that we wanted a jukebox, too. Incidentally, I say my claim to fame is that I put the first nickel in the first jukebox ever on the W campus. Rebecca George[14] and I flipped a nickel to see who would win, and I won. But I don't remember what I played. There were so many tunes I liked, and it was late at night.

So Amanda and I had made a lot of little trips down to the Fairway Amusement Company. We could have gotten into the deepest kind of trouble if we had been caught doing it. We knew a little slot in the hedge over by some of the dormitories. We would go out of the campus and walk down Bell Avenue a little way and then go over to College Street and end up at the Fairway Amusement Company. Those guys were so nice to us. I remember the first time we went in there and told those guys what we were there for, we said, "You mustn't tell anybody we've been down here; we could get into deep trouble." And they said, "Don't worry, we'll help you whatever way we can." We found out it wasn't going to cost the college anything: people put in nickels, played the tunes, and then once a week they came and got the money out. But 10 percent of it went to the W. That sounded like a good deal. So I told Amanda that it was time for us to call a meeting with Dr. Parkinson and the President's Council, who were the heads of other campus organizations. I said, "Let's just lay it out to him and tell him what we learned, and maybe he won't ask us how we learned it." And he didn't. We went in there and sat very prim and proper, and he said, "Now, what is this meeting going to be about?" And I took a deep breath and said, "Dr. Parkinson, the students want a

14. Rebecca George Croley (1923–91), Class of 1945, served as editor of the *Spectator* during her senior year.

jukebox on the campus in the Goose." "Well," he said, and he put his chin in his hands, and he looked around the room. For the longest time he didn't say anything. And I thought, "What is going on?" And finally he said, "What is a jukebox?" Then I said, "It's a nickelodeon." And he said, "Oh, I think I've heard of that. Is that a musical instrument?" And I said, "Yes sir, it is." He asked me to describe it to him. "What does it play?" he asked. And I said, "It plays records; the students want permission to put a jukebox in the Goose so they can dance." "Dance?" That was a serious word, because we had some strict rules about dancing. And I'm talking about girls dancing with girls, because there weren't any boys here. And they wanted to jitterbug in the Goose. I didn't use the word *jitterbug*, because that would have upset him something terrible and we would have lost the case. So I just said they wanted to dance in the Goose. "Well," he said, "we can't afford it." And I said, "We've learned that it won't cost us anything. They'll put it in, and they'll give 10 percent of the money back to this school, and we can use it, if you permit us to, for planning other recreational things." And so he thought a while and he said, "It looks like we may be able to do this, but I'll have to go home and think it over." Translated, it meant go home and tell his wife. So we held our breath for a day or two, and he called us back over and said, "I think we can do this." We were just absolutely thrilled! I thought, "She really doesn't know what a jukebox is either, but why tell her?" A musical instrument sounded not too bad.

The agreement was that only Rebecca George—she was head of the *Spectator* [15]—and I could be in the Goose when the jukebox was delivered at 11:00 at night. That was well after lights out. Everybody was supposed to be tucked into bed, because he didn't want a riot when we got a jukebox in the Goose. So he said, "They will have to deliver it after hours, and you and Rebecca George can be there, and Miss M. Elisabeth Hudson [16] can be there." And I thought, "Uh oh," because she was strict, too.

15. The *Spectator*, begun in 1905 as a quarterly publication, was a combination annual and literary magazine that evolved into the student newspaper by the early 1920s. The *Spectator* is now published weekly.
16. M. Elisabeth Hudson (1897–1970) was professor and head of MSCW's Department of Bible and executive secretary of the Student Christian Association from 1940 until 1963.

And then I thought, "What is she going to think about this?" But we went forward with it, and Rebecca George and I were over there, and there were no lights in the Goose. We couldn't turn the lights on because he didn't want any other students to find out what was going on. Of course, they knew anyway. So a truck came driving around and turned off its lights, and they moved the jukebox in and plugged it in. All the neon lit up, and I thought, "Wow! I don't believe it!" And Rebecca and I flipped the coin to see who could put the first nickel in, and I won it. I wish I had a picture of me doing that, but of course nobody had cameras then, so you'll just have to take my word for it. That's my claim to fame. We enjoyed it very, very much, and students couldn't believe it. And they went over and thanked President Parkinson, and he felt really proud of himself, like he had done it on his own.

Another thing students wanted was to end wearing the uniform. I had mixed feelings about that because I had profited by wearing the uniform. And in my time, we didn't wear exact duplicates of the same navy blue dresses or anything, but we did have to wear navy blue skirts and navy blue sweaters. Different classes could wear different collars, and seniors were the only ones that could wear an all-white collar. We had dickeys under our sloppy-joe navy blue sweaters, and we wore our navy blue skirts. Then of course we wore saddle oxfords and bobby socks. A lot of people just didn't like wearing navy blue. A friend of mine said to me, "I see why you don't mind it; you look good in navy blue. You're blond and blue-eyed." But she said, "Look at me. I just don't look good in navy blue, and I just hate it." Dr. Parkinson had said to me, "You absolutely cannot bring this up. I will not permit it." But I thought there might be some way we could figure out a way, so I decided to read the constitution—the *Mississippi State College for Women Student Government Handbook, 1944–1945*. "What we have to do," I said, "is find a loophole in the constitution, if we can." So we all read the constitution, and I found what I thought was a loophole, and it turned out that it worked.

I wasn't really gung ho about abolishing the uniform because it was cheap. I wore the same few clothes for four years. But I could perceive that the majority of the students thought that it was time to end it. I found this in the constitution: "Amendments to the constitution, bylaws, and regulations may be proposed by the student council or fifty students may bring an amendment to the president who shall present it to the association." I looked at that, and I thought, "That's it!" Dr. Parkinson had told me, "I do not permit you to have a discussion of this in any meeting of the student body." We had two regular meetings every month, and I had to preside. But here it says "Fifty students may bring an amendment to the president, who shall present it to the association." And I thought, "I'll have to do it if fifty people want it." So I went out and found a person who I knew would get this done in a hurry, Gertrude Irby[17] from Jackson. I said, "Gertrude, you get a petition and write at the top that you are giving this to the president of the student body who shall—and underscore *shall*—present this to the association." And the handbook further said, "Amendments shall be proposed two weeks before being voted on and shall require two-thirds vote before passing." Gertrude got out there and easily got way over fifty signatures—she brought a petition with almost every signature in the student body. Then I thought, "Shall I tell Dr. Parkinson before I call this meeting, or shall I not?" I decided, risk everything; don't tell him. Tell him after the fact. So I didn't say a word about it, but I went by the handbook. In two weeks' time, I called a meeting of the student body for a vote. We had it at 5:30 in the afternoon, just before dinner. We all assembled in Whitfield Hall. I got up and I said, "This is not a meeting where we're going to discuss this issue, because everybody's discussed it for a long time. We are going to vote, and we are going to vote on pieces of paper. Now the chapel checkers will pass out pieces of paper." The chapel checkers were the ones that checked the attendance at what was called chapel assembly. Every week we had assembly, and Dr. Parkinson of course presided over that. They got up and passed out these little slips of paper. And then I said, "simply write 'for' the amendment and put in parentheses, 'for abolishing the uniform.' Or write 'against' the amendment, 'not for abolishing the uniform,'" so there would be no doubt about what they were voting for.

17. Gertrude Irby Scott, Class of 1945.

Then we took these up, and then some of us skipped dinner and went over to the student government room and counted these votes. It was an overwhelming response to abolish the uniform. Then I knew I had to go tell Dr. Parkinson, and I did not postpone it. I went immediately over to his house across the street from Main Dormitory, rang the doorbell, and I stood there. I thought, "How am I going to do this?" He came to the door, and he said, "Oh, Eugenia. Do come in." I said, "Thank you." We went in and we sat down. I sat stiffly on the sofa, and I said, "Dr. Parkinson, I have come to inform you that the student body has voted overwhelmingly to abolish the uniform." I took the handbook with me, and I read what it said. Then I said, "I could not ignore the petition that was brought to me, because the handbook says the student body president shall present the petition. I know you told me that I was not permitted to do this. But," I said, "I am the representative of the student body, and I had to do it." He looked down at the floor and he didn't say anything, and I thought, "Is he going to just toss me out the door?" And finally he looked up and he said, "I guess you and I both knew this was inevitable, didn't we?" And I said, "Pretty much so." He said, "That's the way it will be then." So my class was the last one that wore the uniform.

BW: Tell us about your career teaching at the W.

ES: I came because Dr. Ralph Hudson[18] had met my major professor that I had at Columbia in New York at a convention. And my major professor gave a good report on me, which I appreciated a lot. That major professor was one of the wonderful teachers I had. He taught me watercolor. I remember many things that he did to help me along the way, and so I was very proud. When Ralph Hudson phoned me, I was in Clarksdale, Mississippi, as art supervisor for the city schools over there. My salary was eighteen hundred dollars a year in Clarksdale. He said, "I met your major professor, and he said you were very good in all of your classes at Columbia, and he gave you a glowing report." Then he said, "I

18. Ralph Hudson (1922–94), professor and head of the art department, taught at MSCW from 1945 until 1969.

wonder if you would be interested in coming over here for an interview for a job at MSCW?" I just couldn't believe it. I thought, "Mercy! Sure I will be!" So I came over here, and he hired me. And because I had the master's degree, I started teaching as assistant professor of art. I started in the fall of 1949. I was barely older than my students were at that point because I had graduated in 1945. I spent two years in New York getting that master's degree and then taught in Clarksdale. So I had to work really hard to stay ahead of my students.

MSCW has always attracted good students, really good students, because they know when they come here that we don't have football and a lot of the social life that sororities could provide. But students come to the W because they want a good education. So most of the time it was very easy to teach students like that, and very pleasant, too. When I came over here I thought, "I'm not sure I want to stay." I wasn't all that sold on spending my career here. But it was such a great place because of the wonderful students that I decided, year by year, to keep on teaching here. I taught for thirty-four years here and enjoyed every minute of it. I often thought, "Oh, if the people in Mississippi, just ordinary people, knew why I'm teaching up here and getting paid for doing it, I'm not sure they would approve." A lot of people dismiss art as a sort of a frill and not really important and as something that doesn't require much thinking or brains. They think you just do what you can already do. That's not true at all. Art takes concentration, and for me, it takes total concentration. I remember one time a student came to a painting class and brought a small portable radio. And she was over there in the corner playing this music and sort of doing this and that and now and then stroking some paint on the canvas. She was just having a good time. I went over there and said, "You can't bring a radio in here." She said, "I did." "Yeah, but turn it off." I said, "I didn't realize I had to make a rule that you can't play radios in this class." Then she said, "But I can't do this work if I can't play a radio." And I said, "That's just wallpaper music you're playing if you have to have noise." She said, "I can't stand silence. I can't put up with myself that long without something else." And I said, "Why don't we talk about it this afternoon. Come by my office about

3:00," because I tried never to discuss personal things with students in front of the rest of the class. So when she came to my office, I said, "From what you tell me, I don't believe you need to continue working in art, because it's not just a lifestyle, and it's not something that you can do while listening to the radio and jiving at the same time. You just can't do that, because it requires real concentration. You're not doing much in class, and you've got to turn the radio off and concentrate." She said, "I guess you're right. I don't belong in art, but can I continue?" I said, "You can, but you can't bring the radio." She said she'd try it, but she cut class a lot then. And I kept warning her that if she didn't produce much, she was not going to pass this class. So she ended the semester, and sure enough she flunked. It was not too easy to flunk art. Most of the students in classes were truly interested in art. And they really did work hard and they produced wonderful works. Most of them were here to do that. I told her this in the privacy of my office after she failed. I said, "You know you flunked just because you didn't do anything." And she said, "Yeah, I know. I don't really want to be here. My parents wanted me to come to school." I said, "You're wasting their money. Don't you feel bad about that?" She said, "No, I don't, because this is where they want me to be, so I'm here." I said, "But you're trying to flunk out to get back at them aren't you?" And she said, "Yeah, I guess you could say that." I told her, "I really don't think that's fair to your parents." She said, "They don't care if I flunk." The next semester she came back and signed up for the same class. Then I said, "You know you can take this under somebody else," because there was another person teaching it. She said, "No, it's more fun to flunk under you than him, so if you don't mind, I'll just take another semester." I said, "Are you really going to work?" She said, "I might, I don't know." But she flunked again. Then I said, "This is it." She said, "Yeah, I guess so. My parents told me if I would come two years, that was enough. Don't feel bad about it. It's not your fault. It's my fault, and I really did have a good time flunking." I thought that was a compliment, and I guess it was.

Anyway, I enjoyed the superior students that we got. And I learned a lot from those students myself. Goodness, I knew that I had many,

many students that were far more talented than I. My method of teaching is to try to help each student develop original subject matter and original style because I think it's wrong to have students copy what I might demonstrate. If I were to get up to the board and paint a painting quickly and say, "Now do like this"—in other words, do like I do—that would be very wrong. In the first place, it's really hard to define what art is. It's much easier to say what it is not. It is not a copy of anybody's work. If you were to copy somebody's poem, would you say you wrote that poem? No. You might say, "I copied Byron's poetry," but you couldn't claim that you did it. Copying in art would be wrong for the same reason. So I never tried to force any style of mine, or, for that matter, any kind of style, on my students. I would show a lot of slides at the beginning of the semester, and I would travel a lot to take these slides in museums or at exhibitions so that they could see a lot of different styles. I divided the slides into figure painting—not portrait painting, but figure painting—landscape, still life, and abstract, and so on. I wanted them to see all the different kinds of art so that hopefully they would see something that would appeal to them, where they would say, "Aha! That is the kind of subject matter I want to do. I want to be a figure painter, or I want to be a landscapist and so on." It worked for the really good students. I knew that some of them would far surpass my ability, and they did. I could name a few who have.

I think that my approach to teaching was misunderstood sometimes. I had all different kinds of work going on in my class. I would go to each student and confer with that person and encourage and then mention some famous artist that she could go look up in the library to see different approaches to that subject matter. In art you have content, or subject matter, and then you have style. I was anxious that each student select her content, because if I had said, "Okay, everybody paint a landscape today, and here's how to do it," that would have cut off the possibility that that student would have had a much better idea than I had. Most of them enjoyed that kind of approach. In painting classes, I wanted to teach them everything about painting—that is, stretching their own canvases, because it's much cheaper and better to make their own, and making frames and entering exhibitions. I took a class in woodworking one summer just to learn how to build picture frames and to build the framework to stretch canvas. So I taught them a lot of tips about handling tools. After they took my class, they knew how to miter corners, glue and clamp frames together, to put nails in the corners, build a framework and to stretch the canvas on it.

SP: Did you ever feel that as a woman your art did not get the respect it deserved?
ES: No. The strangest thing is that I really never felt discriminated against as a woman. I guess I should have, because I knew that our salaries on this campus were two or three thousand dollars less than men made. Whether they were married or not, men made more. And I had friends who said, "Let's band together and start a lawsuit." I said I wouldn't do that because I didn't want to get involved in stuff like that. I wanted to stay involved with art and teaching. I really didn't feel much discrimination as a woman. I would submit works of art to juried shows, and I was either accepted or rejected. I don't think people who were judging those shows ever knew whether I was a woman or not. I had works accepted in about eighty juried art shows over my career, which was a pretty good record. When I first started submitting works to juries for shows, I had to ship the real work to that person, to a place where he saw the real works in front of him. Now people send slides, but I had to build crates. Again, my woodworking class came in handy. I built many a wooden crate. I learned how to pack paintings safely and ship them off. It cost a lot of money to ship a work. Then if we got rejected, we had to pay for it to come back too. If the painting got accepted, they would pay to send it back. But I had enough success that I don't remember thinking that I was discriminated against in the world of art.

SP: What do you think are the W's greatest strengths as an institution?
ES: I think the focus on academics. Dr. Limbert[19] has stated that the

19. Claudia Limbert (b. 1940) became president of MUW in 2002.

focus is going to be on academics here. I think that's one of the greatest strengths. The curious thing is that when men were admitted, I was all for the admission of men to this campus. I had a little friend in town. He was a cute little boy that would come by my house and bring his pieces of art, and I would talk with him. I just kind of taught him on the side. He was a wonderful guy, and I saw him grow up and become eligible, I mean age-wise, to come to classes at the W. But he and I both knew that he could not. And I felt awful about that. Here he was, living just two blocks from the campus, and he could not attend. He said, "If I could just come and sit in on classes and not get any credit, you wouldn't have to say a word to me in class. I could just come listen, and then I could do it on my own." I asked if he could have permission to do that. Of course, it was no. I felt awful about it, because he would have then had to go to the University of Alabama, and his mother simply did not have the money. She cried, and she said, "I just feel awful that he can't come over to the W." I did too, so I thought it was the right thing for the taxpayers in Mississippi to be able to send their sons as well as their daughters to the W. We have had a good many men to apply, and we still have a good many men over there.

Another curious thing is that a certain lawyer in town tried to stir the men up to change the name of this school, and a group of about a hundred of our men students signed a petition that they did not want the name changed. They said, "We came to this school because it has a good reputation under this name, and we're not ashamed of having a degree from MUW. In fact, we're proud to say we're getting a degree at MUW, because everybody knows it's tough to get a degree, and we want it to keep the name."

SP: What is the philosophy behind your artwork?

ES: A painting named *Back Porch Still Life* is the very first painting that I ever did that I was really satisfied with. One of the things I always told my students is that, among other things, you have to have a healthy capacity to remain dissatisfied. And they would say, "Huh?" One student said, "Look, I have not got time to be dissatisfied. I've got to get on with this and do some works that I like." I said, "Yeah, but you didn't listen to my explanation. If you are satisfied with what you are doing, you're not going to strive to get better. So don't get too satisfied too soon in your career." I told her about the great French painter Cézanne, who was never satisfied with what he did, and mercy, he's one of the most famous. If I were to list ten names in the whole history of art, he would be one of them. He always would say, "I'm just not yet satisfied; I have not done it yet." Mercy, his works sell for millions, and they did during his lifetime. He was a success if you ever had one. But he said that he was always dissatisfied. That struck a note with me. I felt it was okay to feel dissatisfied. In fact, it's not only okay, it's healthy. It makes you strive for something different, and it moves you on.

I had a teacher one time who would come up, and if you were just standing there staring at your painting, he would say, "Do something, even if it's wrong." I thought that was pretty good advice, too, because you can't stand there forever afraid of making a mistake. And he would say, "You've got to put paint on canvas if you're painting a painting, and because you've got a palate knife, you can scrape it off if you don't like it. You can get another piece of paper if you are working on paper. Every painting is not a life-and-death matter. So don't get so scared of doing something wrong." I think that it's important to keep on keeping on. I invented a little term that I've never really spoken of until right now. It was called Operation Bootstrap. When I would send a painting to an exhibition, if I got the postcard back and it said "Rejected," I would feel really down for maybe an hour or two, really unhappy about it. And then I finally realized, I can't be so unhappy that I might quit painting. I'm not going to do that. I have known people who did quit if they got too many rejections from submitting works to juried shows. When a work was rejected, I decided that I would start another painting before that day ended. I called it in my mind Operation Bootstrap. I would make sure that even if I had to stay up late that night, I would get out another canvas or another piece of paper and start another painting, because you can inspire yourself by your own work. You never know when you're going to do something that is going to suddenly tell you,

"I didn't know I could do that. Did I really do that?" You can't afford to sit around and say, "I can't do anything today because I'm not inspired." It's your job to inspire yourself. Just thinking of painting sometimes can inspire me. I can lie in the bed at night if I have insomnia—I don't often, but sometimes I do—and I can just mentally paint. Sometimes I mentally paint something that I get up the next day and actually do paint. I certainly enjoy working at it.

BW: What is your philosophy of life? Do you have any wisdom you want to share with future generations of W students?
ES: Oh, that's kind of a deep one, isn't it? This is the very first time anybody has ever asked me my philosophy of life. My goodness. I could handle this on a lighter scale. My tendency is to invent little slogans, as I told you. "Not beautiful, but better," is such a slogan. When I go out in my backyard and I get dirty and a mess—my hair's all falling down and I've worked hard and I'm sweaty and dirty—I come in and I get in the shower and wash my hair. When I'm rolling it up, I think, "I'm not trying to get beautiful, I'm just trying to look better." So I kind of invented a little slogan: "Not beautiful, but better." I always come out looking better after I've washed my hair, put some rollers in it, and combed it nicely. So I guess that slogan in a broader way could apply to a lot of things that I think and do.

I also have to say that to a large extent a good sense of humor is a part of my so-called philosophy of life because, oh my, I can remember very many times when humor pulled me through some tedious and difficult situations. One summer I went to the Art Institute of Chicago to take a landscape painting class. I had a teacher who I thought was a very difficult person, and he gave me a very hard time at first. In fact, he ruined the very first painting that I was working on by smearing phthalo green all over that painting and telling me, in a sense, "Do it again." I didn't appreciate his messing up a painting that I actually liked. He could have said, "Get a new canvas, and do another one." I really got angry. I was so angry I thought, "I'm going to drop this class and go home." But then that night I thought, "Hmm, I really can't afford to drop this class and go home." I had paid a lot of tuition in advance, and I wouldn't get it all back. Anyway, I wanted to stay there, and I thought, "Surely I can get over this somehow and go on with this class." So the next day I went back to class, and I thought, "Maybe he'll just ignore me today." All of my classmates had sympathized with me when he ruined my painting. He was telling everybody that they shouldn't get satisfied with what they were doing, because he said, "I want you to do something different." So he came up to me first in class, and he said something uncomplimentary about the painting I was working on. I just suddenly started laughing. I don't know what told me to laugh, but then all the other people in class started laughing. When I quit laughing, he said, "Is something funny?" I said, "I think you're funny." And he said, "You think I'm funny?" I said, "Why would I be laughing if I didn't think you were funny? I like it that you're funny." Everybody was still laughing. He couldn't figure that one out, so he walked away. I thought, "I can't figure that out either, but maybe it will work." Gradually he began to come over and say some complimentary things about some of the paintings I was working on. And he found out that I could draw well in perspective. Since he had some people in class that couldn't, one time he asked me if I would mind helping another person with the perspective in her painting. I felt complimented. I went over and I took my sketchbook and I explained some things to her. After that, he unofficially appointed me as an assistant to help people with their perspective drawing. Gradually, he and I liked each other very much. And I learned so much from him about color. The name of one of the paintings that I did in Chicago is *The Pink House*. We were drawing in the slums of Chicago, and I did what he said. I was following the principle of color that the Impressionists used. He would not, in any circumstances, let us have black on our palettes because he said the Impressionists taught us that there is no such thing as black. Black is an absence of color. But you can mix dark colors from primary colors. He would let us have only the primary colors on our palette, and that made us learn how to mix colors. So when I started teaching, I would tell my students, "I do not want to see black on your palette. You can make black if you want to by mixing red, yellow, and blue in such proportions that it will look the same as black. If you try mixing some yellow with some black paint, you get green. So that black paint is not really an absence of color; it has a color of its own." I learned so much from that man. After I continued to teach, I wrote him several times and told him how much I appreciated his teaching me about color. But humor got me out of trouble with him and set us on the right course.

Another situation that was a lot more serious was that about six years ago I got cancer. I had a very deadly kind of cancer and the statistics for my survival were not good. I didn't know how I was going to cope with the illness. At first I came home, and I was so upset that I just started throwing away all my clothes. Then I thought, "This is really not the way I ought to respond to this." Suddenly I thought, "Maybe I can make some cartoons, and maybe I can start laughing about this." Lo and behold, I did. If you know that funny cartoon named *Close to Home*, a lot of their episodes are outlandish things that happen to patients. So I decided to start a series of cartoons that I was going to draw to chronicle my experience with taking chemo and radiation. I nicknamed the chemo room the Drug Den. I told them out at the hospital, "I'm nicknaming this room the Drug Den and I'm telling everybody I'm into drugs." They laughed and said, "This is a drug, but there's not much funny about it." I said, "It's going to be funny in my cartoon." Then I thought of a cartoon with two of my garden club members walking down Main Street, Columbus, and one of them says to the other, "Did you know that Eugenia is deep into drugs?" And the other one says, "Surely not." And the first one says, "But I overheard her telling somebody that she was heading toward the Drug Den." Then I nicknamed the radiation room the Voodoo Room because they drew all kinds of things on my chest so that the technician in there would know where to aim that huge machine that went over me and then back. I had radiation at the same time I had chemo. None of it was fun, but I thought, "If I just think up these things, it will help me." And it did. Somebody one time saw these markings that came up out of my blouse collar, and she said, "What is that on your neck?" I said, "It's a voodoo drawing." So I had a cartoon about the Voodoo Room and the Drug Den and so on. I had one cartoon that I drew among the first, and it was in three sections. It was in response to this doctor who had taken so long to tell me the result of a test that told me whether I had cancer. I really had the feeling that I did have cancer, but I kept getting put off by him to see the results of my test. It took so long that I decided to put him into a cartoon. My friend and I were sitting in this man's waiting room, and I was about to have an interview with him where he would finally tell me the results of the test. So I was telling my friend, "In this cartoon, the patient is lying peacefully and beautifully in her coffin with arms crossed and looking so sweet and her hair fixed nicely. In the second frame this doctor walks by, and he has a bunch of papers in his hand and he stops and he says, 'We finally got the results of all those tests, so now I can tell you why you died.' And in the last frame, the patient is still lying there, only under her neatly crossed arms are all the papers so she can read why she died." Everybody in the room laughed. I didn't know they could hear me. I was trying to whisper, but I guess they heard me. And my friend said, "But that's not funny!" I said, "They think it's funny, and I think it's funny." So when I went into see this doctor, he was so solemn, and I was struggling not to laugh because I was still thinking about that cartoon. I started to tell him, "When I die, please bring me the results of my tests." Anyway, he went on to tell me, "Yes, you do have cancer." But I kept thinking about the cartoon, and it made it easier to take. I still came home and threw away a lot of my clothes. But I also kept thinking all along the way of these jokes I could make. A good sense of humor can pull you through a lot of things.

Mary Glynn Williams Lancaster
Class of 1947

JULY 12, 2006

INTERVIEWED BY AMBER KING

TRANSCRIBED BY RACHEL FORESTER

MARY GLYNN WILLIAMS WAS BORN IN BOLTON, MISSISSIPPI, on July 1, 1925, to James Harold Williams and Mary Verdie Noel Williams. She spent a year at Hinds Junior College (now Hinds Community College) before coming to MSCW, where she was a member of the Bach Society, the Glee Club, Sigma Alpha Iota music honorary society, and the Wesley Foundation. She served as a librarian during her senior year. She received a bachelor of arts degree in piano and subsequently taught music in the public school system for thirty-five years. When she graduated in 1947, she was asked to direct the Methodist choir in her hometown, and she remained as the group's director until 1996. In 1950, she married C. D. Lancaster Jr., a school administrator and cattle farmer. She still lives in Bolton and is active in the Jackson Metro Chapter of the MUW Alumnae Association, her garden club, and the United Methodist Women.

ML: I was an only child. My mother was determined that I was going to college, and she's the one that picked the W for me. I knew nothing about the W at that time except that it was a girls' school, and that was all right with me. But the thing that bothered me was that I had never shared a room; I had never had to share a lot of things with anyone. I knew I was going to have a roommate, and I thought, "I don't know if I'm going to like this business of a roommate," so my mother set me down and talked to me very strongly about sharing and being nice and not letting little things bother me. She was a big help. So when I got to the W and I met my roommate, Mary Ellen Rea,[1] from McComb, she and I got along just fine. Of course once in a while, things would get a little rough, and we'd have to sort it out, but as a whole, we really were good for each other and we stayed together the three years that I was up there. We're still big friends, and our husbands are very good friends, too, so we've had a lot of good times since then, traveling together.

AK: What was your first impression of the school?

ML: When I got to the W, I thought it was the biggest place in the world. I had always gone to one-room type schools, except I did go to Hinds Junior College, and that had a few buildings. But I liked the W. I immediately liked the atmosphere, since the students were friendly. Of course we had uniforms, and it was during the war and you couldn't get navy blue cloth. All the navy blue went to the navy. My mama spent the whole summer before I went to college dyeing my clothes navy blue and putting those little blue stripes on the white collars and all of that. But I loved the uniform. It was so much fun, just to get up in the morning and not have to worry about what you were going to wear. You just grabbed a blue dress or a blue skirt and a blue blouse and that was it. I liked a lot of things about the W. It was a good feeling all the way around for me.

1. Mary Ellen Rea Taylor, Class of 1947.

I started out majoring in music, working on a bachelor's of music. I loved my piano teacher;[2] he was just wonderful. He was a single man, and he played with another single man as a piano duo. They had come from Michigan, and they played beautifully together. He talked me into changing my major. He said a bachelor's of music didn't mean much and that I needed to get a bachelor's of arts with a major in piano. I'm so glad he changed my mind because I found out that that was really what I needed to do.

I remember getting on the bus, going to school by myself, because we didn't have the gas to get in the car and drive to Columbus. When I got there, I had to get a taxi. And that was a new experience for me; I had never ridden in a taxi in my life. I got in my taxi and told the driver what dormitory I wanted to go to, and he got me to the dormitory. It was a lot of first experiences for me, but I liked it all. And luckily there were three girls on my floor that were music majors, all the same class I was, because we were separated—I suppose they still do this at the W—by classes. One dorm was for sophomores; another dorm was the junior dorm. Those three girls and I became very good friends, music-wise. When you majored in music, you lived in Music Hall. We stayed in Music Hall all day long, just about, and practiced. I looked forward to being with the girls because I never had had many girl friends, and being in Bolton, I was limited as to friends. But I couldn't get my daughter to go to the W to save my life. I heard, "No, I'm not going to the W!" I think I had talked about the W so much, I had turned her against it. But every now and then she wants to go to see Columbus, and then we go back to the W and I show her the campus.

AK: Where did she go?

ML: She went to the University of Southern Mississippi—the opposite direction. She said she didn't want to go up that way, since there weren't any boys. And there would not have been. That was before they made

2. Richard S. Johnson, assistant professor of music, taught piano at MSCW from 1943 until 1945, when he took a position at Stephens College. He remained there until his retirement more than two decades later.

that change. Southern was her father's school, so she went there. But you ought to hear my family when they speak of the W. They never speak of it in a normal voice. They whisper, "The W." My husband will tell her, "Your mother is going to the W next week for something," and they tease me about it because they know I'll say, "You're not changing my mind. I still think it's a great school." My husband always called it the "quality college." He would say, "Your mother knows how to do this and that and the other because she went to the quality college." So they love to tease me about it.

I liked the fact that during my sophomore year, our room was in the dormitory that had the dining hall, Shattuck. All we had to do was wait for that second bell and run down the steps and get there before the doors closed to the dining hall. We learned how to serve English-style in the dining hall. Everybody had to take turns: there were eight people around the table, and you had to take your turn in serving plates and finding out what the people wanted to drink. Miss Lawler,[3] who was the head of all of that, came around to see that you did it right, and if you didn't do it right, you were called in to talk and then you were told how to do it. If we got sloppy with our table manners, we had a chapel meeting and Miss Lawler got up and preached to us about our table manners, that they did not want the W girls going out eating like that. We were really jacked up, and we toed the line, I can tell you. Then in the dormitory we had those dorm mothers, I reckon we probably called them. Ours was a very strict dorm mother, and she called us "termites." She said that we all were undermining the good name that the W had. Now, I don't know what we did that was so terrible that we had to be called termites. I don't think we did anything real bad, but anyway, that was her name for us. But we lived through it and got through that first year, and then, when we went back the second year, it was even better, because I was used to everything. I knew people, knew some of the faculty members. This would have been my junior year. But my piano

3. Nell Lawler (1899–1982), Class of 1920, served as student counselor at MSCW from 1942 until 1948. For the rest of her career, she was dean of women at Delta State University.

teacher didn't come back. He went to Columbia, and that really hurt because I had to change piano teachers. But I learned to like the one I got and also learned to like other faculty members.

The last year that I was there, the boys started coming back from World War II, and that was interesting, too. But, boy, we were chaperoned so closely. We had to be back on campus at 10:00, and in sophomore year we couldn't even go to town by ourselves; we couldn't go in a group; we had to have a senior chaperone. And we had to have that hat on, couldn't leave campus without that hat. We bought these little small beanies. They were just about as big as a pancake, and we'd sit them right up here on the back of our heads since we didn't like to wear those things and wanted the smallest one we could find. But when we were there, they did away with the uniform after the first year. And there we all were, stuck with navy blue. When they did away with the uniform, a lot of us didn't have money to go buy a whole new outfit, a new wardrobe. So then we dyed our clothes again, trying to get a different color and trying to put some color with that navy blue to keep it from looking too navy. We went out of the uniform that year, and I really hated that. I voted for the uniform all the way through, since I liked the uniform, but we were outvoted. After that, they got a little bit more lenient about the dress code for going to town. I think senior year we didn't have to wear hats! But we'd have Thanksgiving dinners and Christmas dinners and Easter dinners and boy, we really dressed up; we almost had to wear gloves to those dinners to eat! They were trying to teach us to be ladylike. They wanted their W girls to stand out. I'm glad I had that training because it's come in handy since then to know, for example, that we do need to dress up sometimes. And so I never minded doing those things.

When the senior year came, music majors had to have a senior recital. Then our families would come up and attend the recitals. It was a big thing for each student when she presented her senior recital. Sometimes they put two of us together. One of my best friends and I did our senior recital together. She sang—she was a voice major—and I played. In my junior year, I accompanied a violinist, and that was also fun because I got to go to Greenwood, since we always tried to practice the senior recital on an audience before we did it at the W, where we got our grade. So we went to Greenwood, where she lived, to do the recital. We had something funny happen at Greenwood. They had a nice auditorium where we gave our recital, and there were three of us helping, including one of her good friends, who was also a piano major. This friend's mother had gone up and decorated the stage and had it real pretty with flowers and other things. Mary Kate,[4] who was my friend, was going to play the first number. She went out and played a Chopin number and she was slipping all over that piano. She was missing notes; we just could not imagine what was wrong with Mary Kate. It was just terrible. Finally, she stopped. Then she walked off the stage and she said, "That piano is nothing but soapsuds. My hands are perspiring, and it's just foam all over the keyboard." The violinist's mother had gone out there and wiped the keys off with what she thought was plain water, but the stuff had soap in it. When the pianist's hands perspired, it just made the biggest mess on those keys. We had to stop the recital and go out and clean the keys off for the rest of us to play. When we finally got the piano back in playing condition, we went on with the recital.

By my senior year I realized that that was going to be my last year, but I was ready then to finish up college. That year we did have some boys to date. I remember one night we went downtown to a restaurant in Columbus. There wasn't a lot to do because we couldn't go to those bars and saloons and places like that—no way. You would get sent home in a minute if you did that. So we were just strolling around Columbus and talking, and all at once we heard the 10:00 whistle. We were supposed to be on campus at 10:00. So we started running. There were three couples, and all the girls were W girls. We ran from downtown to the college just as hard as we could run, and we just did get in the gate before they locked the gate. Then we had the Old Maid's Gate; we had to go in backward or we would be old maids. So we had to take time and turn around and go through Old Maid's Gate backward. When we got inside the campus, this night watchman saw us and he took out after us,

4. Mary Katherine Pickens Foose (1926–81), Class of 1946.

so we started running again. I ran to Music Hall. I can remember running through Music Hall just as hard as I could. I expect I knew Music Hall better than he did. I ran up in a practice room and hid until he left, because he had to go and hunt those other girls, too. I finally saw him walking across campus, so I got out of that place and got to my dorm. Luckily they had not locked the door. I thought, "Boy, I'll watch my watch better after this." I didn't want another experience like that.

Later that year, we had a great graduation and the Magnolia Chain.[5] When you go back for your fiftieth anniversary, you do the Magnolia Chain again. When we did that it brought back memories to all of us about when we did it the first time. When we left the W, we joined the alumnae association and hoped to go back every five years. My roommate and I went back every five years together; we never missed. One time I was pregnant with one of my children, and she had to go back by herself, but the rest of the time we went together. And we always stopped in Philadelphia and picked up another good friend of ours, so the three of us always roomed together up there during reunion time. I still always look forward to going back. Remember, your graduating class selects your president in your freshman year, so I had nothing to do with electing Barbara Dean[6] as president. But I grew to love her very much and realized that she was a wonderful president even while we were in school. So many presidents of classes, after the four years and after you graduate, seem to forget about you, and the classes just fall apart, but not Barbara Dean. Our class stayed together.

Barbara would have these mini-reunions where we would get together, and that kept our class in touch with one another. Our class was very close because of course it was during the war when we were there.

5. In 1894, in imitation of some eastern schools, II & C graduating seniors carried a daisy chain from the steps of the old chapel to an outdoor ceremony. In 1913, seniors modified the tradition and carried a magnolia chain. The students still sing the traditional magnolia chain song and carry a magnolia chain at a special class day ceremony before commencement in May. At the end of the ceremony, the seniors rush to the piled chain to claim a bud or flower. Those who get either one will have good fortune, which has been variously defined over the years and for some generations involved being the first to marry.

6. Barbara Dean (1926–2006), Class of 1947.

We didn't have boys to date; they were in the service. We relied on each other for our entertainment on weekends. Having a spaghetti supper was a big thing. Just about everybody had a little hot plate in her room, and a coffeepot, so you could make pancakes and have coffee if you wanted it, but for our spaghetti supper we'd go down to a little room that they had there in the dorm and cook our spaghetti and have a group supper there. And then we could go to the movies, which was always fun. A lot of times on Sunday afternoons my roommate and I would just walk through Columbus, because the homes in Columbus were perfectly beautiful. Columbus is a lovely town. We would enjoy walking and learning about the history of the different houses. We have walked many a mile over Columbus. One of the first things I did after I graduated was to go back for the pilgrimage in Columbus. I went several times because I thought that the homes were just so pretty up there.

We didn't have cars back in those days that we could jump in and run home to spend all of our weekends at home. We stayed on campus. We went to church up there, and we had Wesley Foundation—or, I did. I was Methodist, so mine was Wesley. Other denominations had their clubs that they would go to. We had Vespers at night, so we always had something to do. Movies were also a big entertainment back in that day. We had Wednesday afternoons off, so we could go to the movies then. Of course, music majors had to do a lot of practicing, so we didn't have a lot of time off, but every now and then we'd get together on Wednesday afternoons for the movies. They had a theater uptown that you could pay a dime to go into on Saturday afternoons, and you could pay another dime and get you some popcorn and pay another dime, I think it was, and get a Coke. So for thirty cents you could go and sit in that theater all afternoon and watch one Western movie right after the other if you wanted to. Every once in a while we would do that, and that would be our Saturday afternoon entertainment. But like I said, music majors stayed in Music Hall, and that made us close together.

Oh, the dear old Goose. That was our café on the campus. That's where everybody gathered for a break. It was real close to Music Hall, so we'd run over to the Goose, and we could get a Coke for a nickel, oh, and doughnuts. They had wonderful doughnuts! We would buy a doughnut and sit down and talk and take a little break from practicing and classes. Then lo and behold, some president came along and tore the Goose down. That was heartbreaking. Eventually, they put up a gazebo in place of the Goose, but nothing could ever take the place of the Goose. I just wish they had never torn it down. The building they built in place of the Goose fell down. That was telling them right there that they shouldn't have torn the Goose down. The building just literally gave way and fell down. And so that's when they put the gazebo up.[7] Back before one of our reunions, the president that had torn down the Goose had passed away, and they did a memorial service for him. Our class went to the memorial service, but it was a little hard to mourn for him when he had torn the Goose down. But we behaved ourselves and did so.

I remember my mother came up for my graduation, and she spent several days with me because they had several things for the parents to go to. That was a happy time for her, because that's the first time that she had visited me on the campus. She had never seen the W, and she was so instrumental in my going, and I had told her so much about it. I remember the first time I came home, the first break I had, we sat up until 3:00 that morning, me telling her everything I could think of about the W because I wanted her to know as much about it as I did. When she actually got to see it, it was a great experience for her and for me both. Some of my other family came up for graduation and my senior recital, and it was just a really good year.

I really appreciate the things that the W taught me. They really want their students to be outstanding. They teach you that a great deal depends on how you act and on your studies. They really push those things. As I got out in the world, I could see where I needed those teachings and the other things that they were trying to show us. I've never, never regretted going to the W. Now, when the men came along, I was

7. Charles P. Hogarth was MSCW's president in the mid-1960s when the Student Activities Building, which housed the Golden Goose Tearoom, was torn down. A seven-story administration building, Simmons Hall, was built in its place in 1969. Simmons Hall was condemned during the 1980s after years of structural problems and replaced by a gazebo.

very much against the enrollment of men. In fact, I was against the W ever being a university. I wanted it to stay a women's college. I thought that made it unique, because there are not a lot of women's colleges now. The W never was meant to be a university, I don't think. If we could have just kept it as a small college and let it be just for women. Oh, it used to make me so mad to go up there and see those men walking around! About four years ago, I took three of my grandchildren up to the W to show them where I had gone to school, since they had heard me talk about it for so long. When they came to Music Hall, they were so funny. They all got down on their knees and bowed down and honored Music Hall because they had heard me talk about Music Hall so much. But when we came to the sign where it said, "For men and women," they got up there and hid where it says "men," and I took a picture of them. There they are with their arms above the thing about the men because they knew I didn't like those men going there. So I just wish it could have been kept a girls' college, for women, because I think that's really what the W's all about. I can certainly say that I enjoyed my three years at the W very much. I enjoy going back, and I don't think anybody makes a mistake going to the W.

AK: How did the end of the war affect your experience on campus?
ML: About the only change that we had with the end of the war was that we had some men on campus that we could date. Before that, we really didn't have any dates unless we had a steady, as they called them back in that day. When they came back, they would come up to see their girlfriends. But otherwise, you just didn't see any men. State didn't have any boys over there—well, they had a few, of course. But after the war, the boys started coming back. When I was at the W, I didn't go to the library and read the paper. I didn't have time to listen to the radio; I was at Music Hall practicing, so I didn't keep up with things on the radio. The only time we ever listened to the radio was when they were doing the victory speech or something like that; we would listen to that. We were very much isolated. We hardly knew what was going on. We'd see the newsreels in the movies, but they were quite short. I know the

first time I came home, I felt like I had come back—I hate to say it—to civilization. The W was civilized, but I felt like I had been away on this long trip out in the desert somewhere. I didn't know about anything. Mother and Daddy would be talking about something in the news, and I'd have no earthly idea what they were talking about. So all three years were kind of like that, too. I never did keep up with outside news very much at the W. The W was my life, and it was that way with my friends, too. We lived for the W and what went on up there.

Columbus was a nice town, a nice shopping town. They had nice restaurants, they had nicer clothing places, they had a big department store. Of course, it's grown so since we were in school. I just get completely lost up there now with all the stores and all, but I still think it's a nice place. I wouldn't mind living in Columbus.

AK: After you didn't have to wear uniforms, what did the girls wear?
ML: I had very few dresses. We had to wear dresses to church on Sundays. We'd have two or three dresses for when special things happened on campus that we were supposed to dress up for. We wore mostly just skirts and blouses. And we could mix and match those. For instance, if you had a navy blue skirt, then you could put a red blouse with it or something like that when the uniform went out. And it was easy to do that, to kind of disguise that you were in part uniform and part of the new clothes. Oh, saddle oxfords were in then, and we all wore saddle oxfords. And little black ballerina shoes. And moccasins. That was the footwear. Of course, when we dressed up, we had heels, but we didn't wear heels very much. When we went to church, we had to walk, oh goodness, I reckon it was about seven or eight blocks. We wore those high-heel shoes and oh, it was something. I remember I got a pair of black patent sling-back pumps. I didn't realize that I couldn't wear sling pumps, but I couldn't. When I started to church that day, those things fell off of me. They would slip off of my heel, and I would have to stop every few steps and pull those things up. Oh, it was miserable. But you didn't throw shoes away like you would today—you just toss them and go and get another pair of shoes. No. I put up with those shoes and put

up with those shoes. I was so glad when they wore out and I didn't have to worry about wearing them any more. I never got another pair of sling pumps. That was my one and only pair. And they were very, very popular when I was at the W. I can remember those shoes.

When I look at the dorm rooms now and think about our rooms, I remember that we didn't even have doors on our closets. We had curtains in Shattuck, the sophomore dorm. We just hung our things up there and pulled the curtain. We would go to town and beg for apple crates and orange crates. That was our furniture. We brought those things home on our heads because we didn't have any cars to put them in. We'd walk that eight or nine blocks to town, and we'd put those things on our shoulders and heads and drag those things back to the dorm. The merchants would save them for us. When it was about time for school to open, they'd save them because they knew a W girl was going to be down there digging for those things. We furnished our "kitchen," as we called it—it was just two or three little crates around and about. Then we had a crate to put our toothbrushes, mouthwash, and toilet articles on. Our trunks were also part of our furniture. I had a wardrobe trunk. I wish I had kept that. I was looking at an antique show the other day and they had a trunk just like the one I took to the W and goodness, they were getting a lot of money for that trunk. I threw my trunk away! It was a wardrobe trunk that folded out. I got to use the drawers and it was a big help to me. My roommate had a chest-type trunk that just opened up, and she used hers for a table. She had her books and things on it. So we didn't have much furniture. We had two cots, a desk at the end of the cots, where she had a drawer on her side and I had a drawer on my side, and we had a dresser, and that was the end of the furniture for the rooms. She had a set of spreads and things for her bed, and we would swap out, so the beds would look alike. Today I look at all of the computers and the refrigerators and the fancy hot plates and the televisions and all of that, and I think about what we went to school with. I went up there with a trunk and a suitcase and a box of music, and that was all I took because we couldn't take any more than a taxi could hold.

AK: What other rules did you have to obey?

ML: There were strict smoking rules. You had to get permission from your parents, and then you went down to the smoking room to smoke if you got permission. My roommate and I were not smokers. But when we'd go home, we'd slip back with a package of cigarettes just for the heck of it. One day we were up there just smoking away in our room. If you put a towel over the door, nobody was supposed to come in your room. That was a sign to keep out! So we threw that towel over the door, and we got our cigarettes out. My piano teacher my junior year was also my dorm mother. We heard a knock, and I couldn't imagine who was breaking that towel law because that was just a no-no. She called to me: it was my piano teacher, saying that she had to see me. And our room was full of smoke. You should have seen us fanning. You've seen it in movies how they fan? We raised the window and we tried to get it out; we said we'd be there in just a minute. I know she smelled that smoke, but thank goodness she didn't turn us in. So we didn't get caught, because we didn't smoke enough to get caught anyway. But one or two of the girls got caught, and one girl got sent home, I remember. I don't think it was her first time; I think it was her second or third time. I'm sure if we'd ever gotten caught once, we'd have thrown those cigarettes away, because we really weren't enjoying them. We were just doing it to see if we could get by with it.

AK: Did you get packages from home in the mail?

ML: I remember my daddy was a hunter, and he would quail hunt. He knew I loved quail, so Mother would ship us quail suppers. I don't know how they did it, but this big box would come and when I'd see it I'd know it was my quail supper. We didn't invite anybody in for the quail supper except for me and my roommate. We ate it all ourselves, and we never let on that we had quails. We just would eat away. We never let our other friends know that we had them because they would have wanted to come and eat with us, and we didn't want to hurt their feelings. Mail time was a big time of course then, because that's the only way we had to hear from home. Even though we had telephones, we didn't get on that telephone just to talk. I reckon I talked to Mother maybe once a month. She'd call me. We depended on the mail for our correspondence.

AK: How did you get home between semesters?

ML: Oh, the morning Christmas vacation started we'd get up real, real early. They'd have buses lined up to take us to our different destinations. For example, mine would go to Jackson. I think those buses left at 5:30 or something like that, so we had to get up at 4:00 and go eat breakfast. Of course we'd have our stuff packed up and we'd drag all that stuff—didn't have anybody, any porters or anything to help us—we dragged those suitcases out to where the buses were going to stop. Some of the girls would take the buses to the train station and get on the train because the trains were going to take them where they were going. That was a big, big day, catching those early buses and coming home for Christmas. We always looked forward to that. This would be about a week before Christmas. We would have about two and a half weeks' holiday. I remember one Christmas, Columbus flooded from the Tombigbee River, and we couldn't go back the day we were supposed to go. It came over the radio that the MSCW girls were not to come back to school until they were notified. So we got extra holidays that year. Oh, that was fun. I never thought about the damage or the money that was wasted on all of that flooding—it was just I had extra days at home, and that was great for me. We were about four or five days late getting back that year. We did the same thing at Easter; they had the buses to come and pick us up at Easter, too. Sometimes, since my roommate's father worked for the railroad, she had passes for the train. The train would come through Jackson. We'd come home the same weekend. She'd go to McComb—that's where she lived—and of course I'd come here to Bolton, because that's where I was born and reared. I've lived all my life here in Bolton. To come back, I'd catch the train that she was going on, and we'd ride to Winona and then we would catch the bus to Columbus. We'd get to Columbus about 4:00 the next morning. Then we'd go to the dorm and dress and get to class at the regular time. We would have ridden all night getting back to Columbus. I know we must have been in great shape for class—hadn't looked at a book or anything else or made any preparations for the lesson. We only did that a few times.

AK: Do you remember any of your other teachers?

ML: I had some good teachers at the W, and I had some sorry teachers, I'll have to say. I reckon sociology was my worst class. I had sociology at 2:00 after lunch, and that teacher droned away so slow. She would talk and she would talk, and I would just about go to sleep every time. And I never knew what sociology was all about. How I ever passed that class, I don't know. We had to get up and make reports. Getting up in front of a class and making a report was never hard for me, and I think that the only reason I ever passed that class was because I could make a report now and then and get a good grade. But I had a good French teacher and I had a good history teacher. I loved history and enjoyed my history classes. However, we had one elderly woman who taught history. She wasn't really a faculty member, but her family had given a lot of money to the college, and they just had hired her as a teacher.[8] She had no organization to her class; she taught Mississippi history. One day we might go in and we might study the Indians. And the next day we might go in and study the Civil War. The next day we'd go in, and we might study the early settlers of Mississippi. We never knew what we were going to study. She'd write all of this stuff on the blackboard which surrounded the room. We were supposed to copy that stuff. We would copy it, but we never discussed anything much in class. Then when the test came, that's what our test was on, what she had written all on the blackboard. That's the way we got by, because we could just take those notes and learn them. She was way too old to be teaching. She wore a hat to school, a great big hat to class. I thought that was the funniest thing, that she'd wear a hat to class. That was the only class she taught, the one class. I had so looked forward to having the Mississippi history class because, as I said, I loved history. But I didn't look forward to that class. And I

8. Mary Lou Peyton (1881–1959), Class of 1916, taught part time at MSCW from 1938 to 1945. Her mother, Annie Coleman Peyton, for whom Peyton Hall is named, was one of II & C's founders and taught history there from 1891 until her death in 1898.

minored in social studies. As I told you, I majored in piano and almost had a major in public school music. The only thing I didn't get to do was to do my teaching at the Demonstration School.[9] That was the practice teaching that you did for a degree in public school music. But then after I got out of school, I taught public school music!

I remember we had an arts festival on campus. We had a whole week of things pertaining to the arts. We'd have Glee Club programs, orchestra programs, dance programs, speech programs, and we had plays also. The whole week was dedicated to the arts. I always looked forward to that week. They also had the lyceum programs where they would bring the artists in to perform at night, and we had access to that. The only live performances I had been to were some things in Jackson that Mother and Daddy had taken me to, so all that was fun for me. I looked forward to those things.

AK: What advice would you give to current students?

ML: For one thing, I would say stay in school; make good use of your time. So many students go to school and it's a social thing. They get out of school, and they haven't learned anything. Go to school and really learn something that will help you when you get out of school. I don't know how these students around here learn anything because they're at home all the time. I can't get used to that. They go Monday morning, and then Thursday afternoon, here they are back again. I thought, "When do they ever study? When do they ever go to the library?" That's where we went on the weekends. We went to the library and caught up on all of our papers and things like that. I don't know how they do it. I don't think I could have done it that way. And make friends while you're at school. Make some good friends that you can carry through life. I have friends right now that were my friends at the W. And stay on campus sometimes, where you can learn about it! Don't come home every weekend! I suppose if I had lived in a time when I had a car at my disposal and

9. The Demonstration School, a laboratory school for MSCW student teachers, opened in 1929. It operated as a practice school and as a public elementary school until 2003.

I could have gotten off campus, I would have been off campus. But we look back, and we talk about this a lot when we get together, and we realize that it's the reason we're so close—because we couldn't come home. We did things together, and we stayed together, and now our friendships are so wonderful. I've just lost one of my best friends, Barbara Dean, our president. It was so strange. Barbara Dean had cancer, and we knew that she wasn't doing well, but she lived in Mobile. The last time I saw her, which was last November, I said, "The next time we go to Gulf Shores, would you like to come over and spend the day with us and meet my family?" I said, "You and my husband would have a ball together." She said, "I would love it." And I said, "All right, I'm going to call you." I was thinking about it the other day. I thought, "I really need to call Barbara Dean and tell her that we're going next week." But of course she won't be joining us this year. I wish she could have come one time while we were there. I don't know why I hadn't thought about it before, since she lived so nearby. I reckon I thought maybe it was kind of old hat for her, being so close to Gulf Shores, that maybe she didn't want to come, but no, she was all ready for it. I'm sorry we didn't get to have that experience together. That would have been so nice to have done that. But we can't have everything, can we?

For our fiftieth reunion, I think we had more alumnae back on campus than they had had from any class in a long time. Our class really turned out. We had people coming from all over the United States. People commented on how many of the class were there. After the fiftieth year, they kind of left us on our own and we did what we wanted to, but Barbara kept us together, and we decided to go back every five years. We were going next year for our sixtieth anniversary, and she had already begun to plan for us to go back and do some things. We're hoping one of our classmates that lives in Columbus will pick up the pieces and go on with it, especially through the sixtieth. Then I think we'll have to drop it because so many of our class are not able to go back or they have to get people to go with them, and it's getting to be a hardship. But if we could just make it one more time to the sixtieth, that would be wonderful. We could close it out then.

Frances Mildred Bethea Dent
Class of 1950

JUNE 22, 2006

INTERVIEWED BY AMBER KING

TRANSCRIBED BY LEIGH POURCIAU

FRANCES MILDRED BETHEA CAME TO MSCW from Indianola, Mississippi. She was born on August 8, 1927, in Starkville, Mississippi, to Carl B. Bethea and Julia May Bevill Bethea. A library science major, she sang in the Glee Club for four years. She was also a member of the Spanish Club, the Library Science Club, and the Wesley Foundation Smaller and Larger Councils. After graduation, she began work as a public librarian in Raymond, Mississippi, and she later worked for a five-county regional library. In 1951, she married Robert Miller Dent Jr., who became a brigadier general in the Mississippi Army National Guard. Frances Dent subsequently worked part-time in the Mississippi College library before deciding to stay home to raise her two boys. Active in the Memorial United Methodist Church, in the Bolton-Edwards Garden Club, and in the MUW Alumnae Association, she lives in Bolton, Mississippi.

FD: When I went to the W, I had agreed with a friend that I would buy her navy blue uniforms. Bless her heart, that year they passed the rule that you didn't have to wear the navy. I just let her down—I didn't buy her clothes. But I was saying, "Yay!" the whole time. She was a friend in Indianola. That was pretty funny. She probably wore them to teach quite a while, I imagine.

AK: How did you decide to come to the W?

FD: My daddy said I was going there. I wanted to go to State, but my daddy said no. So that's the way I wound up getting as close as I could, I guess. I just have positive memories. Of course, everybody has a roommate they can't stand, and that sort of thing—just girl stuff—and it blows over. Freshman year, I lived in Callaway, and our social adviser was a senator's sister.[1] She would say, "My brother the congressman says so." This was applied to about every statement that we heard her say. But I reckon I would have been proud of him, too. He was a nice man.

I roomed with a girl from South Mississippi for one semester, and then she wanted to room with somebody else, and so I roomed with somebody else. My new roommate was from the Delta, and I was too. I grew up in Indianola. So Beth and I roomed together a year and a half, and then she got married. Then I roomed with another girl from Brookhaven for my junior year, and then I roomed by myself my senior year. My junior roommate was a business education major, and senior year, she had to have a lot of room for all her technical stuff, so I roomed by myself that year. But I had a lot of good friends. I still do. I'm always glad to see them. When you go back, you find out as you get older and older you'll say, "You haven't changed a bit," and you know good and well they have. But it's really good that you remember all their characteristics, and it's just a lot of fun to go back. I went back for my twentieth reunion. I could have gone more often just to have done it, but I went for my twentieth anniversary. I didn't go to my twenty-fifth one; my

1. Janie Eliza Stennis (1885–1979), an alumna and sister of Mississippi's U.S. senator, John Stennis, served as a social adviser at MSCW from 1943 until 1957.

father had died, and I just couldn't go. Then I went a couple of times later, and then for my fiftieth and my fifty-fifth. I enjoyed them all.

AK: How did you feel about the W when you first got there?
FD: I guess I wasn't as awestruck as I should have been. What really threw me was that I knew about the campus at Mississippi State, and it was so spread out, particularly in those days. They had a lot fewer buildings than are now at State, so they were kind of spread out, and I was used to a great big campus. When I went to the W, here we were fenced in, in that little bitty one-block thing, and I thought, "Good grief! Wouldn't you smother each other?" It was strange that way. But I learned to like it since it wasn't so far to go from one place to the other. And I thought it was pretty. I still think it's pretty.

AK: How did you feel about your classes?
FD: I enjoyed most of them. We had some pretty funny ones. We had a lady that taught sociology, and she was rather dull. So in class our main thing was to tally every time she said, "Uh." We had some pretty good tallies on that. But most of my teachers were very good. I was a library science major. Of course, my freshman year we took just the general things. I was an English minor, so I took several English classes—literature, mostly—and some grammar. One of our librarian instructors[2] lived right across from the campus, and she was a cute thing. I just loved her to death. I don't think she taught us too much, but she was pretty funny. She collected shoes, so every day she would have on a different pair of shoes. Then we had another, an older lady,[3] who was an instructor, and she was pretty straight standing, and she expected us to stand like that. But I liked her. She was good. Most of my instructors were very good.

2. Beulah Culbertson (1886–1990), Class of 1910, taught library science at II & C/MSCW from 1912 until 1958.
3. Probably Alice James Gatchell (1903–91), who taught library science at MSCW from 1939 until 1972.

AK: Did you have a job on campus?
FD: No. I substituted some, though, at the dining hall. In those days, we had a dining room which was seated, and there were eight girls to a table. They had girls that were monitors that served the meal, and they brought out our plates and the trays. I substituted for some girls for that, but that was about all I did. I worked in the summertime at home, but my daddy said, "You need to concentrate on your books," so that was what I did.

AK: What sort of things did you do on the weekends?
FD: They got pretty dull every now and then. But we went to some of the Columbus high school ball games. That was a favorite thing to do in the fall, particularly in the first years there. We didn't date too much because the rules were two dates a week, I think, when we were freshmen. And we always had to go with three people—three girls and three boys. So we couldn't get into too much of a big mess even if we thought we wanted to. Then each year, the number of dates went up a little bit. And finally we could ride in a car by ourselves, and that was fun! Except I didn't really date all that much.

AK: Did you go to many dances on campus?
FD: They didn't have many. Each class had a dance during the year, and then I think they had a final dance for everybody. But they were very formal, and we had our little book with our dances all lined up. So we were trained at the same time that we were entertained. The social advisers would have a little get-together and tell us—of course, most mamas had already told their girls this—how to act and how to greet someone. It's really very good knowledge that everyone should have. We thought it was kind of silly at the time, but it's come in handy quite a few times. We would sit in the gym, and they would give us the instructions on what to do.

AK: Did you take physical education classes?

FD: I had Miss Pohl,[4] and she, bless her heart, tried to teach me ballet, and that was pretty funny. I didn't do ballet very gracefully, so she gave up on me, but she also taught a gymnastics class, and she would give me a workout in there. I also took tennis, swimming, and a couple of terms of archery, which impresses my twelve-year-old grandson, Woods Dent, since he's gotten interested in archery lately. We had to have—I've forgotten now how many—semesters of gym of some sort. I didn't learn too much tennis. I learned to swim better. That was probably the best thing I did, and it was fun. Then we had, while I was there—they timed it so it was held every three years—the Zouave drills. We worked all year long on those things. When you went to gym, you were learning those drills. And it was really an impressive thing. I had a friend who hated every minute of it. I thought it was pretty fun myself. We had all these marches that we had to do, and these ROTC things that they do now for halftime at football games. We did that sort of thing, but it was a thousand or two thousand, however many it was, girls all wearing navy shorts and white blouses, so it was pretty impressive. A friend and I had planned to go back, and she was not able to go, so I never did go and see it as a spectator. I would like to have seen it to see what it really looked like.

AK: Do you have any specific memories of Miss Pohl?
FD: We went to chapel twice a week, and Miss Pohl always had some announcements to make. Bless her heart, evidently she was as blind as a bat when she tried to read anything. So she had these old glasses, and she would stand up and read part of her announcement when she had her glasses on. Then she'd jerk them off when she wanted to look around and say something. Then she'd throw them back on her head and read a little bit more. So it always took her quite a while to get her memorandum straightened out. But she was funny. She was really a riot, actually, and she was old! My daddy graduated from Mississippi State in 1910, and Miss Pohl came to the W while he was still a student. So by 1950—but boy, she

4. Emma Ody Pohl (1880–1966) joined II & C in 1907, when she was hired to develop the department of physical education. She taught that subject until her retirement in 1955.

could still kick as high as anybody else. I know she did it all the time, and that's how she was able to do it. She was very, very active, and she knew everything that went on on that campus. You couldn't fool her. And every year she did a ballet program, which was really lovely. When we had a special program like that, they did it at night, and we were expected to go. We dressed up like we were going to church, and we went through all the good manners and that sort of thing, which was another good education program. We had some very good programs. We had a lot of good acts that came in from other places, so we had quite a bit of cultural advantage which I had not had because I was from a small town.

One time we had some Russian men dancers, and they were one of the most outstanding, because I had never seen that before. You know how they used to do the kicks when they knelt, when they were squatting down and they would kick. How they did it, I never figured out. But it was interesting. And we had several of the big bands go through. At that time, they would tour colleges, and they would play for a dance or for just a band program. So we got to see some that were good. When we had ballet programs, students did the whole program, and it was very good. I always enjoyed that. And I sang in the choir. We had a large choir, and then we had a smaller choir which was the Glee Club, they called it. That group actually had the better voices chosen, which I didn't have, so I sang in the big one. Anyway, we had a program every year and I really liked the music instructor[5] that was the director of the choir. He was very good, and he taught us a lot of music. So I enjoyed that. Then we had a band, a girls' band. My roommate was the drummer in that,[6] so she made a good bit of noise. But they were pretty good. They put on a program every now and then, so we enjoyed that.

AK: Were you in any other clubs or organizations?

FD: We had clubs for our major. I was in Library Science Club, and I'm thinking the English Club, as well as I remember. I was not in the social

5. Harold Richey (1898–1995) taught music at MSCW on and off between 1934 and 1957.
6. Betty Jane Mantz Bourne, Class of 1950, was the drummer and business manager for the Blue Serenaders swing band.

clubs, but I was pretty active in the Methodist Wesley Foundation. They had had a house for each denomination, and I did a good bit of work in that. We had what they call Noonday every day. Right after lunch, we could go down and do a little meditation, and they always had someone to lead it. So it was good, it was meaningful—it got you settled for the rest of the day.

AK: Did you attend church in Columbus?
FD: Yes, they had a program where you could be an associate member of a church, and I joined the First Methodist Church, on the corner of Main and Sixth Street South. We walked to church. They didn't provide buses at that time. I think later on they probably did. But I enjoyed that, and I sang in the choir at the church. We had a special Sunday school class for students of the W, so that was nice.

AK: What did you think of Columbus?
FD: It was a pretty neat town. They kind of left us to ourselves. Of course they were glad to see us in the stores, but aside from that, I guess they were so used to the students, it didn't rattle them either way. Of course we didn't get to go to town all that often anyway, so it didn't upset them too much.

AK: What was your favorite place on campus?
FD: Probably Callaway when I was a freshman. At that time we had South Callaway (Cochran). The doors were cut through so we could go from one to the other.

AK: What did you think about the W admitting men?
FD: At the time, I wondered, "What in the world have they come up with now?" And it was rather a put-down that the first one didn't even pass,[7] which was pretty funny to all of us who were not real thrilled about it. I thought that it was nice to have an all-girls' school, but if men

....

7. Joe Hogan, a nursing major who registered as the first degree-seeking male student, left MUW without graduating.

want to be there, it's okay with me. I went to an alumni luncheon not long ago and met a young man who had been there, and he was really delightful. So he made a better impression on me than some of them had. But I've gotten used to it now.

AK: What advice would you give to the students who are there now?
FD: Enjoy your time. Don't sit in your room and feel sorry for yourself. The more you get out with other people, the happier you'll be. Be sure to take as many good classes of as much of a variety as you can, because you'll be surprised how much you'll use that knowledge later on or maybe just to enrich your own life, but you'll get something out of every one of them.

AK: What was your favorite subject?
FD: It would have to be English literature. I like to read. Of course, I enjoyed my library science classes, but my favorite, I think, was actually the literature.

AK: What did you think about the eating and seating arrangements in the dining hall?
FD: I thought it was wonderful. I had no objection to it at all. It was much more of a family-type thing than now when y'all just go at different times. But the doors were locked, and if you were late, it was goodbye—you didn't get that meal. We had white linen tablecloths, and it was immaculately, immaculately kept. Of course, we thought the food was terrible, and it was really delicious. But I thought the dining hall was very nice, and we had had training there also, although we didn't realize we were getting it. The social advisers and some of the instructors that lived on campus ate with us—they were, I think, assigned an area in the room that they were more or less responsible for, to give us a little oversight. But we always had a good one.

AK: Did you feel like that training gave you some advantages after you were out of school?

FD: I really did. My mother believed in good manners and all of that, and of course she did her best. But still, when W graduates got out in the world, we knew, I guess you'd say, the niceties of what to do when, and it helps wherever you are—just a little polish, I guess you might say.

AK: How would your classmates have described you?
FD: As pretty quiet. I still find myself doing that, just kind of listening to see how the conversation's going. I'm afraid as I get older, I'm getting worse about sounding off when I shouldn't. But I've always just been quiet. I'm not really bashful, but I just don't want to be in the limelight all the time. I'd rather sit back. I was a good student. I was not an all-A student, but I did okay. I think I made all As and Bs, maybe one C. I wasn't in Mortar Board,[8] unfortunately, but I did fine.

AK: Do you recall any major world events that took place while you were there?
FD: We were there right after World War II ended, so a lot of it was reaction to the war and getting our feet back under us. We were rationed on quite a bit of stuff. We had to reevaluate our life, I guess you would say. We did have the states' rights—not convention, but the man that ran for president during those years.[9] My husband and I were talking about that today. The editor of our paper[10] at that time was pretty active in that. She did a lot of articles about that type of thing, but it was not too political, I guess. You know how college students do. In fact, they do it more now than they did when I was growing up. They think they're going to change the world and that it has to be done their way. We were

8. Mortar Board National College Honor Society was founded in 1918 and elects members based on scholarship and campus leadership.

9. In 1948, southern Democrats split with the national party after President Harry Truman, a Democrat, integrated the armed forces. The southerners formed the States' Rights Democratic Party, or Dixiecrats. In that fall's presidential election, Senator Strom Thurmond of South Carolina ran as the Dixiecrat candidate and carried Alabama, Louisiana, Mississippi, and South Carolina, although Truman won reelection.

10. Mary Dowd King Riesterer (1926–2002), Class of 1948, served as editor of the *Spectator* in the spring of 1948, while Perian Collier Connerly, Class of 1949, took over the position the following fall.

not particularly like that, but we did keep up with some of the politics. Like I said, it was such a relief to have the war over that I think people were just sort of coasting and enjoying peace.

AK: What was your favorite thing to do on campus?

FD: I read a lot. Being a literature minor, I always had some book reports I had to make. And I got a lot of reading done then. Most of my friends played bridge, but I just did not care for bridge, so I was the one that would fix the food and that sort of thing. Then I would go to bed and read while the rest of them were playing bridge. We'd get together in somebody's room. The funniest thing that happened, though, was when we were in somebody's—I can't remember whether it was in my room or somebody else's room. Before the war there were no plastic containers. Then after the war, they had learned to use plastic. So I had a plastic bowl. We had popped some corn in a pan, and we decided there was too much oil in the pan, So I just poured some into that plastic bowl, and the thing just melted. Here the table is with this big puddle of oil that had gone through the bowl. I learned a lot about plastic that one time! We had a lot of things that came into being in during World War II that we've used ever since. But I always thought that was one of the funniest things because I was so dumb. Here I am thinking, "Why is that thing melting?" So naturally, that bowl went to the garbage.

AK: Do remember any specific traditions that you took part in?

FD: When we were going to be going home for Christmas and Thanksgiving, we always had a formal dinner with the whole nine yards in the way the tables were set, and another schooling on good manners and the different courses of the meal and so forth. It was much more formal than our usual meals were. And also, at Christmastime, nobody had a car, so everybody had to ride a bus—almost everybody—going home. So they would contract with the bus lines to have all of these buses waiting for us at 7:00 in the morning to head home, and they would just park all around the campus. I guess they had signs about which one you were supposed to get on. But that was pretty impressive to see several hundred girls out scrambling around getting on all those lines of buses. Of course, they would go through town and all the Columbus people were probably saying, "Oh, thank goodness. We don't have to see them again for a couple of weeks." But going home for Christmas was the main thing. When I was a child, we had always stayed at home for Christmas. We didn't have anybody to visit or come visit us. So it was just our family.

AK: How often did you get home?
FD: Not very often. The first couple of years, I think, unless there was some very special reason, I think we got one extra day. We had to have an extra day because we had classes on Saturday then—take a break on our Friday classes and our Saturday classes, so we could have two nights at home. Then we'd have to come back on Sunday afternoon. I think we got one every nine weeks the first couple of years, and then a few more after that. I had one friend that lived in Leland, which was close to Indianola, and her mother was very sick. So she got permission to go home every weekend. But of course she didn't take a break every time. She'd just go home for one night after Saturday morning classes—we didn't have afternoon classes on Saturday. So she had a quick trip. But most people were limited to the number we could take.

AK: Other than those big breaks at Christmas and Thanksgiving, how would you get home?
FD: By bus, most of us. We would just kind of pool to get a cab to get downtown with our luggage. They had big bus stations in those days, so that's the way we got home. Even if you were lucky enough to have a car, you couldn't have it on campus until you were a senior. I didn't have one anyway, so that didn't do me much good. There were just no cars on campus. It was pretty quiet!

AK: Were they strict about having visitors on campus?
FD: They were. We could have visitors, but it would have to be at night, and I probably never even thought about it aside from the weekends. If you had a date, you had to sign out and sign in, and you durst not be

late. I had a date with this boy that I did not like at all one time, and he almost made me late. I was so mad at him. That was my one and only date with him, because it was pretty bad if you were late getting in. We had to get someone to let us in, or the social adviser. We got demerits if we were late. And after so many demerits, we paid some kind of a consequence. I've forgotten now what it was—probably not to get a weekend off. Thank goodness I never acquired enough of those to find out.

AK: Did you know people who did?
FD: I actually don't. I'm sure there were some that just didn't tell it. But I feel that because we couldn't smoke and we couldn't do this and we couldn't do that, that some were just determined they were going to do it. For freshmen there was no smoking. In some of the other dorms for the higher grades, they had a smoking room. Good grief—it was awful in there! It's a wonder they all didn't catch something sitting in that thing smoking because it got pretty bad in there. Of course I just would pass by, because I didn't smoke. You had to have a written permission from your parents, so that's the way they limited it. There were some that smoked, but I don't know what the rules were—how many times you were allowed. I don't know if there was a time limit. I never did find out that part.

AK: What was your typical day like?
FD: Breakfast was at 7:00. The laundry had this whistle or horn or something that went off, I think, at 6:30. And that was what we woke up with. Then we just threw on some clothes and went to breakfast. All the classes were controlled with that device, whatever it was, that went off from the laundry. We got ten minutes between classes. So the whistle would blow at 10:50, and at 11:00 it would blow again when the class was supposed to start. It wasn't just a tweet. It was a loud noise! You heard it all over campus. If you look back on it, that's pretty funny now to people I'm sure. But I didn't even have a watch when I was in college. I got a watch for my graduation. We just didn't keep up with time. We had a clock in the room that we had to wind or we were in big trouble. But we were just timed by that thing. And we just learned to live with it.

AK: How long did each class last?
FD: Fifty minutes, and we had ten minutes to get to the next class. We had Monday, Wednesday, and Friday classes and then Tuesday, Thursday, and Saturday classes. On Monday and Tuesday and Thursday, we had afternoon classes. But they were all scheduled out so it gave you some extra study time or whatever you chose to do.

AK: What did you choose to do?
FD: Not much. Just go in someone's room and talk, or eat a little bit and that kind of stuff. We had lunch, and then at 1:30 or 2:00, they had scheduled time to go to our denominations building. All of them had a program of some type every day. We had labs on Monday, Wednesday, or Thursday afternoon. That was a favorite time for them to schedule those, but I never did have much lab work. I worked in the library some—that's what I did for lab work. I didn't teach. We had to do practice work, so we had a semester going to the Demonstration School,[11] which was for elementary grades, and a semester for high school and a semester of working in the college library. Library science majors did hands-on in the library instead of practicing teaching.

AK: What have you done since you graduated?
FD: I came to Raymond after I graduated and worked in the public library there—the county library. And then we evolved into what they call an area library while I was there, so that involved quite a bit of travel and so forth. Then I stopped when I had my children, and I went to work at Mississippi College in the library, working part time there for several years. At that time you didn't have very much chance of anybody taking care of your children, and we didn't have day cares in those days. I had two sons, so I mostly stayed at home with them.

11. The Demonstration School, a laboratory school for MSCW student teachers, opened in 1929. It operated as a practice school and as a public elementary school until 2003.

Joan Crawford Meadows McLemore
Class of 1951

DECEMBER 27, 2006

INTERVIEWED BY AMBER KING

TRANSCRIBED BY AMBER KING AND RACHEL FORESTER

JOAN CRAWFORD MEADOWS, THE MIDDLE CHILD OF James Leon Meadows and Dell Crawford Meadows, was born in Texas on August 24, 1929. The family subsequently moved to Oklahoma and then to Mississippi in 1939. After graduating from Natchez High School in June 1947, Meadows came to MSCW, where she studied for two years. During her freshman year, she was elected house chairman of Hastings and served in the Student Government Association. Also during her first year, she played the clarinet in the orchestra. As a sophomore, she wrote for MSCW's student newspaper, the *Spectator*. She left MSCW after the spring 1949 semester and married Kenneth McLemore (1926–97), a farmer, a year later. After working in a bank for nearly twenty years, she changed careers, completing a bachelor's degree at the University of Southern Mississippi. She served as a public librarian in Franklin County for fifteen years and then as director of the library at Copiah-Lincoln Community College for thirteen years. In 1983, she completed a master's degree in

> library science from the University of Southern Mississippi. She has served on the executive board of the Mississippi Library Association and the Natchez Historical Society and is a member of a variety of heritage organizations. She retired from Co-Lin in 2003 but is now a popular professional storyteller, regularly presenting programs on Mississippi history and related topics. She also frequently discusses and reviews books for programs such as the Institute for Learning in Retirement. She lives in Natchez.

JM: We lived in Texas and eventually in Oklahoma. My dad was born in Oklahoma when it was the Indian Territory. His dad worked for the railroad company. We lived there for three years and then finally got to Natchez. My mother was so happy because she was a Mississippian, and she was back home where they had trees and grass. We came to Natchez in 1939. They were building Armstrong Tire and Rubber Company here, and that was the company my daddy went to work for.

I had planned to go to Northeast Junior College, it was then, in Monroe, Louisiana—it's now the University of Louisiana at Monroe. I wanted to study journalism, but my daddy would not have that. So I said, "I will go to the W." And my folks were not happy about me going to the W, but if I couldn't study what I wanted to, I would go where I wanted to. I was enchanted with the thought of going to a girls' school.

AK: What do you remember about your first year?
JM: During the summer of 1947, styles changed. That was the advent of the new look. My mother had been sewing for months making clothes for me. Oh, she was a professional seamstress, truly. I never had a coat that came from the store until I went to college. My mother made beautiful clothes for me. But that summer, all of a sudden, things that had been knee length had to be ankle length. She put yokes on skirts, and all the dresses had drapes and were down to the ankle. Material with a satin weave or a satin figure in it was real important. And crepes with drapes were very important. And of course hats, platform shoes, high heels—very high-heel shoes, sling-back pumps, gloves, all those were

important things to go to the W. I had two trunks that I had sent to the W by railway express. One was a wardrobe trunk, and one was a steamer trunk. These trunks had belonged to my mother when she was in college, and they're still around. Some member of the family still owns those trunks. It was quite exciting to be going off to college.

I remember leaving home on the twenty-second or twenty-third of September—maybe the twenty-fourth. There'd been a terrible storm down on the coast. Much of the coast had been blown away.[1] Oh, it was awful. And Natchez is so far from Columbus, we had to go by bus. Nobody had a car back then. The war hadn't been over for very long; nobody could afford a car. I rode the bus to Jackson and changed buses in Jackson and got to Columbus. When I arrived at the W, it was a scary place. I had to get a taxi and go out to the school. There was nobody there to greet me. I really felt like the little match girl, so lost and alone. The enrollment was so great that there were not enough rooms to go around. They put me in Hastings Hall in a broom closet by myself. I was miserable. I knew that I was not going to stay there. But after two or three days, people began to drop out, to go back home for one reason or another—same reason, probably, that I was considering going home—and they put me in a room with someone else. I didn't know anybody that was going to school up there. I didn't know that you had a roommate assigned before you went. I didn't know you found a roommate. But anyway, they did assign a roommate to me that was very satisfactory. And they put me into a decent room.

AK: How did you get home from school at the end of the terms?

JM: If we were going home on vacation, we would charter buses. Some people were lucky enough for their folks to come after them and be able to take everything home, but most of us would charter a bus either at Christmas or spring holidays and then at the end of the school session. Christmas vacation was fun. We didn't get home between September

1. A category 5 hurricane struck Florida on September 16, 1947, and then on September 19 passed directly over New Orleans as a category 3 storm.

and December because we had Saturday classes—we got out at 12:00 on Saturday. A few times, we did visit with some of the girls from Florence, Alabama. We could go over there on the weekend. Also, I had an aunt who lived at Montevallo, just south of Birmingham. I would go over there on the bus and spend the weekend—a little break. But I really didn't mind staying at school. I could go to the library and read a book.

AK: What else do you remember about your freshman year?
JM: I was elected to represent the dorm on the Student Government Council. Jean Woolley[2] was president at that time. I didn't make the grades I was supposed to, so I was only on there one semester, but it was fun being a part of the student government. I also was on the *Spectator*[3] staff. I enjoyed writing some silly feature articles, now that I look back on it. I had been editor of the high school paper here in Natchez, the *Echoes*, and I did want to study journalism, but my daddy always said there's no money in that.

I had never seen anything like all of the guys from Mississippi State. The telephone would ring, and somebody would say, "Anybody want a date?" There were blind dates all the time. I met some nice guys and met some doozies. I was dating a young man who was going to school at Millsaps.[4] He would come up periodically, and he came up for the prom. The prom was a big deal in the springtime. My mother sewed and made beautiful clothes for me and then mailed them to me. I remember my freshman year, for the prom she made me a black taffeta evening gown, off one shoulder; the skirt was caught up with a lace insert underneath there. Oh, I thought it was so darling. And the prom was a lot of fun.

I never was really into studying. I should've been, but I played cards. I learned to play bridge, and that's what I did more than studying. I did enjoy my English classes, and I guess English and bridge have served me

....

2. Dorothy Jean Woolley Jennings (1927–99), Class of 1948.
3. The *Spectator*, begun in 1905 as a quarterly publication, was a combination annual and literary magazine that evolved into the student newspaper by the early 1920s. The *Spectator* is now published weekly.
4. Millsaps College, founded in 1890, is a Methodist-run liberal arts college in Jackson, Mississippi.

better than most anything else. I enjoyed the campus life with the girls. I enjoyed physical education. Many times since I have been away from the W, I have met people and talked with people who knew Miss Pohl.[5] She was certainly an institution, and of course, there were some of our wonderful teachers here in Natchez who had been W girls, so they really expected all of us from Natchez to excel. I'm sure I was a disappointment to them, but I just wasn't into studying at that time.

Sophomore year, I lived in Reneau. That year, I guess I didn't really find myself interested in studying because I wasn't in the field I wanted to be in. I did enjoy the English literature classes with Mr. Covington.[6] Miss Spahr[7] taught hygiene and health. One of the girls from Natchez took her class. I remember her coming to my room one day and saying, "Oh, I am just dying. I'm dying. I have gyno-heria. I have all the symptoms Miss Spahr told us." And I thought, "Gyno-heria? What in the world is that?" I thought, "If you're going to have it, you'd better learn to pronounce it correctly." But she was a hypochondriac, and she just got everything Miss Spahr would talk about.

Oh, Dr. Evans[8] was a wonderful teacher, too. Of course, her cousin, Lorraine Shell,[9] had taught us English here in Natchez, and when I first got to the W and saw Dr. Evans, I thought, "My goodness, Miss Shell has followed us to the W." Then I learned that Miss Shell and Dr. Evans were first cousins. Dr. Evans taught zoology. That didn't interest me because I hated frogs and earthworms. My dear friend loved frogs and earthworms, and when we had to dissect a frog, Ann[10] found crawfish pincers in the frog's stomach, and oh, Dr. Evans thought she was positively brilliant. I did learn a lot in botany classes. I remember every Wednesday trotting

....

5. Emma Ody Pohl (1880–1966) joined II & C in 1907, when she was hired to develop the department of physical education. She taught that subject until her retirement in 1955.
6. Frank F. Covington (1885–1972) taught English at MSCW from 1929 until 1952.
7. Mildred Spahr Kennedy (1926–1982) taught in MSCW's Department of Bacteriology, Physiology, and Hygiene and in the Department of Home Economics from 1947 until 1972.
8. Clytee R. Evans (1889–1981), Class of 1911, taught biology at II & C/MSCW from 1912 until 1952.
9. Lorraine Shell (1889–1985), Class of 1910.
10. Ann Greer Wise, Class of 1951.

all over that campus looking at all the flora and fauna. It was interesting, but it was right before lunch, and we'd be so hungry, just starving to death. But botany classes at the W have served me well. I can identify a red maple and the crape myrtle. I have learned what things to put in my yard just from those classes at the W.

During my freshman year, I signed up for the symphony orchestra. Most of those girls that were in there were music majors, but I had played in the high school band here in Natchez, and I enjoyed playing the clarinet. I did not play well. Dr. Wright[11] was the conductor, and he was so talented, so brilliant. He assigned me the solo clarinet chair, and he realized that somebody was playing off key. My career as the soloist did not last long because I was the one that was playing off key and didn't know how to correct it.

Going to town at the W was rather interesting with that long walk down to Egger's and Ruth's Department Stores and then the walk back to campus. I remember one time when we were walking back, Dr. Parkinson[12] stopped and said, "Would you all like to have a ride?" And one of the girls said, "Oh, no. We can't get in the car with any strangers." So we failed to ride back with the president.

Dr. Parkinson was a very charming, very professional man. We had a housemother in Hastings, Caroline McElveen,[13] who came from King's Tree in Aiken County, South Carolina. She had been at a Presbyterian school where the students worked, and she thought that we ought to be working. She was adamant in telling us that we had to get jobs. We were not going to work. We were not there to work. We were there to go to school. Finally, we went to see Dr. Parkinson—thirteen of us from the dorm went and talked to him, and he said, "I can terminate her now or wait until the end of the semester or wait until the end of the year. One thing we have to think about is you might be swapping the devil for

11. Kenneth Wright (1916–87) taught in MSCW's Department of Music from 1944 until 1949.
12. Burney Lynch Parkinson (1887–1972) served as president of MSCW from 1932 until 1952.
13. Caroline E. McElveen (1904–92) served as a social adviser in Hastings during the 1947–48 school year.

the witch." He was very wise. It was scary, but we finally got our point across to that lady that we didn't have to scrub the floors and clean the dorm here. Our fees to the school paid for that sort of thing.

Miss McElveen was an interesting woman. She kept telling us that she was responsible for Minnie Pearl's [14] comedic character. One night, years later, I was watching Ralph Edwards on *This Is Your Life*,[15] and who did they introduce but Caroline McElveen, who was responsible for Minnie Pearl!

AK: Do you remember other extracurricular activities?

JM: The lecture series at the W was very interesting and important to all of us. I recall when the Von Trapp Family [16] was touring the country, and this was years before *The Sound of Music* was made. They gave a concert at the school, and it was just wonderful. Another speaker was Mildred Spurrier Topp.[17] She later was a professor at Ole Miss, taught English, and she lectured on campus one day. She had written a book titled *In the Pink*. I still think about her. She was such an entertaining lady.

Also, one of the fascinating events there was the visit of Frances Parkinson Keyes.[18] She had just written the book *Dinner at Antoine's*. All of her books are set in certain places—unique places. She would go there and live while she was writing the book. She bought the Beauregard House in New Orleans and wrote *Dinner at Antoine's*. After the big celebration in New Orleans—Dr. Parkinson and Mrs. Parkinson[19] had been there to that celebration—she came to the W and lectured and

....

14. Minnie Pearl was the professional name of Sarah Colley Cannon (1912–96), a comedian known for her Grand Ole Opry performances.
15. *This Is Your Life* was a television program that aired from 1952 to 1961. Host Ralph Edwards (1913–2005) would surprise celebrity guests with a series of family members and friends.
16. The Von Trapp Family Singers were a popular touring group in the 1940s and 1950s. The story of their lives inspired the film *The Sound of Music* (1965).
17. Mildred Spurrier Topp (1897–1963), Class of 1917, wrote *Smile, Please* (1948) and *In the Pink* (1950), both of which garnered critical and commercial success.
18. Frances Parkinson Keyes (1885–1970) was a popular and prolific writer in the 1930s, 1940s, and 1950s. Her only murder mystery, *Dinner at Antoine's* (1948), was one of her biggest successes.
19. Dera Dry Parkinson (1887–1979). In 1927, she became the first woman to earn a Ph.D. (in psychology) from the University of South Carolina.

had a book signing. When she walked into Whitfield Auditorium on that stage, she had on this brown print redingote-style dress and a huge picture hat. The lady was rather short; she had a huge bosom, and she had lace-up high-heeled Oxford-type shoes. They were hideous to us. She heaved her bosom up on the lectern, and she started talking. That woman was one of the most fascinating speakers that I have ever heard. She told us how she came to write *Dinner at Antoine's*. She just had that audience in the palm of her hand. I could've listened for hours. That was really a high point.

There were other events. Oh, Bob Hope came! Actually, he came to perform at Lee Hall at Mississippi State, but the place had had a fire, and they couldn't accommodate the students, so he came to the W. Bob Hope's presentation was a bit risqué for us, but everybody laughed at the proper places.[20]

AK: What do you remember about the dining hall?

JM: I guess the redeeming feature of the W was the wonderful meals. Oh, the cinnamon rolls at breakfast were great. Lunches were always good. I remember the chicken pie. Dinner was always such a nice affair. I had heard about the Goose,[21] and it was a treat to go to the Goose and get something to drink. The food at the W was always outstanding. One thing that was very impressive to me was the service in the dining hall. They served family style. There were eight people at each table. You had to take a turn each week being hostess. I guess that really served me well, because I have never been afraid to preside at my own table. I loved those family-style dinners at the W. I loved dressing up on Sunday for dinner or a holiday, a special holiday dinner. Tradition was important there.

One of the people that sat at our table was Alice Hamer,[22] who was the alumnae secretary in those days. She had been a student at the W and

20. Comedian Bob Hope (1903–2003) performed at the Columbus City Auditorium on April 22, 1949. The fire at Lee Hall had occurred in November 1948, and a number of concerts and programs were moved to Whitfield Hall at MSCW. However, Hope was not originally scheduled to perform at Mississippi State.

21. The Golden Goose Tearoom, located on the first floor of the Student Activities Building (formerly the Henry Whitfield Gymnasium), demolished in the late 1960s.

22. Alice Hamer Sanford, Class of 1944, served as secretary of the MSCW Alumnae Association from 1947 until 1952.

later, I understand, went to work for a newspaper in Baton Rouge. And she still wore the navy blue uniforms when she came to work at the W. She piled that red hair high on top of her head, and she wore platform soles, navy blue suit, and white blouse. She was interesting because she knew so many people, and she probably brought a little dignity to our table. We had to be proper with Miss Hamer there. The interesting thing about that is, in recent years, I have been associated with her daughter, Penny Sanford Fikes,[23] and on the occasion of her mother's eightieth birthday, she was having people send her mother a card. I told her that I remembered her mother well. She said, "Oh, you must send Mother a card." And I had a response from that card.

I run across people all the time that went to the W. It's always fun to say, "Oh, you're a W girl!" My husband never forgot that I was a W girl. He said, "You can always tell a W girl. You just can't tell them much." And I really enjoyed my association with the W girls, no matter where I have met them. In fact, we go to North Carolina each summer, each July, for the month. This past summer in the bathhouse I met this young woman from New Albany, and I said, "Oh, I've been to New Albany. I've told stories there in the public library." And then I said, "I knew people who went to the W from New Albany." She said, "Oh, I'm a W girl." It was obvious that I was older than she, and she said, "Oh, did you go when they were wearing uniforms?" And I said, "No, I'm not quite that old." And I said, "What year were you there?" And she said, "Somebody asked me if we used dental floss when I went to the W, and I said, 'No, it hadn't been invented.'" So she said, "I'm older than floss." Isn't that a wonderful little story? I love that.

AK: What do you think about the quality of academic education you received at the W?

JM: I felt that I got my education at the Natchez Public Schools. We learned how to conjugate verbs; we learned how to translate Latin; we learned how to diagram sentences. Of course, the W for us was just an

23. Penny Sanford Fikes is a Mississippi artist known for her porcelain limited-edition sculptures.

extension of that. High standards—we knew when somebody went to the W that they had a classy education. One day, we were served apples in the dining hall, and we chomped into our apples. I love to eat an apple—bite down on it! My mother would be out in the backyard hanging up clothes, and I would be eating an apple in the house, and she would call to me and say, "Quit chomping that apple!" She could not stand chewing gum or chomping apples. Nell Lawler [24] was the counselor at that time, and Miss Lawler was appalled at the way we were eating apples. They marched us to Whitfield Auditorium, and she had a knife and an apple, and she proceeded to show us how to eat an apple. I have never forgotten that—but I still enjoy chomping on an apple.

Another thing that they stressed at the W was walking properly—walking up the stairs—and how to sit down, how to get up. And always before a social event, they went through the procedure of going down a receiving line. They had these little dormitory teas, and Mrs. Parkinson would attend. The first thing they told us about the dormitory tea was, "Do not tell Dr. Parkinson that you love the W." So, my dear friend who shall remain nameless, when we went down the receiving line, the first thing she said, was, "Oh, Dr. Parkinson, I love the W." We have laughed about that many times.

AK: Why couldn't you say you loved the W?

JM: Obviously you loved it, or you wouldn't have been there. It was just not considered the proper thing to say. And we had to go down the receiving line at the proms. It was very formal. We were instructed to say, "Dr. Parkinson, may I present Mr. So-and-so. Mr. So-and-so, Dr. Parkinson." We practiced that. And Dr. Parkinson, in turn, would say, "May I present Mrs. Parkinson," and then we'd go through the whole thing again, and there would be a number of people in the receiving line. I've thought about those hours of instruction many times. Since I left the W, it's certainly served me well. A friend of mine in Meadville

24. Nell Lawler (1899–1982), Class of 1920, served as student counselor at MSCW from 1942 until 1948.

one day said, "You and I are the only two people I know in the state who wouldn't be afraid to go up to the governor's mansion by ourselves and go in." We were prepared for any social event.

After going into that dining hall every day and sitting down at a proper table, I never would let my family eat in front of the television. Even though we might be eating in the kitchen, we had the table set. When my child was quite small, I would have him set the table. We would use the tablecloth and china and silver, even in the kitchen when time was limited, because I thought it was so important to know that and to enjoy the mealtime. Nowadays, when do families have time to interact with other family members? Even now that I live alone, I do not sit and watch television. I sat there in the dining room and had my lunch today right by myself. I just think that's such an important part of life.

The campus whistle would blow every morning at 6:50, and that's what awakened us and warned us that it was almost time for breakfast. I can't remember if we had breakfast at 7:00 or 7:30, but when that whistle blew, we had time to get up and get dressed and go to the dining hall. No hair in curlers. You could wear a scarf around your hair if the weather was bad. And we had to have rain boots. Columbus was the wettest place, I thought, in the whole state until I got to Hattiesburg, and I realized that all the rain from Columbus came down to Hattiesburg. Hattiesburg is much lower than Columbus is. At the W, the rain boots and the raincoats were so very important. No slacks were allowed unless you might be going on a picnic, and then you could wear slacks or shorts. But proper attire was very important. You did not wear any bobby pins or curlers showing in your hair. You did not wear your hair rolled up on campus, and that has stayed with me all of my life. I see a lady around the block from me who walks her dog with her hair in rollers. I would not dare go out with my hair in rollers. When I get up in the morning, I dress as I'm going to be for the day. I learned that at the W and also from Thomas Jefferson—I think he said that a woman should be ready to meet the day when she came downstairs, and that's not a bad idea. You don't get caught at the front door in your nightgown that way.

AK: Do you remember other traditions at the W?

JM: There were a lot of traditions at the W. I remember going to the Goose on Saturday evening. Oh, I well recall a song that said, "Now is the hour that we must say good-bye; soon you'll be leaving, going across the sea,"[25] or something like that. We would play that beautiful record over and over and over again. Oh, and playing tennis—we enjoyed playing tennis. There were wonderful tennis courts at the W, and I took tennis, and later on I gave tennis lessons to some of my friends. For two consecutive years, one of my friends won the country club championship. I couldn't play well, but I could read and knew the rules and knew how to coach her in playing tennis.

I remember the dormitory sings where the students would compose songs about their class and about their dorm and there was a competition. I had been used to this because we had what we called sing-song at Natchez High School. The four classes would compete for this banner. And our teachers had gone to the W, so I know where the tradition came from. I can remember the song from Reneau: the song "Dream"[26] was real popular, and we did a parody on that song. We had something like "Dream when you're feeling blue" and how Reneau was the place to be, and then we had, "Reneau, everybody! Reneau!" Standard Oil Company put out a little booklet every month—*Scenic South* was the name of it. And Reneau had been on the cover of *Scenic South*, and that was part of our song: "This cover girl for *Scenic South*, you made history."

And the wonderful Christmas programs in the music building, Poindexter Hall. Oh, the musicians that were studying at the W, and the faculty—the musical programs, the senior recitals, all of that was very

25. Maewa Kaihan, Clement Scott, and Dorothy Stewart, "Now Is the Hour" (1948). The first verse is as follows:

> Now is the hour that we must say good-bye
> Soon you'll be sailing far across the sea
> While you're away oh then remember me
> When you return you'll find me waiting here.

26. "Dream (When You're Feeling Blue)" was written by Johnny Mercer in 1945.

impressive. MSCW was certainly a cultural center for young women. We didn't have to go to Ward-Belmont[27] or some of those fancy schools a lot of girls from here went to, like Hollins College[28] in Virginia. But we had that element at the W that they found at those more expensive schools—at Brenau,[29] places like that. I'm certainly proud of my time at the W. It was truly worthwhile.

AK: How would the people who went to school with you describe you?
JM: I have no idea. We don't see ourselves as others see us, and I remember learning that from Robert Burns in Dr. Covington's class: "O wad some Power the giftie gie us, to see oursels as ithers see us."[30] I don't see myself as others see me. They probably see me as egotistical, boisterous. And I'm really shy. So I don't know what they would say about me. Oh, Dr. Covington was such a wonderful teacher. He had such a great gift in reading these stories, the short stories that we studied, and the tale was on the campus that he was color-blind and that he never looked up. I do know that he always looked down. He wore those pince-nez type glasses without any sidepieces, and the story was that if you changed shoes, he'd mark you absent because that was the way he checked the roll, by looking at your shoes. He was such a good teacher, and when I've run across some of those stories, I've remembered how great he was with assuming the different character roles.

My daughter-in-law finished at Co-Lin Junior College in 1972. She and my son married that summer and moved to Columbus. Peggy went to the W, got her bachelor's degree two years later, and then went on and got her master's.[31] They left Columbus not long after that, but their daughter, my granddaughter, enrolled at the W as a freshman and graduated

27. Ward-Belmont, a private women's junior college in Nashville, Tennessee, founded in 1913 as a result of a merger between Ward Seminary and Belmont College for Young Women. It is now coeducational Belmont University.
28. Hollins College (now Hollins University), founded in 1842, is a private liberal arts school for women in Roanoke, Virginia.
29. Brenau College (now Brenau University), a private women's college in Gainesville, Georgia, was founded in 1878 as the Georgia Baptist Female Seminary.
30. Robert Burns, "To a Louse" (1786).
31. Peggy Arnold McLemore, Class of 1974.

with a degree in broadcast journalism.[32] When Bethany finished the W, she wanted to work in North Carolina. While she was interviewing in North Carolina, she called a man at a TV station in Chattanooga, and he said, "Please come by. I'd like to interview you." She went over there, and he said, "I'm so glad that you came. I don't have a job available, but my mother was a W girl, and I just wanted to interview a W girl." The W's reputation is well known.

Bethany lived in Hastings, and I was so amazed when I went to Hastings after living there in a broom closet. And then I saw that darling little apartment that she had upstairs. I couldn't believe it! Of course, I understand that's a good way to keep the students on campus, a nice way.

AK: What did you do after you left MSCW?

JM: The summer of 1949, I met Kenneth McLemore. Oh, he was the best-looking thing. I met him right at the end of May, and he started coming to town. He was a farmer. He came every Saturday and Sunday and Wednesday and Friday. Finally, in July, he said, "If you'll learn to drive, I'll marry you." We didn't have to drive in Natchez because we had city buses, and at that time town was small. You could walk anywhere you wanted, and it wasn't unsafe. He got a new car in July 1949. It was a '49 Ford, a beautiful navy blue four-door Ford automobile with a straight shift, and he started giving me driving lessons. So I got a job that September rather than going back to school, a job as bookkeeper at Geisenberger Drug Company, a wholesale retail drug firm in Natchez. I learned to drive and got my driver's license in March. Ken said I was the dumbest woman he'd ever seen, since it took me so long to learn how to drive. But we had fun on the driving lessons. He had given me a ring on the twelfth of October in 1949. When I showed it to my mother, I said, "We want to get married at Christmas." She said, "Absolutely not. Nobody comes to a Christmas wedding. Nobody gives wedding presents at Christmas. The flowers are not blooming at Christmas. You can get married May the sixth." That's what Mother said, so that's what we did.

32. Bethany McLemore Austin, Class of 1992.

On May the sixth, all the Easter lilies were in bloom, and Mother had a friend with a bed of Easter lilies. Our flowers for the church did not cost anything because her friend had all these flowers. We married at Jefferson Street Methodist Church on that Saturday at about 7:00 in the evening, and then there was a reception at my aunt's house.

Then we went on a little trip to the coast, and I came back and settled in to be a dairy farmer's wife. I was a stay-at-home mother for ten months after our child was born. In April 1951, ten months and some days later, I went to work at the bank in Franklin County and worked there for almost twenty years. But I decided one day that I was not cut out for that; I was meant for more. So I went to college. I thought I would get a degree from the University of Southern Mississippi in history, but at the USM branch campus in Natchez, all they gave were degrees in education and maybe nursing, so I took some education courses, but I also took the history classes. At that time I was a trustee for the public library. One day I said to the director of the Lincoln- Lawrence-Franklin Regional Library, "I shouldn't be getting a degree in history; I ought to be getting a degree in library science." She said, "I've been waiting for you to say that." So, that December, the die was cast. I told my husband I was going to USM because I had to have access to the library for those library science classes. And he said, "What about me?" I said, "What do you mean?" And he said, "Who's going to cook for me?" So I taught him how to use the microwave, and his mother had lived with us for many years; she certainly wouldn't let him go hungry. So I took off to Hattiesburg. I registered. That was an ordeal because I was not used to that big a place. I had to go to the library to speak to the adviser, then I had to go to the coliseum, then I had to go back to the library, then I had to go to the registrar's office. I just didn't know if I was going to stick with it or not. But I finally got my schedule, and I attended classes Tuesday, Wednesday, and Thursday and then would come back home. It was a wonderful experience for me. I met so many interesting people over there, and it was so much fun being in the Cook Library at USM. I finished in August 1976, had an internship that summer, and worked in the library at Brookhaven as part of my college work. Then I was employed by the Lincoln-Lawrence-Franklin Regional Library. We opened our new county library in November 1976, and I was the librarian in Meadville. I loved doing that. It was a wonderful place.

Those rural people had never had a public library. It was closed several mornings a week so that I could have the schoolchildren come down and give them classes. I thought, "What's the point in us having a library if these people don't know how to use it?" I worked with the women's homemaker's clubs, the black clubs. I had one really interesting experience: an old black man who was a preacher—I knew him from my days in the bank—came in one day and he said, "Miss, is you got a Bible in here I can get?" I said, "Sure, we've got a bunch of them. Come over here and let me show you." And I showed him one that was a large-print Bible. He said, "Now, Miss, how much is this Bible?" I said, "That Bible's not for sale. You can take it home with you and read it and then bring it back." I said, "This is your library. You can get books here." He was so impressed with that. I realized that was another facet of library service those people needed.

I didn't know before I was hired that I was going to have to do the children's work. One day the director said, "All right, you've got to start your children's story hour." Okay. I had read stories to children but had never told stories. I did not like the idea of a book being between me and the child. So I did continue to read stories, but I would commit the stories to memory. At first, I thought, "Oh, I can learn one a year." Then I thought, "One every six months." Then I thought, "One every three months." And then I was learning a story every week. I would read a story and maybe read some poetry or show a film, but I did a lot of storytelling. People in Franklin County were enchanted with those stories. I then thought, "I can tell them stories about their own people." For example, that county was named for Benjamin Franklin. Those people there were not aware of Franklin and his importance to their entire county. So I learned Benjamin Franklin stories, and I learned stories of Franklin County. There's a gold hole out there in Franklin County where treasure was supposed to be buried. I developed a story about that gold hole and have told it many times. I told stories about the highwaymen on the Natchez Trace. I told stories about people in Franklin County that had always been interesting to me. Another of the things that I did with my storytelling is research the history of the local churches. People love to hear these stories. And I've also learned some of the folktales from other cultures.

In about 1981, I was invited to join the Delta Kappa Gamma Society International.[33] After I had been in there for a while, I would do programs on any subject for anything. I remember when we got computers in the library, I put together a little booklet and did a program for teachers in the local Delta Kappa Gamma chapter on the terminology: *monitor, keyboard, interface*. That was one thing that I learned at the W: public speaking was so important. I am not intimidated by a small group or a large group. In fact, at the story hours, if only one child came, I went on with my stories. I loved having programs at the library. I also did programs at a men's club, maybe it was the Civitan Club, telling them the library story and what useful things there were at the library. I would also go to the Board of Supervisors and tell them about new things that we had at the library. If they had questions—"What's the population of our county?" "What's the secretary of state's telephone number?"— I delighted in giving out that information.

As I went on with Delta Kappa Gamma, I found out that they had what they called the International Speakers Fund. I applied for that, and one year the state society in Alberta, Canada, invited me up there to be their keynote speaker and tell stories. I told stories about the South, and I found that Mississippi was much like Alberta. We were both settled by the French in the 1700s; agriculture, oil, and tourism were important to Alberta as well as to Mississippi. I was able to tell them the family stories and traditional stories from Mississippi. Then that afternoon at 3:00, they said, "We would like our guest to give us her thoughts." I can't remember what went through my mind, but I thought, "God, please put words in my mouth." It must have been all right, but I was truly speaking extemporaneously about my philosophy of life and what Delta Kappa Gamma had meant to me.

33. Delta Kappa Gamma is an honor society for professional women educators.

In the summer of 1995, I was selected as one of 30 women from the 160,000 or so membership of Delta Kappa Gamma to go to the Golden Gift Seminar, a leadership training program at the University of Texas. That was quite an experience. We had people to tell us how to dress, how to wear our hair—personal appearance consultants. They taught us how to travel for a week with a skirt and a blouse and a blazer and pair of shoes and a pair of pants, mixing them up. It was most informative, and the University of Texas is the place to be! It is the Harvard of the South. I really enjoyed that. Another thing they did there was very important, but it was almost unheard of then. One of our speakers was a young woman, an attorney, who went to law school at the University of Texas. She was talking about lawsuits dealing with improper actions on the part of women teachers. She talked about the number of lawsuits on behalf of students against women teachers. This was before it was common knowledge; it's such a common thing now. In other words, she discussed young women teachers acting improperly with their male students. This was truly interesting in 1995, but here, in the year 2005, it's not an uncommon thing to hear about.

I have been honored by being invited to speak for different groups. I'm a member of the Daughters of the American Revolution, was an organizing member and a regent. I am a member of the Dames of the Court of Honor, which is a heritage organization—you can be a member if your ancestor was an officer in any of the armed services from the colonial days until 1865. I'm a state officer in that. It's so important here in the area where I live, your family's history. The first question they ask is, "What was your mama's maiden name?" And I'm a member of the Colonial Dames, Seventeenth Century, and a member of First Families of the Twin Territories, which is in the Oklahoma Genealogical Society. Organizations like these are a way of promoting local history. I'm a member of the Natchez Historical Society and on the board of trustees and really enjoy doing that work. I still speak often; I haven't counted last year's, but two years ago I gave 112 programs in fifty-two weeks. This past year, I went to Houston, Mississippi, twice to give programs to the DAR chapter. I went to Winsboro, Louisiana, to give a program on Benjamin Franklin. I think that's in Franklin Parish, so that was an appropriate subject. And this year I've done about three programs on the Eudora Welty biography by Suzanne Marrs.[34] I think it's such a wonderful book. Eudora Welty's life was much more interesting than some of her writings, even though I do adore that short story "Why I Live at the P.O." And I belong to two garden clubs. I'm a member of the Natchez Garden Club as well as the Rosecraft Garden Club.

I've joined a Presbyterian church here in Natchez. I was raised Methodist, but when I came back here, the face of the church had changed so much that I didn't know anybody there. I had lots of friends at the Presbyterian church. As a retired person, you could devote your entire life just to the church and stay busy all the time. I served on the diaconate for three years. The association with the ladies at the church is fun. Natchez is a wonderful place to retire because there is so much going on all the time.

I'm also on the faculty of Elderhostel[35] here. This movement began in Boston in the 1970s and it was for people over fifty to tour interesting places and to hear educational lectures. For instance, in Natchez, one Elderhostel program is titled "Natchez: Magic on the Mississippi," and another one is "Natchez: Jamestown on the Mississippi." We have lecturers talking about slavery and the culture of the old fort here, Fort Rosalie, which was established in 1729—the Spanish days, the French days, the English days, and then Mississippi as a province and then eventually about its early statehood. We study about the War of 1812, the Mexican War, the War between the States, the Spanish-American War, World War I, and World War II in connection with the history of Natchez. Elderhostel people tour the churches, the Indian village, Jefferson College, and some of the homes and then hear lectures about the people. It's just absolutely fascinating. I've attended some Elderhostels myself, one in Savannah, and I was just charmed. At that time I was really into researching the history of the Methodist Church, and of course the

34. Suzanne Marrs, *Eudora Welty: A Biography* (2005).
35. Elderhostel is a nonprofit educational travel organization for adults.

Wesley boys were in Savannah.[36] And of course Juliette Low,[37] the founder of the Girl Scouts, grew up in Savannah. Since I was so interested in her, I've been asked a number of times by the Girl Scouts to come tell stories about Juliette Low. Oh, that horrible book, *Midnight in the Garden of Good and Evil*,[38] was set in Savannah. Unfortunately they spend too much time on that book, when they have so many other valuable things to talk about other than that tacky book. I did read it and toured the Bonaventure Cemetery. In fact, I went to Savannah in January 1998. My husband died in May 1997, and I thought, "I can travel by myself. I can drive there. I'm not afraid to do it." So I had my car serviced and bought new tires. I left here one morning at 7:30 on a Saturday, knowing that I should get to Savannah on Sunday afternoon about 3:30. Somebody had written down very detailed instructions, an itinerary which would take me to Columbus, Georgia, and on to Savannah. I got to Columbus, and the highway to take me to Savannah did not exist. It was nighttime, and night comes early in January in those Georgia mountains. I started driving again and I drove and I drove and I drove. There was no sign of life on this four-lane highway, no motels, nothing. I said, "Lord, please help me." All of a sudden on the right side of the highway there were a lot of lights; I drove up and there was a sign that said, "Madame Teresa: Have your palm read." I know what Madame Teresa's is here in Natchez. It's not a place where I wanted to stop, so I just drove on through the driveway and continued to drive. I thought, "Lord, you've just got to send me some relief." All of a sudden there was a sign that said, "Motel: One block past the four-way stop." It was a new motel, so I was not afraid to stop there. I asked the lady if she had a restaurant. She said, "No, but there's one about three blocks down." I knew I would never find my way back to the motel, so I said, "Have you got a vending

36. John (1703–91) and Charles Wesley (1707–88), Anglican ministers and founders of the Methodist movement, came to the Georgia colony with James Oglethorpe in 1736 and stayed for about a year.

37. Juliette Gordon Low (1860–1827) founded the Girl Scouts of the United States of America in 1912.

38. John Berendt, *Midnight in the Garden of Good and Evil: A Savannah Story* (1994), tells the story of a murder and the four trials that followed it.

machine?" She said, "We actually have one, but it's not full; it's empty." Then I remembered I had a pear and some nabs in my basket in my car. I said, "That's all right. Would you give me a room near the office?" She said, "Oh yes." Then I said, "Do you have security?" She said, "No, but the sheriff comes by during the night." She added, "We would have been robbed this morning, but the door was locked and the person couldn't get in." I thought, "Oh, that's all I need." I went to my room and it was no smoking, because it was so new nobody had had an opportunity to smoke: the room was very clean. I was just worn out, so I went in and went to sleep. About 3:00 I woke up and I walked to the window and looked out. My car had been jacked up and there was not a wheel on my car. Somebody had stolen my wheels. I thought, "Oh, where was the sheriff?" I knew that I couldn't do anything about it, so I just went back to bed. But about 6:30 I got up and I went to the window and looked out, and my car was perfectly all right. I had had a nightmare, and I had just dreamed that somebody had taken my wheels off of my car! I got up and dressed and started on toward Savannah. I got to Savannah at 3:30, just in time to enjoy that Elderhostel.

I have researched the history of many of the local Natchez churches. The man who in 1817 built the church I attend, the First Presbyterian Church, came here from New York. His name was Levi Weeks. He had been accused of the murder of a girl that claimed that he was going to marry her. The very first recorded murder trial in the United States of America was in January 1800, and he was the accused. His lawyers were Aaron Burr and Alexander Hamilton, who later fought a duel where Hamilton was killed. Thirteen years passed after Weeks was found not guilty. He went on to Elyria, Ohio, and eventually came down to Natchez, where he was no longer just a carpenter but an architect. He built the Presbyterian church; he built Auburn, Arlington, and the Briars, historic Natchez houses. Auburn is a beautiful mansion, which was then on the outskirts of town. People are fascinated with the history of the churches. They know their early Christian history, but they don't know their local history. I've had a lot of fun developing those stories and telling them.

AK: How do you feel about the W admitting men?

JM: I was opposed to it, but the day has come. It had to be done. I thought it was a wonderful place for training young women who would be future leaders. Notice the women who have been in leadership positions in the state who have been students at the W. Lenore Prather,[39] who became a judge, a lovely person. Presidents of the state garden clubs, which are important entities, of state religious organizations, like United Methodist Women, many of these people who have had those positions have been W students or graduates. Carol West[40] is on the faculty at Mississippi College School of Law. She used to be the director of the library at Mississippi College Law School. Carol is a product of the W. In any organization, you can find leaders who are W graduates. There was a time when all that schoolteachers who finished at the W needed to get a job was their diploma. They didn't have to take any kind of qualifying test.

One thing that I did not like and will still oppose was the movement to name it the Welty University. Eudora Welty[41] only went to school there two years, and her father didn't think it was important enough, wasn't good enough, for his daughter. He sent her on up north. I understand needing to get a different point of view, but I don't think she should be honored with naming the W Welty University. When she won the Pulitzer Prize, I was in Jackson for a luncheon where she was the honored guest. It was so exciting to see this little bitty woman with this camellia almost as big as her head pinned on her shoulder. She came in this room where all the librarians from the state were, and all the members of the legislature, and there was a standing ovation for Eudora Welty. But I do not think that we should name our school the Welty University. Her parents were not even from Mississippi, even though she was probably born here. She didn't have those strong Mississippi roots.

....

39. Lenore Loving Prather (b. 1931), Class of 1953. See the interview with her in this volume.

40. Carol C. West, Class of 1966.

41. Eudora Alice Welty (1909–2001), an internationally known writer, was a native of Jackson, Mississippi, who attended MSCW in 1926 and 1927 before transferring to the University of Wisconsin at Madison.

AK: What advice would you offer current W girls?

JM: When my daughter-in-law was there, they offered a course in flower arranging. I said, "Take it." I said, "Learn to play bridge, and by all means, learn to swim." There are things there that will serve you all your days. I'm sorry they don't have the family-style meals anymore, because knowing how to preside at your table and making that an important part of your life is still important. Where else can a family have interaction, learn about the day's events, if they don't have supper together? And for many families, breakfast is in such a hurry that they don't have time to sit down for breakfast. I think that going to school there probably gave self-esteem to many young women because they were not in competition with each other. In my day, at Mississippi State, there were three thousand guys and seventy-five girls. But we knew why those girls were going over there. They wanted to be cheerleaders or something of that sort. And they were just so overwhelmed with men. Perhaps they've had an editor of the newspaper at State that was a woman, I don't know, but in my day, all those positions went to men. When I was at the W, Perian Collier,[42] who married Charlie Conerly, was a student there. He was a really important professional football player. He went to Ole Miss and then went on to play for the New York Giants. Perian has written a couple of books. But she couldn't have been editor of the newspaper if she had been at State. Those things at the W serve the women well. I imagine even with a small male population, women are certainly more in the leadership positions. Another thing about the W is that the campus is small enough. I'm so overwhelmed by Mississippi State's campus, and that's not even one of the biggest. On the campus at the University of Texas, they have a shuttle that comes by every fifteen minutes. You have to be able to get on the shuttle, or you'd never get around. You can walk everywhere at the W, and you can walk to town.

42. Perian Collier Conerly, Class of 1949, served as editor of the *Spectator* during her senior year and went on to write several books, including *Football Fundamentals for Feminine Fans* (1963) and *Backseat Quarterback* (2003), which describes her life as the wife of a New York Giants football player.

I encouraged my daughter-in-law to go to the W, and I encouraged my older granddaughter to go. But my second granddaughter is a graduate of State. There was no encouraging her; she had made up her mind where she was going. But nowadays I would say this to anybody: You've got to go to college. That is so important. I'm also a firm believer in going to the community college. I did not feel that way when I started college. I thought, "Junior college?" That was really misnamed. A community college is different. You can live at home and go to the community college. We have dorms here at Alcorn,[43] and the coed students can live there, but most of the students don't because it costs so much. You can live in the dorm and pay all your room and board at Copiah-Lincoln Community College at Wesson for what it costs to live in the dorm at Alcorn. It's terribly expensive because it is a four-year university. But you have to have at least one degree now, and I think you need two. Life was certainly different for me after I got my professional degree. It meant so much to me personally. Nobody else knew it, but I knew it. I came to the community college to work after I was sixty. Can you imagine changing careers when you're sixty years old? Several of the students have told me that I have been an inspiration to them. I have encouraged young women to go to the community college in their thirties and forties. Maybe they didn't see the importance of going on to college earlier, but they have to have those degrees if they're going to do anything. People pay you for what they think you know. And there's a way to go to school, no matter what. You can find money. In fact, my second granddaughter went on that critical needs scholarship.[44] The first year that she taught they paid back one year. The second year that she taught they paid back the second year. She got a letter in September, during her third year of teaching, that her debt had been paid: over forty thousand

43. Alcorn State University, founded in 1871, was the first state-supported higher educational institution for African Americans, and it remains predominantly black.

44. The Critical Needs Teacher Loan/Scholarship Program is open to juniors and seniors at Mississippi's colleges and universities. In exchange for financial aid, each student agrees to earn a class A teacher's license and to take a job in one of the state's "critical needs" areas immediately after graduation. For every year of teaching, one year of loan obligation is eliminated.

dollars. Is that not incredible? They need teachers, and I think education is a wonderful field.

The librarian's place in an educational institution is a very powerful one. I've often thought about the importance of being honest in book selection. One has to choose books that present all sides of an issue, but if one were not honest, you could have only Karl Marx books, for example. I considered the job a very important job. I didn't go around telling people this, but I tried to make sure that I had every idea represented. It was there whether they wanted to read it or not. I love the library world—a world of books.

Lenore Loving Prather
Class of 1953

APRIL 3, 2006

INTERVIEWED BY SUSAN PUCKETT AND BARBARA WHITE

FILMED BY CHRIS JENKINS

TRANSCRIBED BY RACHEL FORESTER AND CHRISTIE COLLINS

LENORE LOVING, BORN IN WEST POINT, MISSISSIPPI, on September 17, 1931, is the daughter of attorney Byron Herold Loving, who served as a state representative and state senator from Clay County, and Hattie Morris Loving, who was educated at Draughn's Business College in Jackson, Mississippi, and who served as deputy circuit clerk and as election commissioner for Clay County. A speech major at MSCW, Lenore Loving participated in the Theatre Guild, the Forensic Council, the Student Christian Association, College Oratory, the Debate Team, the President's Council, and Tournament Plays. She earned a certificate in parliamentary procedure, directed the radio program, and was elected a student government representative. During her senior year, she was elected class secretary-treasurer and chosen as a senior chaperone. She went on to receive a law degree from Ole Miss in 1955 and began practicing law in West Point with her father. She married Robert

Brooks Prather (1931–97), a businessman and attorney, in 1957. In 1965, she became West Point's municipal judge, and in 1972, Governor John Bell Williams appointed her as Mississippi's first female chancery judge. She served in that position until 1983, winning reelection in 1975 and 1982; Governor William Winter then appointed her as Mississippi's first female Supreme Court justice. She won reelection to the court in 1984 and 1992 and in 1993 became presiding justice. From 1998 to 2000, she served as chief justice of the Mississippi Supreme Court. In 2001–2, she served as MUW's interim president. She is a member of the Mississippi Bar, the Mississippi Bar Foundation, the American Bar Association, and the American Judicature Society. An MUW Medal of Excellence and Alumnae Achievement Award winner, she is also a member of the University of Mississippi Alumni Hall of Fame. A member of St. Paul's Episcopal Church in Columbus, she has served on the vestry and on a variety of other church committees. She lives in Columbus.

LP: My early education was all through the public schools of West Point, Mississippi. At that time we didn't have kindergartens or things like that, but twelve years entirely in the West Point High School building, which is still standing. At that time it only had one classroom per grade. West Point was small. But that was my early childhood training, and it got me prepared for admission to the W in later years.

BW: Why did you decide to go to the W?
LP: I don't know that I thought about anything else. I had had a half-sister[1] who attended the W. It was just kind of an expected thing. Most of the young ladies of that time considered furthering their education at a women's college. So with that expectation and the closeness to my hometown, I applied for the W and spent four years there.

1. Margaret Ponder Loving Noonan, Class of 1944.

SP: What did you study?

LP: As I began college life, I don't know that I had an idea exactly about what I wanted to do. I like to preface this with a little bit of background about my age and the time in which I lived. Since I was born in 1931, still the throes of the depression era, I think my whole lifestyle was set by the events of the preceding depression and the lack of a lot of money, the lack of a lot of affluence, generally, in society. I think with the World War II years and the sacrifices that we all had to go through, we had kind of a change in our attitudes about life in general. So when I came to the W, I didn't have a specific major in mind. I didn't know that I wanted to go to law school, but I took the required courses. And among those courses was a required course in speech or communications. With that, I was introduced to a first-year professor that was head of the speech department, Harvey Cromwell.[2] He was my major professor. And his influence, I think, on my life was immense. As a freshman student in that required course, I learned to know him and enjoyed his instruction. He had as one of his classes debate work, and he tried to interest me in joining it, and I didn't think I could do that. But he insisted that I try it. Dr. Cromwell was the sponsor of debate at the W, and he promoted participation in what at that time was a debate organization among all of the institutions of higher learning in Mississippi. Debate clubs within the state debated each other, and we had tournaments in debate work. And that kind of led me to some consideration of law school. Certainly the participation in the debate program at MUW for four years was a very definite influence on the rest of my life. With debate work, we got to know people within the state and outside of the state. We went to regional tournaments. When I was a senior, the MUW Debate Team went with Dr. Cromwell to Notre Dame, in South Bend, Indiana, for a tournament and participated in a debate on the assigned topic. In that day, a competition topic was selected for the Southeast, perhaps throughout the nation. Everybody debated the one subject, and we competed

2. Harvey Cromwell (1907–77) served as director of speech and theater, dean of arts and sciences, and dean of the graduate school at MSCW between 1949 and 1975. In 1977, the new Harvey Cromwell Communications Center was named for him.

against each other in all the tournaments. So we went to Notre Dame and participated, and we didn't win. We also competed individually in other things like oral interpretation. I did oratory, and I had a speech that Dr. Cromwell suggested that I do on the "newer South." I thought it was really distinctive for the W to have an opportunity to participate in programs like that. I don't think they do that any more, and it's a shame.

I think the genes from my father had some effect on my choice of law, since my father was a third-generation lawyer. I grew up around the courthouse in West Point. My daddy's office was right behind the courthouse, and as a child after school I spent the afternoons at the courthouse yard, and I remember interacting with some people who also became judges—Billy Coleman, from Columbus, whose father was an officer in the courthouse.[3] I remember back in the era when you didn't have air-conditioning, you waited until night when it cooled off to go have supper. We'd sit out in front of the old courthouse in West Point and listen to all those wonderful stories about the law and lawyers and the jury system. That had a major effect on my later decision to go to law school and see if I could get through. I wasn't sure I could make it, but I just wanted to see if I could tackle that and get a graduate degree.

SP: What else do you remember about campus life at the W?

LP: Oh! I could tell you lots about campus life. I think the campus life was a real awakening because of the wonderful advantages that MSCW had to offer. We had musical programs at the auditorium. We had Miss Pohl's[4] wonderful ballet dancers, and we had visiting celebrities that sang. I remember one year we had an opera singer, a male who was very handsome. We had those types of activities that were not available in the small town that I grew up in. So we had a broadening experience at college, with some of the cultural things that we missed as younger

3. Judge William Coleman Jr. (b. 1929) retired from the Hinds County Circuit Court in 1996 after twenty years as a circuit court judge. In 2006 he was appointed by the Mississippi Supreme Court as a special judge to help relieve the backlog of criminal cases in the Hinds County Circuit Court.

4. Emma Ody Pohl (1880–1966) joined II & C in 1907, when she was hired to develop the department of physical education. She taught that subject until her retirement in 1955.

children. Now, the year that I was a senior, I was president of the Theatre Guild, and we asked to go to see a play, a staged Broadway play, *South Pacific*,[5] on tour in Birmingham. We had about two busloads. Those were some of the extras that I didn't have as a younger person but was afforded at college. And of course, Miss Pohl's ballet dancers were always a treat and very professional. I know any W graduate will remember the Zouave. That was a wonderful opportunity that the students participated in that everybody would come to see. The pictures of Zouave remind me of a lot of happy memories, even though it was a lot of hard work getting there.

BW: What was your social life like? Did a lot of boys come to the campus?

LP: Oh no. Again, we didn't have social life as it is today. Of course, first of all, it was a girls' school. When I came as a freshman to MSCW, I knew or understood exactly what the rules were. I think when I came to school as a freshman, we understood that we were going to have closed weekends for six weeks—couldn't go home for six weeks. It would be unheard of today. My roommate that freshman year left early and got married. I think the closed campus was first an encouragement to get students over homesickness and then also to have them there, hopefully, long enough to get accustomed to the curriculum. There were a lot of other rules and regulations that today seem rather unusual. I remember that we had a certain hour that we had to be in the dorm at night. I think the doors were closed at 10:00. Then we had a certain hour that we had to have lights out. My dormitory was South Callaway. If you've ever been to South Callaway, it's a very small dorm, but the rooms that the individual students had were very large—much larger than a typical room today. And the door had a glass transom, so the light in the room was visible from the hall. At 10:30, we had bed check and lights out. We became very ingenious about how we were going to get everything done. In South Callaway, what we would

5. *South Pacific*, a musical by Richard Rogers and Oscar Hammerstein, opened on Broadway in April 1949.

do was get in the huge closets after lights out with our textbooks that we hadn't finished reading for the next day and use a flashlight so we could finish reading our lessons. I don't know whether the other girls were able to do that since their closets may not have been that large.

There were other rules about certain things, like we couldn't wear a scarf while walking to town. I don't really know a justification for that. On campus, when we went to gym—and gym was required—we had a regimented uniform, blue shorts and a white shirt. When we left the dorm and walked to the gym, we could not walk without a wrap. We had to have a coat or a raincoat on. We didn't walk across campus in a pair of shorts. But I have to say that those classes at the gym were good for everybody, and one of the first things that we did in gym class as freshmen was to have a posture test. Miss Emma Ody Pohl would have everybody come in. I don't remember exactly what our costume was, whether we were in a swimsuit or whether we were in our uniform, but we would have our picture taken. I thought that was kind of crazy, until I realized that some of them would discover after the test that they had a curvature of the spine that might have affected swimming and so forth. We had a certain regimen that we had to pass off in freshman physical education. We had to do some terrible things that I can't even imagine how I did them now, but we had to develop muscles that helped hold the body up straight to maintain good posture, and we had to learn how to swim. There were many students that would have come to the campus without knowing how to swim. I could swim, but if you didn't know how to swim, you had to learn how to swim before you could graduate. That was all well and good, because certainly everybody needs to know how to swim in an emergency.

SP: Were you interested in or influenced by the student government on campus?

LP: There was a strong student government, and not only that, but there was an organization called Civic League.[6] Civic League had to do with

6. The Civic League, organized just after the turn of the twentieth century, was a student organization that took responsibility for the neatness and cleanliness of the dormitories and campus.

the monitoring of the condition of your dormitory room, and I don't remember anything else, but you had to have your room cleaned up and presentable, and the Civic League checked it. We also had organizations that featured the highest-rated academic students. We were encouraged to keep our dorm room clean, to make good grades, and to go to the events that were offered on campus.

I remember one time looking at some of Daddy's financial statements and seeing that in my freshman year, the tuition for the W for the full nine months was just under five hundred dollars. Five hundred dollars. Included in that was all the instruction, of course, but we also had three meals a day and laundry service! Now the laundry was less than desirable in some situations. We sent our sheets and our towels, but with clothes, we had other arrangements that we made. But that was a pretty small amount to pay by today's standards for what we got.

The meals I'll have to comment on. I think many of us gained a lot of weight because the food was so good. And participating in the meals taught several things. We had a whistle at ten minutes of the hour, and another whistle on the hour. The ten-minute whistle reminded us that we had ten minutes to get to the dining room. If we didn't get there, the doors closed, and we just missed the meal. We just couldn't go in after that. So we learned to be punctual. I remember seeing that some of the students that got up late would throw on a raincoat on top of a pair of pajamas and wander to the dining room for breakfast. They had to sit there with their raincoat on the entire meal, but they made it through the door before it closed. We had wonderful meals, absolutely wonderful meals. I never had had spoon bread before, which is supposed to be one of those southern dishes that we all like. And in addition, we stood until the blessing was said. Sometimes we sang the blessing and other times it was given by someone else. We were moved around from time to time to different tables so that we got to know different people. A certain chair at the table was designated as the hostess chair, and whoever sat there (or if that was the only place left if we got there last) was the hostess. The hostess had the responsibility of passing the food or getting additional food. At Shattuck, we had fellowship between the students of the various classes. The seniors would sing to the freshmen, and the freshmen would sing to the sophomores. They each had class songs, which was a unique part of the life in the dining hall.

BW: What can you tell us about required chapel?

LP: We had required chapel, and all students attended. With chapel we had assigned seats. Each seat in Whitfield auditorium had a number on it. And the dean of women, Dean Keirn,[7] had certain persons that she designated as chapel checkers. These were always seniors, and I was selected as a chapel checker. I was so honored; it was a real pleasure! The chapel checker sat on the end of the row. When the program began, the chapel checkers would get up and go from row to row to see if there was a vacant seat down that row. If there was, we were supposed to write down the number. At the end of the program, we took the names of the absentees from chapel to Miss Keirn's office. Now if you were in the infirmary, you got an excuse there, but if you didn't have an excuse, you got a demerit. And if you got so many demerits, you were restricted to campus for the weekend.

I mentioned earlier the wonderful opera singer we all enjoyed. His name was Jerome Hines, and he was a handsome, tall man who had a gorgeous, beautiful voice.[8] When he came to campus, he had a wonderful program that the audience completely loved. We demanded that he had to sing some encores. We clapped and clapped and applauded. And we then clapped and clapped and applauded. And we clapped, and the poor man just stayed on stage just forever that night. The next time we had chapel, Miss Marguerite Goen[9] said, "You need to be instructed that you do not demand more than four encores of a party. It was very, very impolite to ask for all those encores." That's the first time I've ever heard

7. Nellie Sutton Keirn (1885–1975), Class of 1906, was hired at II & C in 1906 as a teaching fellow. She taught until 1919, when she became dean, serving until 1955. She also held the post of acting president of MSCW in 1929–30.
8. Jerome Hines (1921–2003) was a very popular bass with the Metropolitan Opera. He performed at MSCW on April 30, 1951.
9. Marguerite Goen (1896–1977) held a variety of posts at MSCW between 1928 and 1963, including teacher of secretarial science, student counselor, and dean of students. Goen Residence Hall was named in her honor.

that! It was one of those instructions that we received as a part of our education from the social adviser, I believe was her title. And she would also instruct us from time to time about what was proper etiquette. So we learned we could not and should not demand more than four encores of a guest artist.

SP: What can you tell us about the administrators?
LP: Dr. Parkinson[10] was president three years while I was there. The rules that I talked about earlier, about time limits and lights out and doors locked, were just part of the expectation he and Mrs. Parkinson[11] had. We had many, many rules and regulations. I didn't have a lot of contact with the Parkinsons. I, fortunately, had no reason to go see the president. I did take a parliamentary procedure course with Mrs. Parkinson. She taught on the side. It was not a required course; it was just something for our general knowledge. It was another plus for the W that the girls were afforded the opportunity to learn about parliamentary procedures. She taught it every year, and she was very good. I don't know much about Dr. Parkinson and Mrs. Parkinson. Maybe it was because I was often on debate trips that I didn't have many activities with them, but in my senior year, Dr. Hogarth[12] came as president. In that year, there were a number of rule changes that were more in keeping with the lifestyle of that era, and some of those restrictions we had had earlier were removed.

BW: How would you compare life in law school with your life at the W?
LP: Law school certainly wasn't as regimented as the rules and regulations of the W. None of that type of regulation existed at all. At law school, we were graduate students. As such, we lived either off campus or on campus. I lived in what was considered the graduate dorm at Ole Miss. The female graduate students and law students were allowed to be housed there, and I think most of us did live there. My good friend Mary

10. Burney Lynch Parkinson (1887–1972) served as president of MSCW from 1932 until 1952.
11. Dera Dry Parkinson (1887–1979). In 1927, she became the first woman to earn a Ph.D. (in psychology) from the University of South Carolina.
12. Charles Pinckney Hogarth (1911–97) served as president of MSCW from 1952 until 1977.

Libby Bickerstaff[13] and I were both in Ricks Hall. There were no restrictions other than just get to class and answer the questions. We had freedom of movement in the law school. I don't think I ever felt intimidated or resented at all by the professors or the students. There were just three women in the freshman law class that August, and that was the largest number of female students that they had had in any one class up to that time. There was a fourth female that came during our two-year period in law school, but we entered the class with three females.

The coursework was intimidating. We just hoped to be able to make the grade. We were given a case assignment book with all the cases that had been decided in the past and from which we were supposed to be able to pick out the root of law. In the classes we would be asked questions by the professors, and what was intimidating was our being able to answer them correctly and those professors being the ones who decided whether or not we could make it in law school. There was one professor of note, and he was John Fox, sort of the Great White Father of the law school.[14] He was a tall, stately man, snow-white hair and a bellowing voice. I was always hoping and praying that he didn't call on me for one of the questions. But as we went through law school, he usually had a person that he liked to argue with in class. Of course it was a wonderful experience for a person who aspired to be a lawyer to be able to argue back in a setting where there wasn't going to be a verdict for you or against you. All you had to worry about was whether you got out of law school or not! In law school, I didn't feel any intimidation, but it wasn't one of those fields that many women entered. Evelyn Gandy,[15] for example, was ahead of us, but there were very few. Now today, it's quite a different story. My daughter went to law school, and when she was in law school, the class was about one-third female. Today in law school,

....

13. Mary Elizabeth Bickerstaff Payne (b. 1932), Class of 1954. See the interview with her in this volume.

14. John H. Fox Jr. (1909–65) taught law at Ole Miss from 1932 until his death.

15. Evelyn Gandy (1920–2007) graduated from law school at the University of Mississippi in 1943, the only woman in her class. She was elected to the Mississippi legislature in 1948 and became the first woman elected to statewide office in Mississippi in 1959, when she won the post of state treasurer. She served as lieutenant governor from 1976 until 1980 and ran for governor in 1979 and in 1983.

you'd find basically half women and half men. So it was a unique time for us to get through it and survive. The main thing is, we survived.

SP: What did you expect your career and your life to be like when you got out of law school?

LP: I had no idea except that I knew that I was going to go back home and practice with my daddy. And I did that. Other than that, I didn't have any aspirations. I just wanted to practice law. There is opportunity in law to help a lot of people, and I thoroughly enjoyed my association with clients and the chance I had to help them with legal matters. But I had no idea that that would lead to other things. In 1960, my father died, and I was alone in the office. But I managed to make a few dollars and stay afloat. I was married, and then later my husband went to law school. After we managed to get through that two-year period, he came back, and he and I practiced in West Point for a while. But it's pretty difficult financially for a two-lawyer marriage to make a living out of the income of one law office when we had children coming along. Three children were an expense. So Bob didn't stay in West Point for very long but went on to Columbus to set up a law practice in Columbus. That allowed us to have two offices instead of the one in a smaller town. As I said, it was hard to make ends meet, so to supplement things, I started teaching at Mississippi State University in the speech communication department. That was when communications became required in all the state curriculums, not just for the communication majors. When they made that conversion in the core curriculum, they found out they needed a lot more speech teachers. From the entire area, we had three W graduates, I think, that taught in the speech department at Mississippi State. I did that teaching about seven years, going to campus three days a week, coming back to the office in the afternoon, and staying there to make a few dollars out of the law office, taking any opportunity for a little income. Along the way, I had been offered the judgeship of the city court in West Point, and that was a recommendation that came from the male city attorney. For about seven years, I was city judge. On certain days, I was going to Mississippi State for class, and the rest of the time I was spending in the office. My mother was my secretary, so between all the family members, we managed to make it.

Those were busy days, hard days, long days, but really enjoyable when I look back on them. And of course all this experience afforded me the opportunity for further advancement. As city judge, I didn't have anything to deal with except the city ordinances, although I did bind over to the grand jury if there was a criminal case of enough significance. But it gave me the opportunity to be considered for an appointment to the Chancery Court bench. I was lucky enough that Governor John Bell Williams appointed me to the Chancery Court. That was a post that was extremely important and probably one of the most enjoyable posts I have had, because that court deals with people and issues involving family, although the jurisdiction covers more than that. It was a wonderful opportunity to try to help people resolve family matters that were before the court. It dealt with child custody, which wasn't always enjoyable to make a decision on, but it was an interest I had because I loved the family. And I always tried to see what was best for the children in those cases. So I was able, because of that small job in the city of West Point, to have a track record where I was open to an appointment on the Chancery Court bench. Then from there, I was happy to have the opportunity to be appointed to the Supreme Court bench. In 1982, I went to the Mississippi Supreme Court as a justice.

BW: When you were practicing law, what kind of cases did you take on?

LP: Anything that came in the door! In a small town, I pretty well took any cases that came in. Collections were part of it; divorces were part of it, loan closings on real estate sales. I didn't do a lot of criminal work, although I did when my daddy was alive. Daddy was a wonderful criminal lawyer. With him I participated, but I didn't prefer the criminal defense work myself. I dealt more with family issues or real estate matters, business issues, tax law. In a small town you do some of all of it.

SP: Did you have to run for election to the Supreme Court?

LP: I did. I was appointed initially but had to stand for election in a short period of time. I was elected without opposition for two consecutive terms, and that was equal to eighteen years on the Supreme Court bench. In my last campaign for reelection, which was in 2000, I was defeated, and it was all right.[16] It was time for me to come home and enjoy life.

BW: How did the judges on the Supreme Court treat you? Was it kind of an old-boy network?

LP: I think women have advanced a lot in women's rights in this last quarter of a century. There is more openness to women in any field they want to follow. When I was appointed to the court, Chief Justice Neville Patterson[17] went out of his way to make me feel welcomed and to give me help and instruction with anything that I wanted to know. He was a gentlemen and a scholar, and he was very helpful in my adjustment to the court. In addition to that, when I became chancery judge, my chancellor at that time was Chancellor Robert Sugg[18] from Eupora, Mississippi. I learned a lot under Judge Sugg. Then Judge Sugg was offered a position on the Supreme Court by John Bell Williams, which made the vacancy in the district Chancery Court. I was appointed as successor to Judge Robert Sugg. When I was appointed to the Supreme Court, Judge Sugg was still on the court. So I had my teacher and my mentor from the chancery bench also as a wonderful help on the Supreme Court. Neville Patterson was also a former chancellor, so I felt right at home with the men on the court. I didn't feel any hesitancy at all to ask questions if I needed information or help in anything. They were very nice to offer. And I'll tell you, the system was very organized. I knew what was expected out of me. We knew how many cases we were going to get.

16. Chuck Easley defeated Prather in the 2000 election.

17. Neville Patterson (1916–87) served on the Mississippi Supreme Court as a justice, presiding justice, and chief justice between 1964 and his retirement in 1986.

18. Robert P. Sugg (b. 1916) served as a Chancery Court judge from 1951 to 1971 and on the Mississippi Supreme Court from 1971 to 1983.

We knew how much time we had to get a decision ready and how much time we had to circulate. The organization was already in place, so all I had to do was follow it.

SP: What important cases came before the Supreme Court in those years?
LP: I guess the most earthshaking, emotionally draining cases were the death penalty cases. We did have two death penalty executions while I was on the court. Those were really the most difficult ones. It's a hard decision to make, and I remember that with those two executions, we stayed at the court until the execution was carried out. They usually did it late at night. It's hard to have an agreement to execute somebody, even if they did heinous crimes. Two executions were traumatic for all members of the court, and we haven't had any since then either.

BW: What social or racial changes have you seen in Mississippi?
LP: I'll speak to that from the standpoint of the Supreme Court. Shortly after I came, Reuben Anderson, who was the first black judge on the Mississippi Supreme Court, was appointed.[19] I remember when Reuben Anderson came for his swearing in, Mike Sullivan[20] put his robe on him. Reuben was an easy person to like and to work with. When he left, Fred Banks[21] came. Both were very hard workers. They were astute, and they both made a wonderful contribution, and I enjoyed serving with them. Now another female, Kay Cobb,[22] is one of the minorities whose term began while I was there, and I was so delighted to have a short time to work with her before I was defeated in 2000.

19. Reuben V. Anderson (b. 1942) served on the Mississippi Supreme Court from 1985 until 1990.
20. Michael D. Sullivan (1938–2000) served on the Mississippi Supreme Court from 1984 until his death, at which time he held the post of presiding justice.
21. Fred L. Banks Jr. (b. 1942) served on the Mississippi Supreme Court from 1991 until 2001; from 2000 to 2001, he held the post of presiding justice.
22. Kay Beevers Cobb (b. 1942), Class of 1963, served on the Mississippi Supreme Court from 1991 until 2007. From 2004 until the end of her tenure, she served as a presiding justice. She was the court's second female justice. She served as president of the MUW Alumnae Association from 1983–84.

SP: What did you do from the time you graduated from the W until you started law school?

LP: I went back home to West Point, and I was offered a job at the West Point radio station. I had been a communications major. We had a radio station on campus. We'd broadcast from Orr Hall. We had microphones, proper insulation on the walls, and we were on the air each day for thirty minutes on the Midsouth network. That was a small network in this general geographical area. So having done radio work at the W as part of a speech major's responsibilities, I had experience. At the W, we had to take part in every activity in the speech department. So this was the summertime, and I was offered a program on "Sandwich Time." I was to write a script, be my own editor, get all the information, give the recipes that I wanted to give, and have a fifteen-minute segment, which I did. At the end of the week, I think I got paid like three dollars for one fifteen-minute segment. So I had about fifteen dollars pay coming to me from that little activity, but that wasn't enough to make it if I was going to be on my own. So I decided I might look for something a little bit more productive from a financial standpoint, and I decided to try law school.

SP: When did you meet your husband?

LP: It was after I came out of law school. He was at Mississippi State as a student, and his major was hotel/restaurant management. He was working part time as a student at a local hotel in West Point, and I met him there. It was just one of those things. We began dating, found out that we had mutual interests, and we married about six months afterward. Then we lived in West Point. After he graduated from State and was working as a resident manager, he went on to be the head of food service for the Henry Clay Hotel in West Point. And we stayed there probably six months. I haven't really thought about it in a long while. Then he had an opportunity to be manager of the country club in Columbus, so we moved to Columbus. And that's how we met and married.

BW: When you were on the Mississippi Supreme Court, where did you feel like you had the most influence?

LP: I was a chancery judge for a long enough time to see some inequities in the laws dealing with women's rights. My background had showed me that something had to be done by the Supreme Court with reference to the custody of children and to the equitable distribution of property between husband and wife when divorce occurred. As a chancery judge, I could not take away title to real estate under the law at that time. So if the husband of a family had all the property—the real estate—in his name, I could not divest title from him and share the real estate with the spouse. There was one case that I remember where everything was in the husband's name, and the only thing that I could give to the wife as a distribution of her share for her contribution to the relationship was just a money judgment, and I did that. I didn't know how she would collect it, since there was a mortgage against the business and a mortgage against the home. But all I could give her was just a money judgment. In the meantime, I was offered the position on the Supreme Court. I followed that lawsuit with another judge. I was trying to see how she came out, because I believed she needed to have some part of that which had been acquired over a long period of time in the marriage. She tried to seek a judgment to take that one hundred thousand dollar money judgment and place it against the husband's business, but the chancery judge refused to do that. So she didn't get anything out of that marriage, and it had been a long-term marriage. And she had made a contribution, I felt. I felt badly about that, and I wondered what could be done about that.

BW: When you were on the Mississippi Supreme Court, where did you feel that you had the most effect?

LP: There was a case assigned to me, just by chance. It was not a case I picked. All cases were assigned and we had to take the case we were assigned. With this case, I could tell from the first that there was an opportunity to do something about distribution of property between husband and wife at the time of divorce. I did a lot of research and found out what other states were doing, and I decided to propose a change in our law in Mississippi to have a more equitable distribution of marital assets. Following that lead, I proposed an opinion. Needless to say, it was an earthshaking change in Mississippi law. There was a lot of discussion in the chambers of the Supreme Court about that case and what should be done. Then there came another case of similar nature, and it was assigned to another judge by rote, not because he picked it. For two full years we were working diligently, trying to decide how we could decide these two cases. What effect would this change in the law be? Finally after two years, the two cases, *Ferguson v. Ferguson* and *Hemsley v. Hemsley* (1994), came down the same day. We knew the two cases were going to cause very drastic changes in the Chancery Court all over the state. But we did make equitable distribution to women in divorce cases. I think perhaps the courts are still dealing with the change in that law.

Another important area that I dealt with was how you determine which parent should have custody of children in a marriage. That was something that again I had noticed a need to have some better guidelines, and I wrote another decision with new guidelines to follow in making decisions about custody of children in divorce. This case was *Albright v. Albright* (1983).

SP: What were your plans when you left the court?
LP: I didn't have any. I had planned to stay on at the court and be able to do that longer. But with the change of circumstances, I came back home, and I didn't know exactly what I'd be doing. However, my mother was sick shortly after my coming back home to Columbus. I was able to help her through a medical procedure. Then as time moved on, I realized I might have another job offering.

BW: What was that?
LP: As the events of that first year that I was home progressed, there was a resignation by the president of MUW, Clyda Rent,[23] whom I had always supported and loved. I thought she did a wonderful job with her years as president of our university. But she resigned from the W, and I was

23. Clyda Stokes Rent (b. 1943), MUW's first noninterim female president, held the post from 1989 until 2001.

offered the position of interim president. I was completely flabbergasted but welcomed with open arms the opportunity to come to my university and help it out in a time of need. I hated to see Dr. Rent leave, but I was happy to lead the W for a short period of time. I think I came in on August 1, 2001, and I had so much help from all those wonderful people. The W has a wonderful staff. Dr. Rent had such a wonderful working relationship with all the people in her office. They knew everything, and they knew every alum. So it was a great time for me, a wonderful, enjoyable event. I was glad to pay something back to the university that gave me such a wonderful beginning.

BW: What were your major contributions as interim president of the W?

LP: I hope I made a contribution. I thought that the W needed to give reassurance to alums, to faculty, and to students about how strong our university was. And that it was here to stay. I also tried when I came in to develop relationships with all those separate groups at the W. I met with the faculty to tell them what I had in mind for the year. The staff were loyal beyond words, and we tried to help them out a little bit. I remember for the staff that first year, I knew they hadn't had a raise in a long time. Just as a little appreciation, and without knowledge of the college board, because I didn't ask permission since I didn't want to be refused, I decided to give them the Wednesday before Thanksgiving off. So that gave them a long weekend from Tuesday until the next Monday in appreciation for their efforts. The next semester, I got hints saying, "Are you going to do that again this year?" It just happened that the Fourth of July fell on a Thursday that year, and typically on Friday, we'd have to come back to work. So I exceeded a bit of what the college board requires, but we gave them another holiday for that. And everyone appreciated that, getting two nice long weekends during the school year for the staff as well as the faculty. But with all that, I think I was most interested in trying to assure everyone that the W was long term and that it was here to stay. And I wanted to encourage students. I had an opportunity early on in my tenure there at the W to do something that I thought that the students would enjoy. That was to change some of the planning that had been done. They have a wonderful food service at the W—wonderful food and a wonderful chef that prepares it. And as other things were being changed around the W, there was a change in the seating arrangement for the student cafeteria. I was asked if I would consider changing that again, because they didn't think that what had been changed was what students today like to see in a dining room. I said to the staff, "Why don't you just bring me a plan and let me see what you have to offer me." The plan that was in place was more like a dining-room-style arrangement. The food service contractor wanted to make it a food court. Many of the colleges have food courts, and apparently that is what most students liked. I considered that change and thought it was necessary for us to be in line with what students want and what is common in other colleges and universities. So I made the plan to change it, and they drew up a plan to make it into a food court, which turned out to be extremely popular. Students really like it.

In the year that I was there, there was a selection of a new president, and interviews were being held on campus for the final candidates. When a candidate was selected, which was Dr. Claudia Limbert,[24] of course, she announced that she could come in on July 1, 2002, so I served until that time. And I tried to offer her as much help as I could during that transition.

BW: What people or places or events have been the major influences in your life?

LP: Goodness, there have been so many. But certainly my parents above all have been major influences, and also my husband, who has been my greatest supporter and my greatest promoter. He did everything to promote me rather than himself, and he was very, very unselfish about what came my way. He was responsible for a lot of initiative that was taken in my receiving judgeships. And my children have always been supportive of me. As I got to the Supreme Court, they were getting older, but we

24. Claudia Limbert (b. 1940) became president of MUW in 2002.

had one daughter still left in high school—Melinda was a senior when I went to work at the Supreme Court—so it was not a difficult job there from the standpoint of their ages, since they were at or near college age. But it was hard on my husband, since I was away during the week. But the Supreme Court position was something that my husband encouraged me to take, so there wasn't much trauma with that. I was sorry that he was alone, but he had Magellan, our dog!

SP: How have you juggled being a wife, mother, grandmother, and judge?
LP: I had some household help. When the children were little, I had household help each day of the week. As they got older, I did not. I had one of best chefs in the world, my husband. He had been a hotel/restaurant manager. He loved to cook, and he could throw together a wonderful meal anytime. And we didn't always stay at home. We enjoyed eating out and visiting places that were renowned for good food when we traveled. We traveled a little throughout the world. We enjoyed doing that, and we always found a good first-class restaurant to eat at. But I had some wonderful household help. And of course my mother was an invaluable help when I was working those years at Mississippi State. She was at the office in West Point, and she would go pick up the children after school. So my family has helped support everything I've done, and I couldn't have done it without them.

BW: What have you learned in life that you would like to share with future W students?
LP: I can certainly say that in order to be successful and to have some of the privileges of life with a few of the luxuries that go along with it, any student today needs to get all the education they can get. The W has a wonderful faculty. They had a wonderful faculty when I was there, and I found that to be just as true when I returned to be interim president. The faculty affords them an opportunity to get a superior education and to be successful in life in whatever their chosen field may be. But today, you don't just need an undergraduate degree. I think that you have to

go forward beyond that to be successful in most of the professions. I encourage students to get all the education that they can beyond the undergraduate degree. I feel, too, that taking advantage of the extracurricular things in a college or in a community was extremely important to me. Being involved with public affairs is another area that W students should stress. W students are still taught to take part in events in school. You should continue to make participation in a variety of events a priority in the future. With public issues, try to make a difference in making some change that needs to be made. I guess that's what you can say I tried to do as I was given opportunities throughout my life.

Mary Elizabeth Bickerstaff Payne
Class of 1954

APRIL 3, 2006

INTERVIEWED BY SUSAN PUCKETT AND BARBARA WHITE

FILMED BY CHRIS JENKINS

TRANSCRIBED BY AMBER KING

MARY ELIZABETH BICKERSTAFF WAS BORN ON MARCH 27, 1931, in Gulfport, Mississippi. Her mother was Emily Augusta Cook Bickerstaff; her father, Reece O. Bickerstaff, represented Harrison County in the Mississippi legislature from 1936 to 1955. Mary Libby Bickerstaff spent two years at the W, during which time she was active in a diverse group of organizations, including the Forensic Council and the Student Christian Association. She transferred to the University of Mississippi and graduated from the Ole Miss law school in 1955. She served as a professor of law and as founding dean of the Mississippi College School of Law before she was elected to Mississippi's new Court of Appeals in 1994, the first and still only woman to serve on that court. In 1955, she married Bobby R. Payne, who eventually became director of central records for the Mississippi Employment Security Commission. She has served in all three branches of state government, first drafting legislation, then holding the position of executive director of the Mississippi Judiciary Commission, and finally becoming assistant state attorney general. Payne retired from the Court of Appeals in 2001 to devote more time to her public speaking engagements and to write down her family history. She is also working on a history of the Mississippi College School of Law. In 1998, she helped begin Mississippi's Task Force on Gender Fairness. She has received the Women in Higher Education Mississippi Network Woman of the Year award, the MUW Alumnae Achievement Award, and the MUW Medal of Excellence. She lives in Pearl.

MP: I grew up in Gulfport. My daddy was in the legislature. My mother ran a boardinghouse or did whatever she could to help supplement our income, because at that time, the legislators had to pay all their expenses except mileage one way to Jackson at the first day of the session and mileage one way back at the adjournment. All the rest of the expenses—staying in the hotel and things like that—had to be paid by our family. So that's why Mother worked. Mother did other things also. Eventually, she took the exam to become an employment interviewer with the Mississippi Employment Security Commission. She got a job as a file clerk, making seventy-five dollars a month, but that was sure money.

I was born the year that all the banks closed. I don't remember the depression much, but I have a depression mind-set because I never throw anything away. I believe you can always find somebody who could use whatever you've got. Daddy was a lawyer, and that really didn't impress me much when I was a child. What did impress me was after my having begun ballet lessons in the first grade, the following year I went to MSCW for my cousin's[1] graduation. In those days, graduation was a week of festivities, and one of the events was Miss Pohl's[2] ballet. So I knew from the second grade on, I was going to MSCW, and I was going

1. Ida Frances Cook Klages, Class of 1940.
2. Emma Ody Pohl (1880–1966) joined II & C in 1907, when she was hired to develop the department of physical education. She taught that subject until her retirement in 1955.

to study ballet under Miss Pohl. I didn't have any late epiphany that made me decide to go to the W. Nobody recruited me. I went to the W because I knew I was going there to study ballet. I did continue studying ballet through the twelfth grade and went on to the W. In the meantime, however, along about the eighth grade, I guess, I learned that if I were to become a ballerina, in order to make a living, I'd have to move to New York, and I knew I couldn't stay that far away from my daddy. I'd get too homesick, so I had to look for something else. Ultimately, I came to realize that God was calling me into the ministry of jurisprudence and that I would be going to law school. I didn't want to spend all that time way up in Oxford, so I went to the W for the first two years and loved it. If they'd had a law school, I never would have left.

BW: Tell us about your high school years.

MP: We lived right across the street from the school, so I would sleep late. When the first bell rang, I would leave home, dash across the street, get my books from my locker, and get in my seat by the second bell, which was five minutes later. It was just wonderful living right across the street. Of course, when I got to the W, I had to walk across campus. In high school I was in the speakers' club. I was in each of the plays that I was eligible for. I was in oration contests. I never won first place, but I did love public speaking. At Gulfport High School, at that time, we had a Book of Golden Deeds, I think it was called, and if you had enough points in that book, you got a literary letter. It was in English script rather than like an athletic letter, and I earned one. I never could afford to buy a sweater to put it on, so I've now got it in a shadow box. I was very much involved with extracurricular activities. Speakers' club met every Tuesday night. We had something called Y Teens in connection with YWCA. I hope it's not immodest, but when my group was talking about who they were going to vote for for elite titles, I figured that since I'd always been number one in my class, that it was a foregone conclusion that I'd get Most Intellectual. And so I asked Patricia Barrett, "Who is our crowd voting Most Likely to Succeed?" And she said, "Why you, of course." And I was flabbergasted. But I got it! Never have

I been quite so surprised as I was by that. Oh, I was also involved in our radio program. We had a high school radio program that we put on once a week. That's about all I can remember about high school except I was dead in love with Billy Overton, who didn't reciprocate.

BW: What are your first memories of the W as a student?

MP: This was before the days of the ACT or the SAT, so we had about four days of entrance exams. I was terrified of them because I even hated the Weekly Reader tests in grammar school that they would give us where we had to read everything fast and we had to answer by multiple choice. I always found multiple choice difficult, because none of them was exactly what I would answer. I would argue with the answer rather than put something down. Anyway, at the W, we had English proficiency, and we had other proficiency tests; we knew that the grades would be in on a Friday, and we were not registered until we qualified with all those exams. I knew I was a slow reader, and on the bulletin board, Miss Goen[3] had written five names of people to come to her office that day. Mine was one of them. I went in fear and trembling, and she said that the grades had come back from national, and I thought, "I am going to have to run away. I'm going to disgrace Gulfport High School. They're sending me home, and I was the first in my class." Anyway, she went ahead to talk about it, and then she said, "Of the girls from the W who took the test, five of them were in the ninety-fifth percentile, and your grade was the highest." Then she said, "Therefore, Miss Bickerstaff, what I think you need to know at the beginning of your college days is that if you don't make straight As, both you and this institution will have failed." When I told somebody that later, they said, "What pressure!" I said, "Pressure? It was such a relief. I thought I was going to be sent home, and all I had to do was make good grades." Except for a one-hour course in personal use typing and those gym classes that didn't count, I did make straight As. I made a C in personal use typing, and I

3. Marguerite Goen (1896–1977) held a variety of posts at MSCW between 1928 and 1963, including teacher of secretarial science, student counselor, and dean of students. Goen Residence Hall was named in her honor.

probably would've made an F if I hadn't gotten sick and had the opportunity over the Christmas holidays to practice and practice and practice until I did all of it perfectly. We were also required to take zoology and botany. I had been very skillful in avoiding the science hall in Gulfport High School. It smelled bad. So I had taken two semesters of first-year algebra, two semesters of plane geometry, two semesters of second-year algebra, trigonometry, and solid geometry. But that left me four more semesters of science that I had to have to graduate. So I took four semesters of home economics. I may have gotten more out of the home economics than anything else that I'd studied, but when I got to the W, I could not avoid those frogs in formaldehyde. I had to take that. And it just so happened that my zoology class was just before lunch—that was when I had to deal with those old dead frogs. But I loved botany. I still look at tree bark and leaves and point out to myself what each of those is. But I didn't want to take either one of the classes. At the end of the first year, Miss Cheek[4] called me in, and she said, "Miss Bickerstaff, I see that you do well in science. Would you like to consider majoring in biology?" I said, "No, ma'am! I certainly would not." And she said, "But you made such good grades." And I said, "Miss Cheek, that's your teaching, not my learning that made those good grades. You're such a marvelous teacher I couldn't help myself. But no, I am not interested in any of your courses that I am not forced to take." But Miss Cheek was a wonderful teacher!

BW: Tell us about campus life.

MP: It was so well regimented with us having to go to sleep on time and eating three good meals a day that I gained nine pounds the first nine weeks I was there. I almost couldn't wear my clothes that Mother had bought me in New Orleans to wear to college. I got that off as soon as I got adjusted to the fact that one piece of bread would be enough. We did have good homemade bread. We did a lot of singing. I think that's my favorite memory about the W. We would have dormitory songfests.

4. Maude Cheek (1898–1978) taught biology at MSCW from 1922 until 1961.

Shattuck Hall was my favorite experience my sophomore year because we got to pick where we wanted to be. We were just assigned our other roommates, and I stayed in Columbus Hall my freshman year. I had a wonderful freshman roommate,[5] but she and I had different study habits. She was an art major, and I was a political science major. I needed quiet in order to study and concentrate. She was doing all this artwork, and she just loved using that time to converse. We were required to stay in our room and study from 7:00 to 9:00 or something like that. We did not room together the next year, although we are still good friends. But I loved the people I was with. I loved the fact that the dining hall was two flights down. It was like being in high school again. I could sleep late and still get to breakfast on time. There was a song that was popular called "Sweet Violets,"[6] and our Shattuck songfest did a parody on that. It ended, "Covered all over from roof to floors, covered all over with sweet sophomores." We did a lot of singing. You didn't have to be a voice major to have fun with music.

We had breakfast, and after breakfast, we would then go to the post office, which was in the basement of Hastings, and we would have Morning Watch. At noon, after we had lunch, during the thirty minutes between the time that we got through with lunch and the time that classes started, we would go to Noonday at the Baptist Student Union. We had Saturday classes, and I lived so far away I seldom got to go home. So I was there on Sunday. On Sunday afternoon, we had quiet time; we had to be in our rooms and be quiet from 2:00 to 5:00. I usually took a nap, a pattern I continue on Sunday until this very day. Some students studied, but I thought that I should not do labor on Sunday, so I didn't study on Sunday. Then at about 6:00 every Sunday—I can't remember if it was before or after supper—in Poindexter we had Vespers. There was more encouragement for spiritual growth and moral and cultural enhancement at the W than I've ever found anywhere else. We also had a group that was called the Student Christian Association. I think now it's the Interfaith Council.

5. Maurine Clower Tunnell, Class of 1954.

6. Joseph Emmet wrote "Sweet Violets" for his 1882 musical, *Fritz among the Gypsies*. Dinah Shore recorded a version of the song in 1951.

Sara Barry[7] was the head of that, and she helped coordinate Westminster Presbyterian Fellowship and Baptist Student Union and all those other religious organizations. That was an important part of the campus.

We had chapel, which was required, and I enjoyed it. Everybody thought I was an oddball, but I loved it. We had a variety of programs, but two things stand out in my memory about chapel. One was when Dr. Underwood[8] from the Department of Health came and predicted that within not too long a period of time there would be a vaccine to do away with polio. Now, you have to understand that from my earliest remembrance until I was a freshman in high school, Franklin Delano Roosevelt was our president, and he had had infantile paralysis, which is polio. There had been many ways polio had affected my life: they would close the swimming pools—I spent most of the summer in swimming pools. They had canceled Girls' State between my junior and senior year in high school because there was a polio epidemic, and they couldn't risk having that many girls from all over the state together. I already had my cards printed up. I was going to run for the Girls' State legislature and then run for speaker of the house, and Daddy had gotten my campaign cards printed. It was almost too good to believe for Dr. Underwood to say it. But it came to pass, and people who are my grandchildren's age have no more idea than a jaybird what polio is, and isn't that a blessing? The other thing was that I was impressed with was Dr. Parkinson's[9] prayers, and very often he would pray, "Lord, grant us a true sense of relative values." That has stuck with me even though it's been more than fifty years, because he left when I left. I teased people, saying that Dr. Parkinson couldn't stand to stay at the W if I wasn't there, since he retired in 1952, at the end of his twentieth year. But he had an impact on me. And of course Mrs. Parkinson[10] did also, because

7. Sara Barry, Class of 1951, a Presbyterian, served as president of MSCW's Student Christian Association during her senior year.

8. Dr. Felix J. Underwood (1882–1959) served as head of the Mississippi State Board of Health from 1924 to 1958.

9. Burney Lynch Parkinson (1887–1972) served as president of MSCW from 1932 until 1952.

10. Dera Dry Parkinson (1887–1979). In 1927, she became the first woman to earn a Ph.D. (in psychology) from the University of South Carolina.

she taught parliamentary procedure. I got the certification for parliamentary procedure and have used it considerably since.

BW: What else do you remember about professors or administrators?
MP: Oh, I have one memory of Miss Keirn,[11] but maybe I ought not to tell that. We had closed weekends before exams, and my cousin who had been in the navy—this was in 1951 and I had not seen him in years—was going to be in Artesia, Mississippi, visiting his parents. There was a rule that you couldn't cross the Tombigbee River bridge without being signed out as if you were going for a weekend. Artesia is across the Tombigbee River. My aunt, Ann Cook Spurlock,[12] who those two years just happened to be president of the alumnae association, was a good friend of Miss Keirn's. So she thought, "I'll just go and get a waiver of this closed weekend rule, and I can take Mary Libby over to Harvey and Hazel's to see Harvey Jr."[13] But Miss Keirn said, "No! It is a closed weekend." And Auntie said, "Don't you let people date?" Miss Keirn said, "Oh, yes, but they can't cross the bridge!" And my aunt said, "Why do you have this closed weekend?" "Oh, that's to make sure that students' grades don't get adversely affected." "But she could date so long as she stayed on this side of the bridge?" "Yes." "And that wouldn't adversely affect her grades?" "No, we don't think so." So my aunt said, "Nellie, Mary Libby's grades are not going to be affected no matter what she does. She is a lot better student than some of these people who are going out on dates. Now, you give me permission to take her with me!" Miss Keirn said, "Annie, we have never done this before, and we are not going to do it now." And Auntie said, "Just because you've been wrong for the last twenty-five years doesn't mean you've got to be wrong again!" I didn't get to go see Harvey Jr., but I do have memories of Miss Keirn. I was not participating in the conversation. I was only witness to it.

11. Nellie Sutton Keirn (1885–1975), Class of 1906, was hired at II & C in 1906 as a teaching fellow. She taught until 1919, when she became dean, serving until 1955. She also held the post of acting president of MSCW in 1929–30.
12. Ann Harvey Cook Spurlock (1889–1982), Class of 1911, served as president of the MSCW Alumnae Association from 1950 until 1952.
13. William Harvey Cook (1894–1987), brother of Emily Cook Bickerstaff; his wife, Hazel Vandiver Cook (1899–1989); and their son, William Harvey Cook Jr.

BW: Why did you leave the W, and what did you do after that?

MP: When I entered the W, I knew I was going to be going to law school, and Ole Miss had a program where if you got all of your required courses in your first three years, you could get admitted to law school, and your first year of law school constituted all your electives for your fourth year. Then you got your bachelor of arts degree at the end of your first year of law school. In order for me to get seven years in five, I had to take the Ole Miss core curriculum at the W, which was not easy because that meant that I had to have twelve hours of foreign language. At Ole Miss, they had intermediate Spanish and second-year Spanish for those who had had Spanish in high school. At the W, you had second-year Spanish as a freshman, so I got stuck with all the majors and minors in Spanish taking third-year Spanish with Dr. Caulfield.[14] I had taken Spanish, but it didn't take on me. I just memorized well. So anyway, at the end of the first semester in third-year Spanish, where we were studying Spanish literature, Dr. Caulfield came to me and said, "We are thinking about organizing a class in business Spanish. Would you be interested in taking that course?" I said, "Yes, ma'am!" because the only thing that was going to be offered other than that in Spanish was medieval Spanish poetry, which I was afraid I never would be able to pass. So I missed that bullet; I did take business Spanish, and I can still say "very truly yours": *su seguro servidor*. That's about all I remember from that course, but I didn't have to take Spanish under Dr. Longest,[15] who had flunked my daddy in Spanish in the 1920s. He was still there at Ole Miss. I was scared to death of him. I also took all my math that was required by Ole Miss at the W because my uncle, Dr. T. A. Bickerstaff, was head of the Ole Miss math department.[16] His students had said that he would write with his right hand and erase with his left and say, "You understand that? You understand that?" I was terrified of not doing well and embarrassing

14. Ruby Caulfield (1887–1974), Class of 1908, was an II & C/MSCW faculty member in modern languages from 1909 until 1952.

15. Christopher Longest (1874–1962) taught modern languages at the University of Mississippi from 1908 to 1951.

16. Thomas Alton Bickerstaff (1904–76) served as chair of the mathematics department at Ole Miss from 1947 until 1971.

my whole family if I took math under my Uncle Alton, although I'm sure I could have learned it. At the W I had Mr. Grossnickle,[17] and he was a wonderful math teacher. There was another teacher—she taught English history,[18] and besides our book and other assignments, we had to read 150 pages a week and turn in note cards in addition to everything else. It was a good thing we had open library stacks, because I went and took that list. I looked at the size books and the size prints and the size margins. I read some books that I didn't have any interest in that had to do with strange parts of English history because they had wide margins and big print. It sounds as if I was a goof-off. I really was not, but after I was fifty years of age, I discovered that I really do have a learning disability, and it has to do with eye-motor coordination and reading across the page. I did always read my 150 pages, but sometimes they had fewer words on them than some of the pages that others had read. She was a fabulous history professor.

BW: Tell us about your student life at Ole Miss and what you did after you left the W.

MP: When I went to Ole Miss, I already knew I was majoring in political science, and often I was the only girl in my class. When I entered law school, there were two other girls in my class, so it was three times as good as being there by myself. In fact, the only non-A I made in undergraduate school at Ole Miss was a B+ I made under the head of the political science department. He was Daddy's good friend, but he really didn't believe women had any business being involved in political science. The next semester when we were studying constitutional development—we'd studied constitutional history the first semester—he had to give me an A. There wasn't any way that he could get around it. I still have my term paper. This was 1953, and it was on integration of the races

17. Russell Lowell Grossnickle Sr. (1894–1989) served as professor and head of the math department at MSCW from 1926 to 1964. In 1979, Grossnickle Residence Hall was named in his honor.
18. Probably Minnie Clare Boyd (1898–1983), who taught history at MSCW from 1934 until 1963, serving as head of the department until 1948.

in public universities. I did a whole lot of research over in the law library, and he handed it back to me with an A on it and said, "Very interesting concept." Then he said, "You did a really good job although I know you don't believe this." And I thought to myself, "I do believe it." I knew that the progression of cases was such that the next case going before the Supreme Court was going to have to deal with integration—not like at Louisiana State University where they let a black student come and they made him sit in the special part of the cafeteria, but true integration. In the spring of 1954, I was studying constitutional law under William P. Murphy at Ole Miss law school when *Brown v. Board of Education* came down, where the Supreme Court said that segregated public schools, not just institutions of higher learning, were discriminatory. It was discrimination per se to have segregation. So I think it's important that I kept a copy of that term paper.

All the classes that I took that one year of undergraduate school at Ole Miss were political science, speech, and history. We had to have a major and two minors—one related minor, which was history, and one unrelated minor, which was speech. I was not in any plays, although I tried out for one and got a part. But I found out that they did a lot of their rehearsals on Sunday mornings, and I just didn't believe that was God's will for my life to miss church for play practice, so I turned it down. I soon found out that at Ole Miss sororities were really big things, but I knew I didn't have time to mess with a sorority. They required pledges to study in study hall. It may be good for freshmen, but I was a junior; I had good study habits established. I didn't need to be in that, and the sororities fined you if you didn't go to the meetings. They had the meetings on Wednesday night, and that was prayer meeting night. And I couldn't afford the fines, even if I could've afforded the dues. They had open house the first day of rush. Anybody could go to the open house, and I knew I'd never get to see the inside of those buildings if I didn't go to the open houses, so I went. Then I got this call from the dean of women saying that I had failed to pay my rush fee. I said I wasn't interested in the rush. Then somebody else called and said, "Oh, you need to be in such-and-such sorority, so go ahead and pay your fee because our sorority wants you to pledge." I said, "I haven't got time for this, and I can't afford it." She was the wife of a law student and from the coast, so that may have been supposed to impress me. Anyway, I said, "I appreciate this. I have prayed about it. I do not have time in my life for a sorority." And then, would you believe, they had my aunt call me, Dr. Bickerstaff's wife,[19] and suggest that I go out for rush. I said, "I am not interested in something that will take away from my studies. I am going to have to work summer and winter, and I am not interested." She said, "You are exactly right. You've made the right choice." But do you know, there were some girls who left Ole Miss that next week because they didn't get in a sorority? I thought maybe it was really good that nobody ever invited me into a social club at the W, because I didn't know how important rush was supposed to be. I was very much involved in Baptist life, but that was the only extracurricular activity I had, and I think that Mrs. Marian Leavell,[20] who was the Baptist Student Union director at Ole Miss, was one of the greatest influences in my life in my higher education years.

All the law students were afraid of one professor in particular, Mr. Fox,[21] but especially the first-year students. He was tall, red-faced, white-haired, with a booming voice that almost rattled my teeth. He rattled my nerves as well, and he called on me every day. I never did quit shaking whenever I was in his presence, even after law school graduation. There were always rumors swirling around university campuses about prominent professors, but Mr. Fox's name struck the most terror. To make matters worse, he taught four required courses that no one else taught, beginning with Contracts. Those courses equaled fifteen semester hours over four semesters. Rumor had it that there were three types of students he did not like: females, offspring of successful lawyers, and particularly offspring of legislators. I was guilty on all counts, so even before I entered law school, I realized I would be a target.

19. Lillian Russell Bickerstaff (1909–85).

20. Marian Leavell (1905–75) served as director of the Baptist Student Union at the University of Mississippi from 1931 until 1967.

21. John H. Fox Jr. (1909–65) taught law at Ole Miss from 1932 until his death.

We had covered offer and acceptance and were going to discuss cases involving consideration in that day's class. He asked me, "Miss Bickerstaff, what was the first promise?" "Where had that question come from?" I thought. I answered, "I'm not sure, Mr. Fox. Do you mean what was the first promise made to me, the first promise I can remember, historically what was the first promise?"

"I asked, what was the FIRST promise!" he shouted back. By that time I was trembling and wishing the floor would open up and swallow me. Desperate, I exclaimed in a shaky voice, trying not to cry, "I don't know, Mr. Fox, unless it was in Genesis 3:15 when the Lord promised to send the Messiah." He glowered down at me, snorted, walked to the other side of the room, paused, turned on his heels, and stormed back in my direction, all the time turning red in the face. He faced me down with another question: "What was the NEXT promise?" Trembling, I stammered, "Oh, Mr. Fox, I have no idea." His response was booming and intimidating: "IT AIN'T GONNA RAIN NO MORE."

Thankfully for me, he walked off to interrogate the next victim he could find. I have little recollection of anything else that was said that day. Surviving his onslaught was memory enough for that day. I retreated to my dorm room the next hour between my classes to lick my wounds.

Later that afternoon, I learned that my friend, Lenore Loving, had left class and gone to the alumni house grill, where she settled herself in a far corner to study for the next class and drink a cup of coffee. Before long, in came Mr. Fox and several other law professors for their coffee break. They did not notice Lenore. Mr. Fox said something like, "Never before in all my teaching have I been left speechless by a student." The colleagues showed interest in hearing the full story. He told them about his questioning of me and my response. Then he asked, "Do you reckon that really was the first promise?" One of his colleagues suggested, "Why not go to the library and look it up? Since she gave the exact reference it should be easy." He replied, "I would. But it seems somebody's stolen the Bible out of the law library." At that the whole group broke out in uproarious laughter. The reason that this whole thing was such an affront to Mr. Fox was that for years he had taught that the rainbow was the consideration for the first promise made by God. That promise is in the ninth chapter of Genesis, after the flood, considerably later than God's promise of the Messiah when he drove Adam and Eve out of the Garden of Eden.

About the time the laughter subsided, Mr. Fox spied Lenore sitting on the other side of the room and asked her, "Miss Loving, does Miss Bickerstaff really know the Bible verse by verse?" Without a moment's hesitation and with a desire to return to her anonymity, she simply answered, "Yes, sir."

BW: What did you do after you finished law school?
MP: I got married to my Prince Charming. I couldn't get a job. I took the *World Book Encyclopedia* training course, and I bombed out when I tried to be a salesperson. If people told me they couldn't afford the books, I packed up and left. I just believed them. The law firms wanted to know how many words a minute I could type. They didn't want to think about me as an associate but as a typist, and that's the one subject that I made a C in before I ever got in law school—I made two Cs in law school. Typing was not what I was trained to do. I finally did get a job as a secretary for a lawyer. Why people don't tell you things like this beforehand, I don't know, but I was so desperately in need of a job—I later found out he had been disbarred and reinstated. Anyway, I had beaten him in a lawsuit that a Clinton lawyer had just thrown my way. It was sort of a trash suit, he thought. It was about child custody, and I won. Anyway, the lawyer I defeated hired me to be his secretary, not a lawyer. He was to pay me $50 a week. But if he was not there on Friday when he was supposed to give me my $50, we started a new week the next week. He thought he didn't owe me for the week before. That job got a little expensive for me. After he got $180 in debt to me, I decided, "I can't afford this job anymore," so I began padding the pavement.

It was around this time that I taught for the first time. I had been planning to practice with my daddy when Bob got out of undergraduate school at Mississippi College, but my daddy died. In the meantime,

Dr. Spell,[22] who was academic dean at Mississippi College, had asked me to teach business law in summer school. I said, "Oh, I would love to do that, but I'm not qualified." I said, "I never did get a teacher's license. I didn't take any courses that would qualify me to teach, even in public schools." He just chuckled and said, "I didn't either." Since he was academic vice president, he felt that he could hire me to do that course. I made $100 the first semester and $100 the second semester. We bought a seven-piece dinette set at Montgomery-Ward with that first $100.

Then I got hired as a secretary at a title insurance company, and I worked for them for a few months. I got fired for incompetence, and I was an incompetent secretary. I'm so glad now I wasn't good at that. I might never have done what God had called me to do, be a lawyer. So anyway, I was padding the pavement looking for a job as a secretary at the other title insurance company, but they didn't have any secretarial jobs, nor any other kinds of jobs. But Mr. O. B. Taylor Jr. called Mr. W. Roger Jones with Henley, Jones, and Henley and said to me, "I know this man needs an associate. He's looking for someone." I just heard Mr. Taylor's part of the conversation. I heard him say, "Yes, Roger, she is, but she's got the best record of anybody I have ever referred to you." So I got an appointment to be interviewed as an associate. I may be the only lawyer in the world who ever had to take an entrance exam to get a job, but they gave me an abstract to examine. That's about determining what the value of the title is, and they said they'd pay me for it, but they wanted to see if I could do the work. I wasn't intimidated by that. I had made an A in titles, and I had made an A in real property. My daddy did all kinds of real property work, so I knew a little bit about the language and the law anyway. I brought it back, and what surprised me was how surprised they were that I'd done such excellent work.

Anyway, I got hired, but in that same year, I got pregnant. I worked until a week before the baby was born, but I got fired because there wasn't any such thing as maternity leave. We were really poor, and I

22. Howard E. Spell (1902–92) served as professor of Bible at Mississippi College from 1941 to 1947. He subsequently became academic dean, serving until 1969, and then returned to the faculty until his retirement in 1973.

needed to get back to work, but I had a health condition that wouldn't let me go back to work full time at my six-weeks checkup, so they hired somebody to take my place. I talked them into letting me come train him. While I was training him, I realized that they had more work than two people could do. I suggested that Mr. Jones let me work for them Tuesday, Wednesday, and Thursdays, and he said, "That'd be fine. In fact, that'd probably be good. What do you want me to pay you?" I've never known how to ask for money, so I said, "Just three-fifths of his starting salary since I'm just working three days a week." He said, "That sounds fair. We'll do that." When I got my check at the end of the month, three-fifths of his starting salary (the fellow I'd trained) was more than five-fifths of my salary before I got fired. Now, you can't beat that with a stick. Having that baby and getting fired did me a lot of good because I could make more in three days than I'd been making in five. Yet when I got pregnant again, I decided I was tired of getting fired. Although I never had any more children after that, I realized there wasn't a lot of future in that law firm for me, and I didn't go back there. But no other law firm wanted to hire me either.

Eventually, after I had done a stint at freelance legal research, Joe Bullock[23] had been appointed by Ross Barnett[24] to the Agriculture and Industrial Board, but we were a year and a half into Paul Johnson's[25] administration and Joe hadn't been replaced. Joe had a law office that was empty in Brandon, so he told me, "Just go put your daddy's books there"—because I still had Daddy's library—"and you just keep the office open until I know what I'm going to do." So I ended up staying five years and practicing law by myself and doing well, because when I left, I was making as much as the statutory salary for a circuit judge. Somehow or other, I had made a successful living practicing law. I had what I called a threshold practice—that is, anybody who came across the threshold with a cause of action was my client. I had a lot of poor people

23. Joe Bullock (1919–66) served as executive director of the Mississippi Agricultural and Industrial Board from 1960 until his death.
24. Ross Barnett (1898–1987) served as governor of Mississippi from 1960 to 1964.
25. Paul B. Johnson (1916–85) served as governor of Mississippi from 1964 to 1968.

who were my clients, but poor people pay their bills; they just pay it five dollars a week, and my fees weren't that high anyway. I think the highest compliment I have ever received was when a man from three counties over came to get me to take care of some legal problem he had which really any lawyer could've done. I said, "How did you get here?" So he said at White Oak, he had turned right onto Highway 18, and I said, "Wait, I have asked the wrong question. How did you come to choose me to be your lawyer when you had to pass by all those law offices in those other county seats?" He didn't hesitate. He said, "They says there's a lady lawyer in Brandon won't let nobody take advantage of you." I was thirty-five years old; I had achieved my life's goal. I wanted to make a difference in people's lives. I wanted to give a voice to the voiceless. I wanted to see justice done to the poor. And somehow I had managed to get that reputation, and it had traveled three counties over. I guess that's what I remember most about my private practice in Brandon.

But it was hard not having a partner or a mentor or somebody to bounce ideas off. However, John McLaurin[26] was right across the hall, and he would throw his dog practice—the cases that were not very profitable—my way, and he hired me sometimes to do briefs if he was taking cases to the Supreme Court. My vision of what I would be as a lawyer was that I would be in a partnership with a lawyer who would be a litigator, and I would spend my time in the library doing research to make sure that everything he tried to prove or needed to prove, we knew in advance, and we knew how to defend it under the law. I loved the research. I guess my vision was that I would be the equivalent to a law clerk to a judge, but judges didn't have any law clerks back then.

BW: Do you think the world is an equal place for female attorneys now, or do they still struggle with some of the issues that you faced?

MP: It's more insidious now, but there are still issues. After I got to be a judge, when I would be on a panel with two men and we were asking questions of the people who were giving oral arguments, sometimes the

26. John McLaurin (1926–2004) was a trial lawyer in Rankin County.

lawyers who were arguing before us would say, "Yes, Judge; yes, Judge." But if I asked a question, it was, "Yes, Mrs. Payne." Now this was in 1997. I always made sure that I did not ever let the insensitivity of the lawyer inure to the detriment of his client. But after oral argument one day—it was a medical malpractice case, big bucks—when the three of us on the panel went into robing room to take off our robes to go to lunch, I said, "Did y'all hear what I heard?" They said, "What are you talking about?" I said, "Did you hear what the attorney for the hospital said when you asked, 'Did the doctors count the sponges?'" And they said, "Yeah, we heard that." I said, "Did you hear the answer? The answer was, 'No, the girls do that.'" I said, "Do you know who those 'girls' are? They are highly trained, certified surgical nurses who are due as much respect as the doctors, but that's a 'girl's job.'" And that was in 2000. So there's still much that's ingrained, although there is much progress that's been made. There was a cigarette ad for Virginia Slims, that said, "You've come a long way, Baby." We had! We'd come from here to here, but we didn't realize that the first here is where zero was. And we were just a plus five, although we had made fifty points. Am I making any sense? I think that my concern with today's women law students and younger women lawyers is that they are not aware that there are any vestiges of discrimination left, so they can get blindsided by normal prejudice.

I do want to brag a little bit about Mississippi College School of Law, that was started by two W girls. Carol West [27] was our first employee after me. She established our law library, and she's still at Mississippi College Law School—this month she is being honored at the Mississippi Bar Foundation. Anyway, in 1996, the American Bar Association commissioned a study of law schools to see which were female-friendly. Out of 169 law schools, Mississippi College School of Law was twelfth from the top. And the first three tenured faculty members at Mississippi College Law School were female. Two of us were W girls. The other was Shirley Norwood Jones, a Millsaps graduate, who held the first chair of law at Mississippi College School of Law. Our first law review editor-in-chief,

27. Carol C. West, Class of 1966.

Anne Porter Veazey, was female. We have always had a history of women in leadership at Mississippi College School of Law, and I think it has to do largely with the fact that there have always been many more women in leadership roles in the faculty and the administration at MC than in the average law school.

BW: How did your association with Mississippi College School of Law start?

MP: First I have to mention where I was between Brandon and MC, so I'll go from 1968 to 1975 first. In 1968, the legislature had the longest session that they've had in the history of the state. While I was in Brandon, I worked part time for the legislature as a legislative draftsman when they were in session, so my law practice was just about fizzled by the fall of 1968. In September 1968, I finally got to start practicing full time. The legislature had created the Mississippi Judiciary Commission, which was an eighteen-month study group. I was fortunate enough to be selected as the executive director. When we had done all of our surveys, we went out of business. All of it had to be done from scratch; this had never been done before. We made our report to the legislature. After legislative adjournment, the commission died, but that was the year Mississippi had the reorganization study. The next week, I was hired to be the full-time head of the drafting and research office that was being established by the House of Representatives. I stayed there until 1972, when A. F. Summer,[28] the attorney general, called me to see if I'd be interested in coming to work for him. Of course, I'd been wanting to do that for years, because the predecessor attorney general,[29] had been a good friend of my daddy's, but he had told me that he didn't have any openings. Then two weeks later, he hired somebody that had just barely squeaked through law school. But I loved being an assistant attorney general. Now I didn't have the background in that field that I had in legislation, but I

28. Albioun Fernando Summer (1921–81) served as attorney general of Mississippi from 1969 until 1980.

29. Joseph Turner Patterson (1896–1968) served as attorney general of Mississippi from 1956 until 1969.

went to work on Tuesday, and by Thursday afternoon, I had opinions to be considered by the opinion review committee, so I wasn't a liability to Summer. He was a wonderful boss, and I loved him, but the story's too long to tell about how God led me to give up that wonderful job and go to Mississippi College.

I went to Mississippi College thinking I would be the interim dean. There was a man under contract to be dean who said he needed an extra year where he was in Delaware. Then he reneged on his contract, and I ended up being the only dean that we had through those years. Nobody ever told me how much fun teaching was going to be. There were two things I was never going to do: I wasn't going to be a secretary, and I wasn't going to be a teacher. I never took a single hour of education courses. I had taught that class in business law in 1956 but had then gotten the secretarial job. Then after that I had been lawyering.

When I went to Mississippi College, I found out how invigorating college students could be to an old woman of forty-two. However, I really had a very difficult time trying to take an unstructured, profit-making, evening law school and fashion it into the academically excellent branch which would match everything else at Mississippi College. So there are lots of stories. I'm writing the history of Mississippi College School of Law, so you'll have to read about that later. The thing that kept me going was there were some students who were very dear and so fabulous. At the end of this week we'll have an alumni reunion—in my eyes, every student I ever had was an A student. I don't know what they made; we graded them anonymously. It didn't matter. I loved the students. That's why it was so hard for me to answer God's call to run for office and be a judge.

Bob and I were so sure we had our lives planned out after I went to work at Mississippi College. My mother had gotten sick in 1989, so I had the care of my mother until she died, but we just knew what we were going to do. Bob was going to retire in 1995, and in the summers we were going to go to Alaska to do home missions work. Two things happened. One was that, without our permission, our friends who were missionaries to Alaska retired before Bob did. And the other one was that Evelyn

Gandy[30] was speaking at a women's continuing legal education program in the fall of 1993. Mother had died in July 1992, and I was just about to get my strength back from being so exhausted when Evelyn said, "There's a new Court of Appeals. Which ones of you women are going to run for those judgeships?" I was sitting at the table with her looking at those sixty women, and not a single hand went up, and I said to myself, "What is wrong with these women? We need at least one woman on that court." So I began to think, as I was coming back from Vicksburg, who I could snooker into running and then help her get elected. And the more I thought of the women in the Third District, the more I realized that they didn't have sufficient networks to be able to win. I had no idea that I would be able to win, but I knew that I had a better chance than others. I began to hear in my ears Mordecai's words to Queen Esther, "But who knoweth whether thou art come to the kingdom for such a time as this."[31] And so I ran, and I got defeated, and it was wonderful. I didn't have to give up Mississippi College, and I didn't have to be rebellious to the Lord. But that was a very peculiar year. The law was changed, and those elections were invalidated, and then we were on the ballot in different configurations because they doubled the size of the court. There were four other candidates—men—that I was running with. I came in second in the general election and first in the runoff.

I can tell you that one of the most truly invigorating experiences that I ever had was the challenge of beginning this new court. I had no idea that at age sixty-two I would change careers again. But it was fabulous, and the men that I worked with were just wonderful, and we all loved each other and still do. Two of them have gone on to be with the Lord, and there were people who would resign or other people who would get appointed and then they'd get defeated, and then there would be new people coming in. I think I served with sixteen different men

30. Evelyn Gandy (1920–2007) graduated from law school at the University of Mississippi in 1943, the only woman in her class. She was elected to the Mississippi legislature in 1948 and became the first woman elected to statewide office in Mississippi in 1959, when she won the post of state treasurer. She served as lieutenant governor from 1976 until 1980 and ran for governor in 1979 and in 1983.

31. *Esther* 4:14.

during the seven years that I was on the court. But it was a fabulous time! And it was icing on the cake to be part of something brand new. Lenore Prather[32] said something about all of the systems on the Supreme Court being in place, and all she had to do was get in step with them. We had to start from scratch. Nothing was in place, and that was exciting to me. I think that I have really found my place in society as someone who starts new things. After they get to running, I am perhaps not as excited about them as I am as we start. I would hope I never slack off in doing my very best in my work, but the invigoration comes from the new challenge.

My running for office was an outrageous thing to do except for the fact that I knew that it was God's will for my life. Somebody said to me, "You never intended to run for office, did you?" I said, "You've got it wrong. I intended never to run for office," because we had sacrificed so for my daddy to be in legislature. He had to make several races. He was in five terms. I think in at least three of them he had contested elections. But talking about contested elections and uncontested elections, I was up for reelection in 1998, and praise God, I didn't have an opponent. That's the way to run. You either run scared or unopposed, and I've done both. Unopposed is a lot easier.

BW: Which of your contributions do you feel were the most significant?
MP: Our court was established to eat up the backlog of appellate cases that were before the Supreme Court. We did it! And we did it within about two years. I think perhaps my greatest contribution to the judiciary was in efficiency. I never missed a deadline. I had my office organized so that my clerks knew exactly what was expected of them and when their deadlines had to be in order for me to meet my deadline. I had perfectly wonderful staff. I found out later that the clerks said that everybody knows that Judge Payne's clerks work twice as hard as everybody else, and I'm sorry about that. I worked on Friday afternoon, even though other judges may not have. I wanted us never to let justice fail because we were not efficient. Efficiency is only important if nothing is

32. Lenore Loving Prather (b. 1931), Class of 1953. See the interview with her in this volume.

sacrificed. We would certainly never sacrifice justice. There were times when I might have gotten permission from the chief judge to have an extra week, but it never meant that it was delayed long enough for us not to meet our statutory deadline, so number one was efficiency. I wanted to be a role model for seeing to it that we got our cases out on time. When I left, although the required limitation was 270 days, our average was 180 days. All of us working together did a really good job, and we didn't miss any deadlines.

The other important thing is the cases in which I dissented where the Supreme Court then reversed the Court of Appeals. Now that made me proud. There was one case when the Supreme Court had handed down two opinions, so there was no relief. We had to follow what the Supreme Court said because we couldn't overrule the Supreme Court. But the effect was blatant injustice. So I said in my dissent that even though the Supreme Court's ruling in the case of such-and-such versus so-and-so must be followed, and therefore we have to affirm this judgment, if I had the authority to write what I think would be a just resolution, it would read this way. So what I did was that I prepared for the Supreme Court, when they got this case, not only an outline but a manuscript of how they could reverse this case and bring justice to this particular issue. I was proud of that. The first dissent I ever wrote, the Supreme Court agreed with me and reversed us. I was pleased with that.

But what I will mention in regard to women has to do with two other cases where I wrote a dissent. I could not get enough men with me to flip it to make it be six to four on either one of them. There were two librarians who were the subjects of sexual harassment—a very hostile environment. To keep their sanity, they had to resign. They filed for unemployment compensation, and they were turned down because they quit. I said they had cause to quit—that it was virtual termination, unjust termination. There was a hostile environment, and the U.S. Supreme Court had already handed down a case about hostile environment. Since our cases were not published those first two years, they were not precedential. That meant they did not establish a precedent. We had another one that was not quite as strong a case, but it was also concerning a woman who quit because of sexual harassment. I wrote a dissent, and I only got three men to join me in that one, but two years later, the Supreme Court by Mr. Justice Sullivan[33] said, "As a matter of first impression we are holding that sexual harassment is grounds for leaving and the person is qualified to get unemployment compensation." That didn't do those first three women any good, but at least somebody got the message, and somebody came up with justice for other women. There were a number of cases where I cited *Hemsley v. Hemsley* and *Ferguson v. Ferguson*[34] to make sure that women got equitable distribution. But primarily, we were the worker bees. Each of the ten of us wrote about eighty cases a year, and we all had to vote on all of them. It was hard work. Bob can tell you that.

BW: Since you left the court, what have you been working on?
MP: Not nearly as much as I thought was going to be doing. First, Bob was diagnosed with cancer, and we had to take care of that. And then we realized that I couldn't get any work done because our house was in shambles. All we wanted to do was just lighten up the den—paint the den. And you know how that goes. We had to start by doing something to the foundation. We couldn't do anything with the foundation without voiding our termite contract. So then we had to have all these traps put around the house. It took, oh, six or eight months. Then, in the meantime, we went on an Elderhostel[35] trip, "Music on the Mississippi." Carolyn Vance Smith,[36] a W girl, was in charge of that Elderhostel. You just find W girls everywhere you go. Then I did some writing and got some things accepted. One of them was for an Internet magazine; of course, that just goes off the radar screen, so it's a good thing I kept a copy of that. I'm now working on the history of Mississippi College School of Law, and I find that it's a good thing that I'm a pack rat because

33. Michael D. Sullivan (1938–2000) served on the Mississippi Supreme Court from 1984 until his death, at which time he held the post of presiding justice.
34. Precedent-setting 1994 Mississippi cases that define a wife's contribution in "equitable distribution of property" in divorces.
35. Elderhostel is a nonprofit educational travel organization for adults.
36. Carolyn Vance Smith, Class of 1960.

very few records were kept by the law school. I'm interviewing some of the people who were involved back in those early days. I'm finding a lot of new things that were behind the scene that I was not aware of. It's going slow. I'm used to support staff, and I have none, so as a secretary I still make a good bricklayer. But I'm enjoying that. Also in 2002 into 2003, I worked on my autobiography, and I decided it was swallowing an elephant, so instead of starting with when I was born, I decided I would start with my career. I've gotten part of the way done on that. In the meantime, I also had been working on a piece about women in elected office in Mississippi because I knew most of the early ones—judges and legislators and statewide candidates. I sent out surveys and got very few back. Eloise Scott,[37] who just retired from the legislature, a W girl, did send back the survey. I guess my problem is I am all over the map, and besides that, Bob and I like to travel. Well, Bob doesn't like to travel at all, but I do. And my sister, Emilyann Bickerstaff Raspilair, and I have also traveled some together. I'm still involved in all the extracurricular activities I was doing before I retired. I'm on the Women in the Profession Committee of the Bar and the Bench and Bar Committee of the Bar. We are also very involved in our church. And my unmarried son and I celebrated his fortieth birthday at Disney World. We have this mouse addiction. And we are headed to Disney Land because it's the fiftieth anniversary, and it's also our golden wedding anniversary.

I guess the group that means the most to me is my Dragon Slayers group. It's a group of women. Our requirements for being a Dragon Slayer—you can self-invite—is to be a high-achieving woman whose life demonstrates that the highest goal in her life is to live in the center of God's will. I've got my campaign manager, Shannon Warnock; I've got my mortgage banker, Anne Lewis; my physical therapist, Dene Fulton; and many others. We were kind of heavy with lawyers, so we reached out to others: Ellen Dabbs, who's a CPA, and Sherry Lanier, who's involved in ministry. Anyway, there are about twenty now—could always be

37. Eloise Hale Scott (b. 1932), Class of 1953, served in the Mississippi House of Representatives from 1988 until 2003.

more—who meet every two or three months to encourage one another in the Lord. We pray for one another, and we tell what all God's done in our lives to bless us, because we're all more blessed than we're willing to acknowledge, I think.

We're called Dragon Slayers for a specific reason. My mother's brother, Everett Cook, was a lawyer in Gulfport. He and my daddy practiced together way back, probably before I was born. Anyway, Uncle Everett was married to Irene Griffin, who was an artist. Much of the artwork in my house, Aunt Irene did. They had one son, Joseph, who teaches at the law school at the University of Tennessee in Knoxville. Uncle Everett had died in 1980, while I was still teaching at Mississippi College. In 1993, Aunt Irene died, and Joe, her son, wrote me how much he appreciated my being there with him at the funeral because he was an only child and that I might not know, but I was Uncle Everett and Aunt Irene's favorite niece. He said that Uncle Everett had followed my career with great interest, and he looked on me as something of a "dragon slayer" because of all the things I had had to face in the legal profession. When they liquidated all of Aunt Irene's worldly goods, one of the last things that was sold was her kiln in which she baked her copper and enamel artwork. In that kiln there was a disk that has a beautiful green dragon on it and a little tiny knight who is going to slay the dragon, because his sword is right at the dragon's throat. I didn't have thirty-five dollars to buy it, but I had to have it, so I think I must've borrowed thirty-five dollars from Bob. The first thing that went on my desk as a judge the day I was sworn in was my dragon slayer disk. I wanted to remember that I had a mission in life, and that was to slay the dragon of injustice. My campaign manager, who had been one of my students—still one of my dear, dear friends—said, "I want to be a dragon slayer," and it was from that that this group evolved. A lot of these women would have no reason to know each other except for their connection in this group, so I really like that.

I think that the other thing besides the writing that I have done since my retirement, the thing that has really characterized my life, has been public speaking. I have the joy of doing original Bible studies at least one month out of the year at First Baptist in Jackson. I'm not a member of that church anymore, although we were until 1967. As a law professor at a Baptist school, I was invited to speak beginning in 1985. After I went to the court, I've just been bootlegging the Gospel ever since. I do enjoy that. I tried to do two things. I tried to make copies of manuscripts of speeches, and that was hard because until 1985, I didn't even have a computer. I have three-ring binders full of speeches that I've made that take up about this much bookcase space. But I am working now on doing a small book with just twelve of those Bible studies in it. Just yesterday I located a transcriber. A friend of mine said, yes, she would like to transcribe audiotapes of my speeches. After she does that, I'll have manuscripts in a database. We're going to get started on that, and I hope to be able to submit that to somebody. I'm sure it will be rejected, but I have been rejected before. I've been turned down more times than a bedspread, but I'm still here.

BW: Do you have any advice for future generations of W women?

MP: When I was growing up, I was taught that God has a plan and a place and a purpose for every life, and it was my job to seek to know him well enough to discover that plan and place and purpose. Before I did that, I was to accept his will sight unseen, and then all he had to do was reveal it to me. Now, there have been times when I haven't said no, but I've said, "Lord, are you sure I'm the one?" I'm so glad Gideon and Moses and some others had this kind of discussion with God, because I have done that myself, but never have I wanted to rebel against God's will for me because I know it is exceedingly, abundantly above all that I could ask or think—beyond my wildest imagination. It doesn't really matter whether or not you're accepted. It doesn't matter whether or not there are roadblocks in the road. Accept God's will sight unseen; walk daily in his path, and God will do some amazing, outlandish, hilarious, wonderful things for you and through you. So if I had to say one piece of advice, it's "Trust in the Lord with all your heart and lean not to your own understanding. In all your ways acknowledge him, and he shall direct your paths."[38]

....

38. *Proverbs* 3:5–6.

BW: How do you feel the W made a difference in your life?

MP: Oh, in all kinds of ways that I didn't know to look for—didn't even know I needed. And I'm glad you brought that up because that's very important to me. I got a barrier-free education. The W does not have the white male preference that permeates coeducational institutions even to this day. It's not as pervasive now as it was in the 1950s, but it still exists. At the W, I did not have to hide my brains in order to have dates. Of course, I had no dates except when I came home, but there were airmen who came to our church from Keesler Air Force Base, and they didn't know I was supposed to be unpopular. So I had lots of friends in uniform. There's something about a man in uniform. I brought girls home from the W on weekends, and some of those airmen would entertain those girls, and the one who was the best friend that I could always count on to entertain W girls that I'd brought home was a friend named Bob Payne. Then summertime came, and there were no more girls brought home from the W, so he had to date me, and by the time I got to Ole Miss in September, I was engaged to be married to that Prince Charming in my life. We were engaged three and a half years, and then we got married. And we just celebrated our fiftieth wedding anniversary.

Since I did not know how intimidating college could be in a coed institution, by the time I got to Ole Miss, I was just as eager to volunteer and I was just as sure of myself as any of the men. I was already engaged, so I didn't have to worry what boys thought about me. I received from the W that confidence that one needs. I heard historian Gerda Lerner[39] say that women have been acculturated to doubt their own best judgment. I've had a lot of that in my life, but not nearly as much as I would've had otherwise because the W encouraged me to think creatively and to express new ideas and didn't laugh at us. I had to do a great deal of speaking in the 1980s and 1990s about protecting the W and the women's mission. I was very much involved in fighting

39. Gerda Kronstein Lerner (b. 1920) is a feminist historian and a founding member of the National Organization for Women.

the legislation.[40] They'd call me up at 4:45 and say, "There's going to be a hearing of the Universities and Colleges Committee of the House. Can you be there at 5:15 and speak for the W?" And I'd say, "Yes, of course I could." And being at a private institution, I didn't have any of the limitations that I would have had had I been on the state payroll. But we worked very hard to preserve the W, and one of the things that I am proudest of is a video called *Common Ground*, where we were arguing against closing the W and the Valley.

It's very important that women have equal opportunity and that women also have the right to fail. I never knew I had the right to fail. I didn't even get that from the W. But taking risks is something that's necessary in order to be able to grow professionally and personally, and there have been studies done even in kindergarten that show that little boys are bragged on for attempting new things; little girls are bragged on for keeping their desk clean. In 1989 the American Council on Education said it was very important that we give women equal opportunities, provide the equal playing field that male students have always had.[41] They emphasized that institutions of higher education have the responsibility to counter all those insidious, invidious things that were still current in higher education in America. A study in 1982 about the "chilly climate" for women in the college classroom showed that women who were from single-sex schools had much more confidence after their higher education.[42] Then there was the Tidball

40. Severe state budget constraints led Mississippi governor Bill Allain (b. 1928, in office 1984–88) to suggest closing some of the state's eight institutions of higher learning. In 1986, the Board of Institutions of Higher Learning in Mississippi (IHL) voted 9–3 to close Mississippi Valley State University and Mississippi University for Women. Payne was a leader and a spokesperson in the organized political fight MUW alumnae waged against closure in the media and on the floor of the legislature, and the IHL subsequently reversed its previous recommendation. The issue resurfaced nearly a decade later, when the IHL responded to the U.S. Supreme Court's 1992 decision against the State of Mississippi in *Ayers v. Fordice* (which sought to equalize state funding for Mississippi's historically black colleges) by recommending the de facto elimination of MUW and Mississippi Valley State University by merging them with two other state universities. W alumnae and President Clyda S. Rent again mobilized political pressure to block the plan.

41. See American Council on Education, *Educating the Majority: Women Challenge Tradition in Higher Education* (1989).

42. See Roberta M. Hall and Bernice R. Sandler, *The Classroom Climate: A Chilly One for Women?* (1982).

study,[43] which found that the overwhelming percentage of the women who were in *Who's Who in America* were women who had attended single-sex schools. This study drew the conclusion that these women had not been limited in their education by their goals having been disparaged. Their ideas had been valued by their faculty. I still think that we need to be very careful that we don't fall into or stay in those old patterns which give men students longer time to answer, interrupt men students less often, disparage women's but not men students' goals. I loved it when Dr. Joyce Brothers [44] spoke here, and she talked to us about having been asked to step down from graduate school so that a man could have her place, because he would use for society's betterment this training in psychology that she was going to waste. Now, who today doesn't know the name of Dr. Joyce Brothers? It is intangible, and it is hard to explain, but there's just something about a W girl, and part of it is that she knows she has value no matter what the circumstances around her might be. And that's what the W did for me, even when I didn't know I needed it.

43. See M. Elizabeth Tidball, "Perspectives on Academic Women and Affirmative Action," *Educational Record* (1973).

44. Joyce Brothers (b. 1929) is a psychologist, writer, and television celebrity.

Sylvia Camille Duck Clark
Class of 1956

APRIL 28, 2006

INTERVIEWED AND TRANSCRIBED BY RACHEL FORESTER

SYLVIA CAMILLE DUCK WAS BORN IN LOUISVILLE, Mississippi, on July 24, 1934, to George M. Duck, a railroad manager, and Camille Langham Sullivan Duck, who owned and operated a women's clothing store in downtown Louisville. At the W, she majored in elementary education. She was active in many organizations, including the Glee Club; the Silhouettes, a freshman-sophomore social club; the Hottentots, an organization for campus leaders; the Jesters, a social club for juniors and seniors; the Baptist Student Union; the Religious Emphasis Week Committee of Fifty; and the College Singers. Her numerous campus leadership positions included junior usher, vice president of the Theatre Guild, president of the Baptist Student Union Executive Council, and president of the Student Christian Association. Elected a class cheerleader in each of her four years at the W, she served on the President's Council during her senior year. In 1958, she married Robert Earl Clark, a tree farmer and real estate investor. She served as president of the MUW Alumnae Association in 1995–96 and has been recognized as the Louisville/Winston County Woman of the Year and as Queen of the Junior Auxiliary Charity Ball. She now lives in Louisville.

RF: How did you hear about the W, and what made you decide to attend?
SC: We lived sixty miles west of Columbus, and it seemed that the girls who went to school during the 1940s and 1950s came to the W. It was an economically priced school, so a lot of girls who were not able to go to other places chose the W. It's always had a wonderful reputation, so my mother and daddy chose for me to come here. I was unsure at first, because I was very interested in church-related occupations. I enjoyed activities at our church and I thought maybe I was destined to go to a church-related school, but upon my parents' urging I came here, and I have never been sorry. To my great surprise, the things that I was looking for in more spiritual matters, I found here. They had many activities here that dealt with different denominational groups. The church that I joined downtown was just open arms to all the college girls who came there. And we had plenty to do. We had Morning Watch, and that was a devotional time every morning after breakfast in the post office lobby. People just lined up down there. And we had Noonday at the different denominational houses, where you went for about thirty minutes before lunch. There were all sorts of activities that met that need, so I felt very fortunate here because practicing religion was a sincere thing. It was not a church-related school, so any activities along that line were very sincere and very well done, whereas if you go to a church school, it's expected. So I was very pleased, and I never thought about transferring. I was determined to go from freshman to graduation.

RF: What did you do during the Morning Watch?
SC: It lasted about five minutes, I guess—Not more than ten. There was a piano down there, and somebody would play. We would sing a hymn, and then the person that was leading for that day or week would give a

thought for the day or short devotional, and we would have a prayer, and then we'd go. It was Monday through Friday. It was very, very worthwhile. The post office was downstairs in Hastings Hall. And we would just make a semicircle of five or six lines. We didn't get tired of standing there or anything. It wasn't that long, but it started your day right and disciplined us to think about things like that every day. It would be right after breakfast, so I would say it was probably 7:30 in the morning. And most everybody, believe it or not, came to breakfast. Whether you just drank a cup of coffee or ate a hot breakfast, you did it in the dining hall because we didn't have anything else to eat between that and Noonday. So everybody was pretty good about eating breakfast. Now, we didn't look too hot, I'll tell you that.

RF: The W today is still the most affordable school in Mississippi. Was it the same then?

SC: Yes. I'm sure that it was, because church schools were higher. They still are, I guess, more expensive. And not very many girls went to Mississippi State. It was just a small group at that time. I guess it was rather expensive to go to Ole Miss, too; there were so many other things to do up there. So the W was very reasonable. We had city girls, and we had rural girls and girls from small communities as well as larger towns. It just met the needs of everybody financially. It was surprising that there weren't very many scholarships then. You could work as a monitor in the dining hall, serving meals and cleaning up afterward. That was a way to make money. And then you could work as a desk assistant in the dormitories—that was another job. Or you could work for a teacher. That was another way to pay for college. And there were little jobs like in the gym, somebody to test the swimming pool water, things like that. But there were not all these scholarships that people have now. But we have thought back about it all. We mostly dressed alike; we were not in uniforms. That had already passed, but you just didn't notice what other people had. If someone didn't have as many changes of clothes as somebody else, she just went on and attended. We just judged them for their character and who they were inside. And I will frankly tell you, there were some girls here who didn't come with much, but they were accepted, and many of them were scholars. It just all worked out really well.

RF: Did you have to work to put yourself through college?
SC: No, but I'll tell you, when I look back on it now, it was so inexpensive. Because we had our meals, our dorm room, and our studies. And I think it was $250 a semester. Now can you beat that? I'm sure there were some people really struggling it out, but it was very reasonable along that line.

RF: Where did you live during your freshman year?
SC: Hastings Hall.

RF: How did you feel on move-in day?
SC: I didn't register until August. Now, that would be strange now, wouldn't it? You wouldn't get in if you waited until August. My roommate[1] and I had gone first through twelfth grade together, and we decided we would room together over here. We didn't have any preconceptions about where we should live. A lot of girls who came had sisters who had been here before, and I think everybody probably wanted to be in Callaway, but I don't know what made that dorm seem to be the place to live. We were just tickled to death with Hastings, because it sat right there on the green where you could see people going in Shattuck Hall, and the front steps were right under our window where we could see who was coming in and going out. We were the smallest dorm, I guess, at that time. And we had the sweetest housemother.[2] She just couldn't have been beaten. She was wonderful, and took such good care and good interest in us. So we were just thrilled to death.

I found myself this past weekend, during Homecoming, seeking out those girls that I had known first. You just kind of get to know them best. Our sophomore year, we could either live in Reneau or Shattuck.

1. Alice Freeman Sharp Stone (1934–92), Class of 1956.
2. Janie Eliza Stennis (1885–1979), an alumna and sister of Mississippi's U.S. senator, John Stennis, served as a social adviser at MSCW from 1943 until 1957.

So my roommate and I decided that we'd rather live in Shattuck, because it was right in the middle of everything, and we could wait until the last minute to come down to meals. But I guess one of the biggest disappointments was that that summer, Shattuck burned.[3] So that threw us at the tail end of everything, because our friends had already selected their rooms over in Reneau. So we lived in three different rooms in Reneau that year. We moved from a two-girl room to a three-girl room to a bunk room. We moved three times that year because they were putting a few into Fant Hall and shuffled us around. What a year.

RF: How was it to live with three girls at once?
SC: It worked out. It was a larger room. It was the size of two rooms or maybe was a room and a half, but we had three single beds in there. It was just for maybe three or four months, I think, and we managed okay. The three of us that lived together,[4] we had all gone to first through the twelfth grade together. My long-standing roommate, she was a sleeper. And she could concentrate thirty minutes and get more done than I could do in three hours. Then she'd lie down and go to sleep. The other friend, she was a music major, so she just lived in Music Hall. It was rare for us to all to be together there, so it worked out fine. But they moved us all around and we had to go to a bunk bedroom and that was murder. It was tiny.

RF: Was that two bunks?
SC: Just two. But just two girls. Our third roommate got married midyear that year. Since her husband was in the service, they went on. But it was just a top bunk and a lower bunk. I remember the closets were just so tiny. You brought your clothes at the first of the year, no matter what season, you brought them for the whole time. And they were just stuffed in the closets and everything would be so wrinkled when you took them out. It was just a sight! I think we were on the third floor, and it was hot

3. The fire at Shattuck Hall in 1953 resulted in the loss of the top two floors of the building, although it was repaired and used again as a dormitory and dining hall.
4. Bettie Davis Marshall Woodward, Class of 1956.

up there, really hot. We had no air-conditioning; we just had to raise our window.

Then our junior year, we went to Peyton, and I guess of all the dorms, I liked that best because it was shady over there and cool, and we could just walk out the front door and down to the dining hall. They got the dining hall fixed back up. The building didn't burn down, just part of it. I guess it burned upstairs or something, where the rooms were. So we were able to be in the dining hall all four years.

It really was nice. They made us try to have good manners, and there was a housemother that sat near us if she didn't sit at our table. They tried to help us be ladies.

RF: Tell me about the housemothers.

SC: These were mature ladies, older than our mothers. They had an apartment in each dorm. They stayed out front most of the time. When men would come and go, they were always at the desk. The fellow had to go to the desk and ask for the date, and then she would call up the girl over the loudspeaker. She knew what was going on, and she had to be around when it was time to come in. We had curfew hours. When we dated as freshmen, double-date or triple-date, however it was, we had to be in on Friday and Saturday nights at 10:30. Then on Sunday night, I think we had to be in earlier than that. And if you had a problem or anything like that, they'd help. I'll tell you this little tale that I had never heard before that that a friend who lived across the hall from us our freshman year told me this weekend. One of my roommate's grandparents passed away, and one of the family members called me and said, "Would you ride the bus home with her, because she's going to be really emotionally affected?" They didn't want her to be by herself. We had no cars. You would have thought, since we just lived an hour and a half away, that somebody would have come over here and gotten her, but that wasn't an option. So I said, "Sure I will." So we just threw things in a suitcase, and I don't know whether we walked to the bus station downtown or what, but we went downtown and we rode the bus to Ackerman, which is a town eighteen miles north of Louisville, and somebody met us there. But anyway, this friend this weekend told me, "After y'all left, I passed your room"—we never locked the doors; even at Christmas, we never even closed the doors in our rooms—she said, "I passed your room and y'all had not been able to straighten up." She said, "I went in there and I straightened your beds and picked things up and got it where it didn't look bad." She said, "One of the maids in the building saw me in there." So the maid went to the housemother and said, "She's in the room. What should we do?" So our friend had to go down to the housemother and explain the situation and all that. Oh, I felt guilty. I said, "I'm so sorry. I'm so sorry that you got in trouble," because we should have been better housekeepers than we were, but we had to move fast. My roommate was the Civic League[5] person for our floor, and that meant she had to check the rooms from time to time, and we were terrible housekeepers. We got a big laugh because I lived with the Civic League person, and we kept the worst room almost of anybody.

RF: Was it hard to share a room with someone you'd been friends with before you got to the W?
SC: We got along just fine. We were opposite in a lot of ways, but we cooperated with each other. She was more scholarly than I was, but she had a great sense of concentration. And she could just work fast, whereas I'd have to go to the library and spend every night trying to read and keep my mind on what I was doing. We had always known her family, and they'd always known us, and so we just got along fine. And she was funny. She just had a great sense of humor, so she was very popular in our class. Her name was Alice Freeman Sharp, so we just called her Freemie. All of our lives, we had called her Freemie, so everybody here called her Freemie.

RF: Did you have a nickname too?
SC: Yes, I did. Some of my high school friends started calling me Duckie, so now a lot of my college friends do, and even my husband does.

5. The Civic League, organized just after the turn of the twentieth century, was a student organization that took responsibility for the neatness and cleanliness of the dormitories and campus.

RF: What was your favorite class you took at the W, and why?

SC: As I said, I was not much of a scholar, but I got by. We had to take a few entrance exams after we got here, to place us into different classes. I got misplaced. I got into a real high English class. But I have always enjoyed reading and writing, so I was in a real good English class, and we had to write stories and essays and things like that, and I think that helped me quite a bit. But I always thought, "I'm in the wrong class." They're so smart, and here I am. I had a psychology professor here, Dr. Mikesell.[6] He was only here a few years, but he was a published person, he had a book, and that's what he taught—his book. He just made it so interesting. I never wished to do anything with psychology, but I did enjoy that. I was in elementary education, so we had to take a lot of different things. But I enjoyed him very much. And then you always end up saying, "I need three more hours to make out my year's time." So I took a class called Mothercraft, and it was taught in the home ec building. A lot of people took it—mostly home ec majors, really. But that was such an interesting class because of the teacher. She was a nurse.[7] She was so funny. The smell of alcohol would just send me into deliriums. I just got so nervous with the talk of blood or anything like that. She told about how if you were on a moving train, what you could do if you had to deliver a baby. She said, "Now, after you take this class, if you have to help somebody, you can do it. But you have to have a stack of newspapers. That's very important to have, because newspapers are clean." And I thought, "I cannot picture myself on a moving train, helping deliver a baby with a stack of newspapers." I guess she presumed we would have water and all that. In the process of all this, the blood just left my head. She looked at me and she said, "Miss Duck, are you about to faint?" I said, "Yessum." She said, "Somebody help her into the next room so she can lie down." That was so funny. Everybody just had big eyes. Oh, mercy. But that class was very interesting. And then I needed three more

6. William Henry Mikesell (1887–1969) taught psychology at MSCW from 1953 until 1957.
7. Mildred Spahr Kennedy (1926–82) taught in the Department of Bacteriology, Physiology, and Hygiene and in the Department of Home Economics at MSCW from 1947 until 1972.

hours, so I took a class of cooking in the home ec department. I thought that would do me some good. Of course, everybody in there was a home ec major, and they had to figure out formulas for recipes. I never did figure all that out. But we cooked a few little things. I remember one day I was fixing the hot chocolate for the meal—I guess it must have been breakfast or something—but I had never heard of beating up hot chocolate, whisking it up with a turning eggbeater. I was giving it all I had, but I was talking to the person next to me, and the teacher came up to me, and she said, "Miss Duck, your hot chocolate is flying all over the refrigerator, the stove, the floor, the walls, everything." That was funny. Then I had to learn to clean up after myself. In elementary ed, we had to take a math course, and of course we were always in there with the math majors, and that made it kind of hard. And then we had to take what we called kiddie literature, kiddie lit. That was in the library, and there were lots of library science majors in there. So we touched on quite a lot of things in elementary education, and then we had to do our student teaching down at the Demonstration School.[8] That, of course, just culminated the whole thing, and that was good experience.

RF: What did you do in kiddie literature? We have Adolescent and Children's Literature. Is that the same class?
SC: That's it. That probably was the name of it then. That was fun because I had not read a lot of the material that they required us to read. It was good for me to have that. And then we had art. I remember I had to take nine hours of art. Now, that was really helpful, because I am not talented in that line at all, but it was interesting.

RF: What was your least favorite class?
SC: Oh, I'm sure it was history, history and math. In science, the teachers were awfully good with us—in biology and zoology. And I had had biology in high school, so it was a little more familiar to me. We had to

8. The Demonstration School, a laboratory school for MSCW student teachers, opened in 1929. It operated as a practice school and as a public elementary school until 2003.

bear down on those, too, but I liked those okay. But math and history were hard!

RF: What social clubs were you in?
SC: I was in Silhouettes to begin with. We were only the second pledge class in the Silhouettes, since it had just started a couple of years before we came. That lasted two years, and then we went to the junior-senior club, which was Jesters. And then I was also in Hottentots. Somebody asked us this weekend, "Now, what were your objectives in Hottentots, and what were your projects?" We said, "We didn't do one thing!" We got together at Christmas, I think, and maybe at the end of the year, and that was about it. But I think it was just sort of an honorary for people that were leaders on campus.

There is definitely a place for social clubs on the campus because it brings us all back. We want to see our friends that we were with in those clubs. There were only three freshman-sophomore clubs, so twenty pledges and twenty members—that was a very small number. And there were only, I guess, three to begin with in the junior-senior clubs. It was about the same number in there. Actually, there were fewer there. Then they organized one or two more while we were here. So it really involved not a very large group of people. But that didn't seem to matter. Nobody held it against you for belonging, and you didn't hold it against those that didn't belong.

RF: What do you remember about pledging?
SC: We had to wear these little books around our necks. And we had to acknowledge, by name, all the other members of the club, the sophomore members. This was for Silhouettes. We had to know their names and where they were from. Then certain people had jobs at night to go over to the dormitory to find out if the sophomore members wanted anything from the Goose.[9] And I think we had to have a program maybe

9. The Golden Goose Tearoom, located on the first floor of the Student Activities Building (formerly the Henry Whitfield Gymnasium), demolished in the late 1960s.

once a week, or something like that. There was probably less to do in the freshman-sophomore clubs than there was in the junior-senior clubs. We really had fun pledging people when we got to be sophomores, and I thought we had some pretty clever parties. They were real cute. We would pick a theme for our party, and then we would pick a place. Sometimes it would be outside or off campus. One time we went to the YMCA uptown, and they let us have a party there. And then we had our sort-of dress up party, the last one. We had it in the hotel, where we sat down and had dessert or something. I just remember that we had cute decorations and a cute program, which we provided for the hopeful pledges. Then we had a party out at one of our members' homes here—she lived here in Columbus, so we went out to her parents' home and had one out there. I thought they were real clever. Our lead person when we were sophomores, she was number one on the line, played the piano real well. In another social club, their pianist fell by the wayside, and so they came over and asked her, "Would you mind coming and playing for our party?" And she said, "I don't think so. We're trying to get the same people y'all are. How can I go and play at your party?" They said, "We'll put up a screen, and they won't know who's playing the piano." She told me that story this weekend, and I had not heard it. I thought it was funny. You just had to do what you had to do.

But when you got to be in the junior-senior clubs, I don't remember them doing parties. They knew you by then. They didn't have to get acquainted. They just called you when it was time. But we had to work hard on our programs when we were juniors, I'll tell you. They were tough on us then. And they wanted services done for them, too. But we are still very close to those with whom we were in a social club, and I think there's some good in that. I do. It helps retention in the college because you want to come back to be with those you pledged with.

I shouldn't have been in so many things, but it was so interesting to me because when you go to a small, rural high school, you don't have a lot of things to do. I wanted to see what those things were like. I didn't want to study, anyway. I'd rather do the fun things. Yes, we were pretty busy. Of course, we couldn't have cars. But my last semester of my senior year, I knew I'd be going to work somewhere, so my mother got a car for me, and I brought it on campus. And do you know, most of the time the battery just went dead because I didn't have enough time to get out and go about and use it.

RF: You were president of the Baptist Student Union and the Student Christian Association. Were you elected to those positions?
SC: In the Student Christian Association, yes, I believe I was elected there, and the Baptist Student Union, I honestly don't know how I got it. Maybe we just moved up. Maybe the Executive Committee would just get people to run for offices.

RF: What did you do in those clubs?
SC: In the Student Christian Association, I think the little devotional we had downstairs was under that. And believe this or not, but I think our freshman year, they had what was called Meditation. After we had lunch in the dining hall, we had to go to our rooms and study for an hour and a half. We couldn't play the radio, and of course we didn't have a TV. I guess we could nap if we wanted to. But I think they wanted us to read. And maybe that was under the Student Christian Association, but I don't know how we could control that. And then once in the spring we would have a spiritual week. We would have little meetings of Bible study, I think, and speakers for Religious Emphasis Week. I think we had to work with the denominational houses to have special things for that week, and that was one of our main responsibilities. We had a lady named Miss Hudson[10] who was our religious director, and she also taught some Bible courses here, too. She kept us going straight in the programs that we would have. Believe it or not, we had chapel every Wednesday over in Whitfield. It was required; they checked the roll. They would have a little devotional to begin that, and then they would have different kinds of programs, but that was part of our doing, too. Like I said, it was a

10. M. Elisabeth Hudson (1897–1970) was professor and head of MSCW's Department of Bible and executive secretary of the Student Christian Association from 1940 until 1963.

very spiritual campus for a state school, really. So I was happy with that. Then over at the Baptist Student Union, we had Noonday every day. We had lots of parties and entertainments over there, and we would invite the boys from the Baptist Student Union at State, and they would come and then would invite us over there to theirs. And it was a good place to go get a Coke or cool off. They had a nice living room and a kitchen if you wanted to cook on the weekend. It was very comforting to us to have that.

RF: Did you ever get into trouble while you were at the W?
SC: I got on the edge with my grades. They would give you warnings about that. Some classes I would make real high in, but the weak things I wouldn't do very well in. I remember that junior exams were coming up, and it was the last time they were going to do Zouave on the front campus with the whole student body. I wanted to be in it so badly, but it looked like I was really going down the drain with history. And I decided I just had to get out of Zouave. It didn't do me any good to get out; I should have stayed in it. I wouldn't have made any better or any worse. But that was kind of scary. And they gave demerits here if you didn't sign out properly or sign in properly when you left the dormitory. And surely, certainly, I did something wrong there—I can't remember really. If you got so many, then you were restricted to campus. I didn't ever get that close, but I'm sure I must have gotten a few. And if your room wasn't clean, they'd give you demerits on that too. Isn't that something?

RF: Did you ever get demerits for your rooms?
SC: No, we slid by, somehow, some way. But we just accepted all this. It wasn't strange to us or anything like that. Today, it would be very strange.

RF: What other traditions and events did you participate in?
SC: We had a new president. When we came in, he came in with us. It was Dr. Hogarth.[11] His inauguration was huge here. Of course, they

11. Charles Pinckney Hogarth (1911–97) served as president of MSCW from 1952 until 1977.

get representatives for an inauguration from every college all over the United States if they can. But what was so thrilling about it was they wouldn't let anybody go home that weekend. I believe it was a weekend. Everybody had to stay. And they even told us what to wear. Everybody was to wear a suit. And that was the most thrilling sight I have ever seen. I just happened to be in the Glee Club and we were up in the balcony of Whitfield, now Rent Auditorium. And when we looked down and saw hundreds of young women march in with good posture and nice-looking suits on, that was thrilling to me. Then of course there were so many people here in caps and gowns from other representing colleges. That was a thrilling sight.

RF: Did you ever do the Freshman Serenade?

SC: Oh, yes. We had what we called dormitory sings, and we sang divided by dormitories. We would pick a theme for our presentation, and then we would write songs to the tunes of popular songs and dress according to our theme. There was the Student Activities Building, where the gazebo is now, right out in the middle of the yard out there. It was a beautiful building which underneath had the Goose and then upstairs was a large reception room, and it had a winding staircase outside on both sides. So then, according to the dormitory that you were with, everybody would get on those steps, and then the cheerleaders would lead the songs. There were judges to judge who was the best. We had to pick our theme, write the songs, rehearse, and get it good. Then we put on some kind of little costume that would go with the theme, and we'd get up there and do it. It was like Songfest.[12] I came to Songfest. I have a daughter who's a W girl[13] and a daughter-in-law who's a W girl,[14] so I came to most of the things our daughter was in. The dormitory sings were very much like that.

....

12. Songfest is a song-and-dance competition among the women's social clubs held at MUW every spring.
13. Camille Langham Clark Ball, Class of 1988.
14. Gwen Luke Clark, Class of 1984.

When I was a student, we all had to be in Mag Chain,[15] too. There was no, "Are you going to do it or not?" It was not like that. I think we had to wear a white dress or a white blouse and skirt underneath our cap and gown. We marched from the music hall, and then the bleachers were up there on the front campus. The cheerleaders would lead us, and I was a cheerleader all four years. We were in high heels! We didn't think anything about that either. That was just part of it. Then I think somebody would give a talk. But we didn't run for the magnolias; we didn't do that part, I don't think. Magnolia Chain was part of the graduation. We had to be in graduation, and we had to be in Mag Chain.

RF: What did you do as a cheerleader?

SC: We would lead cheers at basketball games when our class played basketball or some other team sport. We would get out there and the few people that would come to watch, we would lead in cheers. And sometimes we would have marches to the dining hall at night. I think it was before Junior Night or Senior Night. We would lead the class. One time we made torches to lead the class in. It's a wonder we didn't burn each other up. Then we led Mag Chain. Now, all the alumnae cheerleaders get up on the stage and lead "Hail to Thee"[16] every time we come to Homecoming. It's fun.

RF: What was a typical day like for you?

SC: There was a whistle on the laundry or somewhere back there on back campus, and it would blow to get us up in the morning. It's just strange how we didn't set a clock unless we were going to get up earlier than that.

15. In 1894, in imitation of some eastern schools, II & C graduating seniors carried a daisy chain from the steps of the old chapel to an outdoor ceremony. In 1913, seniors modified the tradition and carried a magnolia chain. The students still sing the traditional magnolia chain song and carry a magnolia chain at a special class day ceremony before commencement in May. At the end of the ceremony, the seniors rush to the piled chain to claim a bud or flower. Those who get either one will have good fortune, which has been variously defined over the years and for some generations involved being the first to marry.

16. "Hail to Thee," MSCW's fight song, was written in 1920 by Eola Williams (Class of 1920) and Jane Williams (Class of 1921).

We just listened, and the whistle blew. And then it would blow again for breakfast. And then it would blow for the first class. It just went like that all day. And I'm trying to think if at night it blew. I don't know. But it would blow when class was over, and you just got up and left. And we heard the trains. I can hear a train whistle now, and it just puts me back—there I am again at the W.

RF: What was your favorite thing to do on the weekends?
SC: Sometimes we would have dates and go to the movie uptown. Or when we got to be upperclassmen, we could go in a car single-dating, so we would go a lot of times to eat dinner at night somewhere. But there really wasn't a lot of money flowing for boys. So usually I guess the movie was the thing. Then, if we knew somebody at State who was in a fraternity, sometimes we would get asked to go over there for formals. And then football games at State. Also, sometimes they would have concerts at State. Big bands would come through there, and when there wasn't a football game, maybe they'd have a concert in the afternoon and then they'd have a dance at night. Most of the time, these were formal dances. There were places we could stay over there. If we knew a girl in the dormitory over there, she'd let you stay and dress in her room. And sometimes we'd just come on back to the W afterward. Then the denominational houses would have parties. We didn't go home every weekend. Some of our friends went home religiously every weekend. We didn't—maybe every third week or something like that, because we lived close enough that either we could get a ride with somebody or we'd ride the bus, and maybe our mothers would bring us back.

In the dining hall, the food was excellent. We just had good food here. I'm telling you, I came in fairly slender, but boy, I rolled out in four years. I ate a lot of butter and drank a lot of milk, and it was just delicious. My mother was a professional person, so she didn't cook a lot at home. So I ate things at the W that I had not experienced before, and I enjoyed it, I really did.

RF: Do you remember any major world events that happened during your time at the W?

SC: I think there were still people in Korea, and a lot of our high school boys had joined the National Guard. Some of them were too young, but they did anyway, and quite a few of them had to go. I don't know if they went overseas or if they just went to another part of the country. But I remember in high school, when General Douglas MacArthur was discharged of his duties in Korea, he made a farewell talk and they stopped school and opened the little talkie system that we had, and we listened to that.[17] Then General Dwight Eisenhower was running for president, and he was running during our freshman year here. I remember that we had a little radio, and we kept it down real low that night; we wanted to hear the returns. And he did win.[18]

We were very protected here. It was a time in life when we had one newspaper in every dorm, so if we read our newspaper at home when we were growing up, we got out of the habit here because it was used by so many people that we just sometimes didn't read it. And no TV. And we just didn't listen to the radio religiously either. So we didn't really keep up with a lot of things. Things went on that we were not concerned with and were not upset with, like we are with things now. It was the best of times for me to be here, because I could take care of my work here and enjoy being here. And we enjoyed the things that went on in our classes. You didn't look toward another class and say, "I just can't wait to get there and do that." You just enjoyed the things that you could do your freshman year, and your sophomore year, and all the way up. I'm sure everybody will look back on her years at the W and say, "That was the best time that I could have ever been there," but that's the way I feel about when we were here. It was the best time, because we were still under control of the rules of our parents, the way they taught us. And when we

17. On April 11, 1951, President Harry S. Truman relieved General Douglas MacArthur of his duties as commander of the United Nations forces in Korea because of his public opposition to Truman's conduct of the war.

18. Republican Dwight D. Eisenhower (1890–1969) defeated Democrat Adlai E. Stevenson (1900–1965) in the 1952 U.S. presidential election.

came here, it was continued here. They expected the same things from us. So we just didn't have a lot of things to get in a jerk about, really. We just floated along and did what we were supposed to do.

RF: Did you meet anybody here who changed the course of your life or influenced you greatly?

SC: I think the greatest thing that happened to me was the friends that I made here. Some of them were different from people I had known growing up, but most of them were just like we were. But I have made some forever friends. We held on to the same values that we felt were right for us. We just didn't have a lot of bad people here. We just didn't. One or two people were excused from school for doing things that probably girls now would think, "My word. That's very mild." But usually they'd let even the one or two that that happened to come back eventually, or maybe they'd have to stay out a semester. But it was all to try to protect us and to try to get us started in life the best that we could. They definitely gave us our money's worth in every area, and for that I am just really, really thankful.

A friend from my class that I met after I came here[19] was recommended to me by our pastor at home. He had known her growing up, and their two families were good friends, and he said, "I want you to meet this person when you come to the W." And down in South Mississippi he told her the same thing, that he wanted her to meet me. So we have stayed really, really close friends. After graduation we decided we would go to Dallas, Texas. That seemed like a big city to us. She had majored in library science, so she immediately got a job in the public library there. But they wouldn't let you teach there unless you had lived in Texas for a year. We had to get immersed in the Texas way of life and the history and all that. Since I couldn't teach that year, I got a job in the library, too. We were in two different libraries, but I was in a children's library. I didn't intend to go anywhere with it, just be there long enough to be able to teach the next year. So we both took the teachers' test and

19. Janet Clare Smith, Class of 1956.

passed it, and the next year, we got assigned to schools there. We only worked for the library one year and stayed to teach one year, and then I decided to marry a boy that I had gone to high school with. He was graduating from the military academy at West Point. He had gone to Mississippi State two years, so he had to start over when he went to West Point. Those two years were good for me, because we couldn't marry yet anyway. So we married, and then my friend said, "It's time for me to go back home anyway." We both came back home, and we've been friends ever since. We roomed together last weekend, during our reunion.

RF: How often do you talk to your W friends?
SC: Fairly often. Not every week, but we stay pretty close, and every year, twelve or fourteen of us go on a trip somewhere. We've been to Callaway Gardens. We've been to Gulf Shores. We were at Lake Tiak-O'Khata in Louisville three times before we started branching out—we would meet there. This year we're going to Blowing Rock, North Carolina. We've been to Florida to one of our friends' sons' homes. He let us have it for a time there. We pick nice places and we stay about three or four days. We've been to Charleston, too. So we'll make it all around before it's all over.

RF: What is the most valuable thing you have taken from the W in the past fifty years?
SC: I think friendship and how to accept people, all types of people. The values here were very high, and I think that's helped me. Also to know girls from every corner of the state as well as from other places. They taught me things, and I hope I've taught them some things, too. And they certainly taught us to be organized here. I don't know that I absorbed that as well as I should have. And to be high-minded, to think upon the better things of life. I could certainly recommend the school, and I hope it will always be here.

RF: What advice would you give to a current W girl?
SC: Go with a determination that you're going to succeed in life, that you're going to be able to do something with your life professionally. If

you should plan to be a homemaker all of your life, then be prepared in case that doesn't work out or if your spouse should die. Be able to do something that would help you to support yourself. Just learn as much as you can about as many things as you can. And stick with it until you finish your college degree, because whether you do anything with your major or not, there is a finishing quality here that holds you until you are mature enough to break out into life. I know there are people that are smart and don't have to come here to learn, but there is a finishing quality here that helps put you on the right track throughout life. I'm proud of the W, and I'm happy with the things that I learned here and the people that I met and the experiences that I had.

Barbara Ann Garrett
Class of 1956

APRIL 21, 2006

INTERVIEWED BY VALLERI TEMPLETON

TRANSCRIBED BY LEIGH POURCIAU

BARBARA ANN GARRETT WAS BORN IN YAZOO CITY on November 20, 1934, to Ezra W. Garrett and Mary Eleanor Bishop Garrett. While she was at the W, her numerous activities included the Student Christian Council; the Committee of Fifty; the Baptist Student Union; the Women's Athletic Association; the Rogues, a freshman-sophomore club; the Jesters, a junior-senior club; the Hottentots, an organization for campus leaders; class volleyball and basketball teams; the Tournament Play cast; the Physical Education Club; and the Theatre Guild. She also served as class secretary and treasurer her sophomore and junior years. A member of the staff of the *Spectator*, MSCW's student newspaper, she served as the assistant business manager during her junior year and as business manager in her senior year. She was named Most Athletic during both her junior and senior years and earned a degree in physical education. After earning graduate degrees and teaching at two other universities, she joined the MSCW faculty in 1967. She retired in 1991, when she was named Faculty Member of the Year. In both 1970 and 1991, the yearbook, the *Meh Lady*, was dedicated to her. She later received the MUW Alumnae Achievement Award and the MUW Medal of Excellence. An expert in nonverbal communication, she is the coauthor (with N. F. Greenwald) of *Non-Verbal Interaction with Adult Clients* (1994). She lives in Columbus.

BG: I grew up in Yazoo City, Mississippi. I was, as an only child, very spoiled, particularly by my daddy. We were just the best of friends. I grew up in an environment of parks, even though Yazoo City only had a population of about ten thousand then—it's not too much larger than that now. I lived across from a block that was just a playground, and it had two tennis courts in it. I convinced my dad to buy me a badminton racket in a drugstore when I was about eight years old. I thought it was a tennis racket, so I'd go out and bother all the people who would come to the park to play tennis. These were old clay courts that had a lot of gravel, and people would have to line them off with lime for the lines, which was very tedious. I sat in the backcourt area, out of the way of their swinging rackets. I'd just sit there and watch and watch, and then when I was eight they let me play because they didn't have enough people for a match. I didn't realize it then, but actually one of the first people that let me play with them and also play doubles with them turned out to be my basketball coach in high school, and she was a W alum. She had graduated in the late 1920s—Margaret Hester[1] from Philadelphia, Mississippi. We'd be playing on this court, and I'd go for a forehand, which was on the same side I was holding a racket, the ball would hit a rock, and all of a sudden it'd be on my backhand side. So my agility skills were sharpened by that type of tennis court. As I was advancing in age, the city actually built two concrete courts there, so I enjoyed playing even more. I later got to play with the men, and I was the only woman on the Yazoo City men's tennis team. They let me play in the sixth position, but I would usually beat my opponents because they were young fellows, and I played with the fellows

1. Margaret Hester (1907–94), Class of 1927.

all the time. You can see I was interested in athletics from the beginning. I grew up with a tennis racket or a basketball in my hand.

I also enjoyed running and riding bicycles, that sort of thing. I was really a tomboy. Give me a tree, and I would climb it in a minute. For college, though, I was offered a basketball scholarship. I was an all-state forward, and I was offered a basketball scholarship to go to Holmes Junior College. I'm so grateful that I didn't accept it. Instead, there were six of us that came to the W. One of my dear friends at that time was planning on coming to the W, so there was no question in my mind that I would come here. It was really because of these friends that I chose the W.

Not knowing much about higher educational institutions at that time in my life was really a blessing in disguise. I had grown up in a very nurturing family environment—churchgoers. I got to the W, and Miss Pohl[2] was big in dance. Of course, Southern Baptists didn't dance then. Some of my Southern Baptist classmates did, but not Barbara!

I had never been to the W. When I landed on campus, that was the first time I had seen it, and of course it was wonderful. I had been to camps before, and I'd always enjoyed that atmosphere. Growing up near the park, I had had the opportunity of being with other kids, but when you're an only child in a family, it's an attraction to go somewhere else. In fact, as my parents and I arrived on campus, I realized that I had forgotten my pillow from home. So my parents disappeared to go find me a pillow. While they were gone, I got so involved, I didn't see much of them after that. I just unloaded my stuff, and I was ready for college. I'm sure they were a little disappointed as they drove away because my attention was already geared to what was going on around me.

VT: You weren't homesick?

BG: No, no, no. I got too busy. I had a great class, too. That made a big difference. There were six of us that came from Yazoo City. Three of us graduated from the W, and three did not.

2. Emma Ody Pohl (1880–1966) joined II & C in 1907, when she was hired to develop the department of physical education. She taught that subject until her retirement in 1955.

VT: What were your general thoughts about attending college?
BG: It was, at that time, just something to do. It was just the next step. I thought I didn't want to teach. And I didn't want to coach because I had been on teams, although I loved that aspect. I loved competition, and at that point in my life, I was probably a natural athlete. I wasn't going to coach or teach, but I wasn't sure what I was going to do. Even though I wasn't sure about the teaching, I started out my first semester in elementary education! I changed my major my second semester to physical education, but my sophomore year I decided it was physical therapy. I had heard a physical therapist who was a W alum come to speak at chapel.

Chapel was always interesting. It was held in Whitfield in what is now Rent Auditorium. We had chapel two days a week, and we were supposed to be in our seats or we could be reprimanded. They had checkers, so you sat in the same place every year in an assigned seat. Chapel is where we learned and sang the W songs. Singing the songs was done repeatedly, and we then would have a speaker or announcements. Also often we'd have a devotional or that sort of thing. Just to see the classes—the students—walking in mass to chapel was impressive. In those days, we wore saddle oxfords and socks. It was just a sea of saddle oxfords and full skirts, A-line skirts. That was pretty much the dress for everyone. One of the beautiful things about it is that we didn't know who among us might come from a family of wealth or one who had very little. In those days, when we came in 1952, I think the cost per semester was $250. That was everything. But that was something that was very difficult for some parents to pay even in that time, because it was not too long after the Second World War. And, of course, my parents lived through the depression. Because of that they spent their money wisely and were conservative about how they used their money.

How we dressed was important, though. For physical education we wore blue shorts, white shirts, white socks, and our tennis shoes. Our sneakers were all the same kind. Converse was a big brand, but we didn't have many varieties of sneakers—one for running or one for all the other different sporting areas or events like we do today. Since we were physical education majors, our junior year we wore maroon shorts and white shirts for our physical education classes. That distinguished us from the others as being majors. And of course in intramurals, the majors would usually be the officials because we took courses in officiating and in different sport techniques.

In my time at the W, there were probably closer to a thousand students as far as enrollment, but everybody lived on campus unless they lived in the community and commuted. Very few people commuted from a distance. There were no mature students, and of course there were no African Americans at that time. Integration happened in the 1960s, and I was on the faculty when that actually occurred. That's one of the interesting things in my experiences at the W, because I've seen it go through so many transitions, and it's just fascinating to see how it's all melded together. It's been a great experience. I never intended to come back to the W to teach. I had no intention of doing that. Something just opened up.

VT: What was your roommate at the W like?

BG: My first roommate was one of my dear friends from home,[3] but sometimes that doesn't work out. Another wonderful friend actually came in and told me right before my zoology exam that my roommate was changing roommates at the beginning of the second semester! She didn't know that I did not know—that the roommate hadn't told me. It was a little shock. She was my growing-up friend from home. Our mothers were just the dearest of friends: both their maiden names were Bishop, and they both had gone to the same college in Clinton—a women's school at that time, maybe some of the beginnings of Mississippi College. But anyway, Callie[4] happened to be on campus, too, and it bothered her more than I think it did me when Ina told her. Ina and I are like family because we both were only children, but we had never had to live with each other. She was Most Beautiful, and I was the tomboy.

3. Ina Rae Aven Coggeshall, Class of 1956.
4. Carolyn Lammons Kirk, Class of 1956.

In fact, she was Most Beautiful at the W at least two of the four years, maybe three, and I was Most Athletic the last two of our years. When we were little girls, we would ride our bicycles to grammar school, and our parents would drive. They would be together in a car behind us until we got there. Hers is the only family that still calls me by my family nickname, Boots. Ina still has her family call me Boots. In fact, her children only know me by Boots. I think they still don't know my last name. It's just Boots.

When I changed roommates, I moved to South Callaway. I was on first Callaway, but then I moved upstairs and was across from Ina. I roomed next door to Douglas Stevens. We called her Doug, but she goes by Ann now, Ann Graham.[5] We were next-door neighbors for the next three and a half years, which is really a great experience in itself. We watched each other. Our relationship started when we would sit in the middle of our beds during exam times and eat what her mother and dad sent us. They would send us pork and beans and jars of pickled pigs' feet, which were a delicacy in those days. I still like to have some of those occasionally. It's a rare occasion, though. We had two spoons and a platter. Those are the only dishes we had, because we all ate in Shattuck. We'd be there for three meals a day, most of us. There were no hamburger places, and the Goose[6] just had potato chips. I can't even remember getting a hamburger at the Goose, but surely there were sandwiches or something there too.

VT: What was Shattuck like?

BG: Shattuck was wonderful. We had a group that we would sit with—since we were assigned, we didn't swap. But we were allowed to get up and visit, and that was time you could catch up with people that you needed to find. You could find them at mealtime. Noon was really a wonderful time to do that. The dining hall was great, not only because of the experience of being together but also because traditions were so strong.

5. Douglas Ann Stevens Graham, Class of 1956.
6. The Golden Goose Tearoom, located on the first floor of the Student Activities Building (formerly the Henry Whitfield Gymnasium), demolished in the late 1960s.

We would be singing class songs, making big major announcements like about Stunt Night and junior-senior rivalry—the things going on on campus. On the day of Stunt Night, it was announced in the dining hall by the senior class president. My roommate was class president for four years—Lu Lee.[7] You're in the know if you're the president's roommate!

Callaway has always been a great dorm, and when I was a student that was freshman row. Hastings, which is Hastings-Simmons now, and Columbus and Callaway were all freshman dorms. We would walk from Callaway through Columbus, and we would go down into Hastings. We had Morning Watch on the first floor area of Hastings, where the post office was. I can't remember if it was before or after breakfast. Somebody from the Student Christian Association, which Duckie[8] was the president of our senior year, would have a devotional. Somebody would be playing the piano, and we would sing, We'd make a semicircle around the opening in the door and have several lines of people. When I came back to the W as a faculty member in 1967, Morning Watch was held in Carrier Chapel. That was a carryover from the post office days. We'd stand and sing our songs, and we'd have a brief devotional and go on our way.

We went to class by the whistles. The whistle was not electric; coal actually, I think, was the fuel for the whistle, but it would blow ten minutes to the hour, and it would blow on the hour. We were supposed to be in our seats by the second whistle. I would sit trying to cross my Ts and dot my Is because papers were handwritten—they were not typed in those days. Thank goodness! Since I had been a basketball player in high school, and typing and basketball practice were the same hour, I didn't have typing skills when I got to the W! But I would be sitting there in the dorm when the ten-until whistle would blow. I would still be there when the hour whistle blew, but I could make it to my class on the second floor of Painter Hall and into my seat before the whistle had stopped blowing. Of course I always had a good classmate, like Janet

7. Lula Bullock Lee, Class of 1956.
8. Sylvia Camille Duck Clark (b. 1934), Class of 1956. See the interview with her in this volume.

Smith,[9] who was the editor of the *Meh Lady*,[10] who would check my papers for me, and I still give her credit for helping me through some of my English classes.

The second year we lived in Reneau. Now, of course, Reneau houses the College of Business. Being the roommate of the president, I had the first choice of rooms, and we had a three-girl room which is now actually an enlarged classroom—they put two three-girl rooms together to make a large classroom on the third floor of Reneau. During sophomore year, we had physiology together, since all three of us were physical education majors. After lunch, we didn't go to classes until 2:00, so we'd go back to the dorm and hit the bed. Most of the science classes were in Martin Hall. When the whistle blew—the ten-until whistle—we would get up and go to our class. Reneau was the back campus then. There was no Fine Arts Building, and there was no Fant Library as there is now. When we were students, what is now Welty Hall was Fant library, and that is where we would spend a lot of time taking books back at night with our pajamas rolled up under our raincoats. We were trying to get them in before whatever time they were due, before the whistle blew at night for us to be back in our dorms.

VT: Did you have a dorm mother?

BG: We did. We had dorm mothers. In fact, Senator John Stennis's older sister, I think her name was Jane, was our housemother freshman year in Callaway.[11] Another unique thing about Callaway is at that time it had the stacks. These were black structures, like silos, with a roof on each one. They were slides for fire escapes. There was one behind Callaway that was right behind Miss Stennis's room. She was in a room that was right next to the smoker. People could smoke, but they could only smoke in the smoker. Of course, smoke would come out of the open windows. There was no air-conditioning in those days, and we didn't get out of school until June. Our sophomore roommate, the one that roomed with Lu and me our sopho-

9. Janet Clare Smith, Class of 1956.

10. *Meh Lady* was the W's college yearbook, published between 1902 and 2005.

11. Janie Eliza Stennis (1885–1979), an alumna and sister of Mississippi's U.S. senator, John Stennis, served as a social adviser at MSCW from 1943 until 1957.

more year in the big fine three-girl room, had a silo right by her bed. The interesting thing is, we always just disregarded people's beds because we'd go right over them in our dirty jeans, go down the silo and back up the steps and go down the silo again, and we got to the point where we could actually go to classes that way with our books in our hands. There was an entrance from second floor and third floor. People would be sliding out, and there was also a third silo that was back behind the west wing for all three floors. So you might have people flying out of three different silos at times for class changes. I'm sure we were waking Miss Stennis up from her naps, so she decided that all the sliding needed to be stopped. The administration decided the silos were no longer to be used; the doors were bolted and we could not slide from the third floor to the ground level anymore. When I came back to the W in 1967, the silos were gone.

VT: What did they do for fire escapes after that?
BG: There were the doors—the areas between the dorms, the enclosed old wooden connecting walkways, that were considered fire escapes. The old silos I guess were the things they had used primarily before that. Anyway, they were unique. Not many places had silos for fire escapes that you could go sliding down in circles.

Our dirty blue jeans went to the laundry. We had laundry bags with our laundry numbers on them. Once a week, our laundry went to the W laundry, and when the clean clothes came back, we could stand our jeans up, they were so well starched and pressed. That was wonderful. We didn't have to worry about washing clothes. But if we had to wash our socks out, it was sort of hard to wash a dozen pairs of socks and hang them up somewhere in our room, because there were no washers and dryers in the dorms or even an extra corner.

VT: Did you like any teachers in particular?
BG: Quite a few. I loved Dr. Covington, my freshman English teacher.[12] I remember his mannerisms. He'd always hit his left foot as he'd go

12. Frank F. Covington (1885–1972) taught English at MSCW from 1929 until 1952.

around the desk to talk to us, to come closer to us. And then he'd go back, but repeatedly he'd hit that foot. He was such a gentle soul, such a sweet man. But it was my science teachers, like Luna Austin,[13] who really prepared me for the courses I'd take at Duke in physical therapy. She was marvelous, a marvelous teacher. Miss Berryman was my adviser—Romayne Berryman.[14] She helped advise me regarding physical therapy. She helped me select Duke because there were no physical therapy schools in Mississippi or in the Southeast. Duke was the closest at that point. I applied and was accepted. That in itself was quite an experience. To this day, not everybody gets to go to Duke for a graduate degree.

I have seen the W teachers from different aspects—as a student and then from being a fellow faculty member. I had said I was never going to teach, but I became very quickly aware as I began practicing physical therapy at Vanderbilt University Hospital that I taught every person with whom I worked. I learned that teaching is not always just in the environment of a classroom. It could be around a patient's bed or it could be outside or when we teach our own children and our families. Even though I had gone through phys ed as a major, it was actually in a teaching program, so I practice taught. I had my teacher's experience, but I didn't really plan to use it. So I was a surprised person when I realized my teaching skills. But I don't think I would have been the teacher that I turned out to be if I had moved right out of undergraduate school into the teaching role. I first worked with individuals. I did do group work, but much later in the profession. I was initially more sensitive to what individuals need and how they learn. I think this really better prepared me for the role that I was to assume later.

VT: Was physical education your favorite subject?

BG: Really that was not so. I was just a competitor. I loved competition. I have an article from the *Yazoo City Herald* that I found in my mother's things, saying, "Freshman Wins Tennis Tournament." As I began to read,

13. Luna Austin (1895–1985), Class of 1916, taught hygiene at MSCW from 1923 to 1961.

14. Romayne Berryman (1901–84) taught physical education at MSCW from 1924 until 1966.

I realized that "Barbara Ann Garrett from Yazoo City" was the winner of the tennis tournament, the school tournament, that year. It was back in those days that the W began to compete with Memphis State. My sophomore roommate, Jane Standefer Steen,[15] and I played doubles together. We went to Memphis State to play, and they came here to play us, and we beat them both times in doubles. I think we won our singles matches as well. And then Mississippi State came over and played us, and there were no girls' teams in those times. There were no women around in sports. You didn't see anything about women playing in the newspaper either, so the fact that the local paper had my name in regard to that tournament was unusual. The W tennis courts at that time were in the area by Poindexter Hall. The two dorms, Keirn and Taylor, were not built yet. We had eight courts—great courts at that time. I was a competitor, and I knew how to play tennis. I remember Miss Massengale,[16] whom I first knew just from hearing students talk about her. The name that they gave her was "Fess," short for "professor." I called her "Fess" to her face my freshman year, not knowing any better. But Fess and I were later the best of friends because I was a pretty good volleyball player as well as a tennis player. Tennis was her sport. And my being a major, that helped. Majors often were playing on the courts for classes. We had to pass tennis to be able to graduate, like you had to pass swimming, and it was tough. I had a classmate from San Antonio, Texas, who really had to struggle in tennis to get out of the W, just to pass the course. We had physical education every semester for four years.

I enjoy the sciences. At the W, we learned to appreciate subjects outside of our majors. I am fascinated with Mary Lib,[17] my classmate from Amory. Because of her art professor, the head of the art department,[18] and his interest, she took art appreciation instead of music appreciation.

....

15. Jane F. Standefer Steen, Class of 1956.

16. Grace Massengale (1894–1987), Class of 1916, taught physical education at II & C/MSCW from 1916 until 1969.

17. Mary Elizabeth Barrett Francis (b. 1934), Class of 1956. See the interview with her in this volume.

18. Ralph M. Hudson (1907–98), professor and head of the art department, taught at MSCW from 1945 until 1969.

Over the years, wherever she was, one of the first places she went and where she took her children was to the art museums. Now she's been on the board of the Amory Museum ever since its inception. I took music appreciation, and while listening, I could see people running through the fields—my interpretation was really very basic at that time. There was so much to know, and we had experiences in such a wide area in our classes. This was one of the beauties of the W, in our years particularly. We were given an opportunity to open up to different experiences. Even though in high school we'd had some exposure, at the W it was much broader exposure. They had recitals and the performers they brought monthly, and some of us were ushers, so we'd have to be there at the performances. However, the whole student body usually showed up. I think the closeness of being on campus and not going anywhere else—everything was centered on the campus—probably proved to be very beneficial to us. And we'd have to wear our fine ball dresses to be ushers. We just didn't wear slacks.

VT: What was your least favorite subject?
BG: My least favorite subject? I called it secretarial science. It was typing, personal typing. I was a scared freshman. It was my first semester, and I was the only freshman in the class. The majority of the people in the class—since I was the only freshman and most of them were juniors and seniors—guess what they were doing? They were pledging two-year clubs. The head of the secretarial science department was our teacher.[19] Unfortunately, bless her heart, as far as nonverbal communication is concerned, she had very many negative behaviors. One is that she never gave us eye contact. She would look at the aisles instead of us as she walked up and down. I was very afraid because I'd never had typing, and I wanted to do well. When she was not in the room, we'd have our assignments to do—she would leave and then she'd come back. I was always behind because the keys were not lettered. They were blank keys

19. Clarice Robinson (1897–1982) served as professor and head of secretarial science at MSCW from 1950 until 1955.

so we could learn the keyboard. When she would come back into the room, my fingers would never be on the right keys. Maybe this is why I don't really care for computers—or part of the reason. As a physical therapist at Vanderbilt, I did have to type my patient records, so I did develop some skill, but very basic at that point. I was in that class with all the upperclassmen having a wonderful time, some of them already with some typing experience, enjoying college life to the hilt because the teacher wasn't in there most of the time.

Nutrition was another course that was not my favorite because, being an only child, I rarely had to wash a dish or cook or that sort of thing. In nutrition we had to cook, and it was not my cup of tea. We were divided up into groups. One group cooked one day a week, and the other two were in the classroom. On one particular day the teacher was out of the room, and we were making some kind of pastry—jelly rolls. We were working and doing whatever we were supposed to do for that day. One of my sophomore roommates was over in a kitchen on the other side of the big room divided into kitchens. She called my name and said, "Catch!" And I went up in the air. Here was pastry flying across from one side of the room to the other, and I had to jump to get it and I caught it. Just as I caught it, the teacher walks in. This teacher was another little lady who used nonverbal behaviors. When she would talk to you, she'd get right in your face as you were eating that meal. But those were just classroom experiences. They were just part of college life, so I accepted them.

VT: Was Zouave still going on when you were a student?

BG: My junior year we had Zouave. That was the last time Miss Pohl directed it, since Miss Pohl retired at the end of my junior year. Zouave was right before graduation, and it was part of the graduation ceremonies, so that spring we had all been practicing. Every class in physical education at that time was involved with Zouave. On March 5, I fell over a chain playing tag with my roommate's niece who had been at Girl Scout camp with me my freshman year. That day was the birthday of one of our classmates, one of our juniors. And we had celebrated her birthday by having a cookout. Afterward Lu and I took the extra hamburgers over to the Goose so security could come and get them. Then the kids said, "Oh, let's play tag!" As P.E. majors, how could we refuse that request? So we were running back over to where the barbecue was, and the chains were like a fence around Peyton dorm. I turned around to tell them watch out for the chains and when I did, one threw me. I hit it, and it threw me over. Afterward I had a stiff neck, but I didn't think anything of it then. My parents came up the next night and took us out. Then after that we went over to the Baptist Student Union center and watched George Gobel [20] on television. That was the only television on campus, and we had it because one of our group's pledges had a boyfriend who was in the military at the base. He had given a TV to the Baptist Student Union center. While I was there, my neck started to bother me. It turned out that I had a fractured vertebra in my neck—the seventh cervical vertebra. I had just had anatomy so I was a little aware of what was happening. It was a process that articulates with the vertebra above it. So I had to wear a brace, and I had to sleep in the infirmary for several months, and I could not be in Zouave. After that, every afternoon I'd go out and watch the practice, but I did not participate in it. However, I think I could have done about every move that was in it. It was amazing, because everybody was taking physical education since it was required. Then everybody in each class learned what they were supposed to do, and finally it was put together. To watch Miss Pohl was fascinating.

VT: What can you tell me about junior-senior rivalry?
BG: During the junior-senior plays, there was a competition. We'd have a person from our class directing us. Doug Stevens was our class director, and she wanted me to be the preacher in the play. So I was the preacher and Janet Clare Smith was my wife. I still have the program for that. The judges said that my attire was very fitting—I had little glasses that I had worn when I was in the third grade, silver-border-rim glasses that I wore

20. George Gobel (1919–91) was a comedian who hosted *The George Gobel Show* on NBC from 1954 to 1960.

down on my nose. And I was made up with the haircut and had the collar. I never knew which denomination or what affiliation I was, but I was the preacher. It was a great experience. Of course if she asked us to do anything, we didn't turn Doug down. For Stunt Night, we did things which had once been sort of cruel toward faculty members. We had been asked not to be so mean-spirited about them in our skits, so we tried to avoid ridicule. The theme that year was movies and musicals, and Lu and I had *Harvey*.[21] I was Harvey, and she was Jimmy Stewart. I had the rabbit ears on. Those are the kinds of things that we did, but we would do it as a class, and at that time there was still some of the two-year club influence on the rivalry. It was a little calmer in some respects, but still a competition between the classes. We did not go and steal things from others' rooms to show off at night. That all developed later over the years. And of course it's been toned down now, since it got really out of hand. But we would sing as a competition. We sang by classes, and we would usually sing on the steps of the old Goose. Songfest[22] was usually held on the steps, and we would be sitting on those or maybe on the steps of Poindexter. Everything was more class-oriented for us. There was a unity that you really felt as a class that you don't have now. When people hear about the sophomore-junior rivalry, if they haven't been there and seen it happen before, they have no idea about what's going on. Even the people who are supposed to be the leaders don't know what's supposed to be done, so the traditions are really lost as there is no continuity as there was previously. When I was here, we were all on campus. We were captive audiences and captive participants. But we did it willingly, because it was just what everyone did. There was no other entertainment. That changed quickly, though. When I came back to the W in 1967 as a faculty member, I was teaching a conditioning class right after lunch. Shattuck Hall was still open. I had gotten back from my lunch and had parked the car. All of a sudden, everybody was running like wild to the dormitories.

21. *Harvey* (1950) starred James Stewart as a man with a friend who was an invisible six-foot rabbit.

22. Songfest is a song-and-dance competition among the women's social clubs held at MUW every spring.

I'm trying to remember what soap opera was on that day, but there was something big that was supposed to happen on that program that day. Quite a few people were not in my class, and it was one of those classes that met two days in a row and then skipped a day—Monday, Tuesday, and then Thursday. The next day—it must have been a Monday that this particular program was on—I said, "How many of y'all enjoyed that episode?" And all these hands went up before they realized they were admitting they hadn't been in class the day before. Then everybody just cackled because they realized I had caught them. That was in the late 1960s. Having been here on faculty for twenty-four years and living in the community since 1991 after my retirement, I've seen many evolutions.

VT: What do you think about the campus today?

BG: One of the wonderful things is that we by far have the prettiest campus in the state of Mississippi. In fact, we have one of the prettiest campuses in the Southeast. When I was tennis coach, we went to Auburn, Alabama, Duke, UNC–Chapel Hill, and other big campuses for tournaments. Ours is the most beautiful. Just the ambience, the feeling, the environment, I think, is one of the things I'm most grateful for. Within that framework, I feel that we have really been nurtured in an academic and social group. We have been given more than just a classroom experience. I know here I was growing up in an environment where I knew my professors personally. Some of them were sponsors of clubs I was a member of. They didn't have to be at meetings. But you knew them and they knew you, and they were interested in you. And if you needed them, if you were brave enough to express that you needed them, they were available. And there was a lot of loyalty as far as the faculty was concerned. I saw the campus, and I saw the people as a part of the campus. I always felt this very strongly. When I was out in the professional world for years in physical therapy at Vanderbilt and at the University of Alabama, if I said I was a graduate of the W, people would say, "Oh yes, that's such a fine school." People from all over the Southeast and in other areas would say, "Yes, I really understand.

It's the Stephens[23] of the South." Fortunately, money has been made available these last few years to keep the campus updated, because it was really beginning to crumble. Now universities are building structures that they'll have to change within twenty years to keep them current. This is something that the administrations will have to face, but we are very fortunate in our facility, and I think we're very fortunate in this community. We are a part of the community, and students don't realize sometimes how important that connection is. It's also important for the community to realize that the W is a very essential part of their lives. It works both ways, and it's unique. When the W's not in session, something's missing. The campus is there, but the students are not. Our society has gotten to where we have so much to do that we don't have time to be still. And yet that's something that's so important for us to learn how to stop and really appreciate the beauty around us.

VT: What did you do on weekends while you were a student?
BG: Usually we would sleep late. Since we didn't have cars, we couldn't go out and get a hamburger, and really there were not many hamburger places. There was no McDonald's or anything like that. The old Holiday Inn—it's now Master Hosts—was the last building on Fifth Street North, which becomes Highway 45 North. There was nothing after that. When I came back in 1967, there was a trailer out there that had good hamburgers. And there were a lot of residences, homes out along the strip, not close together but spread out—sort of in a flood area. It's been interesting to watch the whole Highway 45 strip open up since I came back in 1967. But in the 1950s, we would stay on campus, and we would just bum around. If somebody was going home, we might go with her. During my junior and senior years, two of my classmates had cars. I was privileged to be able to drive both of them. And I would often drive them home, but going to Yazoo City, the car would be packed. We'd fill it up to go home. Marie,[24] the owner, would let me drive it a lot of times,

23. Stephens College, a private school for women founded in 1833 and located in Columbia, Missouri.
24. Marie McGraw May, Class of 1956.

and she'd just be in the car. Duckie had a car, and she lived in Louisville. Occasionally we would drive there, but we didn't go many places unless it was to State to a ball game or something like that. Not many people went to Alabama at that time; it was more Mississippi State. We would just stay on campus and catch up and do our hand washing—things we didn't want to send to the laundry since they starched so heavily. Then we'd go to church on Sunday, most of us. They would have a van for the churches. It was a bus then, I guess. They would pick us up; we would go to Sunday school, and we'd get back and go to Shattuck for lunch—really fine meals on Sunday. Then we'd go to Sunday evening services, and some organizations would have different events on Sunday afternoons.

Time conflicts between events rarely happened. At the Baptist Student Union and at Wesley there was Noonday every day. So according to our denomination we would go to Noonday after lunch because we didn't have to be in class until 2:00. Our junior year, I believe it was, the Baptist Student Union burned. A fire started in the stage area. After that, we would go over after class and help take debris out and that sort of thing. One of the lumber companies that was owned by Baptists was helping. For all the time we put in it, they would put in supplies. They made a rate of time and money. When we'd go for supper after being out of class and working there, our friends would say, "Oh, I smell a Baptist!" because we'd smell like the smoky building we'd just been in.

I think back on my experiences—of the skills that naturally developed within me because of my love for competition, my love for movement, and also in the area of nonverbal communication. I once saw five books of the Bible in the American Bible Society in New York City, a stack from the floor to the height of a table, that were in Braille. They were Helen Keller's. We think how remarkable she was to learn to communicate, but we don't realize how remarkable it is that 92 percent of our process of interaction with each other is not verbal. It's the meat of the process. Every word we say is wrapped in nonverbal clues—that's paralanguage. How we say what we say can cut off a communication process immediately or make it continue. The fascination for me is that in a relationship, all the nonverbal dimensions work together—you see me moving my hands, you see me looking at you and moving my head. That's kinesic behavior. And the verbal communication we use is interrelated. If you can read a passage of something, you can read the nonverbal in something. It's all a part of it.

Our perceptions work differently because of our age, because of our experiences in life, because of experiences of our background—socioeconomic, educational, cultural. This is so important. Because how do we work with people in groups or classes? How do we relate to family members? How do we relate to a patient? How do we relate to our students? How do we relate to somebody who's going to be reading our materials or following us through a museum one day? Nonverbal communication is really the foundation of our language, yet we spend so little time on it. To me it's one of the most fascinating things to be attuned to. I think that the experiences I've had just observing somebody have taught me so much. I will watch somebody and look to see if their pelvis is level or their shoulders high, or if their head's to one side. I notice these clues because of what I've learned in working with patients over the years and working with my students over the years. Observational skills are so important, yet we spend very little time in developing these skills. Now they are beginning to teach babies sign language. It's not the signing of those who have a hearing deficit. It's signing to get them to communicate earlier. Who does the baby mimic? The person who is around him or her.

I worked with a child at the University of Florida—I was there on leave from Alabama—a child that the doctor's prescription for treatment was for us to give as much tender loving care as we could give. The child was thirteen months old, but it looked like it was eighty or ninety years old: skin drawn, no expression, just gazing in one spot. I did range-of-motion exercises with the baby and just spent time rubbing and talking to it. But the baby died because the child was ignored from birth. The child never had a chance to develop any of its sensory skills because there was no input into it. This lets us know how precious life is and how important it is to learn how to relate one to each other, and that our world would be a much stronger and better place to live in now if we could just communicate with each other sensibly and peacefully.

We're all so much alike, regardless of the freckles on our skin or which part of the world we come from.

After I was practicing as a student and a professional physical therapist, I began to realize the importance of nonverbal communication. It does not make you a mind reader, but it makes you much more attuned to the individual with whom you are working. Through observation, you know when you should talk with somebody about something, and you know when you shouldn't. These are social skills that are very important, and they're not taught in med schools. Some of the med schools are beginning to teach empathy courses. Can you imagine? I can remember hearing a physician at what's now the University of Alabama at Birmingham say that one of the most difficult things for a male physician to do is to learn how to touch somebody else—a person they do not know. This is because usually they're not caregivers. They usually don't babysit as teenagers (this was in the 1960s). When you think about it, there are a lot of females now who are in the same situation.

VT: By the time people are in medical school, is it too late to teach observation and empathy?

BG: I'm not sure. Sometimes some people you would think are incapable of learning still can, at least if they can think. When you work with seminar groups teaching nonverbal communication, the biggest thing is simply to bring it to the awareness level. My mother, who had Alzheimer's the last years of her life, always was so irritated with me if I would run out of the house, particularly on a wet day, without shoes on. On a cold day, she would get angry. Almost at the end of her life, she told me of an experience that had made her react that way, and I doubt if she realized this herself because it was a memory. She told me that her mother died of pneumonia, and it was three days after she'd gone out to see a relative off somewhere and she'd had on little footlets to go outside. She didn't have on shoes; I guess they were slippers. My mother associated the lack of shoes, catching pneumonia, a cold, and death. All those were all nonverbal messages she had as a child. She was eleven years old when her mother died. We often don't know the impact of specific actions. I was told when

I was in fifth grade to stop singing in a class. I didn't sing again until I was out of Duke and then sang in a college choir—even sang a solo one time in a contest. I was as tall as the fifth-grade teacher at that time. She was standing right next to me in the middle of the class. Rarely did she do that; my desk was in the middle of the room, and she usually taught from the front. We had the little yellow golden book to sing out of. Her name was Miss Key—I can remember it was Frances Scott Key. This particular day, she was standing next to me—she was standing on my left—and she barely looked down at me and said, "Barbara, stop singing." She never told me why. A child back then never asked, "Why did you tell me to stop singing?" But how she said what she said—it wasn't the kinesics (the turning of the head and looking at me). It's how she said what she said that made me believe something was wrong with my voice. All of those years I could have enjoyed singing. I did enjoy music, but didn't think I had a voice to sing because of her. That day I did stop singing. It was very possible that I was singing so loudly that she couldn't hear anybody else sing, not necessarily that I was singing badly. But I had no idea about that.

VT: How do you think your classmates remember you from the W?
BG: Probably as a tennis player. I think my classmates would probably remember me as an athlete. However, I was involved in everything. I was in Theatre Guild because of my enjoyment of backstage work. I was on the *Spectator*. My sophomore year I was the secretary of the class. I was a Rogue. And of course I was a Jester junior and senior years, and I was a Hottentot my junior and senior years. I would not be perceived as having been a scholar, because my interests were not very scholarly. However, I loved the sciences and I had math—I was the only girl in plane and solid geometry in high school. So they will remember me as a tomboy maybe, athletic certainly, but hopefully as a good friend.

VT: How do you feel about being a Golden Girl now after fifty years?
BG: I feel very happy because we have reached our financial goal. We have over $80,000 that we've gotten in the last fourteen years, and there

are a number of people in our class that have given other scholarships. Personally, I have given an annual award in my mother's and in her nurse's name for the graduate nursing program. Several people have given awards in honor of their parents. Several husbands have given scholarships in honor of their wives. Mary Lib and I set the goal fourteen years ago—that if we each gave $50 a year for fourteen years, it'd be $750 per person, and if a hundred people gave, that would be $75,000. So over fifty of our class have given, and we have reached over $75,000. One of the great things now is to hear my friends' voices, like for example Jane calling from Jackson to see if I know the words to the alma mater—it's changed since we were students.[25] And to hear people calling me from San Antonio or talking to classmates from Missouri and hearing about their families and what the families are accomplishing. My having taught the daughters of alum friends at the W has been special because I could see the similar characteristics of their parents in them. There are wonderful, wonderful students who come from alums.

There are a lot of W memories that have been incorporated into many things that we do now. And it doesn't take long—we have popcorn and sit down and start chatting. When our group gets together every year—this is a group of twelve to fifteen—it is just like we were back in the dorm together. We just go right back to being our old selves. One of the beautiful things, one of the remarkable and wonderful things about being so close is that we know each others' strengths and weaknesses. If somebody was strong in something, those were the responsibilities they took over in the group, on campus and later. It was in learning to live and work with each other that was the growth period for us—not in just competing on a field but in getting something together for an event and realizing that we knew how to do it. We just did it, and we learned how to enjoy it. It was just a natural

25. The original alma mater was written by Frances "Frankie" Jones Gaither, Class of 1909, and begins "In our heart of hearts rests a sacred retreat . . ." According to students who had to sing it often, the song had a difficult tune and range for most voices. In the late 1950s, a student committee was organized to produce a new alma mater in time for the W's seventy-fifth anniversary. The new song, "Serene as the Dawning," was first sung in May 1959 at the Magnolia Chain class day exercises.

thing, a process. Yet that still exists—appreciation for each other still exists. This will be a great adventure for us to reach our fiftieth reunion and to share with each other again. It will be two days of sharing experiences and just getting back together like we used to. Catching up is a big thing!

Mary Elizabeth Barrett Francis
Class of 1956

AUGUST 2, 2006

INTERVIEWED AND TRANSCRIBED BY RACHEL FORESTER

MARY ELIZABETH BARRETT WAS BORN IN NEW ALBANY, Mississippi, on November 24, 1934. Her mother, Mary Rawls Barrett Martin, graduated from the W in 1931; her father, Raphoral Lee Barrett, attended Mississippi State and taught agriculture. While at the W, Mary Lib Barrett was a member of the Debate Team; the Blue Serenaders band; the Hottentots, an organization for campus leaders; the orchestra; the staff of the *Spectator*, MSCW's student newspaper; the Mississippi Youth Congress; the Southern Intercollegiate Association of Student Government; the National Student Congress; Mortar Board, a national college honor society; the President's Council; Lockhearts, a freshman-sophomore social club; and Black List, a junior-senior social club. She was elected secretary of the student government during her sophomore year and served as vice president in her junior year. Chosen Miss MSCW and elected president of the Student Goverment Association during her senior year, she earned a degree in mathematics and English. In

1956, she married Jack C. Francis, who owned and operated an insurance agency. She taught mathematics before turning to a career in real estate, and she served on the Mississippi Real Estate Commission for four years. President of the MUW Alumnae Association from 1976 until 1978, Francis has received the MUW Alumnae Achievement Award and served a term as treasurer of the MUW Foundation Board. She is also a civic leader in Amory, where she now lives.

MF: My childhood was perhaps a little different from most. It certainly affected my life, although I guess it was normal the first few years. Both my parents were schoolteachers. They met teaching school and married, and then my brother was born, and then me. My father was an agriculture teacher in Minter City, Mississippi. Apparently it was customary then for the school to provide a house for the agriculture teacher, so we lived in a house on the school grounds. My brother is just thirteen months older than I, and he got to go to school first. When my turn came, which I had been waiting for, I was sick. I didn't get to go, so my mother taught me at home.

Then the war came—World War II—and my father was called into service. He went in as an officer because he had been in ROTC at State. Because of that we were able to move around with him for his training up until the time he went overseas. So that's when my childhood became different, with the combination of not going to school and then our family moving around with him. Before a move, he would go first with his battalion, and then when he could find housing for us, we would move there. When he was transferred, we would move again.

We went to Texas first, and I was able to go to school there, but it was always confusing to me. I had been taught at home and didn't have a school record, and in Texas you had to go to kindergarten first. I was ready to go to the second grade, but they thought I should start at kindergarten. I went for a couple of weeks, and then they moved me to first grade for a couple of weeks and then they put me in second grade, but they called it third. I'd only been to school a few months but

I was in level 3! The next move was to Kentucky. After Texas I had a school record, and it said grade 3, so they put me in the third grade. My mother said, "No, she's supposed to be in the second grade." We had to go through this with every move. For example, when I went to school in Texas, they were teaching me to print, but my mother hadn't bothered with that. We went straight to cursive at home. So when I finally got to the right level, it was okay, but for a while there, I thought, "I don't know what everybody else is doing." One day in Kentucky we went into the gymnasium, and I'll never forget it. All the students in the stands stood up and sang "Remember Pearl Harbor,"[1] and I had never heard that song before, so again I had that feeling of not knowing. It was always like this everywhere because we wouldn't be in one place long before we moved again. After leaving Texas, we went back there once, and we also went to my mother's parents' home in Hernando, Mississippi.

During another move we went to California when my father was having the desert training. We lived in Indio, and housing was hard to find there. There was a family that owned acres and acres of orange trees, and they had a big house with a pool in the backyard. Behind the pool was a guesthouse, and they let us live in the guesthouse. We were out in the middle of nowhere, living in those orange groves, just my mother and my brother and I, and we didn't go to school while we lived in California.

Then we went back to Minter City when my father went overseas, and I was young enough so that I didn't really understand about the war. It wasn't a traumatic thing for me, but it was very different because we were writing letters to him back and forth on what they called V-mail, Victory Mail. Do you remember when you were a beginning writer that you probably wrote larger than you do now? We would have one piece of paper, and I would start trying to write something, and I'd soon run out of space. My children now don't know what we're talking about when we talk about this kind of mail, but our letters were photographed and reduced in size, and they were also censored. In the letters that we received from Daddy, if he shouldn't mention a place, the censors would

1. Don Reid and Sammy Kaye, "Remember Pearl Harbor" (1942).

blot it out. He was overseas for over three years, so this V-mail was our communication, because there was no such thing as a phone call. These letters took a long time, maybe two months, getting to or from the person.

Before, in Minter City, we lived in a house provided by the school. The school officials had assured my father that his job would be waiting for him, but when his time stretched into years, they really needed that house. The last year of the war, my mother went to Greenwood, which was not too far from Minter City, found and bought a house, and we moved to Greenwood. This was the summer before I would be in the fifth grade. And the letter to my father about the move didn't reach him. He was allowed to come home on leave that summer, after he had been over there over two years. But when he came home, he went to Minter City instead of Greenwood because he hadn't gotten the letter. At any rate, we had that brief visit and then after the war he came home. Since he no longer had the agricultural teaching job, he worked for the Veterans Administration.

In Greenwood I had a wonderful fifth-grade teacher who caught me up with the subjects I'd missed because of the irregular schooling my first years of my life. I feel like she's one of the teachers that had a profound influence on me. I finished high school when I was seventeen, and I was valedictorian of the class, but that would not have happened if she hadn't caught me up at that time. I had wonderful teachers in Greenwood. Then I didn't know otherwise, so I didn't really appreciate them until I came to the W, even though some of them influenced me to come to the W. I found that when we got to the W, some of us were placed in classes that indicated whether or not we had a good educational background. Then I realized, as I watched some other students struggling with some things that were easy for us, that I should really appreciate those Greenwood teachers.

RF: Why did you decide to attend the W?
MF: It was not a decision that I made. As my brother and I grew up, it was understood that my brother was going to State and I was going to the W.

Of course, as I mentioned, many of the good teachers I had were from the W, and this influenced me also. Now this seems really weird, but I'll say it, although it may sound strange to you. At Greenwood I was president of the student body and I was Miss Greenwood High School. One of my teachers there told me, "You'll go to the W and you'll be president of the student government and Miss MSCW." I didn't think anything about it at the time, although it was a strange thing for her to say to me, but it all came true. The teachers influenced me too, but the decision was really my parents'. My father had died when I was in the ninth grade. It wasn't easy for my mother, so my brother and I pretty much did what she said.

RF: Do you remember anything in particular about your first few weeks at MSCW?
MF: It wasn't a big deal. I had always known I was coming to the W. I roomed with a friend from Greenwood, whose aunt, incidentally, was Miss Nellie Keirn,[2] dean at the time. We immediately made really lifelong friendships. And that was wonderful. We were at that time all here together. We didn't have cell phones. We didn't really have regular phones, although there was one in the dormitory. And we didn't have cars. We had Saturday classes, so we didn't go home much. And I loved it because I think I had, after all those years, some stability—not because there was anything wrong with my parents. They were certainly solid citizens and had the right set of values, but with the turmoil of the war, my father's being gone so much, and then his early death, I guess that these were my most peaceful years, and that was what I needed.

RF: Did campus social clubs help you bond quickly with the other students?
MF: I was in social clubs, and those girls, I suppose, were my closest friends because we were thrown together more, but it was never my priority. If I hadn't been in a club, I don't think it would have made that

2. Nellie Sutton Keirn (1885–1975), Class of 1906, was hired at II & C in 1906 as a teaching fellow. She taught until 1919, when she became dean, serving until 1955. She also held the post of acting president of MSCW in 1929–30.

much difference, but it was nice to be asked, and my friends were asked. So there we were, doing something else together.

RF: What do you remember about pledging social clubs?
MF: It was kind of fun as a freshman because pledging did help, since you had to memorize everybody's name and where they were from. It helped you learn about people, and your social club big sister was a person who looked after you, not just in a social club but in general. In addition to that, every freshman had a junior big sister. Since I never had a real big sister, I loved it. So those were the things, low-key things, that made me feel like I was being looked after. It was a safe learning environment. We didn't have a lot of worries that students now have about safety or about conflicting opinions. Now there are so many different groups and such strong ideas about religion. We were all pretty much alike, since we were raised in Christian families. I think our parents were the ones that are now called the Greatest Generation. It was a good time for us to be at the W.

RF: Who was your favorite professor?
MF: I guess the professor I saw the most of and admired tremendously was my math professor, Mr. Russell Grossnickle.[3] In every math class he was my teacher. I had a double major in math and English. I had a lot of different English teachers but only the one math teacher. I knew him better perhaps because of that. And he in my mind was the way a teacher should be. Of course, he had taught my high school math teacher, too, and she was an excellent teacher. I was well prepared for his classes, and they were not hard for me, but they were for some students. I observed that he had a strong belief in helping students as long as they were wanting to learn. He would give them as much time as it took to teach them. I marveled at his patience. Some of these students would ask questions

3. Russell Lowell Grossnickle Sr. served as professor and head of the math department at MSCW from 1926 to 1964. In 1979, Grossnickle Residence Hall was named in his honor. At the dedication ceremony, Barrett spoke of her memories of Grossnickle and announced a scholarship in his name.

which seemed so elementary to those of us who had had these things before, and he was always so patient with them. He would look them in the eye and keep talking to them and explaining and explaining until finally they said, "Oh!" and then he would grin from ear to ear and then move on. But he would also meet with them after class if they needed extra help. He was a really intense teacher. He would come into the classroom and he'd look around and grin and he would tell a joke. Then he would enjoy the joke as much as we did, but he would get the attention of the students. As he taught, his eyes were darting around the room the whole time. He could tell if somebody wasn't getting it, and then he would work on her. I had not planned to be a teacher and didn't get a teacher's license, but after I married and went to a small town, that was my one option. So I became a teacher. I had not had the courses in education, so in my mind the way to be a teacher was to try to be like him. I taught math—first-year algebra, mostly.

One of my students was having a hard time understanding math, but he really wanted to learn and he wanted help. Given the example I'd had with Mr. Grossnickle, I believed that helping this student was what I was supposed to do, so I met with him before school and after school and during my break period and during my lunch hour. I helped him a lot, because that's what I had seen Mr. Grossnickle doing. Personally I was inclined to enjoy the good students more, but I tried to not ever let him know that and to do what I thought Mr. Grossnickle would have done. He made it through that class, and he grew up to be a math teacher, surprisingly. He lived in the same community as I did, although he taught in Aberdeen, which was twenty minutes or so away. But in all of those years that this man taught, if any student from Amory needed extra help, and some of them would need somebody to tutor them on the side, they would naturally go to him because he lived in Amory and they knew he knew the subject, although he was a teacher in another town. He did that for anybody in Amory who asked him for help all the years that he taught, and he wouldn't accept pay from them. He would say, "This is because of Mrs. Francis." So I was more than repaid for the extra help I gave him, because I don't know how many people through the years came to me and told me what he had said.

RF: Was it difficult to be a double major in English and math?
MF: It was a very strange combination, but no, it wasn't difficult. I liked both of them so well I couldn't decide, and I was able to do enough to get a double major.

RF: Did you have a least favorite subject or professor or another class or professor that you particularly remember?
MF: I guess I could mention one other class, but it certainly wasn't a least favorite. However, it was so entirely different to me that I'll mention it. A one-hour-credit class was offered in art appreciation.[4] While the Greenwood schools were wonderful, I never had any art. I had an aunt who was an artist, and I think I quickly determined that I couldn't draw because I wanted to do what she could and I couldn't. But that was about all my exposure to art, so I took this course in art appreciation and it probably affected my life as much as any other course that I had. It opened up a whole new world. During the time that I was at the W, those of us that were student government officers had to take a trip to Virginia, so we lengthened our trip and went to D.C. and New York City. That was my first trip to New York City, and it was in the spring of my junior year. When we went to the museums and I saw the originals of the things I had studied about in art appreciation, I was so excited. Through the years I have had opportunities to travel, and always museums are on my agenda. Still I have that sense of excitement. Our teacher taught us that 90 percent of appreciation is familiarity, and that proved true for me. But if it hadn't been for him, I wouldn't have had that introduction to the paintings.

My husband and I went to New York recently for our fiftieth wedding anniversary, and I've been many times over the years. I have a whole

4. The teacher was Ralph Hudson (1907–98), professor and head of the art department, who taught at MSCW from 1945 until 1969.

shelf full of playbooks from the shows we've seen in New York, but the trips to the museums are always the most important to me. Our last trip was the first time I had been back to the Museum of Modern Art since they had remodeled. I went in and found they now have five floors. I kept going and going, but finally I found all my favorites on the fifth floor. I still feel that same excitement. That day I looked at Picasso's *Three Musicians*. I had seen it there fifty years ago when I came as a W student. And also Monet's huge *Water Lilies*. I had to go visit them again. I also later found that familiarity with art affected not just my trips but also my home. I like paintings and books in my house. Many years ago, I started collecting books by Mississippi writers and paintings by Mississippi artists. I know that those things that I learned at the W later influenced me and my family. That's how my children grew up; they were exposed to art, too.

A lot of other things we did at the W, like our meals, for example, have influenced me. When we were students, we ate in Shattuck Hall in the dining room. We sat down with our friends, who had become like family. Every meal we sat together, and we ate all at the same time on tablecloths with napkins. Later, I wanted that for my family, too. So as my children grew up, we had one dining room and seated meals, and I'm sure that was from my W influence.

RF: Do you remember any other professors?

MF: Miss Pohl[5] was in her last years when we were on campus, but she was very much a living legend still. At that time she dressed in what I call a Gibson Girl look. She had these black circular skirts, flat shoes, and a white blouse with a big red floppy bow at the neckline. And that's the way she was any time you saw her on campus. We all speculated about how many outfits she had just like that one so that she could dress consistently. I think the only class I had under her was freshman level, what was called fundamentals. We learned some dancers' arm movements and

5. Emma Ody Pohl (1880–1966) joined II & C in 1907, when she was hired to develop the department of physical education. She taught that subject until her retirement in 1955.

that sort of thing. But Zouave was done once when I was on campus. It was my junior year, so we did get to experience that event and to know Miss Pohl and the things that made her famous, such as her appearance while stalking around the campus. I remember for some reason she called us all by our last names, which was sort of unusual. In my mind I can see her as clearly now as then.

RF: Can you tell me about your experiences on the debate team and at Mississippi Youth Congress?
MF: That was the Greenwood influence again. When I was a senior at Greenwood High School, a teacher came there who was able to teach speech, and I signed up. Then she wanted to have a debate team. There were four of us picked from that class, so I was in the first debate I ever saw. It was a new thing to us. I have to go back to high school to explain why I was involved in these things in college. In Greenwood, we learned what a debate was, and we were in competition with other towns. Eventually we made it to the state finals against Greenville. We debated that team I don't know how many times to get to the state finals. Then when we got to the state finals, we debated them for the state championship, and we won.

When I came to the W, all freshmen had to take speech. The main speech I remember was one where we had to explain how to do something. A new thing to me was that we were all issued laundry bags with a number stamped on it. We put our dirty clothes in the bag, and on a certain day we threw them downstairs, and they were picked up and then returned a day or so later. I still remember my number was 1044. Later, we would go pick up our laundry bag and there were our clean sheets or towels or whatever we had sent to the laundry that week. This laundry bag had a drawstring through little holes that ran around the top. And it was a circular string—it wasn't like it had two ends. When I first saw it, I thought, "How do you fasten it?" This question became the topic of my speech. I went over to the laundry and asked them how to close and fasten it, and they showed me a particular kind of knot that I could use. That was my demonstration speech. The teacher, another surprise, gave me what she said was the highest grade she'd ever given a student on a speech. Her comment caught the attention of the head of the department, who called me in and said he had been puzzled by that grade but then found out that I had been on the debate team in high school. He asked me to join debating at the W. That department head was Dr. Cromwell,[6] and now the building is named after him. So it wasn't, I assure you, that I was a real good debater, but I guess there weren't a lot of high schools that had debate, so with my experience, I was able to be on the W team, too. That was the group that went to Youth Congress. I think the award that I won at Youth Congress was for parliamentary procedure. I had brushed up on that, so I used some issue of procedure or motion to get our team out of a difficult situation. Even though I got some special award for that, I was really not a good speaker or a good debater, but I did have those experiences which came in handy.

I'll elaborate just a little bit more. One thing that the teams were taught which has come in handy through the years is how to chair a committee meeting or lead a group through a discussion, that sort of thing. After the student government people had gotten to Virginia for that conference, I was told that I was to chair a discussion. I don't remember the topic now, but attending were student leaders from all over the South. It was a conference for the Southern Intercollegiate Association of Student Governments. Apparently somebody from my school knew that I was down to chair the discussion, but they didn't tell me in advance. So when I got there I learned about it and didn't have time to plan. However, I had a little bit of training, and it didn't faze me. I just went out there with these girls who were leaders from their schools, and we had a really good group session. A short time later, all the different groups assembled again in the auditorium for the election of officers of that association. I was nominated from the floor for president by somebody who had been in my group and by one of the other students from the W. There were three of us from the W, and one of the W students stood up and made

6. Harvey Cromwell (1907–77) served as director of speech and theater, dean of arts and sciences, and dean of the graduate school at MSCW between 1949 and 1975. In 1977, the new Harvey Cromwell Communications Center was named for him.

a speech on my behalf. The first thing I knew, I was elected president of the Southern Intercollegiate Association of Student Governments. As a result, I had to plan the next annual meeting and was sent as a delegate to the National Student Association held that summer in Minneapolis. I met people from all over the country who were in similar positions as student body presidents, and it was a wonderful experience. That little speech class led to all that.

We often went to different places for the tournaments, but one of them was held on our campus. Of course we were a girls' school, but the teams that we were debating against were not necessarily all girls. I met this boy, and I guess you'd say he had a crush on me. Anyway, he invited me out that night. We were going to debate against each other the next day. He was trying to do something impressive and be very gallant about everything. Most of us kept our notes in little index boxes, and he had brought his along on the date. He thought it would be impressive to give his to me to take in with me that night so I could know what he was going to say and be prepared to debate him the next day. That was something no other boy has ever done! I didn't open it because I felt it would have been unethical. I don't really remember who won that debate!

RF: What did you do on the weekends?

MF: We had Saturday classes. Sometimes we had dates, and in the early years, we had to double-date, but as the years progressed, we had more freedom. Sometimes we didn't have dates, and we would do things with other girls on campus. We could walk downtown to the movie. Somehow the boys seemed more likely to have cars than we did, so on a date we could have more chances to do different things, but there was always a group on campus, so if you didn't have a date you could still have fun. I guess students now would think it was very boring, but it wasn't to us. Some of the girls in the social club might have a party or go out to eat together or just hang out together in a room. I don't remember

7. The Golden Goose Tearoom, located on the first floor of the Student Activities Building (formerly the Henry Whitfield Gymnasium), demolished in the late 1960s.

there being a TV on campus until my junior year. Some people would go over and watch TV at the Goose[7] then. I don't think I did that but once or twice, and there weren't ever a lot of people there. We didn't grow up being used to things like television. We made our own entertainment, I guess you would say. One unusual thing that happened, I only remember it happening once, was that somebody got up a bus trip to Birmingham to see a stage production of *South Pacific*.[8] That night, we rode the bus to Birmingham. That was my first time to see a traveling Broadway show, and it was just a magical night. The performance was wonderful. As I remember, Mary Martin[9] was the star, but anyway, when we came out of the theater, huge snowflakes were falling. Some of the girls from the coast had never seen snow. It was a treat for all of us. Then we loaded back on the bus and came back to campus. That was fun.

RF: Can you tell me any stories about tricks or pranks that people played on others?

MF: I thought all those pranks took place at Mississippi State! You remember now that I was president of the student government, but I guess it's all right to tell this. My freshman roommate was a great person. She was pretty and bubbly and so much fun. And her aunt was the dean. That enabled me to see a different side of Miss Keirn, one that other students never saw—Dean Nellie Keirn as somebody's adoring aunt. My roommate would talk about Aunt Nell, since that's what she called her. We were sometimes invited to her house. She also made cakes for my roommate, beautifully decorated cakes that she had done herself. Of course Miss Keirn would have wanted every student to observe all the rules, but my roommate attracted the eye of an older man in Columbus, and they didn't like the rule about just dating on the weekends. Also, she was the first person I ever knew that had horrible cramps once a month. It was terrible. There was only one thing that would relieve her, so in the

....

8. *South Pacific*, a musical by Richard Rogers and Oscar Hammerstein, opened on Broadway in April 1949.
9. Mary Martin (1913–90) was a stage and film star best known for her stage roles as Peter Pan and as Nellie Forbush in *South Pacific*.

bottom dresser drawer, she kept a whiskey bottle for medicinal purposes. That would have never been approved by Aunt Nell. I spent a lot of my time on campus working on rule changes. Every year the student government would propose rule changes to the administration. We would go to the president and plead our case, and usually we would get approval on some of them.

One of my jobs as student government president was to preside regularly at chapel or assemblies in Whitfield Auditorium. This was a time for the different organizations to make announcements about when they were having meetings and what was due and other things. I would stand there on the stage and say, "Are there announcements from this section?" and then they would raise their hands and they would stand up. I'll never forget the slip of tongue I made one day when a certain place on one of the highways had been approved for our attendance. This place was better than a joint, or they would never have approved it as a place for the W girls to go, but some places like that were not approved. And in making an announcement I said, "There's finally a place off-limits where we can go." And the whole student body laughed. Girls were always wanting to go dancing at certain places, and it wasn't always allowed. It was fine to go to Mississippi State for the weekend, spend the weekend over there and go to dances, but you couldn't go to the local places.

RF: Did you meet your husband at Mississippi State?
MF: No, no. He's ten years older, so he tells people that he came to the W longer than I did. He did date many girls and has his own set of stories about the W, but it was after my junior year that I met him. He was working in Greenwood, and I was home for a couple of weeks that summer, and we happened to be on the tennis courts the same night. That's where we met.

This reminds me of another opportunity that came about because I was at the W. A number of us would be counselors at Camp DeSoto[10] on

10. Camp DeSoto is a Christian camp for girls and young women located in Mentone, Alabama.

Lookout Mountain in the summers. The people that hired for that camp would come to the W and interview students to work there. I think my salary those summers was only enough to pay my transportation there and back. But I learned so much being a counselor at Camp DeSoto. The leaders there were such strong Christians and so intent on making it a good experience for the campers, but they looked after the counselors, too. And most of the counselors were our friends from the W, although there were certainly some from other schools, too. It was a fantastic camp, and working there taught me so much. That experience influenced my family and our life, too. I wanted both of my girls to go there as campers, and so a lot of summers I later made the trip back to Camp DeSoto. It's a funny feeling, too, when your children start singing the same songs you sang and having the same experiences.

RF: What were your favorite traditions at the W?
MF: Oh, I think everybody twirled around backward to walk through the Old Maid's Gate every time we left the campus. And every fall, when the leaves on the ginkgo tree turned yellow and a wind came up, we would all head over and stand under the big tree because if a leaf fell on you, good things would happen.

The other day I ran across a snapshot of Carolyn Smithson Ritter.[11] There's a picture of me putting the robe on her shoulders. She was the incoming student government president. At Mag Chain,[12] we passed down a symbol of our activity to the incoming person who was taking over. When I ran across that snapshot, which is almost faded, it reminded me of that day.

....

11. Carolyn Smithson Ritter, Class of 1957.
12. In 1894, in imitation of some eastern schools, II & C graduating seniors carried a daisy chain from the steps of the old chapel to an outdoor ceremony. In 1913, seniors modified the tradition and carried a magnolia chain. The students still sing the traditional magnolia chain song and carry a magnolia chain at a special class day ceremony before commencement in May. At the end of the ceremony, the seniors rush to the piled chain to claim a bud or flower. Those who get either one will have good fortune, which has been variously defined over the years and for some generations involved being the first to marry.

RF: How do you feel about men being admitted to the W?

MF: Oh, it's okay with me. There's a man now who's an alum who is president of the W Foundation Board.[13] He's a doctor, and he's going to be a good leader. It's nice to know he had his start at the W, too. So there are good things about coeducation, although I do think that now they have discovered that students learn better in a single-sex environment, and many high schools are now dividing their classes. They have good reports from the grades of both groups when they do that, so things go full cycle.

RF: Tell me about your work with the Amory Arts Council.

MF: In 1975, communities across the country were getting ready for the country's bicentennial. So we had town meetings in Amory to decide what sort of project we wanted to undertake. The decision was made to start a museum, and I was in on the beginning of that. We located an old, abandoned building in Amory which had been the first hospital in Northeast Mississippi. The building belonged to the private hospital there, but they had built a new one to replace it. They gave the building to the city, and we raised money to have it redone and made into a museum. I was on the original museum board and am still on it after all these years. Right now, we're working on a million-dollar expansion. We've just raised the money for that, and we'll be letting bids on that within the next month. We met with the architects this week. The museum has been a source of pride for a town our size, and it is not only a historical museum for the area, but it's an activity and meeting place for our small town. It's a place where we've been able to have changing art exhibits and traveling exhibits. We've had lectures there and had writers come and talk, that sort of thing. So it's good to have in our community, and with the expansion, we'll be able to have much more in the way of exhibits and speakers. We're also receiving a generous bequest that will enable us to have money every year now to have some exhibits that cost thousands of dollars, which we've not been able to have before. The

13. Dr. Edward Betcher, Class of 1988, has served as the president of the MUW Foundation Board since 2006.

museum is owned by the city, and that's where our budget comes from, but because of the generosity of some different people, these good things are happening now. It's from the museum board that the arts council has evolved, and right now the arts council and the museum board are working together on this project. The arts and the museum go so well together. There's the possibility that in the future, the arts council might be the umbrella association for other venues for the arts, but right now it's just connected to the museum.

RF: What do you feel is the most valuable lesson that you learned at the W?
MF: I've spent my life participating in and being involved in community activities, and now I'm on several boards. I have had a lot of opportunities with grants committees and charitable foundations, the arts council, the museum board, and the W boards. I look on them as opportunities for service. As I look around the community, a lot of the people that give time to this sort of thing are graduates of the W, and they are people you call on when you're looking for somebody to get the job done. It's amazing how many times the people in those leadership positions are W graduates. I don't know why that is, but it is true. I'm on one board that involves nineteen counties in Northeast Mississippi. Some great people are on that board, but every woman that's on that board—and there are only a handful of us and none of us is the same age—we all have a W background. I don't remember anybody ever telling us to be involved, but we were always involved on campus. At the W, everybody was doing something all the time, and it became second nature. We were expected to do this, and we did it, and we've kept on doing it through life. I would say that that's one of the most important things that the W taught me.

RF: What advice would you give to a current W student?
MF: Take advantage of opportunities while you're here—for education, opportunities for friendships, and for events. Everything that's offered, do it, because you might never have that opportunity again. Just get the most that you can out of your student years.

Janet Carol Davis Gray
Class of 1957

AUGUST 14, 2006

INTERVIEWED BY SARAH SHEFFIELD

TRANSCRIBED BY RACHEL FORESTER

BORN IN JACKSON, MISSISSIPPI, ON AUGUST 7, 1936, Janet Carol Davis was the daughter of Homer B. Davis and Velma Mary Hughes Davis. Janet Davis graduated from the W with a degree in English, speech, and journalism. She participated in the Palette and Brush Club; the Commerce Club; the Glee Club; the Wesley Foundation; the Future Teachers of America; the Theatre Guild; the President's Council; Phi Kappa Phi, a national honor society; the Hottentots, an organization for campus leaders; the Maskers, a junior-senior social club; and the staffs of the yearbook (the *Meh Lady*) and the student newspaper (the *Spectator*). During her senior year, she served as president of the Civic League, editor of the literary magazine (the *Dilettanti*), and assistant director of Tournament Plays. She was a member of Mortar Board, a national college honor society. She married Herman L. Gray, an accountant from Rienzi, Mississippi, in 1957. A piano teacher and church choir director for many years, she is very active in her community and has been named an outstanding citizen of Corinth, Mississippi.

SS: Could you tell me about your early life?
JG: I lived in the country, not next to anybody, and the nearest neighbors were not my age, so I did a lot of reading, a lot of sewing, and a lot of playing with dolls—imaginary things. I had a nice, wonderful time growing up.

SS: What books were your favorites?
JG: Any book. I remember reading *Les Miserables*[1] particularly, when I was maybe eleven or twelve. My mother was a schoolteacher, and sometimes I had to wait on her after school. I would go to the school library, and I made it my personal goal to read everything in the library. That book had fifteen hundred pages in it. I remember reading it and that I was so pleased with myself that I had read it.

SS: Why did you choose to go to college at the W?
JG: I first thought that I would go to Millsaps.[2] I had a scholarship to Millsaps. Then I decided that maybe it would be the best thing for me, since I was an only child and had grown up in Jackson, that I go away from home instead of staying in Jackson. Probably, in this later era, I would have wound up going to Mississippi State because we were Mississippi State fans. But at the time, State only had two hundred girls and umpteen boys. My father was not willing to put me in that situation.

SS: Was it the same kind of situation with Ole Miss?
JG: We really didn't consider Ole Miss because of his affinity to Mississippi State. Nobody even talked about Ole Miss. I was excited to be going to college—that was a big deal. I had done a lot of sewing getting ready to go, sewing clothes and that sort of thing. I did not know anybody,

1. Victor Hugo, *Les Miserables* (1862).
2. Millsaps College, founded in 1890, is a Methodist-run liberal arts college in Jackson, Mississippi.

since I was the only person from my school that went to the W. It turned out that I had met some other people through some church events, and it turned out that my best friend from elementary school who had moved away in the fourth grade was also attending the W. We wound up rooming together. But that was after a couple of weeks of uncertainty and not wanting to hurt anybody's feelings and having our feelings hurt and that sort of thing.

I was in Callaway, first floor, south hall. All three of the front campus dorms, Callaway and Columbus and Hastings, were connected, so you could go through them. All three of them were freshman dorms at the time. I think that Hastings had a fourth floor because I remember some girls that lived up higher had little dormer windows that looked out. While I was there, they were working on South Callaway, and it was opened later, but it was not open when I was a freshman. Orr Chapel was there, but it was not open at the time. Part of it was the speech department.

SS: How did you get to school?

JG: We packed up the car, and we took the car up there. My parents brought me. When we got there, many parents had spent the day fixing up their daughters' rooms. I had a pair of bedspreads, and we had corresponded, but I didn't wind up living with that roommate, so nothing that we had planned worked out. But I didn't have cutesy curtains and all the extra stuff that some of the parents had done. I don't think we knew to do that. Move-in day was scary, but it was fun. I was ready to meet everybody. I wanted to get to know people, I wanted to like them, I wanted them to like me.

SS: How did being one of the youngest members of your class affect you?

JG: I think it made me insecure, and I was also immature socially. I had grown up in a small school, and there were twenty-eight people in my graduating class. I had lived out in the country. I went to a small church. There were maybe a dozen people in our youth group in the church, and that included from seventh grade through twelfth grade. So socially, I did not have a lot of experience. That was all stuff that I learned at the W.

When I was a child, before I started to school, I learned to read. It just happened. And that was not common back then. Now I think most children learn to read in kindergarten, but I did not attend kindergarten. Nobody attended kindergarten unless he or she lived in the city. So when I got to the first grade, the teacher came to my parents midsemester and said, "I've taught her everything she's supposed to know in the first grade. I want to move her over to the second grade. She's ready to be in the second grade." And my parents said, "No, we will not agree to that." So the teacher circumvented them by getting all of the books out of the second grade and teaching me and my best friend, who could also read. And she taught us everything in second grade. At the end of first grade, the teacher called my parents in again and she said, "I've taught these children everything they're supposed to know in the second grade. Now we want to promote them to the third grade." They agreed. So I skipped a grade, but I was already young—my birthday fell in the fall instead of the early part of the year. So when I got to college I was sixteen. There was only one girl, Ellen Young Gunn,[3] who was younger than I, so I was the second-youngest girl. I grew up at the W. I matured at the W.

SS: Did you have a dorm mother?

JG: We had a dorm mother, and her name was Miss Stennis.[4] She was the sister of the senator from Mississippi, John Stennis. Anyway, I was not close to her, although some of the girls were. She lived in the dorm and was a very strict dorm mother. We had to be in by 10:30. Lights out was at 11:00. Many a night when I had to write an essay for English class, since I was not very good about doing things ahead of time, I would not be through when it was lights out. So the lights went out, and I would lie down in the doorway with the hall light and write with the hall light until 12:00. When it was midnight, you could turn on the lights.

3. Ellen Claire Young Gunn, Class of 1957.
4. Janie Eliza Stennis (1885–1979), an alumna and sister of Mississippi's U.S. senator, John Stennis, served as a social adviser at MSCW from 1943 until 1957.

SS: Because the dorm mother had gone to bed by then?
JG: I don't know. I guess because it was the next day, so we could turn on the lights. But my roommate, my good friend, couldn't sleep with the light on. So I spent the night writing, and about 4:00 I would go to bed. Then she would turn the light on to write—we had the same English class—and I couldn't sleep with the light on. I didn't get much sleep. But yes, we had lights out, and we had curfew. We could only date on weekends. We had to sign in and sign out so the dorm mother knew when we were in, and the whistle would blow at 10:20 or 10:25. We knew that we didn't want to leave our date. We'd stay out with the date until the last minute right by the front door so we could dash in to get in by 10:30. Back in those days, we had umpteen crinoline petticoats, and we wore skirts all the time to class—we almost never wore pants. Anyway, when we went out on a date, we wore crinoline petticoats—that was the style. This one friend who lived on my wing on Callaway had a boyfriend, and we were outside. I just had a date, but she was very much in love with this boy. She was hugging him and kissing him, and her petticoat fell down. She just stepped out of it, grabbed it up, and dashed inside.

SS: Do you still keep in touch with any of your college friends?
JG: Some of them. I am very fond of half a dozen of the people. Some of them I keep in touch with, and some of them I don't, but that doesn't change how I feel about them.

SS: Do you remember the first day of classes?
JG: Not really. We took a bunch of testing before classes started to place us in particular English sections. The people who tested high were put in certain classes, and I'm sure that must have been true for some of the other subjects as well—I don't know. I was not really apprehensive about the classes. I didn't have trouble with any of the classes. It was different from high school, so I took copious notes. I don't know where I learned to take notes, since I don't think I had to take notes in high school.

SS: Was English your favorite subject? Was that one of the reasons you chose your major?

JG: I was good at English, and yes, I enjoyed English. I love to read, love to write, and I was good at writing. I was involved in the *Spectator* when I was there, although I never had any journalism classes, but I enjoyed writing. I also thought that speech was fun. There were about three things that impressed me at the W. One, my English teacher was inspiring. He knew so much that he made me want to learn it, too. It was Dr. Bozard.[5]

And the library impressed me. I loved going in the library and finding all of this information. I wanted to find it and grab it. And the other thing, I did not take piano my first semester, and I was miserable, because I had had piano for years, and I didn't realize how much I enjoyed it and how much I would miss it. So as soon as first semester was over, when we registered for second semester, I started taking piano. And I took theory and some other music courses. But if I was taking piano, I had to have practice time. In the music building, as I was practicing, I would hear people through the practice rooms, hear all of these other people practicing, all three floors, all this music going on. It was so inspiring. My friends would say, "How can you practice with all that going on?" But you just shut all the other out or you listen to it and you think, "Oh, if I practice real hard, maybe I can play like that."

I don't think they even had the divisional (multidisciplinary) major when I started out. I think that was developed during the time that I was at the W, and I don't think they have it any more. I think it was one of those ideas that somebody said, "Okay, this is something we ought to do," and then they later decided that wasn't the best idea. I started as an art major. We did not have art as a class in our high school. I had had private art lessons, but I was totally intimidated by the teacher—I think her name was Miss Stringer.[6] She stood up there the very first day, the very first class, in that great big airy room and said, "Now, I want you

5. John Fallaw Bozard (1907–85) taught English at MSCW from 1948 until 1957.
6. Mary Evelyn Stringer (1921–2005) taught art history at MSCW from 1946 until 1987.

to put two"—I can't even remember the terms—"and draw something else that's perpendicular to that and use the foci of such-and-such." And I was thinking, "What is she talking about?" And of course, I didn't know anybody, so there wasn't anybody for me to ask, "What is she talking about?" I tried that one day to do what she said, and the next day I went in there and I thought, "I can't do this. I don't need to be majoring in this." So I changed my major immediately. I changed my major I think every semester until I got to be a junior, when I had to figure out a particular something that I was going to major in. I'm a dilettante, a jack-of-all-trades and master of none, so to speak. I guess I'm a master of music, but that's just because that's what I've chosen to do. But I enjoy a lot of things.

SS: Was there a subject that you didn't really care for?
JG: Economics. It was awful—partly the teacher.

SS: Was that a requirement?
JG: When I was majoring in business, I had to take economics. I would never have chosen to take economics, would never again choose to take economics.

SS: Did any subjects other than music come naturally to you?
JG: The English was easy for me. I had never liked history, and when we took the required freshman course, although I don't remember that teacher's name,[7] that was one of the most inspiring classes that I had. She made history come alive as I didn't know it could. That class gave me an interest in history. She was an amazing teacher. I'll tell you two stories about her. She would sit at her desk, and she had a map of the world behind her. She would take her pointer and point over her head and then would say, "The army started down here in Brussels and worked its way over to . . . ," and she didn't look! She knew where that pointer was going

7. Probably Minnie Clare Boyd (1887–1972), who taught history at MSCW from 1934 until 1963, serving as head of the department until 1948.

to be. And then the other thing was the first semester exam. We went in and we had to take our blue books in and swap them out. When we had our blue books ready, she wrote one question on the board for the survey of world history, "Outline the book." Everybody looked at that question and thought, "Ugghhh." But I had studied that way, and I think that I made an A+. I made a really good grade on it because I had studied by outlining. And I had enjoyed her class, which makes a difference in how you appreciate what you've been taught and what you've retained.

SS: Did you receive any specific awards for your academics?
JG: When I was at the W, they published the grades at the end of the year from highest to lowest—who had the highest grade point, who had the next highest, and all the way. Then, as a reward, you got to choose your dormitory room. The one who had the highest grade got to choose the first room in the dormitory that they wanted to be in, and so on and so on. When I was a sophomore, I had the highest grade average, so I got to choose the first room. It was in the center of the third floor in Peyton Hall. When I was there, those front dorms were for freshmen, Reneau was the sophomore dorm, Peyton was the junior dorm, and Fant was the senior dorm. There was some overflow, but I was always in the main dorms.

Since I had a divisional major in English and speech, that meant that I was involved in the theater productions. One semester, we were having a play, and we were practicing in Whitfield Hall, and the set was up and everything. It may have been *Arsenic and Old Lace*.[8] I know I was in that play. Anyway, I don't remember whether I had a speaking part or whether I was just helping. But at that same time, during play practice, there was a called meeting, a secret meeting, of Mortar Board.[9] We met upstairs, out from the balcony on the east side of Whitfield. There was only one entrance into a small auditorium upstairs off of the balcony in Whitfield Hall. It was normally used by the Glee Club for

8. Joseph Kesselring, *Arsenic and Old Lace* (1939).
9. Mortar Board National College Senior Honor Society was founded in 1918 and elects members based on scholarship and campus leadership.

their regular practices. We were going to meet up there, but we weren't supposed to tell anybody that we were meeting up there. When I got ready to leave play practice, the practice was still going on and my good friend[10] said, "Where are you going?" I said, "I've got a meeting." Then she asked, "Where?" and I said, "I'm just going up in the auditorium to the Glee Club room." Then I said, "Now, don't tell anybody; it's a secret meeting." So I went up to the meeting, and about thirty or forty minutes later she came running up there saying, "Whitfield is on fire." If she had not known that we were up there, I think we would have been trapped. But we were all able to get out safely even though the hall nearly burned down. When graduation time came, we couldn't graduate in Whitfield Hall like everybody else had. We graduated outside on the front lawn on the east side of campus. That's also where Zouave was.

SS: You were involved in Zouave?

JG: Yes, I was in Zouave during my sophomore year. It was great fun. I loved it. We practiced every afternoon. It was with Miss Emma Ody Pohl.[11] She looked like a scarecrow. And even though she was out showing us how to do calisthenics, she had on a full skirt and her hair was all akimbo. I can just visualize her with her hair streaming. It was up, but then it didn't stay up—it just kind of streamed all over everyplace. And her arms going this way and this way and she probably only weighed a hundred pounds. She would be saying, "No. No. NO! That's not right! That's not the way to do that!" Then she proceeded to show us how to do it.

SS: How many people participated in Zouave?

JG: Three hundred, but within that group there was a special group that did calisthenic exercises that were choreographed. We did them in teams of four, and we might do a pinwheel, but we were still doing calisthenics. We did them in a formation that was attractive to the eye, with everybody doing the same formation at the same time. Sometimes the

....

10. Jimmie Meese Moomaw, Class of 1958.

11. Emma Ody Pohl (1880–1966) joined II & C in 1907, when she was hired to develop the department of physical education. She taught that subject until her retirement in 1955.

four would go into eight. It was synchronized and choreographed, and it required a lot of practice. Now, the people who did that were the elite. We were chosen. We tried out, and we were chosen to do that part of it. The rest of the group just did the marching and the turning. That was all synchronized to music, too, but it was not quite as athletic.

SS: Did you have to pass a swim test at the W?
JG: Oh, yes. I was telling my grandchildren about taking swimming, that it was a requirement. I didn't want to get out of anything. I wanted to do everything that I had the opportunity to do. When I was a freshman, you were required to take a gym class every semester. One of those gym classes was freshman calisthenics, so we all did all these exercises. The other was swimming. When we went to swimming, we didn't take our own swimming suit. They provided the swimming suits. They were woolen, old-fashioned, navy blue swimming suits, some of which were moth-eaten. We had to be careful that we didn't get a moth hole in exactly the wrong place. When I was telling my grandchildren about this, they just couldn't believe it. We took them off, and they sent them to the laundry and sterilized them so they smelled like chlorine every time we picked them up, but we knew they were clean. And of course, we just hoped we got one that would cover us up or that fit. I remember Miss Massengale[12] taught swimming. When I was a freshman, I was not very secure, and this was all a new environment and I didn't know a whole lot of people, but I did know how to swim. But I had never had real swimming lessons to learn beautiful strokes. But she says, "Davis! Davis! Show them how that's done!" And I thought, "Is she talking to me? You think I know how to do something with swimming?" That was interesting that she thought that I could swim properly. That was never a problem for me, to pass any test. I enjoyed all of the sports that we took, except that I didn't like the golf that I took. After we had taken our requirements, we didn't want to go back and take freshman calisthenics again. I had had swimming and I didn't particularly want to take any

12. Grace Massengale (1894–1987), Class of 1916, taught physical education at II & C/MSCW from 1916 until 1969.

more. I liked to swim, but I didn't want to spend hours in the pool doing synchronized swimming. That was not my thing. So I did the ballet classes. We did *Les Sylphides*,[13] and I can still remember Miss Pohl showing us all these moves. I did that two or three times while she was there. And I took tennis and bowling. I think golf was in a segment where we had bowling and golf and badminton, several sports, six weeks of this and six weeks of that, and I didn't much care for the golf.

SS: What type of clothes did you wear?
JG: We all had starched petticoats, or if we didn't have starched petticoats, we had the newfangled nylon petticoats that you didn't have to starch.

SS: Were there any requirements about what you could wear to classes?
JG: I don't recall that there were any requirements. It may well have been against the rules to wear pants to class, because we never did. I can remember a time or two being out and about with my raincoat on over my pants so that they didn't show, so there may well have been a rule that in classes that you wore skirts.

I do remember the rules about being out at night, that we had to sign in, sign out. And I remember from being in South Callaway that some of the girls knew how to flout the rules. Some of the girls who were much more adventurous and much more social than I was would have midweek dates. Of course, they weren't supposed to date during the middle of the week, but they would have a midweek date. They would meet down at Annunciation Catholic Church on College Street and then they would climb up those fire escapes and come in that way. I was inexperienced and I was very naive. I can remember one girl who would come in from her dates and she would be so wired up that I just thought she was absolutely crazy. She was drunk, but I didn't know she was drunk. She had been out drinking, but I didn't know that's what was going on. And certainly Miss Stennis didn't know that that was going on.

13. *Les Sylphides* is a romantic ballet by Frédéric Chopin set in a moonlit park.

These particular girls on my wing cozied up to Miss Stennis and made great big friends with Miss Stennis. Then Miss Stennis wouldn't have believed that they went out and drank for anything in the world.

SS: What other fads were big while you were in college?
JG: I had white buck shoes and loafers with a penny in them. We wore socks—loafers and socks. The skirts were full, like poodle skirts. Some of the girls had poodle skirts, but I don't think I had a poodle skirt, but I had full skirts. I made a lot of my clothes. We also wore sweaters and sweater sets.

SS: What about music or other entertainment?
JG: Television was just getting started. In fact, my family didn't get a television set until I was in college. I remember going home and we had a new television set. We lived in the country. People in the city could get reception, but we couldn't get reception out in the country at that time. Maybe there was a television set in the living room, the social room of the dormitory. I don't remember ever watching it. On television, *The Hit Parade*[14] was big; Elvis Presley was just beginning, and rock 'n' roll was beginning. People jitterbugged still, but then there was a new kind of dance that went with the rock 'n' roll, bebop sort of stuff.

It was during the Korean War, although this did not affect me. But I know that there were people who knew boys who were in the service and away at war. But we—I in particular, and many of us—were oblivious to world affairs. That was not something that intruded on us. I think it was an age thing. I think that young people of eighteen to twenty-two were not concerned with politics. However, there was the integration issue. There was a big states' rights conflict due to that that I was aware of, but we really didn't pay a whole lot of attention to Korea and what was going on over there. The world war, the big one, was over. That other was just kind of localized, and it didn't really affect most of us.

14. *Your Hit Parade* aired weekly on radio from 1935 to 1950 and then moved to television from 1950 to 1959. Each program featured the week's most popular songs.

SS: Did you have any experiences with integration?
JG: No. Integration came after I went to school. My children were involved in integration. We had Chinese girls from the Delta who went to the W, whom I was friends with, but we did not have any blacks.

SS: What was a typical day at the W?
JG: Everybody had the same schedule within a given framework. Classes were from 8:00 to 12:00. Everybody had lunch from 12:00 to 1:00. We ate in Shattuck Dining Hall at family tables. We had assigned places when we were a freshman, so we were supposed to be at a certain table with a certain housemother and certain people. It was not a matter of choice who you sat with. The places were set. The food was served home style; they would bring food to each table. We had monitors. They got part of their room and board, so they were working, and they went to the kitchen and served, brought those trays back and forth. I guess they went early or ate late, I don't know which. All through my years, we ate at Shattuck at a family table. After the freshman year, I don't remember being required to eat at a given table. I don't know whether they did away with that or if that was just a freshman thing.

Breakfast was from 7:00 to 7:45, and then classes were at 8:00, 9:00, 10:00, 11:00. Everybody ate lunch. After lunch, two days a week, Tuesday and Thursday, we had chapel. Required. Numbered seats in alphabetical order. We sat in every place so they could check attendance. If we were not in chapel, we were in trouble. This was a terrible time to go to chapel and to sit there. You've gotten up early, and you've just eaten. It's warm in there, and it's nap time, and somebody's not too entertaining. We had guest speakers, or sometimes the chorus would sing. There were various things that went on. Anyway, it was supposed to be educational. Then in the afternoon from 2:00 to usually 4:00, everybody had classes. Within that, I might have class on Monday, Wednesday, and Friday. We also had Saturday classes—everybody did. So we had classes Monday, Wednesday, Friday and Tuesday, Thursday, Saturday. If you had a Saturday class, you didn't have an afternoon class, so we had Saturday afternoon off. I believe we had three cuts that we could take during the semester. Usually we used those and cut Friday and Saturday so we could go home. Otherwise, we didn't cut Saturday class and couldn't go home. That was basically the schedule. Within that, you either took fifteen hours or you took eighteen hours or you took twenty-one hours. I took eighteen, nineteen, or twenty-one most of the time. A lot of the kids just took fifteen. I don't think we could take less than twelve. Some people might not have an 8:00 class. I well remember that there wasn't anyplace to get any breakfast except Shattuck. If you didn't get there for breakfast, then they locked the doors. From Callaway it wasn't too bad, but when we were back at Reneau and trying to get to breakfast, I can remember running trying to get there.

SS: What other traditions did you participate in at the W?
JG: The sing-alongs—we did them by classes. That was one of the annual highlights of the W life. Each class would perform what their class chose to sing. The songs were popular tunes but had words that had to do with W life. We sang them in harmony and with accompaniment. We'd sing them on the front steps of each dormitory. We'd go and listen to the one class, and then the next class would do their program. Then they would judge to decide who won. We also had Hell-something. When the juniors became seniors, we had to run through a paddle line. This was not the social clubs—this was the whole class. Of course, we also had freshman-sophomore social clubs and junior-senior social clubs.

SS: Tell me about being a Masker.
JG: That was one of the things that was not as fun as it could have been because I did not get to participate. I didn't know what was going on my freshman year, and my roommate got invited to be in a social club. I was not, and I didn't even know that she had been going to these parties. Anyway, they came in and knocked on the bed, banged on the bed and got her. At the end of freshman year or the beginning of the next year, the freshman club took in people to replace those that hadn't come back. My roommate told me, "I put up your name, but nobody knew who you were." I thought, "That's not going to happen again." So I made a

point to get to know everybody in my class, but that was not very forward looking, because freshman year had already happened and what I should have been doing was trying to make friends with the juniors, the class right above me. So again, when we went to the next year, I didn't get asked to be in that club, but I was asked the last year. When I was in Reneau Hall, they formed the Mam'selles club and they picked a bunch of us. I was one of the ones they wanted to start the club, and I said, "I'm not interested in being a part of the leftovers."

SS: How many clubs were there at that time?
JG: There were four freshman clubs and maybe three junior-senior clubs. The freshman clubs were the Gauntlets and the Lockhearts and the Silhouettes and the Rogues, probably. I think that's right. The people that I stay in touch with were all Silhouettes. Those were the people that I was friends with, and then those people became Jesters. So that's the set of people that I felt most comfortable with.

SS: What were the Hottentots like?
JG: We met two or three times a year, but we didn't do a lot. It was sort of an honorary social club.

SS: What did you do in Columbus on the weekends?
JG: We went to the movies a lot. The big deal was to get to go to State to go to the big dances. The big bands actually came over to Mississippi State, and Jimmy Dorsey[15] and Glenn Miller[16] and all of these old-fashioned groups. We actually went over there and danced to those bands. Those happened maybe three or four times a year. If you had a date, that was fun to do. And the football games, of course, were a big deal. Now, we didn't go over to the football game just to go to the football game—we went over for the weekend. We spent the night at somebody's house that our dates rented for us to have a place to sleep.

15. Jimmy Dorsey (1904–57) was a prominent American big band leader.
16. Glenn Miller (1904–44) founded and directed a big band, the Glenn Miller Orchestra. After his death, Tex Beneke (1914–2000) took over as the band's leader.

SS: What about shopping trips in or around Columbus?
JG: We walked. Nobody had cars. I don't imagine freshmen were allowed to have cars, but beyond that, in the era in which we grew up, most of us didn't have cars. All the cars were family cars. So we were limited in what we did to walking. We shopped at Ruth's Department Store.

Some of the kids went to church at the various downtown churches. I usually went across the street to Wesley United Methodist Church (now Central United Methodist Church) on College Street instead of downtown to First United Methodist Church on Main Street. The Wesley Methodist Church was pretty formal to me because I had grown up in a little church.

SS: What do you remember about the Wesley campus organization?
JG: Wesley was very much a part of my life. There was always something going on at Wesley. We had Noonday. We'd go over there every day for Noonday, and I was in charge of that one year. I don't think we did a lot of cooking over there. If we had food over there, it was kind of a special occasion. Everybody just loved Mrs. Mack.[17] She was warm and loving and kind. It was a nice atmosphere.

SS: What do think about changes at the W since you graduated?
JG: The one thing that distresses me about the W is that they let the music department go. Their music department may be better now than it was, but it just fell apart and was nothing for years there. I know they are renovating Poindexter. But when I was there, it was a premier place to be in music, and it bothers me that that reputation does not exist any more. I also think that the requirement of having everybody be able to swim is not a bad idea. I just think everybody, W or not, ought to be able to swim. It's a safety thing. I don't think it's bad for a college to require it. And I think the social skills that we learned at the W were important. I don't know how much of that exists today, because the atmosphere is different and it's much looser. Nobody has rules any more of any sort. But

17. Gabriella McWilliams directed the Wesley Foundation at MSCW from 1956 until 1960.

that's true not just at the W; that's true everyplace. In order to compete, they felt like they had to do away with those things and come into the twentieth century or the twenty-first.

SS: Did you learn any valuable life lessons at the W?
JG: I learned to be a leader. I learned to excel. I learned to do my best. I learned to compete with others who were top students in top areas. I learned to lose. I think those are all things that I learned at the W that I might not have learned in the same way or to the same degree had I gone to a coed college.

SS: What advice would you give to a current W girl?
JG: Grab it all. Do as much as you can. Take advantage of the wonderful opportunity that college provides in every area. Don't say, "I'm not good at this," or "That doesn't interest me." Try it and discover for yourself whether it really is something you don't like or it's just something you haven't ever been exposed to.

SS: Is there anything else that you would like to share?
JG: We didn't go home every weekend, so life on the weekends was more a matter of relaxing and playing with your friends and maybe going to the library and catching up for the week or maybe when the weather was nice, playing tennis—just for fun, not because it was a class. The Goose[18] was another important place. You all still have a Goose, but it's not like it used to be. Then it was kind of a big hangout. If there was nothing planned at State, a lot of times they would have a disc jockey and music at the Goose. Or they would have a W band made up of the girls that played instruments.

I also remember that they used to tell about Paderewski playing on campus.[19] Paderewski came to play at the W in what is now Orr Chapel,

18. The Golden Goose Tearoom, located on the first floor of the Student Activities Building (formerly the Henry Whitfield Gymnasium), demolished in the late 1960s.
19. Ignacy Jan Paderewski (1860–1941) was a renowned Polish pianist who performed on campus in February 1905, a concert that remained much talked about for decades thereafter.

which was the auditorium, at the time. He went upstairs and he played up there. That was one of the stories that I remember still being told in the music department when I was there.

SS: Did you hear much about when the college was still II & C rather than MSCW?
JG: Not really. There were pictures and things like that. In our age group in the middle 1950s, we were pretty insulated from both the past, the future, and even the present. It was just us, and that's terrible, but that's the way we were.

SS: How do you feel about the fact that many of the professors at the W when you were there were very important in shaping the school?
JG: It's just wonderful to have known those people. For example, I knew Dr. Cromwell,[20] and now the building is named for Cromwell. I enjoyed being at the W. It was a great growing experience. I was there from the time I was sixteen until I was twenty, so that was my growing-up time. Physically, I was grown up when I got there, but emotionally and intellectually, I grew up at the W. There were some bittersweet times that I'd just as soon put behind me, but overall it was a positive experience, and I am who I am because of the W. I've lived in Corinth virtually all my life, although we lived in Memphis for the first couple of years after we married. It's been interesting to notice who the community leaders are—they're all W girls. The women who are leaders have been, in my generation, W girls. I don't think that that's true any more. I think that now there are people coming out of Ole Miss and Mississippi State and other universities, but at the time that I came out, the women who became leaders in their community were W girls. I'm pleased to have been a part of that.

20. Harvey Cromwell (1907–77) served as director of speech and theater, dean of arts and sciences, and dean of the graduate school at MSCW between 1949 and 1975. In 1977, the new Harvey Cromwell Communications Center was named for him.

Beverly Stuart Koch Jones
Class of 1957

APRIL 22, 2007

INTERVIEWED BY JAYDE PETERSON

TRANSCRIBED BY RACHEL FORESTER

BEVERLY STUART KOCH, BORN ON DECEMBER 20, 1935, in Picayune, Mississippi, was the daughter of Alberta Elizabeth Stuart Koch, a schoolteacher, and Stanley A. Koch, a lumber salesman. At the age of five, the family moved to Jackson, where Beverly Koch spent the remainder of her childhood. At the W, she majored in home economics education and was a dormitory sings director and a song leader for both the Wesley Foundation and the Student Christian Association. A member of the freshman-sophomore Silhouettes and junior-senior Jesters, she was elected a cheerleader and a Class Favorite in each of her four years at MSCW. She participated on her class basketball team and in dance productions and was both a participant in and director of the Aquacade synchronized swimming productions. She married T. Nelson Jones, a pilot from Starkville, Mississippi, in 1956. After graduation, she became very active in community and state civic organizations, and she served as president of the

MUW Alumnae Association from 1999 to 2000. She has been named an Outstanding Community Woman and has received the Juliette Low International Friends Award from the Girl Scouts and an award of merit from her local chamber of commerce. She owns and operates an equine boarding facility, the J-3 Ranch, in Starkville.

BJ: My mother had to quit college after two years because her father died and she couldn't afford to come. At that time, she could teach with two years of college. She had a one-room schoolhouse in Louisiana, across the river from Natchez. Natchez was her hometown. So she went home to teach to make money for her mother and to help her younger sister come to college. Her older sister, Gladys,[1] and her younger sister, Mary Louise,[2] both graduated from the W. Mother helped put them through school and was able to teach until she married my father in Jackson.

When I was growing up, it was quite different from now. We didn't worry about security. We'd play outside until dark, and when the streetlights came on, Mother said, "Come back—get back to the house." So in the summertime we'd play kick the can and all the other fun things that kids do, playing outside.

JP: How did you decide to come to the W?
BJ: I was interested in the W a little bit, but we didn't hear that much about it until we were seniors. Some friends from the class ahead of us were at the W, and they invited eight of us from Central High School to come for W Day, they called it, and we spent the weekend. I remember we dressed up with our hats and gloves and got on the bus and rode to Columbus. I have pictures of us all dressed up. Then we spent the night in Callaway. I don't know where all the girls slept, but they gave us their beds, or maybe different ones had gone home. We slept in anybody's bed. And I remember they went to get a black-bottom pie from the Midway, a little tearoom down the way, and that was wonderful. We

1. Gladys L. Stuart McCraine (1904–96), Class of 1925.
2. Mary Louise Stuart Burley (1909–91), Class of 1931.

had a wonderful weekend, so all eight of us decided to come to the W. We had one friend that was off at camp, and when we were ready to go, we were all registered, and Sally Brockway McReynolds[3] couldn't afford to go. So we got busy, and we finally got her to call up and see if she could get a scholarship. And she got a scholarship to work in the dining hall, so Sally came with us, too, and she was an outstanding student. She made As in every class that she was in—every one except one. I never believed that there was a conflict with professors, but Sally definitely had a conflict with this professor, and we were worried about whether she was going to pass the course. But she did. She was Mortar Board[4] because she was so smart, but she almost didn't get to come. After she got here, she got to work for a chemistry professor grading papers, too. She took on two or three scholarships and was able to do it all. That's how we all got here, because of W Day, because of friends that were here, and because Mother had been here and knew what a good school it was.

JP: What do you remember about move-in day?

BJ: Our friend Jo Nell Thomas,[5] her daddy had a little trailer, so I packed all my stuff and she packed her stuff, and he put everything in that little trailer. We have a picture of him backed up to the back door of Callaway, which is not the same back door that it is now. And we unloaded everything; we just moved it all in, and he drove off and left us there. It was confusing, but it was a lot of fun. It was exciting. We had big sisters to come to see us—Student Christian Association big sisters—and then later we had social club big sisters. They came and helped us to be oriented to what was happening, and of course we had dormitory meetings to tell us everything we needed to know.

JP: Did you have a dorm mother?

....

3. Sally Brockway McReynolds, Class of 1957.
4. Mortar Board National College Senior Honor Society was founded in 1918 and elects members based on scholarship and campus leadership.
5. Jo Nell Thomas Hales, Class of 1957.

BJ: Yes, Miss Janie Stennis,[6] and she was kin to Senator John Stennis. I believe she was his sister. She was very large, and she rode the elevator. We had one little elevator, but it was not allowed for us to ride it except for moving luggage in and out. So Miss Stennis would go up to check rooms, to get things quiet or whatever, and she would ride the elevator up. A lot of times the girls from the fourth floor, when they came from lunch, would get on the elevator and ride it up to fourth floor and leave it. And she would get so upset because the elevator was not where it was supposed to be. We had a girl that liked to drink, and she'd come in after dates. Miss Stennis couldn't smell. This girl would come in, and she would just love Miss Stennis and be talking to her, and we'd have to go get her and get her away from Miss Stennis before she found out she was drunk. That's awful, isn't it?

JP: Did you like your first roommate?

BJ: Yes, I did, but we were very different. She was muchly in love and decided to get married at Christmas. She was Jenna Crossley from Laurel. We had a room on the first floor of Callaway, so everybody would come in after lunch. We had an hour before classes started after lunch. Everybody would flop in our room, and we would play records and just cool it until we had to go to class. But she decided to get married, and I remember I rode the bus down to her house to be in her wedding. We had green velvet-top dresses with taffeta skirts and red poinsettia bouquets. Then after that, Sally Brockway McReynolds moved in with me, and I had Sally for a roommate the rest of the year.

JP: Tell me a little more about your closest friends.

BJ: The closest ones that I had were from Jackson. We were still close, the eight of us, but I kind of blossomed at the W. I had a lot of friends, and I really was well liked. I was a Class Favorite all four years. After I was elected a cheerleader, we led the dormitory songs. We sang on the

....

6. Janie Eliza Stennis (1885–1979), an alumna and sister of Mississippi's U.S. senator, John Stennis, served as a social adviser at MSCW from 1943 until 1957.

front steps of the Student Activities Building there, and we made up songs to go with different tunes. Each dormitory sang for that, but for the classes, we also did class songs. As a cheerleader, I took turns with the other cheerleaders leading in chapel. When we were here, we went to chapel every Tuesday, right after lunch. There we always sang the alma mater,[7] and we sometimes did class songs. And sometimes we'd sing a hymn. So we would go up and lead the hymns or the "Hail to Thee"[8] or the class songs or whatever. At first, some of my old friends didn't understand, and they didn't like me being out making friends with a lot of people. They were surprised and said that I was insincere. They wanted me to be close friends only with them, but we got past it, and we got along. We're still friends. We have sixteen of us that still get together every year. We started when one of our friends who was living in South Carolina would come back to Jackson. We'd go down there and have dinner—our husbands and everybody that we could get together. We'd say, "When Betty[9] is coming, we'll go down and have dinner." We did that for several years. Then as the kids got older and we could leave them overnight, we went to Lake Tiak-O'Khata, in Louisville, Mississippi, and spent a weekend. We liked that and we did that several years. Then somebody said, "Why don't we go somewhere else?" One of our friends has a place at Edisto Beach, up in South Carolina. So we all drove up to Edisto Beach and spent a week. And then, from that, we've gone to North Carolina. Last year we went to Boone, and this year we're going to Lake James, near Asheville. Everybody plans a week or five days to go and be together, and that way we've kept really, really close friends from college. The sixteen of us are from three different classes, but mostly Jesters social club. We have the ones that pledged us, five or six, and then five or six 1957 graduates, and then two that are in the class under us. I don't know why we didn't get more. This group has stayed together for all these years.

....

7. The original alma mater was written by Frances "Frankie" Jones Gaither, Class of 1909, and begins "In our heart of hearts rests a sacred retreat . . ."
8. "Hail to Thee," MSCW's fight song, was written in 1920 by Eola Williams (Class of 1920) and Jane Williams (Class of 1921).
9. Betty Howell Ratliff Lewis, Class of 1957.

JP: What other organizations did you participate in?

BJ: We had the Student Christian Association, and that was big at that time. And I was in the Aquacade. We had to swim to music. I remember one theme—I directed that one year—was faraway places, and we had songs about different locations and did the swimming to that. Miss Berryman[10] was the faculty member who sponsored it. And I did Miss Pohl's[11] dances. I did "Apollo's Horses,"[12] and I was the driver of the horses. I was also on the class basketball team because we did class sports. And of course I told you I was a cheerleader, and then I did Wesley Foundation. And, let's see, I was in the Home Ec Club, because I was a home ec major.

I was also a Silhouette. At that time, it was only a freshman-sophomore club. If you didn't get a bid for one of the two-year junior-senior clubs, you weren't in a club after that. But my roommate, Carolyn,[13] and I were both given two bids, Black List and Jesters. We had the afternoon to decide, and then we had to go in there and tell them one by one. We knew who our big sisters would be in Black List because we really loved those girls, but all of our friends were going to be Jesters. So we had to decide. We cried and we cried. We didn't know who our big sisters would be in Jesters, and we just didn't know those girls very well. So we decided it would be better to be with our friends. But it was a painful decision, painful decision.

JP: What do you remember about your favorite teachers?

BJ: Miss Berryman was really sweet and kind, and she was the head of the physical education department. I don't know how she put up with Miss Pohl, because Miss Pohl was always yelling at her. But Miss Berryman was very kind, and I worked with her really well with the Aquacade. We had to get all the records together—platter records for the music, not written records. I remember I once dropped the needle

10. Romayne Berryman (1901–84) taught physical education at MSCW from 1924 until 1966.
11. Emma Ody Pohl (1880–1966) joined II & C in 1907, when she was hired to develop the department of physical education. She taught that subject until her retirement in 1955.
12. From Johannes Brahms's quartet *Der Abend* (The Evening).
13. Carolyn Smithson Ritter, Class of 1957.

on the record for one of the pieces and messed up the record. I had to call in Mother. I said, "Pleeeease, can you find this record?" Miss Berryman was upset. My mother was able to go to Werlein's in New Orleans, a music store. They got the record for me and sent it up, and that made everything right. I also admired and really liked an English teacher, but she was very large and she scared me to death: Dr. Maria Butler.[14] She was young, and she was a wonderful English teacher. Every day now, when I'm using writing, I am so much thankful to her for what she taught me, because I was really a poor student. I had a wonderful time with extra group activities. For Dr. Butler, I just had a hard time memorizing stuff, but then I had to take a test, and she was going around the room, and of course they separated us. When she'd walk, because the floors were just those bare wooden floors, it was kind of like "Boom! Boom! Boom!" while she was walking around the room as we were trying to take the test. She came right by me, and I was just sitting there. I'd studied all night, and my brain was just fried, and I couldn't remember anything. She said, "Are you all right?" And I just burst out into tears and said, "No, I'm not!" It just totally undid her. But I got through the test. Later on, when I got my grade, which was a D, I told her—it was so dumb of me—"I thought you liked me better than that." Like that had anything to do with what I did on the test. It was ridiculous. But anyway, I learned a lot from her.

JP: Do you have a favorite building on campus?

BJ: Callaway. I've been in it in the last five years, but I haven't been in it just this year. We were on the first floor, and we loved that. And I like that they changed it back. For a while there, the doors were different, but they put them back like they originally were, and it looks so much better. And I like the decision to take down some of the big trees that were in front of it. When we were here, those big cedar or pine trees really hid most of the building until you could barely see the tower clock. Now you can see it, and I really like it. I think one reason it was a favorite for me

14. Maria (pronounced Ma-RYE-a) Hogan Butler (1917–99), Class of 1938, taught English at MSCW from 1952 until 1962.

was because it was old, and it had so much history to it, and then it was our first experience. Gosh, we did such terrible things. The floors were this brown linoleum. And I remember one night Jo Ann Doss[15] and I threw water down there and we'd come sliding down the hall. It was so ridiculous! It's a wonder we didn't kill somebody.

JP: What are some of your favorite traditions at the W?
BJ: I like the little ones like Old Maid's Gate. We always walked through the gate backward. But I guess the dormitory sings were a favorite, which they don't do anymore, since they have Songfest.[16] I also enjoyed singing the class songs in the dining hall. I don't know whether they still do that or not, but we loved doing that. And I loved the Magnolia Chain.[17] I hope that they'll get back to doing it the original way. The class stood up on the bleachers. The program was each officer going forward and calling the junior officer up to pass down the office. It wasn't a speaker talking to us, it was us. The class *was* the program. The Magnolia Chain meant a lot to us.

JP: Did you receive any special awards?
BJ: Being a Class Favorite all four years was unusual. And I was elected a cheerleader all four years. I got married in November of my senior year, and that kind of messed up everything. I stayed here and did the Practice House[18] while my husband went to the air force. I finished, and he came back while we were doing Class Day to pick me up to go to Georgia for flight training. I was busy my senior year with getting married and

15. Jo Ann Doss Miller (1935–98), Class of 1957.
16. Songfest is a song-and-dance competition among the women's social clubs held at MUW every spring.
17. In 1894, in imitation of some eastern schools, II & C graduating seniors carried a daisy chain from the steps of the old chapel to an outdoor ceremony. In 1913, seniors modified the tradition and carried a magnolia chain. The students still sing the traditional magnolia chain song and carry a magnolia chain at a special class day ceremony before commencement in May. At the end of the ceremony, the seniors rush to the piled chain to claim a bud or flower. Those who get either one will have good fortune, which has been variously defined over the years and for some generations involved being the first to marry.
18. Senior home economics majors had to spend a block of time running the Practice House on campus.

living in the Practice House and practice teaching in Starkville. So I wasn't here the night that Whitfield burned. It burned our senior year, so we couldn't have our graduation in Whitfield. We had it right out in front here, on the lawn. A big thunderstorm came up just as we finished, and we all grabbed up our caps and gowns—grabbed the hats off our heads—and ran to the old gym, because it was starting to rain. That's the way we ended our graduation, running to the gym trying to get out of the storm.

JP: What did you do on the weekends in Columbus?

BJ: We had classes on Saturday until noon, so we didn't have much of a weekend, and we didn't go home much. When I got to be a sophomore, my parents had moved to Lake St. John, which is right across from Natchez. So it took me five hours to drive home, and we didn't usually have a way a lot of the time. We had to be busy finding rides everywhere. On the weekends, we would have dates, and after we started dating someone, then we would go to Mississippi State. We had all the big bands at Mississippi State. However, I remember one big band, when I had a date with an officer flight candidate, John Birck. He picked me up after the Aquacade with my wet head. In the gym, Miss Pohl had this pipe all the way around the room that had spouts on it. That was the hair dryer. They ran hot air through it. We'd try to do the best we could because we didn't have those automatic hair dryers like you have now. I tried to dry my hair as best as I could and put on my formal with my hoops and a big yellow skirt. He brought me a gardenia corsage, I remember, and we went out to a big band dance at the Columbus Air Force Base. We had a real good time out there. But at Mississippi State we had Stan Kenton[19] and Woody Herman,[20] and I can't even think of all of them that came to Mississippi State. Every time they would come, we would try to go to the dances. They always had them in the cafeteria

....

19. Stan Kenton (1911–79) began touring nationally with his orchestra in 1941 and continued until the mid-1970s.
20. Woody Herman (1913–87) began touring nationally with his band in the late 1930s and continued through the 1980s.

at Mississippi State, since it had a wonderful tile floor. We were in our hoop skirts, and when we would jitterbug, the hoop skirt would keep going one way when you started going the other way. You'd have to undo it, and it was funny. I always wore pantaloons because I didn't want my hoop skirt to tip up. On the weekends, if we stayed here on campus, we'd go to the "Reneau Roof Resort" and sunbathe or up at "Peyton Place," the roof there. They had these wooden racks on the roof so we could lay out on the roof and sunbathe—sunburn, really. We couldn't go swimming just for recreation, but we had swimming classes. And we could walk to town because we didn't have cars. There was a little tearoom uptown—I can't remember the name—but we'd always stop there. There we got this lemon bisque. The lady made it, and it was frozen and it had graham cracker crumbs around it and she wrapped it in wax paper. So we could buy that lemon bisque and eat it on the way home, like a frozen lollipop. It was so good. Mainly we just visited with our friends. And another friend here in my class, Ellen Young,[21] had a cousin here, so sometimes we'd go out to her cousin's house. But the main things here were parties.

We had the class dance in the old gym. What was fun was our sophomore prom. We had dance cards, and we'd get everybody to sign what number dance we were going to dance with them. I remember my future husband, who was my date that night, didn't think about getting a corsage, and he felt so bad because everybody had a corsage and I didn't have one. But it didn't make any difference. I couldn't go help decorate that year because I was sewing my dress. I made all my dresses, and I had a little bitty sewing machine. I put it on a stool and I was sewing all this black net. It was a beautiful dress. It had a velveteen top and black net circle with a big ruffle and a black velveteen bow that came around. It was really pretty over a hoop skirt. In fact, Ellen Gunn wore it for her senior recital. It was a strapless dress, and that's what's back in style now. That's what we wore. And also those that came up and crossed and went around, the halter back. That was in style in the 1950s.

21. Ellen Claire Young Gunn, Class of 1957.

My junior year, I was the youth director in the summer over at the Central Methodist Church, across from campus next to the president's home on College Street, so I stayed down with Mrs. Stone.[22] I had a room down there, and then I would go to the church and walk over to Wesley Foundation to eat lunch. Dean Ransom[23] was here for the summer. We didn't have summer school at that time. So she would walk over to Wesley. She was staying at Wesley, and she would walk over, and we'd eat lunch together. I remember when my fiancé got his first car. It was an old aqua Chevrolet station wagon, and I remember he came over and took Dean Ellene Ransom and me for a ride in this old car. He picked us up from Wesley Foundation, and we rode around Columbus so I could get a ride in his new car.

JP: What is the most valuable life lesson the W has taught you?

BJ: That's a hard one. I would say to be true to myself and to believe in myself. When I came to the W, I was very insecure. I had been in a big high school, so I wasn't one of the leaders because we had five hundred people in our class. But I learned. I was growing, and it seems like the W allowed me to blossom and gave me the confidence and the opportunities to grow into an individual that could believe in herself. And to know that if I can dream it, I can do it. I believe that was true at the time we were here, and for some people it's still this way.

This campus was more spiritual than some of the Christian colleges then. We had a spiritual life retreat for a week once a year. Even though I came from a church that had a good youth group, at the W I was able to claim it for myself and grow in my faith as well as to learn and to feel valued. The W gave that to me because most of our class officers in high school were men—boys—and here we had leaders that were women and showed that we could be leaders, too. We had such good role models on the campus with women teachers and women who worked

22. Irma Futrell Stone (1890–1977).

23. Ellene Ransom (1894–1963) replaced academic dean Nellie Keirn when she retired in 1955 and served in that position until 1960.

with the churches and women administrators. Although Dr. Hogarth[24] was the head of the college, all the deans were women. They were interested in developing us. The W made me mature and then realize that I was equipped to go out. Of course, by the time you get to be a sophomore, you realize you don't know anything. But we learned how to find out what we didn't know. When you leave the W, you realize that even though you thought you knew so much when you got here, you didn't know much. What you have been equipped with is how to research and how to learn, so that you can go and find out what you need to know and how to ask the questions so that you don't have to be ignorant. The W also taught me about service. Giving to others is one of the happiest things you can do in your life, to give your expertise or just to be able to listen to somebody. To give up yourself is sometimes hard for people, but here on the W campus, we were always giving to each other, being a friend and learning to listen. We were learning not to be always the center of attention but to be able to speak up when you needed to. We learned to give. We always did things for Palmer Home,[25] just as students do today, raising money for people that are less fortunate. That was nurtured at the W. It's not like we hadn't ever heard it before, because we had been in Girl Scouts and other organizations, but it was very important at the W. I think that carried over into my adult life, because I've always done church work and community service.

JP: What advice you would give to any future W girl?
BJ: Don't be afraid to be involved. Don't be afraid to step up. Even if you don't think you have the skills, if you have the want-to, you will learn the skills. Somebody will help you with the skills. You learn by doing, and you'll never grow as a person unless you do something you haven't done before. You have to keep on stretching yourself. There's so much to learn; if you stop learning, you might as well stop living. That's the excitement of the W; it's here to teach us. We're here to help the W help students to

24. Charles Pinckney Hogarth (1911–97) served as president of MSCW from 1952 until 1977.
25. Columbus's Palmer Home for Children was founded by Presbyterians and offers a home to children who need a stable environment.

learn in whatever way we can as alums. We help by giving money, but we also like to be involved with students. The members of the Wesley Foundation are coming out to my house on Friday. This will give them a place where they can get away from campus and they can enjoy just being together, having a little devotional and having some silly time. But times like this are where you start nurturing your good friends and the ones that are going to be with you throughout your life. We have friends that we've been through a lot with. At our age now, it's husbands dying or critical illnesses. But we've always got somebody that we can pick up the phone and talk to. And when we get together, it's like we haven't been apart. We don't have to go back and say who we were or where we were; we've been with them through their whole life. We just pick up where we left off. You hurt with them and you laugh with them and you cry with them. But it started here. It was a very special time.

JP: Would you like to make any other comments about the W?

BJ: It just breaks my heart that we're in a crisis[26] now, because I think all of us want what's good for the W. But I don't understand how any one person or group can limit one's freedom, and that's what this whole thing is about, someone saying that you can't elect officers, that the alumni association can't have freedom like we have in this country. When someone threatens our freedom, the hair on the back of my neck stands up. It's just beyond me how they can't see that. And it hurts. We've always

26. In October 2005, the officers of the MUW Alumnae Association, under threat of disaffiliation, signed an agreement severely limiting their self-government. The officers then drafted a set of bylaws, but they did not meet with the approval of MUW president Claudia Limbert or the university's legal advisers, chiefly because of the procedures for the nomination and election of officers. In April 2006, Limbert removed Patsy Lockhart McDaniel, Class of 1963, from her position as director of the alumnae association, which she had held since 1989, and fired the assistant director. On January 31, 2007, Limbert officially informed the MUW Alumnae Association of her decision to disaffiliate the university from the association. The association responded by suing the Board of Institutions of Higher Learning in Mississippi, and the case went to court in May 2007. In October of that year, Judge Dorothy Colom ordered Limbert to dissolve a newly created alumni association and reaffiliate with the original association. Limbert and the college board asked for a stay of the ruling until the case could be appealed to the Mississippi Supreme Court. In February 2008, Judge Colom granted a partial stay, allowing Limbert to recognize both alumni associations as legitimate. The appeal to the state supreme court is still pending.

had problems with outside forces,[27] but this is the first time it's been internal with alumni. The newspapers and the administration are trying to spin it so that it's alums against alums, and it's not. It's alums against the administration that has started this and has tried to tell us that we can't be an independent association. I can't understand how they could think that would benefit the school. When people are free to grow and to help, they can come up with a lot more ideas than when somebody's vision is limited. We have a vision of a much bigger, better alumni association, but they are trying to limit it, to hold it down, and we want it to grow and be better. We're still going to give money to the MUW Foundation. Proof of this is that for this Homecoming we raised $12,500 for the Patsy McDaniel Scholarship in three weeks. That speaks volumes about the people that care about this institution. This crisis will be over someday, and I hope it doesn't draw out too long to where damage is done where students won't come because of the conflict.

27. Since shortly after beginning operation in 1884, II & C/MSCW/MUW has frequently been targeted for closure or for merger with other institutions, often as a consequence of economic crises in the state or conflicts between political factions. Alumnae have repeatedly exerted political and public pressure to block these efforts.

Donette Dunaway Lee
Class of 1957

APRIL 4, 2007

INTERVIEWED BY ELIZABETH SEGAL

TRANSCRIBED BY RACHEL FORESTER

DONETTE DUNAWAY, THE DAUGHTER OF W. A. DUNAWAY, a farmer, and Deloris Pyron Dunaway, a homemaker, was born on July 24, 1935, in Swiftown, Mississippi. At MSCW, she majored in music with an emphasis in organ and earned a bachelor's degree in sacred music. A member of the Torch, Lantern, and Mortar Board academic honoraries, she also was selected for membership in Sigma Alpha Iota, the honorary for music majors. She served as an officer in the Student Christian Association, as regent of the American Guild of Organists during her junior year, and as president of the Baptist Student Union during her senior year. She was also a member of the Glee Club, the College Singers, and of the Jesters junior-senior social club. She was employed as district manager of operator services for BellSouth until her retirement in 1994. In Jackson, she was a church and civic leader as a member of the Advisory Board of Catholic Charities, the Telephone Pioneers, and Habitat for Humanity, and she was Jackson's

YWCA Woman of the Year in 1980. She has served as president of the Mississippi Society to Prevent Blindness, president of the Jackson Metro Chapter of the MUW Alumnae Association, and as president of the MUW Alumnae Association from 2001 until 2002. A recipient of the MUW Alumnae Achievement Award, she currently lives in Douglasville, Georgia.

ES: What led you to MSCW?
DL: I wanted to major in music, and I knew the reputation of the music school at MSCW. There were two girls from my high school who were four years older than I,[1] and we knew their families and knew them, so I asked if I could come over and spend a weekend. They were seniors then. I came and just loved it and stayed.

ES: What did you do that weekend?
DL: It was high school weekend. I guess it's pretty much like W Day. They had activities of all kinds, and we divided up and went to the departments that were in our area of interest. It so happened that I met a person from Ellisville, Mississippi, who was also here just looking around for the first time.[2] She was going to major in piano, and so we kind of knocked around that weekend. Then she said, "Are you going to come?" And I said, "I may." And she said, "Yeah, I'm not sure. What would you think about going on and signing up for a room?" So I said, "Why not?" So we put our names down for a room as freshmen the next fall. This was in April. The next fall we came to MSCW. She and I roomed together for four years, and we are rooming together this weekend at the hotel here for Homecoming. It's just a great, great serendipity.

ES: What did you know about the W before you got here?
DL: Except for those older girls who came, I really didn't know much about it. But my dad always kept saying, "Oh, that is a good school. That is a

1. Mary Ann French, Class of 1953, and Mary Nell Goodwin Kadlec, Class of 1953.
2. Ellen Claire Young Gunn, Class of 1957.

wonderful school. Yes, I'd like for you to go to school there." Nobody in my family had ever been here before, so I don't know if he just liked the idea of a women's college or if he just knew it was an academically good choice.

ES: Tell me about your move-in day.
DL: I don't remember anything about move-in day except that my parents drove me over here on Sunday. We got here that afternoon, and they helped me move all my stuff into the room, and they got back in the car and left. I waved them good-bye from the sidewalk. Later, I learned that my daddy cried when he left. But I didn't cry. I was feeling great! I just don't remember much else about it, except I do remember that other students were helping us move in. That was something that impressed me.

ES: Did you have a dorm mother?
DL: We did, and frankly, I don't remember those dorm mothers very well. They kind of stayed to themselves, and unless we really had a problem, I didn't really have much interaction with the dorm mother.

ES: What dorm did you live in?
DL: I was in Hastings, and at the end of the first semester, one of the tower rooms was vacated—somebody must have gone home. So Ellen and I got permission to move into the tower. We had a huge room. It was neat.

ES: Who was your favorite professor here?
DL: You would usually think that it would be one of your major professors, but I really think the one I look back to with the most fondness was my freshman English professor, from whom I later took English literature when I was a senior—I didn't take it as a sophomore. Her name was Lucy Banks.[3] I came back as a senior and selected her because of who she was. She was reserved and dignified, an elegant, quiet-spoken southern lady. She never married, but she was just the epitome of gracious

3. Lucy Young Banks (1895–1993), Class of 1916, taught English at MSCW from 1932 until 1965.

kindness. And for some reason, she and I hit it off. She taught me to write essays, since I had never done so before taking her freshman English class. I loved to read, and she could just make literature come alive, so we connected.

MUW provided the foundation for the rest of my life. I learned that I could undertake anything that appealed to me, that I could succeed in everything I tried if I worked hard, and that writing and speaking and thinking were valuable tools. I did not pursue a career in my major field, but I was hired into a business management position because I had a degree and could pass their tough entrance exam.

ES: Do you remember any professors that you didn't like very much?
DL: He taught counterpoint, which was one of the required music courses. And he was frankly just as dull as dirt. So I just didn't like the course. I didn't like him. I didn't like having to go to that class, but you persevere. I don't know of anybody that liked him. Everybody was complaining. He also taught music appreciation, which non–music majors had to take, and they didn't like him either!

ES: Did you really like any other subjects?
DL: French. I loved French. And it was just a required course to get my degree. I had never had a foreign language. I got by high school without having to take Latin or anything else, and this was my first foreign language, and I just loved it. Even when I went to France a few years ago, I could still pick up on pronunciations and some of the nouns, names, things that I recognized.

ES: Did you receive any awards at the W?
DL: The ones that come to mind would be the honorary societies, and I also was in Mortar Board[4] my senior year. I graduated cum laude. Those would have been the main things.

4. Mortar Board National College Senior Honor Society was founded in 1918 and elects members based on scholarship and campus leadership.

ES: What did you do in Lantern and Torch and Mortar Board?
DL: They really were not very memorable. It was more honorary than it was activity oriented. The end of your freshman year, you were tapped for Lantern if your grades met the criteria, and in the same way Torch must have been junior year. And then Mortar Board was the senior honorary. It's a national organization, and it carried more prestige than the other two.

ES: What did you usually wear to classes or around campus?
DL: We couldn't wear anything except skirts. Uniforms were gone by the time I got here, but it had been recent enough that you knew what they had looked like and what people wore then. But the only time we could wear blue jeans was on back campus, back behind Peyton Hall, where we'd have picnics. They'd let you wear blue jeans then. And we all wore the same thing to P.E., which was a white shirt and navy blue shorts. I don't know if we had to put on a coat over the gym uniform; I guess not. We could wear shorts going to and from gym for tennis or softball or whatever physical education. Of course, we were required to take P.E., so that's when we wore shorts.

The style that I remember the most were pencil-straight skirts that came about midcalf. They usually had a split up the back so you could walk. And we wore shirts mostly, or sweaters, and socks and loafers or saddle oxfords. So we were all similarly dressed. We all looked alike. On Sundays, if you went to church, you had to wear a hat. I'm not sure if gloves were required, but hats were. It was sometime during my four years that somebody invented a little thing for your head that was nothing more than a clip that kind of fit on the top of your head. It had nothing but a piece of veil. So you could put that little thing up in your hair with the veil over it and call yourself wearing a hat. That kind of gives you a picture of how we looked.

ES: How often did you have to take P.E.?
DL: Every semester. If I remember correctly, I think the only way you could get out of P.E. was with a doctor's certificate saying that you couldn't physically do it. Besides that, you had to pass swimming as one of your

P.E. courses, and if you didn't pass it, then you took it again until you could swim. Occasionally, somebody graduated without knowing how to swim, but it was usually because of extenuating circumstances. You should have seen what we wore for swimming. They furnished tank suits, the swimsuits, one-piece things made out of some sort of wool knit, I think. Navy blue. They were awful. And we hated them. But you couldn't wear your own swimsuit in the swimming pool. You had to wear those navy blue tank suits.

ES: Could you describe a typical day of going to class?
DL: My experience was different than a lot of students because I had to practice the organ; I was an organ major. I had to practice four hours every day. So I had to work that in around my other classes. I would sign up for the practice room from eight to nine in the morning and then go to class at nine, an academic class. It might be in the music building or it might be English all the way over at Painter or a science class on back campus. So we did a lot of running around. We walked everywhere we went. There were no cars; we were not allowed to have cars until we were seniors, and even then we didn't use our cars on campus to go from place to place. It was surprising that there were not as many people that biked as you might have thought because it's still a pretty big campus, but we just walked. We were pretty fit. There were very few who were obese, I'll put it that way. Because we really had to, we got our exercise. We couldn't avoid it.

ES: Where did you practice?
DL: In Poindexter. We had an organ in the Poindexter auditorium and then we had two, I believe, in practice rooms in the back.

ES: What do you remember about the dining hall?
DL: Probably my best memories are of the dining hall. We all ate together all three meals, if you wanted to eat breakfast, which I always did. A lot of people slept through breakfast, and you had to be there by—I don't know if it was 7:00 or 7:15. Anyway, you had to be there before the doors

closed. We would go into Shattuck, which is where the dining hall was located, and we waited out in that big lobby until the doors opened. Then everybody went in and took their places. The food was ready, and it was delivered to your table family style, eight per table. People worked in the dining hall. They were called monitors, and they worked as part of their scholarship. Each year, we got to select which table we sat at and who sat there. So by the time we were seniors, our good buddies were all together! We'd come to the table at breakfast, lunch, or dinner and catch up and have a chance to visit. We had white linen tablecloths and white linen napkins, and the food was prepared from scratch right there. They made all the desserts: the banana cream pie and the graham cracker torte and black-bottom pie. Oh, the desserts were fabulous, as well as all the rest of the food. There just was hardly anything that we didn't think was great. And we were expected to use our manners. Back then, people from outside the W would sort of make fun of us as being a finishing school, which was not the case at all. It was not all about becoming a southern lady. However, we were reminded often that we were supposed to know how to behave ourselves. So at the table we were supposed to use good manners. But I distinctly remember that there was one thing that we would not listen to the dean of students[5] about when she fussed at us. We liked to drink coffee after the meal was over, and we would put our elbows on the table and hold our coffee cup and sip and visit and sip our coffee with those elbows on the table. And it just upset the dean so bad! She would chastise us for our unmannerly way of drinking our coffee. But we got away with it.

ES: Did you sing in the cafeteria?

DL: Oh yes. And we never knew when somebody would start something, but we sort of sat by sections—all the freshmen were in one area. That was just the way it would fall out. All it would take would be one table to start singing, "We are the freshmen, the freshmen are we." And usually if one class started, then the others were popping up and singing their class songs.

5. Marguerite Goen (1896–1977) held a variety of posts at MSCW between 1928 and 1963, including teacher of secretarial science, student counselor, and dean of students. Goen Residence Hall was named in her honor.

ES: Did you participate in Zouave?
DL: It happened my sophomore year. Miss Pohl[6] was still here, but for whatever reason, I did not sign up for Zouave. Most of my close friends did, and I was there that year, when they performed it then. It didn't happen again during my time. That was 1955, I believe.

ES: Do you remember anything about Miss Pohl?
DL: Oh gosh, I can see her. She was just—unique is probably the best word to describe her, because she was not like anything that you'd ever seen before. She had such a distinctive way of walking. She would stride across campus. She was in a hurry to get everywhere she went. So she was always just taking these big, long strides. And she would put her head forward so that when she was walking, you could see how serious she was. And she probably didn't even notice you, but if she did and she spoke to you, it was always by your last name. She didn't care what anybody's first name was. She called everybody by her last name. And of course she was head of the P.E. department. And then she taught all the dance classes, so she had ballet classes and dance recitals that we would attend to watch her dancers. She was quite a character.

ES: Did you participate in any campus traditions?
DL: My favorite of all the traditions is Mag Chain.[7] One reason I loved it so much was that when I was still in high school, two teachers came from the W for their first year of teaching. They adapted the words to the Mag Chain song, and they put it in my high school.[8] So as a senior I carried the Mag Chain in high school, and then I got to the W, and it

6. Emma Ody Pohl (1880–1966) joined II & C in 1907, when she was hired to develop the department of physical education. She taught that subject until her retirement in 1955.
7. In 1894, in imitation of some eastern schools, II & C graduating seniors carried a daisy chain from the steps of the old chapel to an outdoor ceremony. In 1913, seniors modified the tradition and carried a magnolia chain. The students still sing the traditional magnolia chain song and carry a magnolia chain at a special class day ceremony before commencement in May. At the end of the ceremony, the seniors rush to the piled chain to claim a bud or flower. Those who get either one will have good fortune, which has been variously defined over the years and for some generations involved being the first to marry.
8. Mary Ann Ponder Covington, Class of 1950, and Carolyn McRae Temple (1930–2004), Class of 1950, taught at Hollandale High School.

was the tradition here. And of course, part of it was the music because I loved the music and I loved the sentiment behind it and I liked the words set to the music. It combined music and pageantry, singing, flowers, caps and gowns, the out-of-doors in springtime. I just thought it was a beautiful ceremony.

Another tradition that I loved was our Stunt Night. I don't think Stunt Night is still going on now, but the way that tradition worked, it was just such fun. I don't know why they ever dropped it. They would come up with a theme, and they would make assignments. I know the segment I participated in back then was "The Hit Parade." There was a big radio show, where every week the songs that were the most popular were on *The Hit Parade*.[9] So we were assigned that as our segment of Stunt Night. Another group had to do an adaptation of *South Pacific*,[10] the musical. What would happen is that you never knew when Stunt Night was going to occur, but at lunch on a Wednesday, one of the seniors would get up and announce that when lunch was over all of the juniors were to meet in Whitfield Auditorium because it was Stunt Night. As the juniors marched out, the seniors would sing, "Juniors, the seniors are after you tonight." We would march, and they would sing, so it was very ominous. Now, we're talking about 1:00 on Wednesday, we were given our assignments, and we had to have a show ready at 8:00 that night—costumes, all the lyrics to the songs, all the stunts, whatever we were going to do. I remember one of our people who eventually became president of the student body[11] was the Roadrunner. She had to dress up like the Roadrunner, and every now and then during the programs she had to run across the stage saying, "Beep beep. Beep beep. Beep beep." It was just silly stuff, but it was so much fun. We had to work so hard to get ready. And then, of course, the seniors were all sitting out watching and telling you how bad you were doing and what a mess you were and

9. *Your Hit Parade* aired weekly on radio from 1935 to 1950 and then moved to television from 1950 to 1959. Each program featured the week's most popular songs.
10. *South Pacific*, a musical by Richard Rogers and Oscar Hammerstein, opened on Broadway in April 1949.
11. Carolyn Smithson Ritter, Class of 1957, served as president of the student body during her senior year.

how awful you looked. It was just real fun stuff. I guess those probably were my two favorite things.

ES: What clubs were you in?

DL: I was a member of the Sigma Alpha Iota, which was a music fraternity. I wasn't active in the social clubs. I did pledge a freshman club, but I wasn't active. And at that time there were just freshman-sophomore clubs, no four-year clubs, and then you joined a junior-senior club if you wanted to. Fewer people went on into a junior-senior club. But by that time, I had become very close friends with a lot of people in Jesters, and so that was really the group that I bonded with. All of my close friends in my class were pledged by Jesters, and we became close friends then with the seniors. We have stayed friends for fifty or more years. We still get together and take vacations after all these years. And it's mainly that same group that pledged and were pledged when we were juniors and seniors in college.

ES: Can you explain what a social club is?

DL: They have often been compared to sororities, but because they're not national and because they don't have all the Greek associations, they are different. But they provide the opportunity to become a part of an organization of people that you have a lot in common with, that enjoy the same kinds of things, and that you have gotten to know and get to know even better as you are participating in all the campus activities. It's just an identification opportunity, I think, and a friendship opportunity. It provides you with a group where you can develop friendships that really are lasting, and that's what we have found. I don't know that in every case they are maintained in the same way, but we just happened to be in the right group. I don't mean that to sound exclusive. It's just that those women were our friends at the W, and sure enough we clicked to the degree that we stayed friends. We know each other's children.[12] Our children know each other, and we know all the others' husbands

12. While at the W, Donette Lee's daughter, Larraine Lee Durden, Class of 1988, roomed with Ellen Young Gunn's daughter, Beth Gunn Hefner, Class of 1986.

and families. We visit in each other's homes. The relationships formed at the W have lasted a lifetime. I vacation every year with friends that I met fifty-four years ago. That is certainly unique and is very gratifying the older I get. Our common bond from our beginnings at MUW keeps us connected and involved in each other's lives. No other friends outside my family have been more important to me. It's been a lifelong experience that started here.

ES: What did the W do for your life?
DL: Two things come to mind. As I have already discussed, the lifelong friendships that began my freshman year at the W have enhanced the quality of my life in ways that I cannot measure. Secondly, while some students were given a wonderful foundation in the vocations that they would pursue, I did not make a career of my music education. It gave me a love and appreciation for music which I have incorporated into my life through church choirs and choral societies. But more than anything, the W instilled in me the confidence that I could tackle whatever came my way, knowing that I had received valuable life skills and the ability to think and reason. Because we were all women, whatever needed to be done, we did it, rather than deferring to male students to be our leaders. This became especially significant when I became a manager in a traditionally male environment.

ES: What advice do you have for a current W girl?
DL: Fifty years have brought about immense changes in the world as well as at the W. The things that were meaningful to us will have less appeal to today's young people. But the opportunity to build friendships on a small campus, the opportunity to know professors on a personal basis, and the opportunity to soak up wisdom and knowledge are timeless. Taking advantage of these opportunities will be the most valuable thing that a student in any decade can achieve. And in fifty years, they too will have marvelous memories of their time at MUW.

Nell Ann Pickett
Class of 1957

JUNE 15, 2006

INTERVIEWED BY AMBER KING

TRANSCRIBED BY RACHEL FORESTER

BORN IN UTICA, MISSISSIPPI, ON OCTOBER 22, 1935, to Fred Newman Pickett and Eva Reed Pickett, Nell Ann Pickett transferred to the W from Hinds Junior College. She was a member of the staff of the *Spectator*, MSCW's student newspaper; the Religious Emphasis Week Committee of Fifty; the Student Christian Association Council; Sigma Tau Delta English honorary; and the Wesley Foundation Larger and Smaller Councils, serving as financial secretary during her senior year. Also during her senior year, she was the president of the Future Teachers of America and of Pi Tau Chi, a national religion honorary society. She received a degree in English, later completing a master's degree from George Peabody College for Teachers in Nashville, Tennessee, and a doctorate from the University of Mississippi. She taught at Rolling Fork High School and at Delta State University before moving to Hinds Community College. In 1976, she married Harry J. Partin (1927–99), head of the Electronics

> Technology Department at Hinds. She has received numerous awards, including CASE Professor of the Year, and has served as an officer in the National Council of Teachers of English. She has written or cowritten five books, including *Technical English: Writing, Reading, Speaking*, coauthored with Hinds colleague Ann Laster and currently in its eighth edition. She also edited the journal *Teaching English in the Two Year College* from 1988 through 1994. Pickett retired from Hinds in 2001 and in 2005 was among the first group designated emeriti faculty by that institution. Pickett Hall, which houses ninety-six women honors students on the Raymond campus of Hinds Community College, was named in her honor. She lives in Utica.

NP: I have always been a person who enjoyed reading, and we had some books in our home, but not very many. I wanted more, and I read about this book club that I wanted to join, because I could get a book a month for not much money. I talked with Mama and Daddy about it. They said they would pay the initial fee for me to join, and I would get two free books, but after that, I would have to pay for the books myself. I quickly learned that I wanted more books than I had the money to buy and more than my allowance would allow. However, I also quickly learned how I could make additional money. We raised most of the food we ate. We had chickens. We raised biddies, and we had eggs. We also raised hogs and raised beef cattle. In the springtime, we had a garden with a watermelon patch, and we also had cantaloupes. I asked Mama and Daddy if I could have my row of watermelons and cantaloupes, and they said, "Yes, but you'll have to tend to them. You'll have to hoe them." And I said, "That's fine." We were accustomed on Saturdays to taking some watermelons and cantaloupes into Utica and selling those, and I said, "When my watermelons and my cantaloupes get big enough, if I care for them, can I have the money?" And they said, "Sure! That's yours." So then I knew I had a way to earn money to buy those books from the book club. We would take those watermelons and cantaloupes to sell, and Daddy would put mine in a little separate place in the truck. I got that money, and to add to it, my sister, Jane, and I cleaned the church every Saturday, so I got to keep my half of that thirty-five cents we got each week for cleaning the church.

I soon learned how I could bargain with Mama and Daddy if I did some extra chores and get a bonus in my allowance. Later, when I got old enough, I asked a cousin who owned a grocery store in Utica if he would let me help him on Saturdays in the store. I started helping every Saturday, and then he asked Mama and Daddy if I could come in every day and work in that grocery store. By then I was about fifteen years of age, and I worked for that few dollars a week, but I learned a lot about handling money, and I got my first paycheck from that. In the Sears, Roebuck catalog I found a manual, portable typewriter. It was seventy-five dollars. I had to save up money all summer, but I still have that typewriter. That was my first big investment.

The next thing I did was I opened my own bank account. I had five or six dollars. Mama and Daddy said that they would take me to the bank, and then I said, "Y'all just stay out here in the car and let me do it." So I opened my bank account in the Bank of Utica. I think it was five dollars and six cents. Afterward I said, "I will add every week to that bank account." I can say today that things have worked out well for me, and I'm proud of how I learned how to earn money and how to spend it well.

AK: How did you end up going to the W?

NP: It was really a bit of a circuitous route in that in junior high school, I decided that I wanted to major in English and I wanted to be an English teacher. I knew that career would require, of course, a college education, graduate school, perhaps a doctorate. All those things were in my mind. So I thought about what college in Mississippi I would really like to attend if I could get in, the one that I would be the most proud to graduate from. It was Millsaps College.[1] But when I was a junior in

1. Millsaps College, founded in 1890, is a Methodist-run liberal arts college in Jackson, Mississippi.

high school, I got the catalog for Millsaps so my parents and I could study what was offered there. Then we looked at the cost. It was out of our reach—completely. And though I was working every summer and had little part-time jobs and was saving my money, Millsaps was simply out of our reach. My next idea was that I would go to Hinds Junior College for two years, and then I thought again about where I would go after that. I thought, "What public four-year institution in Mississippi would accept me and would best prepare me for a teaching career?" And without a doubt, it was MSCW—Mississippi's Sweetest Collection of Women. So that's what I did. From Hinds, I transferred to the W.

AK: What was it like then for a transfer student?
NP: The first few days at the W were nothing new to me because I had lived in the dormitory at Hinds. I had the experience of having wonderful roommates there. Although my home was only fifteen miles away from Hinds, I lived in the dorm, and I spent a good many weekends at Hinds. There was no problem moving into the dorm at the W.

However, during those first few days, as we were going through meetings for new students, one person suggested that I go by to talk with the registrar.[2] It was only much, much later that I realized that since I was transferring from this little ole junior college, this person was suggesting that I might not be well prepared, although my grades were extra-extra-good. So it was suggested that I go by the registrar's office to see if maybe I needed to have a review of some kind. I went over to the registrar and introduced myself and said that it had been suggested that I come over to talk about the courses I was transferring to the W. It so happened that there were some people in the office sorting a lot of records—folders and other papers—and I said, just offhandedly, "Could I help y'all with those?" They said, "Sure!" So I sat down, and I said, "Are we just sorting these folders only by names, or are there some subsets of information that we need to be aware of, such as where students are from or what

2. George T. Buckley (1898–1980), served as the registrar at MSCW from 1937 until 1958, when he became chair of the English department. He remained in that position until 1964 and then served as a professor of English until 1967.

their major is?" After I said that, the registrar just looked at me and said, "Miss Pickett, it's nice to meet you. Could you come to work for us?" So much for being unprepared! I really enjoyed working those several hours a week at the registrar's office.

AK: So you made a good impression?
NP: I hope I did. I was very much impressed by the staff and their businesslike approach, and I had worked in summers at the agriculture office in the Hinds County Courthouse in Raymond, so I had learned a little bit about working with the public and a little bit about courtesy.

AK: What was your favorite building on campus?
NP: Oh, the library! I loved to read, and I loved all the library staff because I had never been around that many books in my life. As I look back and I think of Miss Eudora Welty,[3] whom I admired so, so much, I recall that one of the things that she mentioned to me is that she had never been in the midst of so much good reading as in the library at the W. We had our study group of English majors. Sometimes we would meet in a classroom, but very often, particularly after hours, we would meet in the library for our study group and go over possible questions and also what we called trick questions that a professor might ask on a little pop test just to be sure that we had read a book. I remember one time we were asked a little question about what kind of shoes a character was wearing. And many of us were totally puzzled, but several of us wrote down it had to be high heels, because the writer said the character went "clicking" down the hall. That was the kind of question that a professor might ask us all in good fun, just to see how closely we had looked at those details.

AK: Did you spend most of your time with your English major friends?
NP: Yes, yes. And some of those persons I still run into, or their siblings

3. Eudora Alice Welty (1909–2001), an internationally known writer, was a native of Jackson, Mississippi, who attended MSCW in 1926 and 1927 before transferring to the University of Wisconsin at Madison

if they're now deceased. I think about June Goforth Cook,[4] who is now a senior minister at Galloway United Methodist Church in Jackson. A couple of years ago, we happened to be on a European trip together, and we renewed our friendship. And I found out she had lived all these years of her married life in Clinton, nearby me. And I think about another person that I was in class with at the W, Martha Dunlap.[5] Again, we were on a trip together, this time Soil Conservation women going to Washington, D.C. We renewed our acquaintanceship and developed our friendship. In fact, just this past week, she came down and spent the day with me at my farm. We cooked lunch together and shared many a good tale about the W.

AK: Do you stay in contact with a lot of friends from the W?
NP: Yes, I'm constantly running into persons who are either W graduates or persons that I knew at the W or someone from the W who had a close relationship with members of my family or a member of my community. I'm just so proud of the W and what it is contributing to higher education in the Southeast.

AK: What traditions do you remember?
NP: One of the traditions then was to have family-style meals. That is, there would be a group of eight of us assigned to a table. It might have been for the entire semester, but it was for at least a period of weeks. We would have all three of our meals every day together, and we got to know each other as persons. We didn't necessarily live in the same dorm. We didn't necessarily have the same major. But to this day, I think, "What is there that shows about a W graduate?" In fact, Martha Dunlap and I were talking about this recently. Martha says, "I can be in a group, and I can spot a W graduate in a conversation immediately." We decided one of those things was is that W graduates can always have a meaningful conversation. I think part of that stems from our family-style meals. Of

4. June Goforth Cook, Class of 1957.
5. Martha Gwynn McClain Dunlap, Class of 1959.

course, there were other traditions like the Magnolia Chain[6] and the Homecomings. And now, I guess, as I move into the fifty-year place, there will be additional traditions that I will enjoy.

AK: You were planning to be an English teacher when you came to the W?

NP: That was my career objective. I had as a backup, should I decide that I didn't want to teach English, that I would go to law school, but I am so glad that things worked out for me to be an English teacher.

AK: Did any professors help you continue in that direction?

NP: Yes, indeed. I enjoyed all of the professors in the English department. Some were a little more peculiar than others, just as some of us students were a little more peculiar than other classmates. But I remember one in particular, Dr. Maria Butler[7] from Yazoo City. She never married, but she came from a large family. She believed in hard work. She believed that when you were studying a period of literature, you also needed to study the art. When I say art, I mean the painting, the music, the whole milieu of that period. And that's what we did in her classes. Particularly I enjoyed the two semesters of British literature—the British romantic literature. Dr. Butler loved to travel in Europe, particularly in the British Isles. She would take pictures and make all these slides for class. She would come back and show those to us to make that literature, that art, that music, that countryside come alive to us. And I have been able to travel just as Dr. Butler did. I have so many fond memories and fond thoughts of Maria Butler, who is now deceased. Not only did we

6. In 1894, in imitation of some eastern schools, II & C graduating seniors carried a daisy chain from the steps of the old chapel to an outdoor ceremony. In 1913, seniors modified the tradition and carried a magnolia chain. The students still sing the traditional magnolia chain song and carry a magnolia chain at a special class day ceremony before commencement in May. At the end of the ceremony, the seniors rush to the piled chain to claim a bud or flower. Those who get either one will have good fortune, which has been variously defined over the years and for some generations involved being the first to marry.

7. Maria (pronounced Ma-RYE-a) Hogan Butler (1917–99), Class of 1938, taught English at MSCW from 1952 until 1962.

have a wonderful friendship as student to professor while I was at the W, but several years later we became colleagues. I was teaching at what was then Delta State College for Teachers, now Delta State University, in Cleveland, Mississippi, and Maria decided to move from her position as professor of English at the W to professor of English at Delta State. She continued to be a mentor to me in my three years that I taught at Delta State. When I run into persons I was with at the W, particularly English majors, Dr. Butler's name always comes up. And my bachelor of arts degree with a major in English has stood me in great stead all the way through graduate school on through my Ph.D. and throughout my teaching career. I can mention the W, and that is immediate recognition and, I know, immediate respect.

AK: So you've done a good bit of traveling since you left the W?
NP: Yes, in fact I just got back a few days ago from a fifteen-day jaunt to Alaska. In October I'll be taking a cruise to the Aegean Sea. We'll be spending a week in Greece on land, and then we will be cruising the coast of Turkey. I never have been anywhere in Turkey. My first love though, and a place my husband also loved, is the British Isles. Oh, I guess Harry and I took at least two dozen or more trips to the British Isles. My favorite thing to do was to go the week after we got out of school. We would have already set up the renting of a car at an airport in London. Then usually we would stay at bed-and-breakfast places anywhere from two weeks to I believe the longest time we stayed was six weeks. We just went wherever we wanted to, and that was all through the 1970s. In fact, Harry and I spent our honeymoon in London. I got married when I was forty, so we didn't have to do things in any traditional way. We got married one weekend—we had the dress rehearsal one weekend, and the following weekend we got married. So we said, "We'll just go a year from now and spend a month in London as our honeymoon," and that's exactly what we did.

Yes, I love to travel. One of the best trips that Harry and I took was to New Zealand and Australia. We've traveled independently, we've traveled with groups, we've been on cruises, we've done self-guided tours. I love it all.

AK: What was your first trip outside of the United States?

NP: It was the first summer after I taught a year at Delta State, and somehow, through a friend, I found out about a full month fine arts tour of Europe for graduate students. It was sponsored by what is now the University of Memphis. So I signed up for that trip, and we traveled through most of the capitals of Europe. I've been traveling ever since. On that trip we went over on the *Rotterdam*, a Dutch liner, and we came back by airplane. It was my first time to be on an ocean liner and to fly, and it was wonderful.

AK: Was there a dress code while you were at student at the W?

NP: Oh, yes indeed. We could wear shorts and slacks only on Saturdays, and even when we went to gym class, we had to wear a long raincoat or a long coat so that our shorts would not be visible. And I will never, ever forget one morning. I guess I had overslept. I jumped up and I put on a pair of slacks and went to class. I believe it was Dr. Butler's class. I went in and she says, "Miss Pickett, I believe you were in a hurry this morning when you were dressing for class." And I looked down. She looked at me. I never again made the mistake of sleeping late and accidentally wearing pants to class. Dr. Butler was very kind. She could have dismissed me from that class. I could have gotten demerits. But later we laughed about it, and that was the end of it.

AK: Did you spend most of your time in Columbus?

NP: Yes. I went home only about once a month or once every two months because Utica, Mississippi, was almost like another state away from Columbus. I was there many weekends, and I attended what is now First United Methodist Church, on Main Street, and went to Sunday school there. People were so kind to us W girls. Very often I was invited to have Sunday dinner with a family, and I have many fond memories. And I remember somehow when I was moving to the W, I failed to bring enough coat hangers. In fact, I didn't bring any coat hangers. And so I said, "I could go downtown and buy some, but I think I'll just go knock on a door or two near the college and say, 'Do you have any extra coat hangers?'" And I did that, and when I came back, I had two big grocery bags of coat hangers that people had given me, saying, "Oh, my dear, yes indeed." Some of them were some of the nicest coat hangers I had ever had—those nice covered, padded coat hangers. That's just an example of how friendly the people in Columbus were to us. And of course, so many of the citizens in Columbus attended programs on campus. Sometimes there would be music recitals, or there would be various speakers, well-known persons who would be invited to come speak to the entire college. All students were not only invited to attend, but we were expected to attend.

AK: Do you have any regrets about your time at the W?
NP: As I think back, I have one regret, *one* regret. I think about it every so often. In my dorm, particularly during my junior year, but also my senior year, there were some transfer students from Northeast Junior College, now Northeast Community College, and they kept saying, "Come spend the weekend with us at Booneville or Tupelo." One weekend in particular they said, "There's going to be this big dance. Come on, Nell Ann, and spend the weekend with us, and we'll go to that big dance and we'll have a great time." Somehow, I did not go, and that is my biggest regret, because the highlight of that dance was that Elvis Presley was performing.[8] That was my one chance to have gotten to meet Elvis, to have danced to his music with good friends. That's the only regret that I have.

AK: How did you feel when MUW started admitting men?
NP: Oh, hooray for the W! Of course, the air force base is there, and why not admit those men legally who had been taking part-time classes? Of course, we had a number of male professors. Many of us had been to high schools that were not segregated from the standpoint of males and

8. On September 26, 1956, three weeks after Elvis Presley's first appearance on *The Ed Sullivan Show*, Presley returned to Tupelo, Mississippi, for Elvis Presley Day and performed at the Tupelo Fairgrounds for the Mississippi-Alabama Fair and Dairy Show. Pickett may be referring to this event.

females. So I said, "Hooray for the W!" But I'm glad we continue to have a female president.

AK: Who was the president when you were there?
NP: Our president then was male, Dr. Hogarth.[9] It's only in recent years that the presidents have been female. But he was a good president. I'd have to go back and look at the list of presidents, but all those presidents were probably males. However, as I said, we did have both male and female professors in the classroom—excellent, excellent teachers. I don't think I could have experienced better teachers than those that I had at the W.

AK: Other than your experience with your teachers, what was the most valuable thing that you took away from the W?
NP: One thing that I think about is that we were a sharing group. I'm not sure if that's simply because we were women, but we were all sincere in our fun. We were all sincere in our studies, and we liked each other. I can't ever remember there being any rivalry. There might have been friendly rivalries in particular among the social clubs and maybe a little friendly rivalry between the Wesley Foundation and the Baptist Student Union. But of course those years were different. I was there from 1955 to 1957. And that was a totally different time. I can't remember ever locking anything. We could leave our textbooks anywhere. I enjoyed my classmates. I enjoyed the faculty, and we had a beautiful, beautiful campus. And I enjoyed the city of Columbus. I enjoyed the Luxapalila River. Many, many good memories. Except I'm sorry I missed Elvis!

AK: Tell me about the books you've published.
NP. The one that we're best known for is the textbook *Technical English: Writing, Reading, and Speaking*, first published in 1970. It was the first book in technical writing aimed specifically for freshman and sophomore college students, and I dare say it has made its mark in the publishing

9. Charles Pinckney Hogarth (1911–97) served as president of MSCW from 1952 until 1977.

world. There had been a number of textbooks for technical writing, technical communication, but they were all aimed at junior- and senior-level students. In fact, the reason that my colleague, Ann Laster, and I began doing some units for the students we were teaching at Hinds Community College is that we kept telling publishers, "We need a textbook for these students in our course in technical writing at Hinds." We kept saying, "Find us a book." And they kept saying, "There is no such book."

In my second semester at Hinds, I was asked to teach technical writing simply because I was reared on a farm and we had a lot of students majoring in agriculture. By virtue of the fact that I knew something about farming, it was thought then that I could teach technical writing. I was handed this textbook, and I read through it immediately, and the first week of class I said, "Students, this textbook was designed for persons who are juniors and seniors at a four-year institution who have already completed all of their general education courses required in the freshman/sophomore years, so let's just start from scratch." So I began preparing a new text with the help of my husband, or the person who later became my husband, Harry Partin, the chair of the Electronics Technology Department. We began doing some study sheets and creating particular writing assignments centered around the students' majors at Hinds. After that, during another semester, Ann Laster was asked to teach technical writing, and her husband was also in technical education at Hinds. So with the help of Harry Partin and other teachers in vocational/technical subjects, Ann and I began cranking out—I say "cranking" out because we used those old-fashioned machines that used purple ink, ditto machines, and each week we would give a new assignment sheet to our students. The next summer, we went to our dean and said, "We want to put together between covers all of what we've done, so we won't have to be doing these handouts every week for our students." The offset printing department said, "Okay." We got a small stipend through the dean to work on that, putting together and shortening and adding to assignment sheets. And so the next fall we had this homemade textbook, so to speak, but it looked nice because it was done by our offset printing department.

Not long afterward, these travelers for publishing companies came by, and they heard about our textbook that we were using. Would you believe, within weeks we had offers in hand from four publishers for that book? A fifth publisher that wanted it dillydallied around a little bit, and to this day they say, "So how did we miss out on publishing that very first Pickett-Laster textbook?"

And by the way, Ann and I have had a good ride with that textbook. For several years, we made more money from royalties than we did from teaching at Hinds! And a few years back, when we published the eighth edition of that textbook, that came out in 2001, we said, "We have done enough." That is, from the standpoint of spending time on more publishing.

Ann and I also published a number of articles based on our experiences, and we also originated the weeklong summer institute in technical writing in 1981. We did a number of workshops across the country, particularly for two-year college teachers. Our career was anchored in technical writing, and that Ann and I learned by doing.

I have an interesting story about the publishing process. In 1970 we had settled with this particular publishing company, and we have since stuck with that company, but several months before it was to have been in its final stages, we began getting these calls from our publisher in New York. They'd say, "We don't need to use Hinds Junior College on that title page," and we said, "We'll think about that." And then in a day or two we received another call from the editor. They said, "We don't really need to use your first names. We'll just use your initials –N. A. Pickett, A. A. Laster." We said, "Waaaaait a minute. We like our names. We like the name of our college." And then we got another call, "We've already contacted a well-known author from a university up east that will write the introduction for your book. You don't have to pay him anything. And we will put his name on the title page and that will such-and-such-and-such." And then we said, "Hold your horses and hold the presses. No, indeed. We're not interested in somebody from a well-known university up east being named as a coauthor supposedly giving our book credibility by writing us an introduction. We will use our full names.

We are women, and we are proud of it. We will use the name Hinds Junior College. We are proud of what we teach and who we are. And if y'all don't like it, just tear up the manuscript." They didn't tear up the manuscript. The book did come out, and it did have our full names. There was an introduction, but it was written by us. We referred to Hinds Junior College. And then later on, sort of by the grapevine, we learned that the editors at the publishing company had said, "Those—I won't use their word—those two women from Mississippi, they cost us a bunch of money." Because we eventually found out that they had already printed the introductory matter; they had already omitted our full names, and they had to reprint that whole part of the textbook. Sure, it cost them money. I wish it had cost them billions. No, no, I'm teasing about that. But only later did we realize what they were trying to do to us because we were women and we were from a two-year college and we were from a rural area in Mississippi! We didn't have the vocabulary at that time to state exactly how we were being treated, but we knew it was unfair, innately unfair.

AK: Can you talk about your leadership roles in teachers' organizations?
NP: I've been privileged to be selected, elected, and appointed to various national posts, particularly with the National Council of Teachers of English and the college composition division of the National Council of Teachers of English—what we call the four Cs, the Conference on College Composition and Communication. I served a four-year term as an officer in that group, and then as a part of that we formed a national organization of two-year college teachers that we called National Two-Year College English Association. I was a founding member of that group, and some years ago the highest award for two-year college English teachers happened to be awarded to me. That honor is now named the Nell Ann Pickett Teaching Award for two-year college English teachers. Of course, I had been most active in the southeastern conference, and there's a session and an award named for Nell Ann Pickett there. I have been so fortunate to have so many good friends and to be able to be a part of groups that really make a difference in teaching.

But I now am retired. I operate three businesses from my home, and I am a full-time farmer. It's so dry now that my main concern is being able to have hay for the cattle for the fall and for the winter. But I love seeing those little baby calves come along. I had thought when I retired, I would have all the time I wanted to read. Now I just try to read at least a book a month.

Since I have retired, I have become reacquainted and further developed friendships with persons in Utica, particularly the Utica Twentieth Century Club, a women's service club. We decided we would keep that name because the club was founded in the twentieth century, back in the 1930s. And for the past two years, I enjoyed serving as president, and we just have a great time together. We meet once a month, and we do a lot of community projects. And also I'm a part of Delta Kappa Gamma, the national teacher honorary sorority, and have a lot of good friends there. So yes, I enjoy every day of living.

Barbara McMillin Webb
Class of 1957

APRIL 19, 2007
INTERVIEWED BY SARAH SHEFFIELD
TRANSCRIBED BY RACHEL FORESTER

BARBARA MCMILLIN WAS BORN ON AUGUST 9, 1936, in Louisville, Mississippi, to Oliver Frank McMillin and Alice Irene Robison McMillin. At MSCW, she majored in library science and was active in numerous groups, including the 4-H Club, the Future Teachers of America, and the Alpha Psi Omega drama honorary society. She served as an officer in the Westminster Fellowship for Presbyterian students. A speech minor, she was also very active in the Theatre Guild, serving as the assistant director and director of Tournament Plays during her sophomore and junior years. She began her career as a librarian at Mississippi State University and subsequently became head librarian at Belhaven College in Jackson, Mississippi. In 1958, she married William Larry Webb of Louisville, a manager in the poultry industry. She served as a high school librarian, speech teacher, and counselor before taking the post of director of Upward Bound at Copiah-Lincoln Community College. In

> 1969, she was honored as Southern Speech Teacher of the Year, and the following year she was the featured speaker at the W's Homecoming. While at Co-Lin, she was a Phi Theta Kappa Top Ten Adviser and president of the Mississippi Association of Educational Opportunity Programs. She retired from Co-Lin in 2000. She has been active in a variety of civic organizations, including the American Heart Association and the Daughters of the American Revolution, and she served as president of Women of the Church of her local Presbyterian congregation. She now lives in Hazelhurst, Mississippi.

BW: I grew up in Winston County, Mississippi, and both of my parents were very supportive, very Christian people. It was interesting that in my childhood, I was programmed from the earliest that I would go to college. It was perhaps very unusual for my generation that both of my grandmothers had college degrees, and my mother had a college degree. So education for women was very important in our family. I had a younger brother who was about eighteen months younger than I was, and we had a farm of about four hundred acres. Our family farmed, and that was our main livelihood. I was very active in a lot of school activities, particularly in 4-H Club work and things of that sort. When my younger brother got into Future Farmers of America and was showing beef cattle, the agriculture teacher did something that was unheard of at that time; he allowed a girl to show. I was the only girl in Winston County that was allowed to show her beef cattle in the FFA contest as well as in the 4-H contest.

SS: How did you decide to attend the W?

BW: My paternal grandmother[1] was in one of the first classes at II & C, so she had a degree from here. I think it was maybe a two-year certificate in business or something of that sort, in one of the very early classes. I had known about the W all of my life, and I was always interested in

1. Ella Watson McMillin (1872–1944), Class of 1889.

it. I had friends that I had known in 4-H that were older than I that had come to the W. But my heart's desire was to go to Mississippi State because I wanted to be a veterinarian. My grandfather had taken a veterinary course and did a lot of the veterinary work for our community, and I always was his assistant, and I helped him do all those things. But my daddy was very emphatic about the fact that nice girls did not go to Mississippi State and live in the dormitory, and that was completely out. At that time, I thought that was the only way I'd ever get in vet school was to go to Mississippi State. So I had to find something else to do, and I decided on a library science degree. Isn't that different from veterinary science? But anyway, I chose to come to the W after visiting here; then there was no doubt that was what I wanted to do.

SS: What were your first impressions of the campus?
BW: I always thought it was a beautiful campus, and I was real excited about living in Hastings, which was *the* dorm as far as I was concerned my freshman year. Of course it was the freshman dorm at that. All of freshman row, I guess, was there, with Callaway and Columbus, too. But I lived in Hastings and I was all excited getting my room fixed up. I had a surprise roommate that I had corresponded with but had never met before I came here, a girl from Searcy, Arkansas.[2] We never had any arguments. We got along fine, but we had nothing in common. Before the end of the year, she moved in with somebody else, and I was left with no roommate, which was fine with me. But I had a very close friend down the hall who spent a lot of time in my room, and eventually we roomed together for the rest of the time, the other two years. We both graduated in three years, so there were only two years after that. This was Judy Mitchell. She's now Julia Mitchell Seals.[3]

SS: How did you decorate your dorm room?
BW: We made curtains and made bedspreads and had everything all to match, and we were excited about that. Other people might have bought

2. Nancy Randall Caldwell, Class of 1958.
3. Julia Mitchell Seals, Class of 1957.

bedding, but there was just never any question for me because money was always scarce. My mother was one of those people that could do anything, and I just grew up thinking that's what you did, so I made my bedspreads and made my curtains.

SS: How did you get to school?
BW: My parents brought me. My daddy brought me in his pickup truck with all of my belongings, including my teddy bear, in the back of the truck. And he said that by the time he moved me home, he thought he was going to have to get a moving van instead of a pickup truck, but I always managed with the pickup truck. I had been to camp and I had been a camp counselor, so I had spent summers away from home, going home on weekends. But being at the W was just an exciting time for me. I don't ever remember being homesick while I was here to the point where I cried and wanted to go home. It never occurred to me that I would leave, that I would drop out of school and go home. In the first place, I had no choice. My parents would have never allowed it anyway. They would have just turned me right around and sent me back.

SS: Did you have a dorm mother?
BW: Oh yes, yes. Dorm mothers were wonderful. We had Miss Settle[4] in Hastings, and she knew us all very, very well. And I can remember right before exams, which of course was right before Christmas that freshman year, Judy, who was later my roommate, and I were making candy in the kitchen there at the end of the hall. Miss Goen[5] came around to do an inspection of the dorm—she was the dean of students—and she got very upset, thinking that we should be studying for exams. Miss Holder[6] was with her, and she looked at her and she said, "Oh no. These are my girls.

4. Elizabeth Settle (1890–1966) served as a social adviser at MSCW from 1951 until 1956.
5. Marguerite Goen (1896–1977) held a variety of posts at MSCW between 1928 and 1963, including teacher of secretarial science, student counselor, and dean of students. Goen Residence Hall was named in her honor.
6. Missie Bridgeforth Holder (1893–1982) served as a social adviser at MSCW from 1946 until 1959.

They know what they're doing. They're A students. They're perfectly all right, and they make good candy, too."

SS: Were there strict rules?

BW: Oh, very strict rules. And of course, at that time, we had curfew—we had to be in at a certain time. We had lights out. And also there were rules about dating. You could not single-date as a freshman; we always had to double-date. It had some advantages, too, because if there was a girl who had a steady boyfriend, she couldn't date either unless she had a double-date, so he'd bring a friend from State and she'd run up and down the hall saying, "Anybody need a date tonight? I gotta have a double." You could always get to meet people that way. Then the Goose[7] always had boys in it. The guys from State came over to the Goose a lot, and we could just go to the Goose to get a Coke and see some guys that way, too.

SS: What do you remember about classes?

BW: I don't remember much about the first day of classes. One of my most vivid memories of freshman comp was the first big theme we had to turn in. I had a comma fault in it, and that was an automatic F. I had never made an F on a major test—maybe a pop test or something like that, but in my life I never had made an F on anything I had studied for. I just thought I had flunked out of college. I was absolutely devastated. But I survived, and I passed freshman English, and I learned all about comma faults.

SS: Did you have a favorite professor?

BW: I had lots of favorite professors. I think the majority of our professors were very concerned about students. They were very personable. They knew their students extremely well. I got a minor in speech, so I knew the people in the speech department very well. Dr. Cromwell[8] was

....

7. The Golden Goose Tearoom, located on the first floor of the Student Activities Building (formerly the Henry Whitfield Gymnasium), demolished in the late 1960s.

8. Harvey Cromwell (1907–77) served as director of speech and theater, dean of arts and sciences, and dean of the graduate school at MSCW between 1949 and 1975. In 1977, the new Harvey Cromwell Communications Center was named for him.

a real favorite for everybody. And Miss Bailey[9] was also a favorite there. Then in my library science department, there was Mrs. Barton,[10] who everybody called Mama B, and we just adored her. She just smothered all of us and took real good care of us, too. I don't have any really bad memories of professors.

SS: Was your major was your favorite subject?
BW: Probably, and yet those speech classes that I got my minor in were just as much fun. I thoroughly enjoyed those, too.

SS: Did you have an opportunity to follow up on any of the things you did in high school with animals?
BW: No more than just to visit Missy Deer[11] every so often. We had Missy Deer in a pen on the back campus, and everybody loved her, and we fed her and did that kind of thing.

SS: What organizations were you involved in at the W?
BW: I don't remember a great deal about us being in 4-H. We probably met occasionally, but I don't remember us doing any great things in 4-H. More of my extracurricular activities were in the other areas. I did a lot in the speech department. I was in Theatre Guild, and eventually I did Tournament Plays, where I was an assistant director one year. Then my senior year I was a director of Tournament Plays. And I was always on the costume committee, the backstage crew. I never acted very much, but I can remember one time when we did a play, I can't remember the name of it, but it was a gangster-type thing, and it had a lot of the gangsters from the Chicago depression era. We had to have a suit with pinstripes, since pinstripe suits were so popular at that time. But on stage you couldn't tell it was a pinstripe suit, so we sewed white yarn on

....

9. Frances Bailey (1899–1987) taught speech at MSCW from 1951 until 1968.
10. Kate Turner Barton (1888–1968) taught library science at MSCW from 1946 until 1958.
11. Missy Deer was rescued as a fawn and became an unofficial campus mascot. Its name was taken from a nickname for MSCW students, "Missydears." *Spectator* editor Betty Boyls Stone, Class of 1951, launched a successful effort to have the deer voted the official campus mascot, and the campus bookstore sold Missy Deer toys.

stripes to make stripes on a suit so it would look like a pinstripe suit to the audience.

SS: What was your least favorite subject?
BW: Probably world history because of the professor. He was a good lecturer, but his tests would be something like "Outline the chapter" for question 1, and question 2 would be "Fill in the outline." So history was never my real big thing.

SS: What did you usually wear to school?
BW: We could wear dresses and skirts. Sweaters and skirts were popular then. Bobby socks and tennis shoes or saddle oxfords or maybe penny loafers. We did not have uniforms for anything other than P.E., but we did have to have our P.E. shorts and shirts. Of course, shorts or pants could not be worn out on campus, on front campus, but we always had a raincoat that we put on over that. They did let us wear jeans sometimes to play practice, particularly if we were working backstage or something of that sort. But everybody had to have a raincoat, because it always rains in Columbus if it rains anywhere in the world. On top of that, you wore your raincoat to breakfast buttoned up if you didn't have time to get dressed or any other time that you didn't want anybody to see what you had on. So a raincoat was an absolute essential.

SS: After Hastings, where did you live?
BW: The other two years we lived in Fant. Reneau was a sophomore dorm at that time, but sophomores were allowed to live on the first floor of Fant. At that time, your GPA was what lined you up for signing up for a room. The higher the GPA, the higher choice you got. I was always fortunate to have a smart roommate. We were one of the first ones in line to choose a room, so as sophomores, we lived in Fant. We were sophomores really only during the first semester and juniors the second semester. By being in Fant, we probably got some privileges we would not have had had we been in a strictly sophomore dorm. Then we lived in Fant our senior year also.

SS: What types of privileges?
BW: We probably got to stay out a little bit later and we got to go out more nights in a week. Freshmen could only go out on weekends, if I'm remembering right. And I think as a sophomore, maybe you could go out on Wednesday night and weekends. And then as a junior you got to go out two nights during the week. I'm not positive of that, but that kind of thing.

SS: Could you tell me about the dining hall experience?
BW: Oh, it was wonderful. You were assigned to a table, I think. It seems as if maybe we were allowed to choose our group that sat together at the table, but you were assigned a table. You sat at the same table every time. We were served family style. We used linen napkins at every meal, and we had tablecloths on the tables. The food was good. Of course, we had things we didn't like, and we complained about those things. But the dietician had been on a trip to Europe one year, and when she came back, once a month she did a foreign meal. On the table she'd have a menu for us so we'd know what everything was and we'd know what was being served. And they used little decorations that fit for Italy or for France or for whatever type of food was being served. It was a very educational experience. And then we had a dress-up dinner once a month, usually before there was going to be a concert or something, so we'd dress up for that anyway, but we had to dress for that dinner. That usually had a special menu also.

Good table manners were expected. We passed the food around, and we had to pass it in the right direction. And another thing that was real special was we usually sang the doxology for grace before the meal. There were students who were on work-study that would bring the food to the table, and they would have several tables that they were the waitress for, so to speak. But they would bring the bowls of food in, and then we served ourselves. I suppose they cleared the tables at the end. I can't remember about that.

SS: What was a typical day like for you as a student?
BW: We'd just have classes, very much like schedules are now. You might

have an 8:00 class, and then you might not have another one until 10:00, or you might have them straight through. We had classes in the afternoon. And we had classes on Saturday. We had Monday, Wednesday, Friday classes and Tuesday, Thursday, Saturday classes. I suppose the whole time we were here we had Saturday classes, though most of the Saturday classes ended at noon. Anything that was a lab was in the afternoon, and they had no labs on Saturday, if I remember correctly.

SS: Was there a scheduled time for extracurricular activities?
BW: Most of the play practices that I participated in and the club meetings were at night. We just fit them in where we could.

SS: Did you participate in the Zouave?
BW: Yes, we did Zouave. Our year was the last year that Miss Pohl[12] did Zouave, and that was quite an experience. I remember that we marched and marched and marched and marched and you did not chew gum. Miss Pohl could see somebody chewing gum half an acre away. She knew everybody by name and called everybody by their last name. She would holler, "McMillin! Get rid of the gum!" It may have been halfway across campus.

Along with the Zouave she also taught a fundamentals course that all freshmen had to take which included exercise, but it also taught you how to get in and out of a car gracefully and how to sit in a chair and how to stand up and all those things—how to walk.

SS: What did you think of Miss Pohl?
BW: She was a unique individual who gave her whole life to what she did. We were always interested to get back in the fall to see what Miss Pohl was going to wear that year, because Miss Pohl would go to New York every summer and pick out her uniform for the year, and she'd buy several outfits just exactly alike. She wore the same thing every day for the year, and then the next year would change.

12. Emma Ody Pohl (1880–1966) joined H & C in 1907, when she was hired to develop the department of physical education. She taught that subject until her retirement in 1955.

SS: What campus traditions did you participate in?
B: I think we called it Stunt Night, where the seniors would just announce to the juniors that Stunt Night was going to be that night. Then you had to get your stunts together and entertain them and everybody else on campus. It was lots of fun. The seniors would just march in together in the dining hall and say, "Juniors, we're going to get you tonight," or something like that. I can't remember the exact words. And it was lots of fun because we were in Fant, and we had lots of friends who were in the junior class and friends who were in the senior class, so they allowed us to participate. That was one thing that Judy and I got to participate in our second year. And then of course we got to participate as seniors during our senior year.

SS: Did you join any of the social organizations?
BW: No. I went out for rush, and I loved it, but I decided that was not for me, so I did not choose to join one of the social clubs. I was in some of the academic organizations, though. I was in the Forensic and the Drama Clubs and then I was in the library science honorary, Alpha Beta Alpha. I was president of that my senior year. That was one of my fun experiences because I got to go to the national convention, which was in Terre Haute, Indiana. We rode the train up. One other girl and I represented our MSCW chapter there.

SS: What were your weekends like?
BW: On Saturday afternoon we'd walk to town, and of course the people in town were wonderful to the W girls. We were always active in church. We went to church on Sunday. We were pretty much expected to, I think. And of course everybody had to wear hats and gloves when they left campus on Sunday for something like that.

SS: Did students do a lot of cooking in the dorms?
BW: We had a kitchen, but it didn't give us a lot of cooking facilities. We learned to do pretty well with a hot plate and an ironing board and a few things like that. We'd cook usually on weekends, but sometimes we might do a little something other than that.

SS: Were there a lot of informal get-togethers in the dorm?

BW: Oh yes. There were jam sessions, and we would all sit around and listen to the radio sometimes. Of course, very few of us had record players or anything like that.

SS: Tell me about the panty raid.

BW: The panty raid was one of the most exciting and fun things that happened the whole time I was here, and this was my senior year. Dr. Hogarth[13] was out of town, and Miss Goen[14] was in charge. One of the fraternities at State called Miss Goen and told her that one of the other fraternities was on their way to the W for a panty raid. Miss Goen just absolutely went berserk. She called Dr. Hilbun[15] over at State, and he told her he'd do everything in his power to stop it. I had a brother who was in school at State at that time, and he said Dr. Hilbun got on the intercom that they had that was heard all over campus and announced that any young man caught on the W campus with the purpose of a panty raid would automatically be subject to draft by morning. And of course, this was at the time that if you were in school, you weren't subject to be drafted, but if you were not in school or were not passing your classes, then you had to go into the service. This time was the only time while I was here that all the gates on campus were locked. We could see patrol cars all the way around the campus. We had the highway patrol; we had the city police. Everybody was all around the campus. We could look out the windows of the third floor of Fant and see all these policemen. They had somebody at the gate. Of course, this happened after girls who had dates had already left the campus for the evening. They had somebody at the gate as the W students came back and brought their dates in, and they took a picture of every guy that came in. Those men had no idea what was going on there. In our dorm,

13. Charles Pinckney Hogarth (1911–97) served as president of MSCW from 1952 until 1977.

14. Marguerite Goen (1896–1977) held a variety of posts at MSCW between 1928 and 1963, including teacher of secretarial science, student counselor, and dean of students. Goen Residence Hall was named in her honor.

15. Benjamin F. Hilbun (1890–1963) served as president of Mississippi State University from 1953 until 1960.

Miss Holder was just the cutest thing in the world, and she got on the intercom and she said, "Girls, we have been alerted that the boys from State are on their way over for a panty raid. Please stay fully dressed and in your rooms. If the boys come, I will alert you. I would not have you miss it for the world." And of course everybody did just what she asked us to do. And we looked out the windows and we saw the police and all that. There was nobody coming for a panty raid. The whole thing was a hoax. But it was the most exciting thing that happened to us for a long time.

SS: What do you remember about major world events while you were at the W?
BW: It was during the Korean War, and at that time, everybody who was eighteen or nineteen had to register for the draft. I don't know how exactly they selected them, but some of them were then drafted, and they had to go into service for a certain length of time. A lot of the young men went ahead and volunteered and went into service. The guy that I eventually married went into service right out of high school. He volunteered for the air force, but that also qualified him for the G.I. Bill, which was started at the end of World War II and then was reenacted for the Korean veterans, which made it very nice. I had graduated from college, and then we were married and then he went to college. On the G.I. Bill and a teacher's salary, we never had very much money, but we had a good time.

SS: How did you meet your husband?
BW: We knew each other in high school, and we dated two or three times as seniors in high school, but that was it. We were mostly good friends, and our families were good friends. Then it was not until later on when he was in service and was home on leave that we went out a few times. We did a lot of our courtship by correspondence because we had known each other always. We had been friends, but we were not lovers yet. And then the whole year that we were engaged he was stationed in Goose Bay, Labrador.

SS: So how did you reconnect?
BW: He came back home on leave, and then we wrote letters all this time, and then we were engaged—he gave me a ring for the Christmas that I was a senior in college, that was December 1956, and then he promptly went to Goose Bay, Labrador. Then he came back, and when he got back to the States and was discharged early in February 1958, that's when we were married.

SS: Did the war seem to affect your time here at the W?
BW: There were lots of girls who were writing to servicemen at that time. Some of them were writing to several or were dating other people—they weren't going steady. But there were some that were engaged to servicemen at that time.

SS: How did you finish school in three years?
BW: I really don't know how we decided to do this. I went to summer school at Mississippi State. At that time, you had to have permission from the W for the specific courses you were going to take at State. I did that in the summertime. And really, I took eighteen and twenty-one hours each semester. Of course at that time, you only had to have 120 hours to graduate. So I had little trouble getting through by going those summers and doing it in three years. I really don't know when I decided to do this. Judy decided to graduate early because she wanted to graduate before she got married, and she was really eager to get married. But that was not the reason I decided to do it.

SS: Are you and Judy still friends?
BW: We're still very close. We talk to each other frequently, and we visit frequently. We have all through these fifty years. It's almost like we still can realize what the other one's thinking. And if there's a time that I really need a friend, she'll just happen to call, and vice versa. So we've been very close for this whole time.

SS: Have you stayed in touch with anyone else from the W?
BW: There are lots of people that I had casual contact with and some that were from my hometown that I had always known and I've kept in contact with that way. But nobody that's been as close as Judy. She's close enough that my children and grandchildren call her Aunt Judy.

SS: Did any of your children go to the W?
BW: My daughter graduated twenty years ago this year,[16] and then I have a granddaughter who is a senior this year who will be graduating fifty years after I did.[17]

SS: How do you feel about the W admitting men?
BW: I really feel like a woman ought to have the opportunity to choose to go to a women's institution if that's what she wants to do. And I can understand why men might feel discriminated against, but in some ways I feel discriminated against because it can't be the wonderful, close women's institution that it was when I went there. I feel like people miss something at a coed institution, just like perhaps I missed something by the W not being coed. But I chose that, and I loved every day that I was at the W.

SS: Did you take any life lessons from your years at the W?
BW: You always ought to do the very best that you possibly can in every situation, and you should take advantage of every opportunity that comes your way.

SS: Is there any other advice that you would give to a current W girl?
BW: I think they should take advantage of all the opportunities. I hope the W still offers opportunities for cultural enrichment. I saw my first opera here, and there were many other opportunities like that that I

16. Amanda Webb Barker, Class of 1987.
17. Erin Gioia, Class of 2007.

would have never had coming from a small rural town and a farming community. I think they need to take advantage of all those opportunities. Some you're going to like, and some you're not going to like, but you'll never know until you try. Always do your very best.

Index